Roman Working Lives
and Urban Living

edited by

Ardle Mac Mahon and Jennifer Price

Oxbow Books

Published by
Oxbow Books, Oxford, UK

ISBN 978 1 84217 186 0

A CIP record for this book is available from The British Library

This book is available direct from
Oxbow Books, Oxford, UK
(Phone: 01865-241249; Fax: 01865-794449)

and

The David Brown Book Company
PO Box 511, Oakville, CT 06779, USA
(Phone: 860-945-9329; Fax: 860-945-9468)

or from our website

www.oxbowbooks.com

Printed and bound in Great Britain by
CPI Antony Rowe, Chippenham and Eastbourne

Contents

List of Contributors

Marina Ciaraldi
Research & Enterprise Services
University of Birmingham
Birmingham, B15 2TT, UK

Janet DeLaine
Institute of Archaeology
University of Oxford
Oxford, OX1 2PG, UK

Simon Esmonde Cleary
Institute of Archaeology and Antiquity
University of Birmingham
Birmingham, B15 2TT, UK

Jeremy Evans
Barbican Research Associates Ltd
Birmingham, B13 9NT, UK

Shawn Graham
Post-Doctoral Fellow in Roman Archaeology
Department of Classics
University of Manitoba
Manitoba, R3T 2M8, Canada.

Jenny Hall
Department of Early London History
& Collections
Museum of London
London, EC2Y 5HN, UK

Ralph Jackson
Department of Prehistory and Europe
The British Museum
London, WC1B 3DG, UK

Ardle Mac Mahon
Research Associate
Department of Classical Studies
The Open University
Milton Keynes, MK7 6AA, UK

Dominic Perring
Institute of Archaeology
University College London
London, WC1H 0PY, UK

Jennifer Price
Department of Archaeology
University of Durham
Durham, DH1 3LE, UK

Damian Robinson
Institute of Archaeology
University of Oxford
Oxford, OX1 2PG, UK

Introduction

The ordinary people who made up the largest section of the population in the cities and towns in the Roman world were largely ignored by contemporary writers and have often been marginalized in traditional studies of Roman urbanism but research into in their patterns of work and social interaction has increased markedly in recent years.

This volume originated in a conference on 'Roman Working Lives and Urban Living' organised through the Centre for Roman Provincial Archaeology and held in the Department of Archaeology at the University of Durham in July 2001. The conference was planned as a forum for colleagues researching into urban space and architecture, commercial and retail structures, organisation of commercial and craft activity and social theory to meet and exchange ideas and information, and the success of the event led to a decision to publish the proceedings. Some participants at the conference were not able to prepare their papers for this volume and other papers have been added since then, resulting in a work which has retained the form of the conference while expanding the content.

The twelve papers have been arranged in two sections. The first, *Urban living and the settings for working lives*, contains five papers, exploring urban space and civic ritual (Esmonde Cleary), private housing as a working environment for the urban rich (Perring), the urban commercial landscape (DeLaine), retail structures within urban settlements (Mac Mahon) and the fittings within retail structures (Mac Mahon). The second, *People at work: owners and artisans, crafts and professions,* contains seven papers which examine the social organisation of production and service activity in Pompeii (Robinson), the role of the River Tiber in the brick industry supplying Rome (Graham), traders and craftworking in London (Hall), production and trends in urban pottery supply in Britain (Evans), glass production and retailing for urban markets (Price), urbanisation and specialisation in plant cultivation for food and pharmacy in Pompeii (Ciaraldi), and medical practitioners in Roman cities (Jackson). The range of topics and variety of approaches in the papers emphasise the wealth of the material available, and we hope that the volume will help to stimulate further research into the lives of the 'silent voices' of Roman urban society.

Acknowledgements
We would like to thank the speakers at the conference for presenting their research and taking part in discussion, and the authors of the papers for their patience and continued support; David Brown of Oxbow Books for agreeing to publish the volume; Yvonne Beadnell, Department of Archaeology, University of Durham for producing Maps 1 and 2 and Yunsun Choi for her help during and after the conference.

Ardle Mac Mahon and Jennifer Price
January 2005

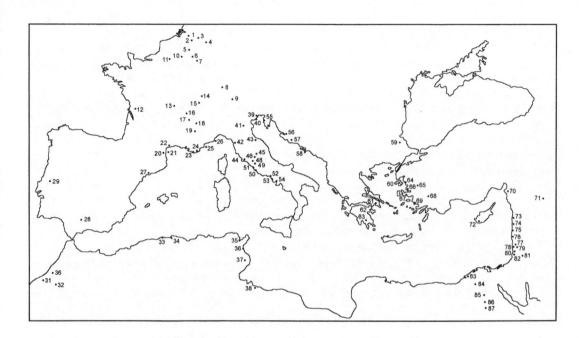

Map 1: Roman Empire – Place names mentioned in text

1. Nijmegen, Netherlands; **2**. Simpelveld, Netherlands; **3**. Neuss, Germany; **4**. Cologne, Germany; **5**. Hambach Forest, Germany; **6**. Neumagen, Germany; **7**. Bliesbruck, Germany; **8**. Augst, Switzerland; **9**. Avenches, Switzerland; **10**. Rheims, France; **11**. Paris, France; **12**. Saintes, France; **13**. Auxerre, France; **14**. Besançon, France; **15**. Villards d.Heria, France; **16**. Lyons, France; **17**. Vienne, France; **18**. Coligny, France; **19**. Vaison-la-Romaine, France; **20**. Chateau-Roussillon, France; **21**. Port Vendres, France; **22**. Narbonne, France; **23**. Gulf of Fos, France; **24**. Marseilles, France; **25**. Embiez, France; **26**. Tradelière, Îles de Lérins, France; **27**. Tarragona, Spain; **28**. Irni, Spain; **29**. Conimbriga, Portugal; **30**. Banasa, Morocco; **31**. Thamusida, Morocco; **32**. Volubilis, Morocco; **33**. Cherchel (*Iol Caesarea*), Algeria; **34**. Tipasa, Algeria; **35**. Carthage, Tunisia; **36**. Sousse (*Hadrumetum*), Tunisia; **37**. El Djem (*Thysdrus*), Tunisia; **38**. Sabratha, Libya; **39**. Aquileia, Italy; **40**. Grado, Italy; **41**. Prati di Monestirolo, Voghenza, Italy; **42**. Pisa, Italy; **43**. Rimini, Italy; **44**. Cosa, Italy; **45**. Otricoli, Italy; **46**. Narni, Italy; **47**. Superaequum, Italy; **48**. Seripola, near Orte, Italy; **49**. Rome, Italy; **50**. Ostia, Italy; **51**. Portus, Italy; **52**. Puteoli, Italy; **53**. Herculaneum, Italy; **54**. Pompeii, Italy; **55**. Školarice-Križišče, Slovenia; **56**. Asseria, Croatia; **57**. Salona, Croatia; **58**. Mljet, Croatia; **59**. Marcianopolis, Bulgaria; **60**. Mytilene, Lesbos, Greece; **61**. Athens, Greece; **62**. Corinth, Greece; **63**. Sparta, Greece; **64**. Pergamum, Turkey; **65**. Sardis, Turkey; **66**. Smyrna, Turkey; **67**. Colophon, Turkey; **68**. Aphrodisias, Turkey; **69**. Ephesus, Turkey; **70**. Antioch, Syria; **71**. Dura Europos, Syria; **72**. Nea Paphos, Cyprus; **73**. Beirut, Lebanon; **74**. Sidon, Lebanon; **75**. Tyre, Lebanon; **76**. Akko *(Ptolemais)*, Israel; **77**. Sepphoris, Israel; **78**. Bet Eliezer, Israel; **79**. Bet She'an, Israel; **80**. Apollonia, Israel; **81**. Samaria, Israel; **82**. Ascalon, Israel; **83**. Alexandria, Egypt; **84**. Wadi Natrun, Egypt; **85**. Karanis, Egypt; **86**. Tebtunis, Egypt; **87**. Oxyrhynchus, Egypt

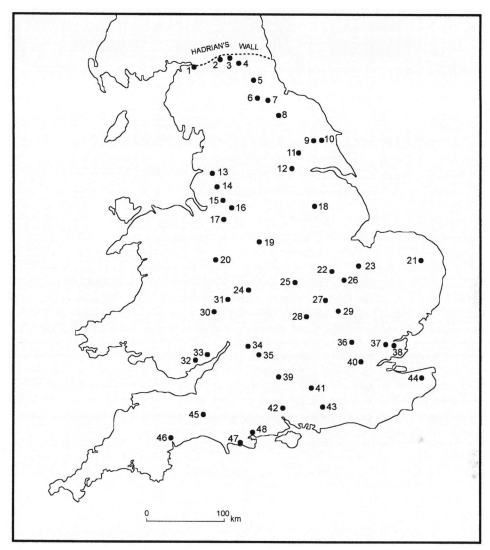

Map 2: Britain – Place names mentioned in text

1. Carlisle, Cumbria; **2**. Vindolanda, Northumberland; **3**. Housesteads, Northumberland; **4**. Corbridge, Northumberland; **5**. Binchester, Co. Durham; **6**. Greta Bridge, Co. Durham; **7**. Piercebridge, Co Durham; **8**. Catterick, North Yorkshire; **9**. Crambeck, North Yorkshire; **10**. Malton, North Yorkshire; **11**. York; **12**. Castleford, West Yorkshire; **13**. Walton-le-Dale, Lancashire; **14**. Wigan, Lancashire; **15**. Wilderspool, Lancashire; **16**. Lindow, Cheshire; **17**. Middlewich, Cheshire; **18**. Lincoln; **19**. Rocester, Staffordshire; **20**. Wroxeter, Shropshire; **21**. Caister-by-Norwich, Norfolk; **22**. Leicester; **23**. Water Newton, Cambridgeshire; **24**. Alcester, Warwickshire; **25**. Mancetter, Warwickshire; **26**. Great Weldon, Northamptonshire; **27**. Piddington, Northamptonshire; **28**. Towcester, Northamptonshire; **29**. Harrold, Bedfordshire; **30**. Kenchester, Herefordshire; **31**. Worcester; **32**. Caerleon, Gwent; **33**. Caerwent, Gwent; **34**. Sapperton, Gloucestershire; **35**. Cirencester, Gloucestershire; **36**. Verulamium, Hertfordshire; **37**. Colchester, Essex; **38**. Stanway, Essex; **39**. Mildenhall, Wiltshire; **40**. London; **41**. Silchester, Hampshire; **42**. Winchester, Hampshire; **43**. Alice Holt, Hampshire; **44**. Canterbury, Kent; **45**. Catsgore, Somerset; **46**. Exeter, Devon; **47**. Ringstead, Dorset; **48**. Poole, Dorset

Abbreviations

AA	*Archaeologia Aeliana*
AC	*Archaeologia Cantiana*
AE	*Année Épigraphique*
AJ	*Archaeological Journal*
AJA	*American Journal of Archaeology*
AJP	*American Journal of Philology*
AL	*Archaeology in Lincolnshire*
AntJ	*Antiquaries Journal*
BA	*Bedfordshire Archaeology*
BAJ	*Bedfordshire Archaeological Journal*
BAM	*Bulletin d'Archéologie Marocaine*
BAR	*British Archaeological Reports*
BBCS	*The Bulletin of the Board of Celtic Studies*
CA	*Current Archaeology*
CAJ	*Cambridge Archaeological Journal*
CE	*Cronache Ercolanesi*
CIL	*Corpus Inscriptionum Latinarum*
CMG	*Corpus Medicorum Graecorum*
CP	*Cronache Pompeiane*
HA	*Hertfordshire Archaeology*
HTR	*Harvard Theological Review*
JGS	*Journal of Glass Studies*
JRA	*Journal of Roman Archaeology*
JRPS	*Journal of Roman Pottery Studies*
JRS	*Journal of Roman Studies*
LA	*London Archaeologist*
LHA	*Lincolnshire History and Archaeology*
NA	*Norfolk Archaeology*
OJA	*Oxford Journal of Archaeology*
PBSR	*Papers of the British School at Rome*
QAL	*Quaderni di Archeologia della Libya*
RIB	*Roman Inscriptions in Britain*
RSP	*Rivista di Studi Pompeiani*
SAHST	*Staffordshire Archaeological and Historical Society Transactions*
TPAPA	*Transactions and Proceedings of the American Philological Association*
TBGAS	*Transactions of the Bristol and Gloucestershire Archaeological Society*
TBWAS	*Transactions of Birmingham and Warwickshire Archaeological Society*
WA	*World Archaeology*
WANHM	*Wiltshire Archaeological and Natural History Magazine*

1

Beating the bounds: ritual and the articulation of urban space in Roman Britain

Simon Esmonde Cleary

'Beating the Bounds' is one of those largely re-invented traditions in which England now abounds and delights, with the excuse for dressing up and doing something faintly ridiculous having usurped its more utilitarian origins and symbolic functions. In essence, on Rogation Day the people of a parish, led by their robed clergy and lay notables, process round the boundaries of the parish 'marking' the various boundary-stones by beating them with sticks (allegedly in some parishes beating the choir-boys also, to fix their awareness of civic and sacred space). However, quaint or ludicrous this practice may now seem, it does embody several features common to much civic ritual. It is concerned with the definition of space; that space is a part of collective memory; the rite takes the form of a procession, ordered according to social structure including age and gender as well as status; it has a marked religious aspect. In rural parishes, because it falls on the day on which God's blessing is asked (Lat. *rogare*) on the crops and the procession circumambulates the farmlands of the parish it has a fertility/seasonal resonance. In modern urban parishes there can be a certain amount of low comedy as the earnest procession passes amongst bemused Sunday shoppers in a supermarket, the building of which may have obliterated the boundary-line; nevertheless, the memory of what was is being handed down.

In this paper I would like to explore the possibility that we may be able to lift the veil on such practices in the towns of Roman Britain and thus gain a small insight into the 'lived experience' of these towns. It will probably not have escaped notice that ritual of the sort outlined above would be remarkable to the archaeologist essentially by its invisibility, save perhaps surviving boundary-stones. Indeed, the cynical may observe that Roman Britain is the ideal test-bed for such a study, untrammelled as it is by any consideration as vulgar as actual evidence. Nevertheless, I think it is possible by laying out general considerations about such practices to give ourselves a series of parameters which may allow us to propose features of the archaeology as explicable in these terms. Accordingly, I want first to outline some common features of civic ritual and the ways in which it can be used to articulate urban space and materialise urban concerns. I want then to move on to a brief consideration of what our knowledge of urban festivals in the pagan and Christian Roman periods may suggest about likely forms of practice. This will then be applied to a series of case-studies of towns in Roman Britain for which we have reasonably full plans.

Urban ceremonial

The place and function of civic rituals in urban life has been the subject of considerable attention for historians of the later mediaeval and early modern periods (*e.g.* Darnton 1984; Hanawalt & Keyerson 1994; le Roy Ladurie 1979; Nelson 1986, all with copious references), as well as scholars working on the central and eastern Mediterranean in the Roman period (*e.g.* Lane Fox 1986; MacCormack 1986; Price 1984, chapter 5; van Nijf 1997, chapter 3, all with references). These are, of course, periods for which quantities of written and pictorial documentation have survived. A number of themes of use to us can be drawn out of this work. Many civic rituals involve ordered movement, processions, from one place to another. These characteristically are the places of interest to the established social and religious order. Equally, places and areas marginalised or excluded by the great and good can be excluded from the schedule of events as a deliberate act of 'social forgetting'. These rituals and processions thus define, articulate and integrate the urban topography, linking separate points into a cognitive geography of urban space. They frequently also move out of the town into its surrounding territory to symbolise the unity of urban and rural, sometimes also marking the boundary between a town and its territory against those of its neighbours. Such processions and rituals regularly incorporate sacred space, deities and priests into their routes and participants, thus invoking or implying divine sanction on/of the current order. The ordering of the participants is generally a self-representation (very often idealised) of the order of contemporary urban society, according privileged places (in ascending or descending order) to the élite and rulers of the city, who are often juxtaposed with the divine. But again, exclusion can be as significant as inclusion; 'out groups' can have their position manifested through exclusion from the procession and rituals. Thus a social geography of the community is displayed and related to the divine, and the individual can situate him/herself in relation to it. However, like all such rituals which may imply a timeless, serene order, they are in fact highly malleable, and their re-fashioning and re-interpretation can be a way in which change to the social or religious order is negotiated. This could be accomplished by agreement, but equally urban ritual and spectacle are arenas for less eirenic interchanges. In later periods they were notoriously occasions on which riot and disorder could ensue, sometimes moderated under the guise of 'carnival', sanctioned disorder. Historians of these later periods see such events as part of the political discourse of urban society and one of the occasions on which more 'popular' feelings could be made overt and pressures for change made manifest to those who might otherwise wish to ignore them. Another feature of these rituals is that they are very often temporally iterative, for instance taking place annually within a liturgical or civic calendar of cyclical time, thus creating a temporal as well as a spatial and social geography of the town. By iteration they help to create and maintain civic memory and thus imbue the geography with a time depth. The rôle of these events, therefore, in creating the ideal concept and actual experience of the town or city can be crucial.

The physical setting
For a period such as Roman Britain lacking documentary narratives or artistic representations, we are dependent on the evidence of urban form. Urban geography is a vast field, but much of it relates quite specifically to more recent periods. However, the work of geographers such as Kevin Lynch has tried to create more generally applicable theories of the elements of the ordering of urban space (Lynch 1960) and the importance of time as a structuring principle (Lynch 1972) – overlapping with the work of sociologists such as Giddens (1984). Lynch's concepts, such as 'nodes' or 'boundaries', give us useful ways of describing the constituent elements of ancient urban space and of understanding their significance in structuring the urban experience.

Some of Lynch's concepts recur in MacDonald's (1986) consideration of the urban architecture of the Roman empire. Some of his categories have use here for the way in which they characterise elements of the urban space within which civic ceremonial took place, and which was in turn affected by the requirements of that ceremonial. He identifies streets as the 'armature' on which the town was laid out and along, or from which its public spaces and monuments depended. These buildings and monuments could be connective (*e.g.* a forum/plaza), or of passage (*e.g.* arches, gates), or (a variety of architecture of passage) the elements he defines as 'way stations' such as public fountains, *nymphaea, exedrae*. These in various ways create, punctuate and articulate space, and passage through them opens up the city to the onlooker. These categories imply the concept of movement, which is central to our discussion here. MacDonald's towns consist essentially of public buildings without the people that use them and the functions that go on in them to give them meaning. His focus on public architecture also means that significant private spaces (*e.g.* the houses of important individuals) and significant other mediums such as sculpture are ignored, nevertheless we shall return to his characterisations since they echo some of the connective functions of urban rituals and the way in which they integrate and give form and meaning to urban space. It should also be remembered that deliberately-planned urban space can be a reflection of a wider cosmological understanding, with the divisions of a city mirroring those of the universe (*e.g.* Wheatley 1971; Carl *et al.* 2000). The prescriptions in Vitruvius' *de Architectura* as to how the various elements of a planned Roman city should be placed and related to each other have explicit cosmological rationales. A city is both its various parts and also the sum of those parts, thus strengthening the rôle of rituals and processions in bringing the different elements into meaningful relationship.

This brief overview of some of the purposes, implicit or explicit, of urban festivals and of their physical setting gives a number of avenues of approach, which will here be used as a way of constructing a series of parameters within which to search for and situate such urban ritual in Roman Britain. The parameters I propose to explore here are: temporality; movement; ceremonies; actors. For each there will be brief overview of what the evidence from the wider Roman empire and from later Iron Age sources may allow us to say about such events. In all these cases, the evidence will be unbalanced: our evidence for practice in the Roman world is copious, essentially due to its being written down (as literary or epigraphic text) and occasionally represented, for the later Iron Age the written sources are few and problematic and more reliance has to be placed on the less coherent witness of the archaeology.

The religious calendar
By temporality is meant the patterning of festivals and rituals in and over time. Particular attention will be paid to evidence for structured iteration of the performance of these rites, which could thus be inscribed on and reflected in the physical evidence of the lay-out of the towns of Roman Britain. The evidence for the ritual structure of the Roman year is extensive. A variety of documents such as the *Fasti Praenestini* (Degrassi 1963, 1–28) allow us to reconstruct the calendar of the late Republic to early empire (*cf.* Scullard 1981 for a convenient compendium). The Codex-Calendar of 354 (Salzman 1990) allows us to do the same for the mid fourth century AD, incidentally also showing the influence of creeping Christianity. Clearly, it should not be argued that one can simply 'lift' these festivals from their context in Rome and apply them to Britain, too many of them are far too firmly rooted in the particular history and topography of the City of Rome (however tempting it might be to appropriate the *Amburbium* of the 27th February when the 'bounds' of the City were 'beaten'). What this evidence does show us is that the Roman religious year was largely organised in an annual cycle (with seasonal elements), though other time-intervals, up to the 110 years of the *saeculum*, were also envisioned.

Public festivals, *feriae*, could be either *stativae*, to be observed annually on the same date, or *conceptivae*, to be observed annually but on a date to be announced. The Codex-Calendar of 354 also allows us to see a development not yet visible in the earlier *fasti*, the huge number of festivals associated with Imperial Cult; at Rome, 98 days a year were consecrated to *ludi* and *circenses* in honour of emperors living and dead and the *domus divina* (Salzman 1990, 131–46). Even when the public performance of pagan rites was outlawed and subsidies to them from the public purse discontinued, Imperial Cult was always specifically exempted (*cf. Codex Theodosianus* II.8). The importance of Imperial Cult is a theme which will recur often in this paper.

Another important source for the annual cycle of religious observance is the *Feriale Duranum* (Fink 1971, no. 117; Nock 1952). Though it comes from the other end of the empire, it is useful in giving us an 'official' Roman provincial religious calendar, and its military origins may be of use in a heavily militarised province, such as Britain. The festivals observed by *Coh XX Palmyrenorum* were overwhelmingly those of Imperial Cult, along with some others generally associated with military deities such as Mars or with Roma. Interestingly, almost all the festivals celebrated at Rome herself are absent, even those such as the *Tubilustrium* (23rd March) with a specifically military orientation and falling within the date-range preserved in the *Feriale*. Nor were towns, even *coloniae*, those fragments of Rome, expected necessarily to observe the Roman festivals, as the *lex coloniae Iuliae Genetivae* from Spain shows (*Fontes Iuris Romani Anteiusitnianae* No.21). It was up to a majority of the decurions to decide which festivals and rites they wished to observe publicly, with the *haruspex* playing an important advisory rôle. So an annual round of public religious observance in the Roman style, especially of Imperial Cult, can be reasonably posited for at least the principal towns (*coloniae*, *municipia* and *'civitas*-capitals') of Roman Britain.

The evidence for the later Iron Age or 'Celtic' religious calendar is far more evanescent and problematical. The most substantial Roman-period evidence is the partial calendars surviving from Coligny and Villards d'Héria in eastern Gaul (Duval & Pinault 1986). The Coligny Calendar shows a five-year cycle of years divided into twelve lunar months, each named. Each month is further divided into two halves dependent on the phases of the moon. Only one festival is specifically named, the *Trinox(tion) Samoni*, the Three Nights of Samain. The name of this festival clearly recalls one of the four main festivals of the year named in later, insular sources, Samain, Beltane, Lugnasad, Imbolc, the 'quarter-days' of the seasonal round. Sadly, these documents vouchsafe no further information.

Isserlin (1994, 44–8) has suggested that epigraphic evidence for dates of dedication of monuments also suggests an awareness of seasonality in Roman-period Britain and Gaul, and goes on to suggest that archaeological work on ritual deposition may yield further results on seasonality. Henig (1982) has also suggested that a seasonal element may be discerned in religious practice in the Romano-British period. Beyond this it becomes increasingly dangerous to go, risking a descent into the crepuscular landscapes of the Celtic twilight. Even so, both the 'Roman' and the 'Celtic' evidence suggest a ritual calendar largely based on a recurring and regular annual cycle. This recurrence is important, since whereas a single ritual event may or may not leave a mark on the urban fabric, pattern and reiteration are far more likely to be inscribed on that fabric and thus readable by us.

Procession and performance
The second parameter I would like to establish is that of movement, that these rituals necessarily involved purposive movement through the urban landscape. The evidence from Rome herself is clear; one has only to think of the symbolism of the route of the Triumph from the *Campus Martius* along the *Via Sacra* to the Capitol. But the Triumph also serves as a

warning, it would be very difficult, if not impossible, to reconstruct its route simply from the plan of the City: processions can be adapted to urban space as much as urban space to processions. More germane to our purposes here is the equally unequivocal evidence for the proceedings and processions of Imperial Cult (*cf.* Price 1984, especially chapter 5). One of the features of Imperial Cult, which distinguished it from most other pagan cult, was that it was not tied to any particular group of worshippers. Anyone could participate, and indeed in the East this seems to have been encouraged, indeed enjoined, with the festivals being occasions when both the civic body and civic space were mobilised. Much other evidence, literary, epigraphic and artistic, might be prayed in aid for the prevalence of processions and street festivals in the Roman world.

Turning to the evidence for late Iron Age Britain, the evidence is less direct but nonetheless a good case can be made for positioning and movement as an integral part of religious observance. Recent work on Iron Age deposition practices (*e.g.* Hill 1995) has shown an emphasis on the placing of certain things at certain places (perhaps at certain times?). Other work has suggested that these practices are strongly related to the conceptualised structuring of space, to the reinforcing of boundaries, to the definition of differing types of area (*e.g.* Gwilt 1997; Parker Pearson 1999). The deposition of human remains at sites such as Folly Lane (Niblett 1999) or Lindow (Stead *et al.* 1986) are all seen as embedded within a sequence of (semi-)public rituals where the place and act of deposition lie at the end of a complex sequence of observances originating away from the deposition site. Many of the extensive, polyfocal late Iron Age complexes generically referred to as *oppida* only make sense when patterns of movement between the various foci are envisaged, structuring and integrating the disparate elements into a conceptual whole. Again, both 'Roman' and 'Celtic' sources allow us to posit a pattern of festivals where an important component was ordered and symbolic movement from place to place, and in which numbers of people might be involved, either passively as spectators or actively as participants.

Ceremonies

The evidence for the types of ceremony or observance undertaken is sketchy. From Rome we have evidence for sacrifices, *supplicationes* (thanksgiving ceremonies), *ludi* (games in the arena), *circenses* (races in the circus) and *epulones* (banquets). The *Feriale Duranum* also mentions sacrifices (including an *immolatio*) and *supplicationes*. Chapter LXXVII of the *lex Irnitana* from southern Spain (González 1986) states that the magistrates of the town should consider which *sacra* (rites), *ludi* (games) and *cenae* (formal meals) should be observed by the municipality. The evidence of the sorts of rites and rituals of Imperial Cult shows the range of observances in the East (Price 1984, chapter 5), for the West our information is more limited but not dissimilar (*cf.* Fishwick 2002). For the indigenous element of the population our information is even more scanty, though the current popularity of 'ritual feasting' as an explanation in archaeology may mean that *cenae* and *epulones* find favour as a ritual form, though one that probably involved a restricted compass of participants. Even if *circenses* are unlikely to have taken place in Britain, due to the lack of demonstrable circuses, some local variant of *ludi* could have taken place in the amphitheatres, whilst *supplicationes* and sacrifices are perfectly possible. Any of these could have been the occasion for public performance and processions.

The actors
Who, then, may have been the principal actors in and organisers of such ceremonials? The
Roman sources make it clear that there was a range of plausible candidates, principal amongst
them, unsurprisingly, the town magistrates in their sacred rôle and the members of the
priesthoods of the various deities. Once again, the Imperial Cult figures strongly. As noted
above, its universality enabled it to be the vehicle for a variety of statements about the imperial
and civic order, with public participation in the rites a *desideratum*. The priesthoods concerned
were the *Flamines* and the *Seviri Augustales*, each having their own reasons for encouraging
public spectacle. The *flamines* were drawn from amongst the local aristocracy and would thus
seek occasions to display their (self-)importance and remind the assembled citizenry of their
euergetism towards the city and its people. The *seviri*, on the other hand, were drawn from the
ranks of freedmen, normally excluded from civic office and honours, but here allowed to assert
a degree of social status and importance. The one inscription of a *sevir* we have from Roman
Britain is that of an imperial freedman in the *colonia* of Lincoln (Hassall & Tomlin 1979, 345).
So both priesthoods, aristocrats and parvenus, would have had their reasons for encouraging
lavish performance of Imperial Cult. Other priesthoods of Graeco-Roman cults might also have
performed in public, where, for instance, did the *dendrophori* of Dunstable (Matthews 1981)
undertake their ceremonies?

How the public cult of indigenous deities was organised is far more difficult to tell. A small
number of inscriptions refer to *sacerdotes*, but only one is from a civilian context, the *sacerdos
deae Sulis* from Bath (RIB 155). Nevertheless, the existence of so many temples of 'Romano-
Celtic' form as well as altars and inscriptions, all derived from 'Roman' practice, suggest that
some sort of priestly cadre existed to service them.

The later Roman period
The discussion so far has been implicitly framed in terms of what one might reasonably expect
in Roman Britain under the Principate. With the Dominate came perhaps an even greater
emphasis on the person of the emperor or on his *simulacra* in the form of statues, paintings and
other images, already potent under the earlier empire (*cf.* Kelly 1998; 1999). A whole
choreography of imperial ceremonial was devised, such as the *adventus* (MacCormack 1986).
These were public events where the strict protocols of order and degree of the late Roman
world were scrupulously observed. Even in the absence of the emperor himself, the icons of the
imperial presence could stand proxy for him, with the added advantage that they would not be
tempted to turn their heads, spit or wipe their noses (Ammianus Marcellinus *Res Gestae*
16.10.9): the destruction of the imperial images in the civic disorder of the Riot of the Statues
in Antioch in 387 brought fear of terrible reprisal on the city.

These ceremonies were also adopted and adapted by the Christian church, with, for
example, the ceremonies for the reception of a new relic imitating those of the imperial
adventus. As the Christian community became a significant presence within urban society and
the bishop became a force to be reckoned with, we may imagine the sorts of modification to the
order of procession needed to embody the new, recreated social reality. There would also be a
developing physical reality as a city acquired a new, Christian sacred topography. That
topography would be articulated by processions in which the bishop, the clergy and the faithful
of all sorts and conditions passed from Christian place to Christian place under the gaze of their
fellow-citizens. Though the full development of these rituals (*cf.* Loseby 1998, 58–67) lies later
than the ending of Roman rule in Britain, it may have been under way during the fourth

century. One area where Christian ideology required a major recasting of public ritual was the integration of the cemeteries into the cognitive map of the city as a zone of public rather than private concern and increasingly as well- rather than ill-omened. The development of extra-mural foci and their placing in the order of symbolic topography and movement would have marked a major shift in the real and imagined patterning of civic space. In addition, the new, Christian liturgical calendar would have altered the seasonal round of observances, refashioning civic time. But as well as adding to the social, spatial and temporal cognitive map of the city, the Church might well also have subtracted from it. With the increasing rejection of the beliefs, rituals and forms of traditional 'pagan' religion, may have come acts of 'social forgetting' as places and persons formerly integral to the materialisation of the image of the city through ritual and procession were expunged from the running order.

It seems to me that a case has been made that the towns of Roman Britain were in essence no different from towns elsewhere in the empire in that we may expect in them a regular cycle of ritual observances and processions, related to both the imported religious practice (above all Imperial Cult) and indigenous religion, consisting of a variety of rituals such as sacrifice and spectacle, carried out by priesthoods both of Imperial Cult and of other Graeco-Roman and indigenous cults, and changing through time, particularly with the development of Christian equivalents or replacements for earlier practice. It now remains to interrogate our available evidence, namely the town-plans and public and religious buildings, monuments and areas of those towns to see if we may identify the effect of such practices on the urban landscape.

Rituals and urban landscape

Before looking at three particular examples, it may be as well to consider more generally where such rites may have been enacted and which elements of the town-plan may embody that practice. First of all, it is important to remember that processions are essentially integrative in nature, by moving from one place or area of a town to another. There is, of course, one element of formal, Roman-style town planning which also has this quality, the street system. MacDonald's (1986, chapter II) discussion of streets as armatures, which structured the placing of public buildings and monuments, but also allowed the onlooker to identify them, is clearly germane here. This warns us against simply looking at individual points rather than the whole. Streets were central to this sort of civic ceremonial as the axes and avenues along which it progressed. In addition, the evidence from the East (*cf.* Price 1984, chapter 5) makes it clear that streets were one of the main arenas for public celebration of Imperial Cult, because of their potential for processions and enactments in front of large numbers of the people. Streets were truly 'public' space, accessible to all. This rôle in ritual may explain the great width of some principal streets at Romano-British towns, for instance Caerwent, instead of/as well as carts and commerce. One slightly odd feature of many western provincial towns, including those of Roman Britain, is that the major 'connective' complexes, such as *fora* and temple precincts, are not penetrated by the armature of the streets. Rather, they lie to one side of them and need to be approached through the passage architecture of their formal entrances before experiencing their connective nature.

To turn to these individual building types; the most important civic complex was, of course, the forum. As has long been recognised (*cf.* Goodchild 1946), Romano-British fora lack the temple precincts that characterise their Gallic and north-Italian counterparts. Since many of the temples in these precincts seem to have been related to Imperial Cult, this would seem to pose a problem for the argument for the centrality of this Cult in British towns. However, imperial statues or images could be housed elsewhere than in temples, for instance an *aedes Augusti*, and one might point to the central *aedes* of a Romano-British forum, behind the basilica, as a suitable place, mirroring the use of the same space in the legionary *principia* which Romano-British fora so resemble. Moreover, the very form of the forum complex allows for public ritual, such as sacrifice, and over time the forum would have been endowed with statuary and other decoration, serving as the *lieu de mémoire* for the *civitas*. One might also note that some *fora* such as Exeter, Silchester and Winchester were surrounded by open areas, suitable for large gatherings. If major, classical-style temples are generally lacking in British towns, other forms of temple, particularly the 'Romano-Celtic' are not. Particular examples will be discussed below, but here it is worth noting that many of them stand within relatively large, open *temene*, precincts, again suitable for large gatherings.

Other structures which would have permitted large gatherings were the theatres and amphitheatres. Rare at the towns of Roman Britain (Canterbury, ?Cirencester, Colchester), theatres of strictly classical plan are well-known from the Mediterranean world as places where society was seated in strict order of precedence and surveyed by an imperial image (*cf.* Zanker 1998, 107–14 for Pompeii). Amphitheatres, more numerous in Britain, were also spaces where large, ordered (if not always orderly) gatherings were accommodated. The Gallo-Roman-style theatre/amphitheatre at Verulamium (see below) and the more classical theatre at the Gosbecks religious complex outside Colchester (also see below) bring us close to the world of the great 'rural sanctuaries' of Gaul, whose large, prominently-placed theatre/amphitheatres were presumably the setting for public spectacles associated with the temple cult. For the later Roman period we should not forget the increasing importance of the cemeteries, though as yet we have little evidence for cemetery churches compared with areas nearer the Mediterranean.

Having established a series of general consideration, it is now time to turn, at last, to some actual instances of Romano-British towns and the possible evidence for the performance and rôle in them of public ceremonial and processions. I am confining myself to the 'large' towns of the island, and in particular those for which we have a substantial amount of excavated evidence. For reasons of space I shall confine myself to three examples, each of which will illuminate different aspects of the argument, as well as providing some commonality. These towns are, Silchester, Colchester and Verulamium.

Silchester (Figure 1.1)

To anatomise the various likely buildings in Silchester of the type considered above is straightforward enough (*cf.* Boon 1974). At the centre (*insula* iv) lies the forum, set back from the streets and thus surrounded by largely open spaces. In the middle of the range on the western side of the basilica was the apsidal *aedes*, presumably housing imperial images and the city's *tutela*. A large polygonal temple lay to the south in *insula* vii, at the western end of a large empty *temenos*, with a possible entrance in the eastern boundary wall. The next *insula* to the east, xxxv, also housed a temple, much smaller, rectangular and at the southern end of an apparently empty space. Associated with the temple were parts of three inscriptions (RIB 69, 70, 71) referring to the *collegium peregrinorum* at *Calleva*. It is worth noting that *collegia*, associations, regularly formed part of ceremonies and processions of Imperial Cult in the East and also had seats reserved for them in the theatres; there is some evidence for them in the Mediterranean areas of the West (van Nijf 1997, chapters 5 and 6, appendices 2,4). In the eastern part of *insula* xxxvi, just inside the east gate, is a walled enclosure containing a rectangular building, which may be a temple or shrine, just by where the road in from the gate

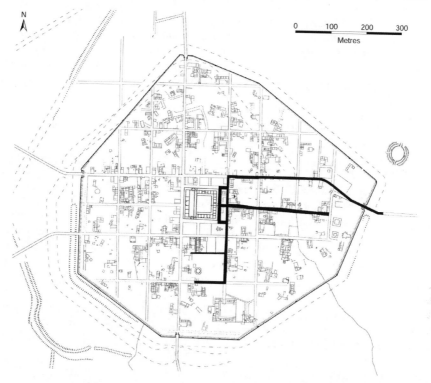

Figure 1.1 *Plan of Silchester with possible processional route*

turns to join with the main alignment of the street-grid (rather reminiscent of the siting of the Triangular Temple at Verulamium). Two *insulae* to the west, the south-eastern corner of *insula* xxi was occupied by a small, rectangular structure with a semi-circular apse, identified as a shrine or *schola*, and opening onto the principal east-west street. To the south of the east gate, inside the eastern walls, lies the principal religious precinct of the town, containing two temples at least (a third has been posited under the mediaeval church) and ancillary structures in the northern part of the *temenos*. Outside the east gate, to the north of the London road, lay the amphitheatre.

How may these have been articulated? One clear element of articulation is the road running between the main entrance into the forum, on its eastern side, and the principal group of temples. This deviates from the main alignment of the street system, running on a slightly more north-west – south-east alignment (in fact, more accurately east-west than the main alignment itself), to arrive near the centre of the western precinct wall. This deviation must have been to link the forum and the temple complex directly. It is not difficult to see this as a processional way from the principal civic complex to the principal grouping of religious buildings. Equally, on leaving the main, eastern entrance of the forum and coming to the major north-south street, wider than average, a procession could have turned either right or left. Turning to the right, towards the *mansio*, would have brought the procession to the *temenos* of the *insula* vii polygonal temple on the right-hand side of the street, passing by the *insula* xxxv temple with its *collegium* inscriptions on the left. Turning to the left, a procession would have come to the main east-west street, and turning right onto it would have brought it past the posited *schola* of *insula* xxi, perhaps a form of way-station in a city notably devoid of other possible way-stations such as arches. This would bring the procession to the possible temple by the change of alignment in *insula* xxxvi, where a turn to the right would have brought it to the main temple complex, or continuing straight on out of the gate would have been the approach to the amphitheatre, where so many people could have sat and witnessed all manner of spectacle (*cf.* Fulford 1989, 187–93).

The defences themselves could also have been a religious as well as a defensive boundary (*cf.* Esmonde Cleary 2003, 79), and thus the circuit may have needed ritual reinforcing on occasion. This religious aspect could in part explain the monumentalisation in stone of the gateways prior to the construction of the walls; the gates could also have served as way-stations on processional routes. Finally, there is the so-called church just to the south-east of the forum complex (though the evidence is that the basilica at least may no longer have had a civic function by this time, see Fulford & Timby 2000, I.6). Standing in an apparently vacant area it could have been the focus for rituals over and above what went on inside its walls.

It is perhaps worth noting that all the identifiable public and religious structures lie on or to the east of the north-south axis. Was this a better-omened half of the urban cosmos? The street-grid is aligned close to the cardinal points of the compass and involved a shift from the later Iron Age orientation, so the urban lay-out may reflect a cosmological view of the place and space of the town. Furthermore, could the directions the hypothesised processions took, and the directions from which temples and other foci were approached also give insight into 'auspicious' and 'inauspicious' directions of movement?

Colchester (Figure 1.2)

Colchester affords us two interesting and contrasting contexts for ceremonial activity. First, intra-murally Colchester contained the Temple of the Deified Claudius, seat of the provincial Imperial Cult (*cf.* Fishwick 2002, 75–91), where annually great festivities would mark the assembly of the *concilium provinciae*, with the representatives of all the *civitates*, the *flamines* of the provincial Cult and its officers all in due order. Though not *sensu stricto* part of the civic ritual of the *colonia Victricensis*, the observances at the Temple left an indelible mark on the physical fabric of the city. Not only was there the Temple, with the great altar all set within a great colonnaded precinct with adjoining classical-style theatre (*cf.* Drury 1984), but to the south was the major complex in *insula* xxx. It is not known whether at Colchester there was a civic and a provincial forum, as at Mérida or Tarragona. The main east-west street can be seen as an important armature, widening out as it passed between the porticoed façade of the Temple precinct and the *insula* xxx complex. At its western end this armature was marked by the arch later incorporated into the Balkerne Gate, an arch which, as so often, marked a boundary and also a significant change in the alignment of the street. This takes us out to the second area of interest.

To the west of the walled *colonia* was a series of extra-mural temples unmatched at any town or city in Britain (*cf.* Hull 1958, 224–40, 259–71). Immediately outside the Balkerne Gate the road was flanked to north and south by temples, marking this as both boundary and liminal zone under divine supervision. Following the London road to the south-west, there was then a branch road leading to the furthest-off and best-known temple. This is the site of the temple and theatre complex at Gosbecks, some 3.5km (2 miles) south-west of the *colonia*. As is well known, this consisted of a temple within a square *temenos* (perhaps originating in a later Iron

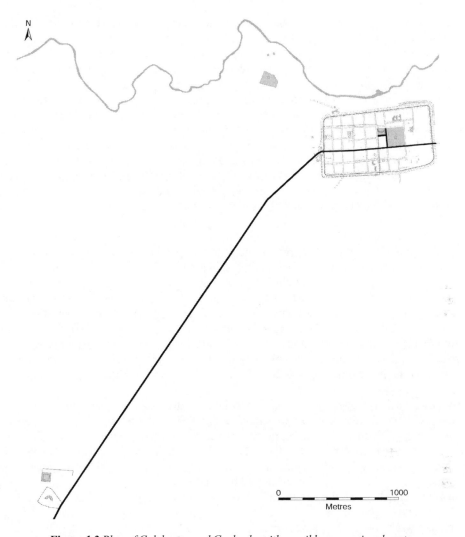

Figure 1.2 *Plan of Colchester and Gosbecks with possible processional route*

Age ditched enclosure), itself set within a larger walled enclosure with another enclosure to the east, and south of that the enclosure containing a classical-style theatre. Crummy (Hawkes & Crummy 1995, 102) has suggested that the temple and theatre were connected by a processional way. It is not hard to see the branch road from the London road also as a processional route as much as simply a thoroughfare, though a processional route which would have passed through the principal cemetery of the *colonia*. Moving along it from the direction of the *colonia*, and soon after leaving the London road was another temple within a walled *temenos*, itself replacing a ditched enclosure of probable late Iron Age date. The precinct-wall had a gate on the south-eastern side for the roadway running to meet the Gosbecks road. To the north-west of the *colonia*, in the area of Sheepen, were at least two other temples, one within a walled *temenos*. Closer in to the walls was another, single temple. None of these has any known formal approach-road, but there must have been an access route of some sort.

Colchester clearly had a sacral geography which extended well outside the walls, integrating a large area of the late Iron Age *oppidum* into the cognitive and experienced map of the settlement. This must make us wary of regarding the walls as imposing a barrier between what was inside and what was outside them; indeed the ancient evidence sees the town and its territory as a unity, not as polar opposites, so the Colchester evidence conforms well to this view. It is worth noting in passing that it seems that in the later Roman period the focus of extra-mural activity moved from the western to the southern extra-mural area (*cf.* Esmonde Cleary 1987, 58–60), with some at least of the temples falling into disrepair. Whether or not the Butt Road building (Crummy, Crummy & Crossan 1993, chapter3) was or was not a church (*cf.* Millett 1995), it again suggests that the southern side of the *colonia* was now the dominant one for burial and other extra-mural, ritual observances.

Verulamium (Figure 1.3)

As so often, it is Verulamium that gives us the fullest range of evidence from a Romano-British town, though we should be wary of letting that suggest Verulamium was somehow typical or a norm to which other towns should conform. Watling Street, running south-east – north-west, was a principal armature along which by the end of the second century we find (from the south-east): the London gate, an arch where the road crossed the line of the late-first-century defences (the '1955 ditch'), the 'triangular temple' in the angle between the alignment of Watling Street and the urban grid, the basilica with forum on its other side, an arch spanning the road between the theatre and temple complex to the left and the *macellum* to the right, a third arch on the line of the north-western stretch of the '1955 ditch', and finally the Chester gate.

Buildings such as the temple, the basilica and the theatre would have announced themselves by their distinctive architecture, and the arches and the triangular temple could also have acted as way stations. The forum was exceptional to Britain in that on the side opposite the basilica there were three temples (or two temples and a *curia*), so the forum in itself would have been a significant arena for civic and religious observances (as Alan Sorrell (1974) percipiently shows in his painting of the Verulamium forum). The road from the north-western gateway of the forum leads directly to the large temple and *temenos*, to which in the mid second century the theatre was added between the *temenos* and Watling Street. Not long after a street, off the main alignment, was driven through *insula* xiv to link the forum and the theatre. The forum/temple/theatre complex was clearly a major area of structured movement in which large numbers of people could participate. Two other temples, side-by-side, lay in *insula* xvii across Watling Street from the theatre. Another single temple lay two *insulae* south-west of the forum in *insula* xxi. These last three are known only from aerial photography, so are difficult to fit into a context.

Since the excavation of the Folly Lane burial, precinct and temple (Niblett 1999), it is now appreciated that there was another important armature conditioning the lay-out and functioning of Verulamium. The road from Silchester to Colchester passed along the south-eastern face of the forum (with its own entrance-way) before passing across the river Ver and past the foot of the hill on which the Folly Lane site and temple stood, having passed the Branch Road bath-house (for ritual as much as for physical cleanliness?). Starting opposite the theatre, another road exited the town, crossed the river and then climbed the hill to the Folly Lane site and

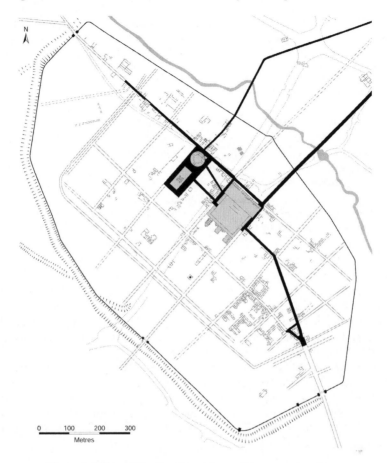

Figure 1.3 *Plan of Verulamium with possible processional route*

temple. As with Colchester, so the physical and ritual topography of Verulamium cannot be fully understood without reference to the extra-mural area, and one must envisage ceremonials integrating the Folly Lane complex into the sacral and cognitive geography of the town.

Verulamium, of course, affords us also the one possible textual description of some sort of civic event or ritual, the *pasio* of Alban. It has long been recognised (*e.g.* Levison 1941) that elements of the martyrdom story conform with the topography of Roman Verulamium.

§14 When he was led like a lamb to the sacrifice, [he came to a river] whose rapid stream divided the wall from the arena where he was to be executed... By which crossing he saw on the further side a great crowd of people of both sexes and all ages and conditions who had undoubtedly been summoned by divine prompting to attend the martyr. [The crowd was so numerous] that they could hardly get across the bridge by evening, and the judge was left in the city without attendants. So he [Alban] betook himself to the stream he had to pass to reach the place of martyrdom, and turned his eyes to heaven. Thereupon the river yielded to his footsteps and provided a dry bed.
§15 When he came to the place appointed for his death...

§16 ...the holy martyr and the crowds climbed the hill, which rose with inexpressible beauty for 500 paces from the arena. It was clothed and coloured with various kinds of flowers, with nothing difficult or steep or sharp about it, its sides in all directions smoothed by nature like a level surface. It had undoubtedly been made ready long since for the martyr; before it was consecrated with sacred blood, its natural beauty had made it like a shrine (sacrum).
(Translation from Morris 1968, 2)

The earliest extant versions of the *pasio* would seem to go back to sixth-century Auxerre (Wood 1984, 12–14), whose fifth-century bishop Germanus famously visited the shrine of Alban. One has, of course, to be careful about how one uses the *pasio*, it is after all hagiography. Thus some parts of it such as the preface derive from other *vitae* (Levison 1941, 345). Even in the short quotes above, Alban makes the Ver behave like the Red Sea, and the flowery meadow of sacrifice is probably hagiographic hyperbole. However, when all is said and done, the circumstantial evidence remains. We have a judicial execution which draws a considerable crowd (as they did in early-modern Europe); the condemned man leaves the city across the Ver conforming to the practice enjoined elsewhere (*e.g. Agrimensores* 47.1) of conducting executions outside the ritual boundary of the town; then after the executioner refuses to kill him in the original spot, they mount a hill; the whole event takes a considerable time. This sounds plausible as a form of civic ritual with integration of different parts of the topography of the town and the participation of many sections of urban society.

Previous commentaries on the *pasio* have argued that the execution-ground may be the hill on the south-eastern side of Verulamium where the Abbey later stood. But could we now posit the Folly Lane hill (*cf.* Niblett 1999, plate I for an air-view of all this area) as the site of this particular ceremony? The Abbey would then memorialise the place of burial rather than the place of martyrdom, and excavations south of the Abbey have indeed shown a fourth-century cemetery with evidence for frequentation and offerings (*cf.* Biddle 1977). Whatever the veracity of this reconstruction, it does suggest that the extra-mural areas of Verulamium may have retained an importance in the sacred and civic geography of the city down to the end of the Roman period, let alone beyond.

Conclusion
Study of the structuring of Romano-British towns has, like our principal source of evidence the plans themselves, conventionally been rather two-dimensional and dominated by building-types or individual buildings. This has often led to the reification of towns: 'towns developed', 'towns declined', 'towns did this that or the other', when of course it was always the people who caused these things to happen. It was all too often left to artists like Alan Sorrell (1974) to people our vision of these towns. I hope that the discussion above has shown that it is possible to approach a significant part of the day-to-day (or year-on-year) lives of the inhabitants of these places. Analysis of the individual town-plans shows that there are elements which make good sense in terms of provision for civic and religious ritual, in some cases better sense that other explanations.

The disposition of streets, public buildings and monuments can well be understood in terms of public observance, ritual and processions. These events would presumably have served to do what they did in other times and in other places. They would have been a means both of emphasising the importance of particular places or structures (equally of ignoring others) and of weaving them into a cognitive geography of the town, both within its boundaries (later walls) and outside them. The very act of doing this would inscribe the memory of this geography onto the mental maps of new participants (immigrants, the next generation), passing on the pattern thus created. This geography would at the same time be a sacral geography, not just of the individual places, but possibly also of their situation in relation to some larger, cosmological patterning of the world, human and divine. The organisation of the processions would also demonstrate to participants and onlookers alike the composition and hierarchy of the urban order; comparative evidence suggests this would be to some extent idealised, a way for individuals and the community to arrange the human world as it ought to be and to relate it to the divine.

If we may argue that there is sufficient evidence to posit the more orderly and seemly elements of this aspect of Romano-British urban life, we sadly do not as yet have the evidence to detect the more disruptive events, ritual and procession as the stage for political action and discourse. However, just as a passing thought, under what circumstances was part of the forum of Wroxeter burnt down in the later second century with the stalls of the traders tipped over, and again at the end of the third century, after which this particular civic monument (and presumably what it represented) was abandoned? Do such events always have to be 'accidents'? However that may be, that such questions can be posed, and that some of the less contentious material and arguments put forward in this paper may be advanced, is, I hope, a way of helping to move on our understanding of the towns of Roman Britain, through putting the people back into the towns and trying to identify some of the round of events that would have structured both their lives and their towns.

Acknowledgements
I am very grateful to the organisers of the 'Roman Working Lives' conference for their invitation to speak (albeit that field-work commitments eventually precluded me from attending), also for inviting me to submit this paper and for putting up with its elephantine gestation period. I am also very grateful to Ray Laurence and Roger White for looking at an earlier version and suggesting corrections and additions which have much improved it.

Bibliography
Biddle, M. 1977. 'Alban and the Anglo-Saxon Church', in Runcie, R. (ed.) *Cathedral and City: St Albans ancient and modern*. Martyn Associates, London: 23–42

Boon, G.C. 1974. *Silchester: the Roman town of Calleva*. David & Charles, Newton Abbott.

Carl, P., Conningham, R., Cowgill, G.L., Higham, C. & Kemp, B. 2000. 'Viewpoint: were cities built as images?', *CAJ* 10: 327–65

Crummy, P., Crummy, N. & Crossan, C. 1993. *Excavations of Roman and Later Cemeteries, Churches and Monastic Sites in Colchester, 1971–88*. Colchester Archaeological Report 9, Colchester.

Darnton, R. 1984. *The Great Cat Massacre and Other Episodes in French Cultural History*. Harmondsworth, London.

Degrassi, A. 1963. *Inscriptiones Italiae: volume 13: Fasti et Elogia*. Liberia dello stato, Roma.

Drury, P.J. 1984. 'The Temple of Claudius at Colchester: reconsidered', *Britannia* 21: 7–50

Duval, P-M. & Pinault, G. 1986. *Recueil des Inscriptions Gauloises: volume III*. XLVe Supplément à *Gallia*. Centre National de la Recherche Scientifique, Paris.

Esmonde Cleary, A.S. 1987. *The Extra-Mural Areas of Romano-British Towns*. BAR (British Series) 169, Oxford.

Esmonde Cleary, A.S. 2003. 'Civil defences in the west under the high empire', in Wilson, P. (ed.) *The Archaeology of Roman Towns: studies in honour of John S. Wacher*. Oxbow, Oxford: 73–85

Fink, R.O. 1971. *Roman Military Records on Papyrus*. American Philological Society Monograph 26. Case Western University Press, Ann Arbor.

Fishwick, D. 2002. *The Imperial Cult in the Latin West: studies in the ruler cult of the western provinces of the Roman empire: Volume III: Provincial Cult: Part 1: Institution and Evolution*. Brill, Leiden.

Fulford, M.G. 1989. *The Silchester Amphitheatre: excavations of 1979–85*. Britannia Monograph Series 10, Society for the Promotion of Roman Studies, London.

Fulford, M.G. & Timby, J. 2000. *Late Iron Age and Roman Silchester: excavations on the site of the forum-basilica 1977, 1980–96*. Britannia Monograph Series 15, Society for the Promotion of Roman Studies, London.

Giddens, A. 1984. *The Constitution of Society: outline of the theory of structuration*. Polity, Cambridge.

González, J. 1986. 'The *Lex Irnitana*: a New Copy of the Flavian municipal law', *JRS* 76: 147–243

Goodchild, R. 1946. 'The Origins of the Romano-British forum', *Antiquity* 20: 70–7

Gwilt, A. 1997. 'Popular Practices from Material Culture: a case study of the Iron Age settlement at Wakerley, Northamptonshire', in Gwilt, A. & Haselgrove, C. (eds) *Reconstructing Iron Age Societies*. Oxbow Monograph 71. Oxford: 153–66

Hanawalt, B.A. & Keyerson, K.L. 1994. *City and Spectacle in Medieval Europe*. Medieval Studies at Minnesota Volume 6. University of Minnesota Press, Minneapolis.

Hassall, M.W.C. & Tomlin, R.S.O. 1979. 'Roman Britain in 1978: inscriptions', *Britannia* 10: 339–56

Hawkes, C.F.C. & Crummy, P. 1995. *Camulodunum 2*. Colchester Archaeological Report 11, Colchester Archaeological Trust, Colchester.

Henig, M. 1982. 'Seasonal feasts in Roman Britain', *OJA* 1: 213–23

Hill, J.D. 1995. *Ritual and Rubbish in the Iron Age of Wessex: a study on the formation of a specific archaeological record*. BAR (British Series) 242, Oxford.

Hull, M.R. 1958. *Roman Colchester*. Reports of the Research Committee of the Society of Antiquaries of London, Oxford.

Isserlin, R. 1994. 'An archaeology of brief time: monuments and seasonality in Roman Britain', in Cottam, S., Dungworth, D., Scott, S. & Taylor, J. (eds.) *TRAC 94: proceedings of the Fourth Annual Theoretical Roman Archaeology Conference*: 45–56

Kelly C. 1998. 'Emperors, government and bureaucracy', in Cameron, A. & Garnsey, P. (eds.) *The Cambridge Ancient History: Volume XIII: The Late Empire, A.D.337–425*. Cambridge University Press, Cambridge: 138–83

Kelly, C. 1999. 'Empire Building', in Bowersock, G.W., Brown, P. & Grabar, A. (eds) *Late Antiquity: a guide to the post-classical world*. Harvard University Press, Harvard: 170–95

Lane Fox, R. 1986. *Pagans and Christians in the Mediterranean World from the Second Century AD to the Conversion of Constantine*. Viking, London.

Levison, W. 1941. 'St. Alban and St. Albans', *Antiquity* 15: 337–59

Loseby, S.T. 1998. 'Arles in Late Antiquity: *Gallula Roma Arelas* and *Urbs Genesii*', in Christie, N. & Loseby, S.T. (eds) *Towns in Transition: urban evolution in late antiquity and the early middle ages*. Scolar Press, London: 45–70

Lynch, K. 1960. *The Image of the City*. Massachusetts Institute of Technology Press, Cambridge MA.

Lynch, K. 1972. *What Time is this Place?* Massachusetts Institute of Technology Press, Cambridge MA.

MacCormack, S.G. 1986. *Art and Ceremony in Late Antiquity*. University of California Press, Berkley & London.

MacDonald, W.L. 1986. *The Architecture of the Roman Empire: Volume II: An urban appraisal*. Yale University Press, New Haven.

Matthews, C.L. 1981. 'A Romano-British Inhumation Cemetery at Dunstable', *BAJ* 15.

Millett, M.J. 1995. 'An Early Christian Community at Colchester?', *AJ* 152: 451–4

Morris, J. 1968. 'The Date of Saint Alban', *HA* 1: 1–8

Nelson, J.L. 1986. *Politics and Ritual in Early Medieval European History*. Hambledon Press, London.

Niblett, R. 1999. *The Excavation of a Ceremonial Site at Folly Lane, Verulamium*. Britannia Monograph Series 14, Society for the Promotion of Roman Studies, London.

van Nijf, O.M. 1997. *The Civic World of Professional Associations in the Roman east*. Gieben, Amsterdam.

Nock, A.D. 1951. 'The Roman Army and the Roman Religious Year', *HTR* 45: 187–252

Parker Pearson, M. 1999. 'Food, Sex and Death: cosmologies in the British Iron Age with particular reference to East Yorkshire', *CAJ* 9: 43–69

Price, S.R.F. 1984. *Rituals of Power: the Roman imperial cult in Asia Minor*. Cambridge University Press, Cambridge.

le Roy Ladurie, E. 1979. *Le Carnaval de Romans: de la Chandeleur au mercredi des Cendres, 1579–1580*. Gallimard, Paris.

Salzman, M.R. 1990. *On Roman Time: the Codex-Calendar of 354 and the rhythms of urban life in late antiquity*. University of California Press, Berkeley & London.

Scullard, H. 1981. *Festivals and Ceremonies of the Roman Republic*. Thames & Hudson, London.

Sorrell, A. 1974. *The Towns of Roman Britain*. Batsford, London.

Stead, I.M., Bourke, J.B. & Brothwell, D. 1986. *Lindow Man: the body in the bog*. British Museum Press, London.

Wheatley, P. 1971. *Pivot of the Four Quarters: a preliminary enquiry into the origins and character of the ancient Chinese city*. Edinburgh University Press, Edinburgh.

Wood, I. 1984. 'The end of Roman Britain: continental evidence and parallels', in Lapidge, M. & Dumville, D. (eds) *Gildas: new approaches*. Boydell, London: 1–25

Zanker, P. 1998. *Pompeii: public and private life*. Harvard University Press, Cambridge MA.

2

Domestic architecture and social discourse in Roman towns

Dominic Perring

The Roman house, unlike its modern counterpart, was rarely a private place. Indeed, one of its chief functions was to provide a stage for the social encounters from which political and economic life was built (Hales 2003). Town houses were consequently as much places for working lives as any other urban setting. Some of the most important work undertaken in the house happened at the court of the aristocratic patron: in his halls and at his dinner table. Here, as much as in the public forum, was where serious business was conducted. Contracts were agreed, alliances established and political careers forged in these domestic settings. Other working lives served these higher goals: large private households supported the needs of the Roman patron, and aristocratic houses became palaces. The social complexity of city living therefore left a clear and visible mark on the design and organisation of domestic space. The study of town houses consequently offers important information on how Roman cities were understood and experienced, and about how such understandings may have differed according to circumstance.

The subject is a large one, and no short summary can adequately address the vast diversity of use and intent that was found amidst the disparate cities of a changing empire. In this paper I will therefore focus my attention the design of the reception quarters of aristocratic houses. These parts of the house served a variety of domestic rituals, such as those attached to the morning greeting of clients at the *salutatio*, or in the entertainment of friends and other guests at evening supper parties. The importance of these facilities is illustrated by the disproportionate amount of space that they took up within the house, by the expense of their decoration, and by the fact that these were the rooms most likely to be extended and improved during the life of a property. This investment in luxury served a purpose beyond that of self-indulgent vanity (*contra* Martins 2003). These places of leisure were also places of work. My emphasis in this paper is therefore on the working rich, although an archaeology of the working poor can also be read from such spaces (for which see Roskams forthcoming).

There are several related points that I wish to make about the design and use of the reception rooms found in Roman town houses. The main path of my argument is that Roman civic life revolved around the encounters that took place here, and that this domestic space was consequently configured around socially acceptable approaches to polite behaviour. This polite behaviour drew on a shared interest in Greek culture that facilitated the educated discourse of elite society throughout the Roman Empire. The use of Greek inspired approaches to domestic ceremony required the adoption of appropriate Graeco-Roman architectural settings. These ceremonies, and the architectures that they inspired, were essentially concerned with reproducing patronal ties within local communities. As a consequence the architecture was not only Graeco-Roman in inspiration, but was deployed in ways that reinforced the distinctive characters of particular civic and regional identities. Most Roman houses managed to combine references to 'universal' cultural values within local design traditions. Here I come close to taking an opposite position to that proposed by Reece (1988), and suggest that far from finding that Roman façades concealed native identities, the urban architecture witnessed Graeco-Roman identities expressed in regional idiom. Design references to Roman authority and Greek ideologies were both widely diffused and widely understood.

A further point I wish to stress is that the full deployment and decoding of this Graeco-Roman architecture relied on understandings of social practice that could only be obtained through an appropriate education. There is a link between the ideas of philosophy, the educational process through which such ideas were elaborated, changes in educated social behaviour, variable expectations of the domestic settings in which housed such social behaviour, and the architectural evidence itself. When describing this evidence it is useful to recognise that classical architecture speaks of a classical education. In order to appreciate the design and spatiality of Roman houses, we must therefore engage with the philosophical arguments that formed the basis of such education (as attempted in Perring 2003a). Art historians have long appreciated the need to set the material evidence within its ideological context (*e.g.* Elsner 1998, who gives proper emphasis to the influence of the Second Sophistic in developments in late antique art and architecture). Such approaches have also now begun to inform the study of Roman domestic architecture (*e.g.* Hales 2003), but the complexity of the relationship between ideas and the built environment continues to be underestimated in archaeological studies. The ideas and arguments alluded to in Roman design were not, in my view, of marginal importance. The use of cultural references in Roman architecture was not simply a casual affectation of the idle rich, but an important component in the articulation and representation of social power.

Houses in the formation of social power

The Roman house obtained potency as both the symbol and product of the power that derived from the ownership of property. Property gave access to civic office and political life, as well as providing the economic leverage through which the ties of clientage could be converted into mutually beneficial advancement. Property, and consequently architecture, was therefore inextricably linked to the ways in which rank was obtained and displayed (Purcell 1990). Such display was a vital feature of urban life. One of the main reasons that towns were necessary to the ancient world was because they established a forum for the networks of patronage and dependency that sustained authority. Wallace-Hadrill has made the telling point that access to power was 'mediated through individuals. It was this inaccessibility of the centre, except through the personal links that generated the power of patronage; and it was through the exercise of this power that patronage placed social integration within limits and so secured social control' (1989, 74).

Town houses provided the main setting for these individual and personal encounters from which power was built. The Roman period witnessed a significant redirection of social and political activity away from the public urban sphere and into the domain of the private house (Perring 1991a; Dupont 1997, 45). Houses consequently drew inspiration from earlier civic architecture, and several design features found in houses made their first appearance in public buildings (examples range from the use of tile coursing in masonry constructions to the use of apse-ended reception rooms).

Navigation of the systems of power relied on shared understandings; on shared rules of social behaviour that facilitated discourse. All complex societies need codes of polite behaviour, supported by recognisable symbols that help guide action (La Gory 1983). Common rules of etiquette and social practice, drawn in large part from Greek models and dependant on educated good taste (*paideia*), were therefore necessary to Roman elite society. The need to provide a suitable setting for culturally defined social behaviour inspired common approaches to domestic architecture: a language of design that presented familiar points of reference and facilitated the measured exchange of deference, honour and intimacy. Wherever there was an identifiably Roman element to the structure of power this was reflected in identifiably Roman approaches to social practice. This in turn gave rise to recognisably Roman forms of domestic architecture. In the language of social theory the design of such space can be described as the product of a contingent, hegemonically maintained system of representation (Natter & Jones 1997).

Regional diversity

The widespread adoption of Graeco-Roman cultural practices was not, however, a recipe for imitative uniformity within the territories annexed by Rome. Houses were resolutely individual, and regional traditions were widely in evidence. This was because there were so many different ways of being Roman. The complexity of empire encouraged variety, and the structure of civic life encouraged competition both within and between communities. There were different routes to power, and these were marked by different ways of describing rank and affiliation. Social display relied on the active and creative participation of a peer community. Such participation resulted in the constant elaboration and sophistication of the cultural language deployed. This created a context for the evolution of different fashions of engagement with the arguments and practices of Rome. The different communities of the Roman world therefore developed distinct and discrete identities, but within the context of a broader conformity to an essential language of power based on Roman authority.

Perhaps the best expression of this argument is found in Woolf's (1998) study of Roman Gaul. This explains how the use of Roman style allowed aristocracies to establish power and status in eyes of local subordinates. Similarly Grahame has shown how in Roman Pompeii 'the target population for stylistic referents was predominantly local' (1998, 176). The same argument can be made in the case of Roman Britain (Perring 2002, 215–7). To take but one example: the aristocratic houses of Roman Silchester were generally entered by means of a large free-standing entrance porch that was linked to the house proper by a long corridor or portico. This style of entrance is not found in other Romano-British cities, and the other urban communities in the province elaborated different regional embellishments to better declare their creative use of Roman style in local competition. Each Roman city was Roman in its own way. Where Roman authority was imposed on pre-existing urban communities, local (but not necessarily 'native') traditions exercised an abiding influence over design. It has been argued, for instance, that the domestic architecture of Roman Volubilis was essentially Punic in character (Daniels 1995). A similar situation may have applied in early Imperial Beirut, where Iron Age architectural traditions persisted in some urban quarters. But in other districts of the city the settlement of a Roman colony introduced radical new types of building that described a distinct colonial identity (Perring 2003b). The very process of colonisation encourages the elaboration of new architectural forms that distinguishes new settlers from indigenous populations.

Notwithstanding the continuing importance of these local and regional variations, and the innovations of imposed colonial settlements, some homogenising tendencies can be described, especially in the Mediterranean basin (*e.g.* Thébert 1987; Alston 2002, 103; Baldini Lippolis 2001). As one might expect these conformities appear to have been a feature of periods of political and social change, when reconfigurations in the basis of authority encouraged approaches to social display that proclaimed affiliation to the broader imperial project.

The most dynamic periods, in terms of the spread and elaboration of Graeco-Roman architectural ideas, accompanied Rome's rise to empire. These and subsequent processes of architectural change can be described, albeit in somewhat general terms.

Some broad trends in the adoption of Graeco-Roman house design

The creation of the Roman empire added impetus to the process of urbanisation, brought wealth to the cities, facilitated social mobility, promoted a massive expansion of citizenship, and offered a range of political and economic rewards to municipal aristocracies engaged in civic administration. These circumstances encouraged investment in urban property, and such property became an ever more important commodity. This is amply illustrated by the growing legislative interest that attached to property in the later empire (Saliou 1994). In the north-west provinces this can also be seen at an earlier stage, in the way in which the ephemeral timber constructions that characterised the earliest urban settlements came to be replaced by more permanent houses of brick and stone. It is common to find that houses built with their main load-bearing posts set directly into the ground required replacement every decade or so. The architects of these houses were perfectly capable of designing more durable structures, but evidently did not see the need to do so. The subsequent decision to invest in more durable materials and structures reflects on the growing importance of real estate as a means of accumulating wealth and representing power. This took place at different times in different provinces, but was essentially a feature of the first century AD. This investment in structural permanence permitted and encouraged more elaborate spatial designs. The pace of such architectural change is likely to have been influenced by political and economic considerations, where increased urban prosperity might have encouraged greater investment in the outward representation of such economic success. But these considerations do not fully account for the particular architectural choices involved.

One of the best-documented trends was the incorporation of Greek visual elements into Roman and provincial houses. This was evident in the design of courtyards, gardens, rooms, fountains, and wall paintings. In Pompeii the precocious adoption of such features dated from the second century BC onwards. This evidence will be considered in a little more detail shortly.

Considerable academic attention has also been given to the changes of the Augustan period, which involved the use of ideas and images drawn from Greek culture in the diffusion of an imperial ideology. This had a significant impact on provincial architecture. These changes attended a 'fundamental relocation and redefinition of authority in Roman society' (Wallace-Hadrill 1997, 6–7). Although the period has sometimes been described as one of 'cultural revolution', the adoption of these ideas took time. As Zanker has observed (1988, 278) the private use of images and symbolism from Augustan public art only reached its culmination in the Flavian period.

In Britain, where some ideas were late to arrive, the creative period in house design continued from the Flavian period into the early second century (Perring 2002, 32–41). Whittaker has also argued that several provinces witnessed a second phase of architectural innovation in the later second century, perhaps marking an intentional renewal of Augustan ideology (1997, 159). This was characterised by the widespread introduction of large and lavishly decorated stone-built town houses (*e.g.* Kondoleon 1995; Perring 1991b, 100).

This highly condensed review suggests that Graeco-Roman architectural ideas were adopted in different ways and at different times by the various provincial cities. The overall impression, in so far as one can be derived, is of the progressive adoption of new architectural forms from the second century BC to the second century AD. By the end of this period few cities had escaped a general trend towards increased investment in high-status urban property, which property incorporated design features inspired by Greek culture. What is more clearly the case is that local architectural histories were closely influenced by the progress of political integration into the Roman world. One of the more interesting questions to ask of local developments in domestic architecture is why some of the more sophisticated Graeco-Roman features (courtyards, gardens, and so on), were only introduced to houses in later phases of alteration and improvement, rather than forming part of the original design. Different communities adopted these elements of the Graeco-Roman architectural package incrementally, rather than wholesale.

Classical architecture and education
One particular idea that I would like to advance here is that the design of reception areas was closely influenced by the spread of Roman-style education, and that this was a process that sometimes required the passage of one or more generations. Full participation in elite culture followed the adoption of a sophisticated range of ideas that drew on years of learning. Greek culture gave people in authority a shared political and moral language, a *lingua franca*, that could be deployed throughout the Roman world and across a range of different social boundaries (Hopkins 1978, 76–80). Access to this language was, however, mediated by access to education. This did not prevent social mobility, but it tempered and controlled the pace of social change. The fact that it took a generation or so for the newly rich to gain social acceptance would have made it easier for elite society to absorb these new elements into political life.

As I have already argued, the introduction of Greek architectural components into the domestic setting was not a superficial cultural affectation. These spaces and symbols provided settings for complex patterns of social behaviour. There was, however, no point in creating expensive settings for particular forms of social practice if people lacked the sophisticated knowledge required to make correct use of them. Ignorant vanity invites ridicule, and thereby defeats the purpose of investment in social display. For this reason many aspects of Hellenistic architecture would have been more dangerous than useful to the indigenous landowners, veteran colonists and merchants from which some urban societies, such as those of Roman Britain, were first formed. I assume here that most members of these social classes would have had but limited access to Greek education. The situation was different for the children and grandchildren born to those who first held authority in these newly Roman urban societies. Access to power was transmitted not only by the inheritance of property, but through the advantages of a proper education.

This is the subject of Tacitus' famous description of the process whereby Britons adopted Roman cultural values under the Governorship of Agricola *circa* AD 80. This deserves quotation because of the relationship that it describes between the processes of education and the gradual adoption of social practices that can be described in architectural terms (colonnades, baths and banquet halls).

> He gave encouragement to individuals and assistance to communities to build temples, market-places, and town houses... Further, he educated the sons of the leading men in the liberal arts... The result was that those who just lately had been rejecting the Roman tongue now conceived a desire for eloquence. Thus even our style of dress came into favour ... Gradually, too, they went

astray into the allurements of evil ways, colonnades and warm baths and elegant banquets (Tacitus *Agricola* 21).

The general point that I have made here, about how the acquisition of knowledge played a critical part in the patterning of architectural language, is best illustrated by taking a closer look at some specific examples of the use of Greek architecture in Roman town houses. Firstly, however, I will make some brief observations about the overall layout of the Roman house.

The organisation of domestic space
It is invariably difficult to ascribe precise functions to the different rooms of the Roman house. The archaeological evidence is not usually adequate to the task (Perring 2002, 11–12), whilst the written sources shed no more than an indirect light on some of the things that were going on in some houses at some times (Allison 2001). There are, however, some common patterns that can be identified.

In large houses it is often possible to distinguish between three main types of domestic space: working and service areas; the residential quarters of the household; and the main reception rooms. In Britain these three types of space were sometimes separated between different wings or blocks, with the service quarters nearest the street and the main reception rooms towards the rear of the house. A fourth century courtyard house at South Shields illustrates this arrangement, and also finds parallels with a range of examples from the Mediterranean (Hodgson 1996).

Some reception facilities are more common than others. The quotation from Tacitus given above describes an emphasis on baths, colonnades and dining rooms. Other sources also call attention to this particular triad of reception facilities. Juvenal offers a good example: 'Your great man will spend ... upon his baths, and something more on the colonnade ... Elsewhere let a banqueting hall arise' (*Satirae* 7.178). Furthermore there are numerous descriptions from both early and late empire of dining rooms reached at the end of long colonnades. The articulation of these key reception areas was an important architectural concern. Private bath houses, where present, were often placed on the opposite and more public side of the house to the rooms most likely to have housed the supper parties. Colonnades and porticoes were used to link these opposed and contrasting reception areas, in a form of spatial dialectic.

The identification and description of possible dining rooms has commanded a fair amount of attention in the recent literature (*e.g.* Dunbabin 1991, Cosh 2001), but the colonnades are no less interesting. Corridors and porticoes established something of a processional pathway through the house, in which the main dining room was the principal destination.

Wallace Hadrill (1994, 58–9) has drawn attention to the importance of hierarchies of space that established an 'ascent of privilege' as visitors penetrated the house. In most parts of the Roman world the main colonnades were usually set out around a garden or courtyard (peristyle), and gave access to a series of reception rooms including dining rooms. In Britain it was more common to find this feature reduced to a portico or corridor along one side of the building, but it seems likely that the purpose was similar. Typically the corridor gave access to one or two larger reception rooms set in a separate wing towards the rear of the house. An early example of this building type has recently been found in excavations at Silchester, reflecting on the precocious trajectory of urbanisation at this site (Clarke & Fulford 2002). Examples are also known from elsewhere in the Roman world: the *Casa dello Scheletro* (III.3) at Herculaneum is a good example.

Peristyle houses

Corridors, porticoes and peristyles were not simply concerned with issues of access; they were an integral part of domestic reception space. Roman peristyle houses owed an enormous amount to Greek practice, where courtyard houses with peristyles and end reception rooms first became popular in the fifth to fourth centuries BC (Nevett 1999, 1). The enlargement of a house through the addition of a peristyle or portico was one of the most common forms of architectural alteration found in the ancient world. In some Mediterranean cities this had been a feature of pre-Roman Hellenisation (*e.g.* Raeder 1984; Ellis 2000, 31). Elsewhere, in both eastern and western provinces, colonnades were introduced to town houses in the course of the first century AD in the wake of Roman annexation (Hirschfeld 1995, 58, 86; Perring 2002, 154–7).

The example of Beirut merits more detailed attention. Here several of the small courtyard houses built when an Augustan colony was settled on the Hellenistic city were altered later in the first century. These alterations involved the insertion of awkwardly small colonnaded peristyles into earlier courtyards, the addition of garden features such as fountains inside courtyards, and the enlargement of an adjacent principal room (Perring 2003b). An important feature of these alterations to the houses of Beirut is that there is no obvious reason why they were not part of the original design. It would not have been more expensive to have put peristyles around the courtyards of these houses when they were built in the Augustan period, by which time this architectural feature was commonly deployed elsewhere in the Roman world. So why was it that the architects of Beirut eschewed this particular fashion when houses were first built for the new colonial settlers, but then went to significant lengths to accommodate it in the course of the following half-century? It is clear that patterns of social living had changed in the course of a few decades: cultural practices had changed, and the house had become a more critical location for elite social display.

In making sense of such changes I am much influenced by a paper by Dickmann (1997) on the use of the peristyle in the Pompeian house. Most typological descriptions of the Roman house rely on identifying different approaches that were adopted in the architecture of courtyards, porticoes and peristyles. Dickmann has given new life to such studies by placing this architecture in its social setting, and this suggests a series of interesting questions about how different house typologies might relate to different ideas and identities. Allison (2001, 186) has taken issue with Dickmann over his use of terms such as *peristylum*, *ambulatio* and *exedra* as labels to describe types of space found in the houses of Pompeii. We do not know if the people of Pompeii knew these places by these terms, and cannot be sure that the social practices described in the sources as taking place in the *ambulatio* and *exedra* were present in these houses.

The evidence of the architecture itself is, however, reasonably clear. This shows that colonnaded gardens were introduced to Pompeii in association with a broader range of Greek architectural features. There was also a clear association between the peristyle garden and the relocation of the main reception rooms, including dining rooms, to the rear of the building.

The idea of the peristyle

Roman colonnades borrowed on an earlier tradition of Greek public building, in which the column was associated with sacred architecture. The peristyle houses of Pompeii made effective allusion to the *gymnasium* and the *stoa* (Zanker 1998, 8; Leach 1997, 59; Wallace-Hadrill 1994, 20–1). This was an architecture of movement and discourse: a setting for philosophical discussion and debate. These were, one might almost argue, the real 'corridors of power' in the Roman world. The presence of these colonnades was a sign of *paideia*, education and culture in the Greek style. It was also closely associated with dining ritual. The purpose of the promenade, or *ambulatio*, was to stimulate conversation and aid digestion. The most important social engagements took place at the supper party. This regulated social encounter drew on the ceremonies and practices of the Greek *symposium* or drinking party. There is an intriguing possibility that the design of this part of the Roman house was modelled on the dialectical contrasts that lay at the heart of Neoplatonic philosophy. A distinction can be drawn between the rational debate of the *gymnasium* (in the peristyle) and the irrational learning of the wine-lubricated supper party (in the dining room). These are concepts touched on in Plato's descriptions of the *symposium*. I am much influenced here by Teçusan's useful review of Plato's ideas on this subject (Teçusan 1990). The reconcilement of the rational and irrational remained an abiding concern of subsequent dualistic philosophy. These arguments derived from Greek philosophy and rhetoric had become an important component in Roman social practice (Wallace-Hadrill 1997, 15). The increased emphasis given to such space may also have been influenced by the effective relocation of rhetoric and debate from public spaces into private ones that took place in the Augustan period (Dupont 1997, 45).

The portico also mediated between natural and human domains: a metaphorical opening onto the natural order (Knights 1994, 140–3). The garden was itself an important symbolic space, with fountains and ponds located to command the views that obtained from the dining room. In the larger peristyle houses of Pompeii a square room was commonly placed opposite the main reception room and projecting into the garden beyond. I have previously (and wholly inadequately) described similar rooms in Romano-British houses as 'garden porches' (Perring 2002, 151–4). Fountains and water features, sometimes described as *nymphaea*, were often found in similarly positioned rooms (opposite the main reception room and projecting into the garden) in Roman houses in North Africa and Spain (for examples see Muth 1998). Dickmann (1997) has identified the Pompeian version of this space with the *exedra*: a place for business meetings, discussions, reading and study (Thébert 1987, 373). Although the case for this identification is open to question (as Allison 2001), the spatial arrangement adds emphasis to the relationship between dining room, colonnade and garden. This both reinforces the point made here about the way in which the colonnade was part of an architectural dialectic, and shows how similar ideas operated in different parts of the Roman world. Although few Romano-British houses were equipped with a peristyle garden, the arrangement of porches, corridors and reception rooms followed a similar pattern and allowed for similar social practices. The space identified as an *exedra* allowed for a form of synthesis between the contrasts posed between rational space (colonnade) and irrational space (dining room), and between human and natural worlds (house and garden). The presence of fountains and other water features in some such rooms reinforces the sense that this space straddled a conceptual boundary between human and divine.

Concluding remarks
Here I have discussed how relationships of patronage were supported by cultural practices that found architectural expression within the house. It has necessarily been an extremely partial survey of the evidence, in which it has not been possible to properly tease out the important distinctions that can be drawn between the reception activities favoured in different periods and regions. Some houses also offered a complex range of additional reception facilities that have

not been mentioned here: such as audience halls, libraries and baths (although these were generally more important in country houses than in town houses). Other parts of the house, including the bedrooms and living quarters, were also accessible to visitors and guests and could be used in business affairs.

It would also be possible to write at equal length about the role of Roman town houses in processes of production and exchange. In most cities the larger establishments dominated entire districts, and were surrounded by lesser properties (Robinson 1997, 143). The rich lived surrounded by their dependants: by slaves and freedmen, clients and tenants. This community was the source of both social and economic power. As patrons and investors urban aristocrats were actively involved in most aspects of the urban economy. This economy involved a significant degree of workshop production, and there was no clear distinction between industrial and domestic premises (Laurence 1994, 55). The importance of these themes is established in other contributions to this volume.

In this paper I have argued that the needs of political life influenced the design of the reception facilities found in private houses. The medium for this was the high culture and philosophical discourse of ancient Greece. Changes in the character of the domestic architecture reflect on the different ways in which such ideas were deployed. Notwithstanding the barriers that the manipulation of knowledge must have placed between educated society and other social classes, this architecture was not just a concern of the aristocratic few. Even small private houses invested in reception facilities that incorporated references to elite architecture. Dining rooms and corridors were attached to comparatively humble properties, such as the workshops and strip-buildings found in the suburbs of second century London (Perring 2002, 58). Similarly although some of the smallest houses at Pompeii lacked sufficient space for a colonnaded garden, most houses here were designed to imitate grand ones (Wallace-Hadrill 1994, 86; Zanker 1998, 10). The standards of educated good taste set by the leading members of urban society were eventually widely copied, and Rome's educated domestic architecture framed many working lives.

Acknowledgements
I am grateful to the editors of this volume for both inviting me to contribute this paper, and for being so patient in awaiting its arrival! I am also grateful to Rana Mikati, Steve Roskams and Letty ten Harkel for their useful comments on an earlier draft.

Bibliography
Allison, P. 2001. 'Using the material and written sources: turn of the millennium approaches to Roman domestic space', *AJA* 105: 181–208
Alston, R. 2002. *The City in Roman and Byzantine Egypt*. Routledge, London & New York.
Baldini Lippolis, I. 2001. *La Domus tardoantica forme e rappresentazioni dello spazio domestico nelle città del Mediterraneo*. University Press, Bologna.
Clarke, A. & Fulford, M. 2002. 'The excavation of Insula ix, Silchester: the first five years of the "Town Life" project, 1997–2001', *Britannia* 33: 129–66
Cosh, S. 2001. 'Seasonal dining-rooms in Romano-British houses', *Britannia* 32: 219–42
Daniels, R. 1995. 'Punic influence in the domestic architecture of Roman Volubilis (Morocco)', *OJA* 14.1: 79–95

Dickmann, J-A. 1997. 'The peristyle and the transformation of domestic space in Hellenistic Pompeii', in Laurence, R. & Wallace-Hadrill, A. (eds) *Domestic Space in the Roman World: Pompeii and beyond*. JRA, Supplementary Series 22, Portsmouth, Rhode Island: 121–36

Dunbabin, K. 1991. '*Triclinium* and *Stibadium*', in Slater, W.J. (ed.) *Dining in a Classical Context*. University of Michigan Press, Ann Arbor: 121–48

Dupont, F. 1997. '*Recitatio* and the reorganisation of the space of public discourse', in Habinek, T. & Schiesaro, A. (eds) *The Roman Cultural Revolution*. Cambridge University Press, Cambridge: 44–59

Ellis, S.P. 2000. *Roman Housing*. Duckworth, London.

Elsner, J. 1998. *Imperial Rome and Christian Triumph*. Oxford University Press, Oxford.

Grahame, M. 1998. 'Material culture and Roman identity. The spatial layout of Pompeian houses and the problem of ethnicity', Laurence, R. & Berry, J. (eds) *Cultural Identity in the Roman Empire*. Routledge, London & New York: 156–78

Hales, S. 2003. *The Roman House and Social Identity*. Cambridge University Press, Cambridge.

Hirschfeld, Y. 1995. *The Palestinian dwelling in the Roman-Byzantine Period*. Studium Biblicum Franciscanum, Jerusalem.

Hodgson, N. 1996. 'A Late Roman Courtyard House at South Shields and its Parallels', in Johnson, P. with Hayes, I. (eds) *Architecture in Roman Britain*. Council for British Archaeology, London: 135–51

Hopkins, K. 1978. *Conquerors and Slaves: sociological studies in Roman history*. Cambridge University Press, Cambridge.

Knights, C. 1994. 'The Spatiality of the Roman Domestic Setting', in Parker Pearson, M. & Richards, C. (eds) *Architecture and Order: approaches to social space*. Routledge, London & New York: 113–46

Kondoleon, C. 1995. *Domestic and Divine: Roman mosaics in the house of Dionysos*. Cornell University Press, Ithaca & London.

La Gory, M. 1983. 'The social consequences of spatial structure', in Pipkin, J.S., La Gory, M. & Blau, J.R. (eds) *Remaking the City*. State University of New York Press, Albany: 180–200

Laurence, R. 1994. *Roman Pompeii: space and society*. Routledge, London & New York.

Leach, E.W. 1997. 'Oecus on Ibycus: investigating the vocabulary of the Roman house', in Bon, S.E. & Jones, R. (eds) *Sequence and Space in Pompeii*. Oxbow, Oxford: 50–72.

Martins, C. 2003. 'Becoming consumers: looking beyond wealth as an explanation for villa variability', in Carr, G., Swift, E. & Weekes, J. (eds) *TRAC 2002: Proceedings of the twelfth annual theoretical archaeology conference, Canterbury 2002*. Oxford, Oxbow: 84–100

Muth, S. 1998. *Erleben von Raum – Leben im Raum: zur Funktion mythologischer Mosaikbilder in der römisch-kaiserzeitlichen Wohnarchitektur*. Verlag Archäologie und Geschichte, Heidelberg.

Natter, W. & Jones J.P. 1997. 'Identity, Space and other Uncertainties', in Benko, G. & Strohmayer, U. (eds) *Space and Social Theory. Interpreting Modernity and Postmodernity*. Blackwell, Oxford: 141–61

Nevett, L.C. 1999. *Houses and Society in the Ancient Greek World*. Cambridge University Press, Cambridge.

Perring, D. 1991a. 'Spatial organization and social change in Roman towns', in Rich, J. & Wallace-Hadrill, A. (eds) *City and Country in the Ancient World*. Routledge, London & New York: 273–93

Perring, D. 1991b. *Roman London*. Seaby, London.

Perring, D. 2002. *The Roman House in Britain*. Routledge, London & New York.

Perring, D. 2003a. 'Deconstructing the Frampton pavements: gnostic dialectic in Roman Britain?' in Carr, G., Swift, E. & Weekes, J. (eds) *TRAC 2002: Proceedings of the twelfth annual theoretical archaeology conference, Canterbury 2002*. Oxford, Oxbow: 74–83

Perring, D. 2003b. 'The archaeology of Beirut: a report on work in the insula of the House of the Fountains', *AntJ* 83: 195–229

Purcell, N. 1990. 'The creation of provincial landscape', in Blagg, T. & Millett, M. (eds) *The Early Roman Empire in the West*. Oxbow, Oxford: 6–29

Raeder, J. 1984. *Priene. Funde aus einer griechischen Stadt im Berliner Antikenmuseum*. Bilderheft der Staatlichen Museen Preussischer Kulturbesitz 45/46, Berlin.

Reece, R. 1988. *My Roman Britain*. Cotswold Studies 3, Cirencester.

Robinson, D.J. 1997. 'The Social Texture of Pompeii', in Bon, S.E. & Jones, R. (eds) *Sequence and Space in Pompeii*. Oxbow, Oxford: 135–44

Roskams, S.P. forthcoming. 'The urban poor: finding the marginalised', in Lavan, L. (ed.) *The social and political archaeology of late antiquity*.

Saliou, C. 1994. *Les lois des bâtiments: voisinage et habitat urbain dans l'Empire romain: recherches sur les rapports entre le droit et la construction privée du siècle d'Auguste au siecle de Justinien*. Institut Français d'archéologie du Proche-Orient, Bibliothèque archéologique et historique 116, Beyrouth.

Thébert, Y. 1987. 'Private Life and Domestic Architecture in Roman Africa', in Veyne, P. (ed.) A *History of Private Life I: from Pagan Rome to Byzantium*. Belknap, Cambridge MA & London: 313–409

Teçusan, M. 1990. 'Logos sympotikos: patterns of the irrational in philosophical drinking: Plato outside the symposium', in Murray, O. (ed.) *Sympotica: a symposium on the symposion*. Clarendon Press, Oxford: 238–60

Wallace-Hadrill, A. 1989. 'Patronage in Roman society: from republic to empire', in Wallace-Hadrill, A. (ed.), *Patronage in Ancient Society*. Routledge, London & New York: 63–87

Wallace-Hadrill, A. 1994. Houses and Society in Pompeii and Herculaneum. Princeton University Press, Princeton.

Wallace-Hadrill, A. 1997. '*Mutatio morum*: the idea of a cultural revolution', in Habinek, T. & Schiesaro, A. (eds) *The Roman Cultural Revolution*. Cambridge University Press, Cambridge: 3–22

Whittaker, C.R. 1997. ' Imperialism and culture: the Roman initiative', in Mattingly, D.J. (ed.) *Dialogues in Roman Imperialism: power, discourse, and discrepant experience in the Roman Empire*. JRA, Supplementary Series 23, Portsmouth, Rhode Island: 143–64

Woolf, G. 1998. *Becoming Roman: the origins of provincial civilization in Gaul*. Cambridge University Press, Cambridge.

Zanker, P. 1988. *The Power of Images in the Age of Augustus*. University of Michigan Press, Ann Arbor.

Zanker, P. 1998. *Pompeii: public and private life*. Harvard University Press, Cambridge MA.

3

The commercial landscape of Ostia

Janet DeLaine

The existence of a variety of locations for the sale of goods or services supplying the needs of its inhabitants is one of the common – if not defining – features of urban centres in many periods, including our own. While originally in the Graeco-Roman Mediterranean buying and selling generally took place in the open space of an *agora* or *forum*, or other similar locations, by the imperial period a range of different structures had been developed to serve the varied commercial needs of urban populations and these made a distinctive contribution to urban living. Ostia, as the river port of ancient Rome, provides a unique opportunity to examine one of the most extensive and varied commercial landscapes which survive from the high imperial period (Figure 3.1). Given the extent of the excavations, it is possible not only to examine the range of types of commercial structures but also to see how these are integrated into the wider urban fabric. While in the past the focus has tended to be on the function of the major warehouses in providing storage for the city of Rome, particularly in relation to the state-controlled *annona* (Meiggs 1973, 272–88; Pavolini 1991, 76–117), this paper is more concerned with the needs of Ostia's own population, permanent and transient. This shift of focus is encouraged by recent studies of the second-century building 'boom' in Ostia, which have reinforced arguments for a much higher level of private or civic, rather than state, responsibility for the construction of many of the commercial buildings, including some of those traditionally associated with the *annona* (DeLaine 2002; Heinzelmann 2002). Although this view leaves the commercial landscape unchanged in a strictly physical sense, it must alter our understanding of how that landscape functioned.

A study of the physical evidence for commerce in imperial Ostia is not without its problems. The difficulties we have in identifying important aspects of Roman urban economics in the archaeological record are well-recognised, and Roman commercial space is no exception. Almost by definition such space is flexible, subject to change not just through time but according to specific function, making use of temporary fittings which have left little or no trace even at a site as well-preserved in elevation as Ostia. In the case of warehouses ('*horrea*') and one- or two-roomed commercial units ('*tabernae*') the temptation has been to append a conventional ancient label to an easily identifiable plan type, and to assume in turn that the identification gives an explanation of function. Recent studies of Roman houses (Riggsby 1997; Leach 1997), for example, have however made it abundantly clear that attaching an ancient label to an architectural space does not mean that the space is understood. Equally, types of structures which cannot be given an ancient name are often overlooked.

The focus in this paper therefore will be on the operation of commerce within the whole range of possible spaces and structures, using the available physical evidence to evaluate the functioning of space rather than simply attaching an ancient label. This will be done in the context of the possible forms of sale and the nature of sellers and buyers, as all commercial transactions can be defined in terms of the nature of the interaction between vendor and purchaser, the nature of the goods, and the scale of the transaction. The paper will concentrate on questions of how the various commercial units operated within the overall urban landscape, and how the physical setting was orchestrated to secure and display the goods of the seller, attract the buyer, and facilitate transactions between the two.

Janet DeLaine

The nature of commercial transactions
It is reasonable to assume that the intensive commercial landscape at Ostia developed to suit the needs of those with goods for disposal. In this context, the broad nature of the markets for them is of more interest than the precise geographical origins of those goods. As well as the permanent residents of the city, there must have been a sizeable temporary population, including those visiting Ostia for business related to long-distance trade or working for the *annona*, those in transit to other parts of the empire, and the contingents of the *vigiles* and the Roman fleet stationed at Ostia in rotation. In addition, Ostia served some of the needs of the long line of villas stretching down the coast to the south (*cf.* Pliny *Epistulae* 2.17.26), and presumably also of Portus, where there is very little evidence for *taberna* units or market buildings.

All these would have looked mainly to Ostia to supply food, clothing, household goods, and objects required in carrying out a wide variety of occupations and for religious ceremonies. Ostia presumably also provided markets for ships and individuals to acquire stores and equipment for long journeys. The small-scale retail market for comestibles would have been particularly high in a city with very little opportunity for domestic food production and a potentially large body of manual workers engaged in ship building and allied trades, dock-work and construction, many of whom would have been paid in cash as day labourers (Howgego 1992, 25–7). High population density and little evidence of domestic production further suggest a high level of outlets selling and possibly producing household goods, including both necessities like clothing and luxuries like jewellery. The presence of ship-makers and seamen must have brought their own demands for specialised items related to shipping, for example from the caulkers and rope-makers attested in inscriptions (*cf.* Hermansen 1982, 58, 61–2). It is thus likely that most of Ostia's population, permanent and temporary, relied very heavily on goods obtained from some form of retail outlet to fulfil their needs.

Traders and middlemen, whether buying primarily for resale in local outlets or at Rome, and merchants and/or ship's masters seeking cargo for an outward voyage, form another group of buyers whose needs could range from whole cargoes of individual basic foodstuffs, to smaller lots of mixed goods for coastal trading, to rare commodities from outside the empire for further distribution, or any combination of these (*cf.* Paterson 1998, 161–4). For example, we know from Strabo (5.1.7) that ships came to Ostia laden with black Spanish wool, and even after the building of the harbours at Portus, there is no reason to imagine that these cargoes necessarily ceased to arrive at Ostia; the large scale *fullonicae* at Ostia might suggest that such material was processed in the town before being sold on (de Ruyt 2001). The high incidence of imported African cooking wares at Ostia compared with Rome (Pavolini 1996, 226–8) also strongly suggests the sale of cargoes at Ostia itself. Rather than a simple dichotomy between retail for Ostia and storage for Rome or foreign markets, the commercial landscape of Ostia should be multi-faceted to cater for this wide range of buyers and sellers.

For most of the transactions envisaged above, where the buyer is purchasing to supply individual need, a straightforward cash transaction is likely. Finds of coins, often in small denominations, are common in Ostia, and here, if nowhere else, the functioning of a monetised economy is perfectly clear (*cf.* Howgego 1992, 16–8; Temin 2001). This still allows a range of physical settings for such transactions, reflecting different degrees of mobility of buyer and seller. The essential need is for buyer and seller to meet. A seller operating from a fixed and permanent location facilitates recurrent trade from a regular clientele with which he/she can

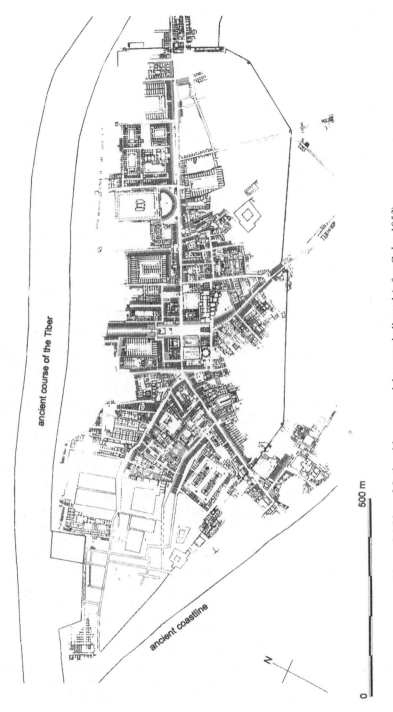

Figure 3.1 Plan of Ostia with commercial spaces indicated (*after Calza 1953*)

establish a one-to-one relationship, but the buyer makes the active choice to patronise any particular seller. Ambulant hawkers, on the other hand, who frequent public places or sell door-to-door, rely more on a 'captive' clientele making passive choices to buy or not. Temporary stalls are a compromise. They might be regular in location, but intermittent in time as in weekly markets (Frayn 1993, 1–9), or regular in time but move location, or be occasional or opportunistic. For merchants and middlemen different conditions prevailed. Direct purchase from ships docked in the river harbour is one possibility, as is the purchase of goods already in temporary storage, the two having the same advantages and disadvantages as temporary stalls or ambulant hawkers on the one hand, and fixed retail outlets on the other. While purchase may have been a direct transaction between buyer and seller on this scale as well, it may have been indirect and competitive, through auction.

Auction was an important form of sale in imperial Rome, used generally for the sale of real estate, slaves, bulk foodstuffs such as grain or wine, luxury goods such as fine linen, and food delicacies, as well as unwanted personal effects (Loane 1938, 151–2; de Ruyt 1983, 360–2). It also covered different levels of sale – from bulk commodities to individual items – and differed from normal sale in many key respects which operate as much today as they did in antiquity. Auctions were brokered by a third party, who was not usually the actual owner of the goods, and were less regular in occurrence and often less fixed in place than normal sale at retail units or periodic markets. In addition they depended on competitive bidding, i.e. they required multiple potential buyers to be present at the precisely same time – the bigger the crowd the better potential earnings. Finally, the buyer had a limited opportunity to view the goods, which were often only brought together for the occasion, and only one opportunity to buy. Where an auction was held presumably depended on what was being sold, both in quantity and quality. Auctioning wine, spices and slaves might all require slightly different physical settings, for example for the display of the goods, but any given setting might allow for the auction of a range of goods. Equally, the same type of goods could be auctioned from different places. The literary sources for Rome suggest a broad range of venues for the holding of auctions, from the street corner where the miserable auctioneer set up his spear to sell a mixed bag of odds and ends as in Horace (*Epistulae* 1.7.63–6) and Juvenal (*Satirae* 7.9–11), to the *forum romanum*, where temporary display areas and auctioneer's posts could be set up in the open space or the rostra co-opted for this use, and to dedicated auction halls, *atria auctionaria* (Cicero *de Lege Agraria* 1.7; *pro Quinctio* 25). The latter were not restricted to the peculiar conditions of Rome, as is attested by an inscription recording the donation of an *atrium auctionarium* to the town of Superaequum by a wealthy local benefactor (CIL ix.3307). We have however no idea what one of these looked like, although the elder Seneca's tale (*Controversiae* I, *praef.* 19) of the orator Hortensius sitting in the auction rooms for a day watching the proceedings, and reciting at the end a complete list of all goods sold and their prices to the astonishment of the attendants, at least gives an idea of the general ambience.

In looking at the physical setting of commerce at Ostia, therefore, all these possible modes of selling to meet the varying needs of different elements of Ostia's permanent and transient population must be taken into account.

Fixed commercial outlets: Servicing the community
For the Roman imperial period the most familiar type of commercial structure is the single-fronted unit with a wide opening to a street or portico, usually labelled '*taberna*'. The distinctive openings provided flexible but controllable access depending on the nature of the

goods or services on offer; they maximised light and allowed a large visible area for the display of goods, attracting prospective buyers and enabling them to inspect the goods on sale, or providing optimum conditions for providing services (Girri 1956, 3). The rear of a unit might have been used for storage, for production, for accommodation, or for any combination of these, depending on the goods or services involved, but this has little impact on the basic selling function. It is thus the open façade which suggests direct sale from a specific place to an ambulant clientele looking for particular items or services and engaging in small-scale transactions. What is unusual about these units at Ostia is their number and density – over 800 in the excavated area – matched only by Rome as revealed on the Severan Marble Plan. In some ways this is a more interesting phenomenon than the number of warehouses, and one given less consideration. The slow death of the city and the nature of the excavations however make it impossible to identify the nature of the goods or services sold (and in some cases also produced) at more than a handful of these commercial units. Rather, it is their distribution pattern which provides the best indications of how retail functioned in the city and what clientele they were aimed at.

Four distinct patterns showing varying degrees of visibility and accessibility can be isolated (Figure 3.1). The first, and most obvious, are the long rows of units flanking the main streets: the east-west *decumanus maximus*, the north and south sections of the *cardo maximus*, and the *Via della Foce* between the *forum* and the river harbour. More concentrations of units line one or both sides of other direct routes from the Tiber to the *decumanus* (*Via dei Balconi*, *Via Epagathiana/Via del Pomerio*), from the *decumanus* to the river mouth (*Via degli Aurighi*), and from the Tiber to the *Porta Laurentina* (*Via dei Molini/Semita dei Cippi*). These are the streets which would be most likely to be used by the transient population and by visitors, as well as by the local population, since they lead most naturally to the centre from the possible places of arrival and out again, and from the interior (down the coast) to the Tiber. Laurence (1994, 88–103) has identified a similar phenomenon at Pompeii, there confirmed by the concentrations of graffiti, a form of evidence not available at Ostia. Many of these groups of units were built as unified projects, notably those lining the northern *cardo* and the eastern *decumanus* fronting the Baths of Neptune, both of which may have been built by the colony as rental property (DeLaine 2002, 64, 67). This contrasts the piecemeal developments along the *Via dei Molini/Semita dei Cippi*, suggesting a hierarchy of commercial viability and different patterns of ownership even between major through streets.

The second group forms clusters around public buildings such as the theatre, the *forum*, important temples and the various baths (Figure 3.1). Although the evidence is less secure due to the limited excavation, a further cluster may exist around the baths of the '*Palazzo Imperiale*' (Spurza 2000) and the temple by the river harbour, tentatively identified as the Temple of the Castores (Heinzelmann 2001; Heinzelmann & Martin 2002, 14–8). These are all areas of the city that would naturally have high levels of social activity, for permanent and temporary residents as well as visitors from the surrounding area, at least on an intermittent basis. In the case of the theatre, the Baths of Neptune and the Forum Baths, the units are built as integral parts of the public buildings, and the commercial viability maximised by constructing them facing the *decumanus* and *cardo* respectively. In the case of the Forum Baths (I.xii.7, 10), some of the units faced inward onto the portico of the *palaestra* and not just outward onto the flanking streets. The one closest to the *forum* still retains its characteristic counter for the sale of food and/or drink, and opens both onto the space in front of the entrance to the *palaestra* from the *forum*, and onto the *palaestra* portico itself. These units would have been accessible even when the baths themselves were closed, as the porticoes and the open space of the *palaestra* were integrated into the circulation routes of the city.

The importance of these two groups of commercial units is emphasised by their association with street porticoes, which also cluster around public buildings, along major routes, and at busy intersections such as the broad piazza just outside the west gate of the original *castrum*, where the *decumanus* intersects the old north-south outer pomerial road and the *Via della Foce*. As well as generally increasing circulation space for crowds and preventing congestion on the main streets, porticoes have a positive function in relation to commercial units, allowing the separation of pedestrians and through traffic and making it easier for the former to stop at will. Generally, the stretches of porticoes found fronting commercial units are concentrated where there are either units on both sides of a street, or units on one side and a public building on the other; that is, where it is the presence of the commercial units that would most likely have caused or exacerbated congestion. They also tend to be more frequent where the streets are relatively narrow, again privileging an ambulant clientele rather than through foot traffic. Architecturally too the porticoes appear designed to enhance commercial activity. The extreme height of many of the well-preserved examples (e.g. on the *Via della Fortuna*) suggests a concern to allow as much light as possible into the front of the units rather than sheltering the public from inclement weather.

Finally there are two groups of units for which visibility and/or access is limited, and which appear to have served more local needs, although the demarcation of entrances by enhanced architectural treatments in some cases would have advertised their presence to visitors (*cf.* Maitland 1985, 69 for modern malls) while others relied on decorative terracotta plaques set into their façades, for example the *Caseggiato dell'Ercole* (Ling 1990). The most accessible of these commercial units are those units fronting minor streets which, although an integral part of the open street network, do not form obvious major thoroughfares within the overall urban structure (e.g. those along the *Via Est delle Casette Tipo*, and along the *Via di Annio*); their location thus assumes a degree of local knowledge. One degree more detached are those units apparently located off dead-end streets, such as that serving I.xiii.2 off the *Semita dei Cippi*. This latter is however linked to the *palaestra* of the Forum Baths through a narrow covered passage, another link in the urban network which would have required local knowledge. A further refinement is where the units face onto an internal street or piazza serving several properties, but which can be closed off from the street system by gates or doors (II.ix.5–6, III.ix.1–23, III.ii.8–10, IV.ii.3, 12–14, IV.v.7 and IV.v.18). Although the evidence for the closing system does not survive in all cases, they are often marked by the presence of a narrowed opening, sometimes showing decorative treatment with pilasters as if for an entrance to an apartment block or commercial premises, or by a covered entrance passage. The fact that each of these areas is also served by a modest public fountain, adds further weight to the identification of these as foci of neighbourhood activity, even if also intended to attract visitors (Ricciardi & Scrinari 1996, 83, 101–102, 114–115, 134, 149, 154–56).

Some of these units opened onto enclosed internal spaces or piazzas, which served relatively few other premises; the nineteen internal *tabernae* belonging to the Garden House complex (III.ix.1–23) are a case in point (Gering 2001, fig. 2; 2002). Of particular note are two ranges of *tabernae* which are fronted by internal porticoes. The row of units south of the *Grandi Horrea* (II.ix.5–6) had a separate upper floor and the open space also served a small group of unrelated structures to the south (Figure 3.2). The internal space was reached from the *Via dei Molini* through a grand portico and central foyer, while a less ostentatious doorway

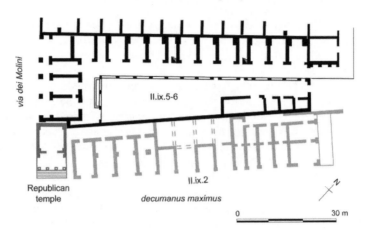

Figure 3.2 *Plan of II.ix.5–6 (Drawing: author) (after Calza 1953)*

gave access to *the Via dei Grandi Horrea*. The grouping is less formal in III.ii.8–10, but it is notable that the open area is immediately in front of III.ii.10 and its portico. Although it is difficult to reconstruct the original layout, as there is no trace remaining of some of the structures on Gismondi's plan (Calza 1953), it would again appear that entrance to the space was restricted. In these examples it appears that the open space had a specific function beyond giving access to the whole group of buildings, and that whatever that function was, it was directly related to the commercial element, or attracted sufficient crowds to justify its presence. All these areas were also served by public fountains. The units opening onto the entrance court of the *Caseggiato del Serapide/Terme dei Sette Sapienti*, onto the *Via Tecta degli Aurighi* and onto the court of the *Caseggiato degli Aurighi* are a natural extension of this last arrangement (*cf.* Kockel 2001, 86).

Finally, there are the completely self-contained groups of units with their own circulation space which could be shut off from the general street system, and where the space itself could be open or covered – in other words a market or bazaar. At least four of these can be identified, although only two (the *Caseggiato del Larario* and the '*mercato*' at III.i.7) normally appear in the literature. Three of these are particularly interesting because they represent a transitional form between street and building (I.ii.5, III.i.7 and III.xvi.4). As with Islamic souks or nineteenth-century arcades and covered markets in Britain, they formed part of the street plan when open, but could be closed off when desired. At the time it was built, III.i.7 formed a link between the *Via della Foce* and the street later superseded by the *domus* of the Tigriniani (Brenk & Pensabene 1998/99, fig. 1), the street itself being flanked by a continuous line of units and giving access onto the *decumanus maximus* (Figure 3.3). Similarly, the *Caseggiato del Thermopolium* (I.ii.5) originally formed a through passage between two important commercial streets, the *decumanus maximus* and the *Via di Diana* (Figure 3.4). In all three cases the internal 'street' forms a straight route with units either side. Even the *Caseggiato del Larario* (I.ix.3) has a main opening on the *decumanus maximus* and a secondary one on the *Via del Larario* forming a through route, both marked out on their respective façades by a pilastered aedicular frame. The advantages here, as with the more modern equivalents (*cf.* MacKeith 1986, 12–14), would have been both security for the units and their contents, and control and protection of the immediate environment onto which the units opened. Conversely, moving around in Ostia outside business hours, whatever they were, would have been relatively restricted and may have made the job of the *vigiles* easier.

Moveable venues: Markets

By grouping *tabernae* according to different degrees of visibility and public access, it is thus possible to see at Ostia a series of superimposed patterns of commercial activity which appear to reflect the requirements of different sections of the population carrying out different activities at different times, from the casual visitor passing through to the inhabitants of local neighbourhoods. This inherent variability provides a useful model for other forms of commercial space less easily identifiable in the archaeological record. Alongside the selling which took place in fixed units, there must also have been temporary stalls set up on a regular basis, daily or at periodic intervals, and ambulant hawkers who frequented public places such as the baths (Seneca *Epistulae* 56.1–2), catered to the needs of buyers and sellers of more substantial goods in the streets and markets, or sold door-to-door. While none of these leave specific traces, it is possible to suggest locations for at least the first of these activities in porticoes, loggias, courtyard buildings, and otherwise undifferentiated open spaces, through their position in the urban landscape and their association with the pattern of units established above. It is important to remember that there is a temporal aspect to these activities, so that the spaces they occupy could also have had other functions.

The clearest case is the covered space open widely on at least two sides and with the minimal amount of internal support, providing a flexible venue sheltered from the elements which has many similarities with medieval English corn markets and Italian Renaissance commercial loggias. The closest typologically to these later parallels is the building in the *Piazza dei Lari*, which originally was a completely open-sided roofed structure with only six supporting piers. It formed a pivotal element in the local street system linking the Tiber to the *decumanus* by way of the *Via dei Balconi* and the *Via dei Lari*, and was a focal point along the *Via di Diana* leading to the *forum* (Figure 3.4). All these streets had high retail density, and more units flanked the small piazza into which the loggia is set. Although alterations to the loggia itself, the blocking or narrowing of many of the *tabernae* openings, and the lowering of the *decumanus maximus* to display the *castrum* gate, have all served to disguise the original commercial importance of this zone, the nodal quality of the piazza is emphasised by the altar to the *Lares vicinales* set up there by the *vicomagistri*, an impression reinforced by the later addition of a cistern/fountain. It is difficult to imagine any other primary function for this structure than as a market kiosk.

A second candidate can be found in the *Caseggiato degli Aurighi* (Figure 3.5). Architecturally, the front of the *caseggiato* is built as a *loggia*, opening from the *Via degli Aurighi* and at the rear onto the internal courtyard with its high arcades. Here again, later alterations to the building tend to conceal the original design. We already have had occasion to note the commercial nature of this whole block, and this may be confirmed by graffiti from the ground floor area of the *Caseggiato degli Aurighi*: one records the purchase of a slave, another gives thanks to Hermes who watches over markets. Here again the wider setting encourages this interpretation. The whole of the east side of the *Via degli Aurighi* is lined with units, and the street itself widens to form a small piazza in front of the *Aurighi* façade. Both these commercial nodes are in high density residential areas, which would have provided a ready clientele for daily food markets. Interestingly, the *loggia* in the *Caseggiato degli Aurighi* did not last very long before being turned into a residential apartment (Mols 2000, 168–71), a

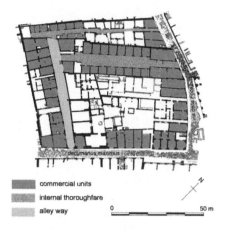

Figure 3.3 *Plan of III.i. SW corner (Drawing: author) (after Calza 1953)*

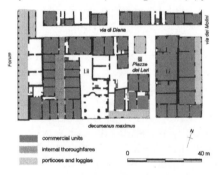

Figure 3.4 *Plan of I.ii and Pzza dei Lari (Drawing: author) (after Calza 1953)*

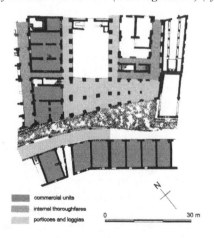

Figure 3.5 *Caseggiato degli Aurighi and facing street (Drawing: author) (after Calza 1953)*

relatively rare case where the changing fortunes of commercial viability can be easily demonstrated.

The function of the other four *loggias* is more ambivalent (Figure 3.1). Two lie at the south end of the northern *cardo maximus* (I.vi.1 and I.v.2) and form the culmination of two long rows of porticoed units leading from the Tiber along the widest street in the city to the *forum*. The loggias may have had ceremonial significance, for example when the urban praetor arrived from Rome to preside over the festival of Castor and Pollux (Meiggs 1973, 343–6) or on other state occasions, or in relation to ceremonies at the '*Capitolium*' or in the *forum*. The long row of *tabernae* flanking the *cardo* however suggest a strong commercial role for this street and the *loggias* at its end. Once more it is worth emphasising that the two functions are by no means mutually exclusive. The same applies to the remaining two *loggias*, situated close to major entrances to the city: the *loggia* of *Cartilius Popicola* just outside the *Porta Marina*, and V.xvi.2 just inside the *Porta Romana*. As these are natural gathering places, any commercial function is likely to have been just one aspect of these multi-purpose structures which served the varied needs of those arriving at Ostia and departing from it.

Now that the *macellum* of Ostia, well-attested in inscriptions (de Ruyt 1983, 122–4), is no longer to be identified with the building just outside the original west gate of the *castrum* on the *Via del Pomerio* (IV.v.2) (Kockel 2000), no permanent market of the courtyard type has been identified. Just inside or outside of city gates, and by the rivers of port cities, are however very common locations for produce and livestock markets (de Ruyt 1983, 329). One possibility suggested originally by Becatti (in Calza 1953, 135) is the so-called '*Foro di Porta Marina*' (VI.viii.1), just outside the eponymous city gate (Figure 3.6a). Opening off a small piazza formed by the widening of the *decumanus*, it takes the form of an open space with porticoes on three sides, what is probably an altar, and an axial apsidal hall or shrine, but has none of the internal units which might identify it specifically as a *macellum* or a fish market. Although Becatti suggested affinities with the Greek *agora*, both the Porticus of Livia at Rome and the Eumachia building at Pompeii provide closer parallels, and the latter at least has always been interpreted as having a commercial function despite its evident religious overtones; the two are not of course mutually exclusive. Even modern markets in British and Italian towns make it clear that periodic selling space does not require integral retail or even storage space. We have ancient literary evidence for this at Rome, in Martial's description of a shopping trip to the *Saepta* (*Epigramata* 9.59), where a medley of antiques, slaves, precious stones and pots could be bought. The archaeological remains for the Hadrianic *Saepta* reveal an open space bordered with porticoes but no evidence of storage space at all. Such mobile markets could equally have been held in the *porticus* behind the theatre at Ostia (the so-called 'Piazza of the Corporations'), or indeed in the Ostian *forum* itself, as we know was the case at Pompeii.

Another likely market space is the partly excavated structure just inside the *Porta Laurentina* (V.i.2), comprising a series regular cells opening onto a large rectangular open space (Figure 3.6b). Traditionally this has been identified as *horrea* because of the relatively narrow (*c.* 1.5m) doorways of the cells, but the cells are not very deep and the amount of open space appears out of all proportion to the storage available for this to be its only function. It would appear that the main entrance to the building was on the south, towards the *Porta Laurentina*, as access to the south of the building was left when the space between the gate and V.i.2 was filled by a single row of units in the Severan period, and marked as important by a wide opening flanked by pilasters, a treatment not accorded the units themselves. Its relation to the *Via Laurentina* would therefore suggest a function as a livestock market particularly for

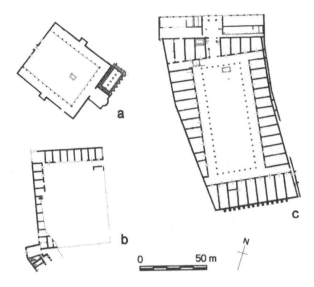

Figure 3.6 Plans of a) Forum of the Porta Marina; b) horrea V.i.2; and c) Horrea of Hortensius
(Drawing: author) (after Calza 1953)

swine and poultry coming from the Laurentine estates. Pigs and chickens were the predominant species found in recent studies of the animal bones from imperial Ostia, and it is striking that the pig bones show both that the species was particularly large in comparison to the standard found elsewhere in Italy, and that whole animals were being butchered in the city rather than the meat arriving as cured joints (pers. comm. Michael McKinnon). The building is usually dated to the mid-first century AD, a period which saw considerable expansion at Ostia with the building of Claudius' harbour and the formation of many of the coastal villas which might have supplied such a market.

Bulk commodities: storage and sale
Both the '*Foro di Porta Marina*' and the '*horrea*' by the *Porta Laurentina* are places where large-scale selling could have taken place, as must have been the quaysides for buying straight from the incoming ships. Unless bulk goods were bought direct from there and immediately dispersed to retail outlets or moved to another vessel for trans-shipment, some kind of interim storage was necessary. The buildings most associated with the storage of bulk goods which changed hands at Ostia are of course the *horrea*. As Rickman (1971, 15–86) makes clear, there are problems in identifying *horrea* in the archaeological record, and many of the design elements thought to be specific to the building type were individuated through a careful study of the buildings at Ostia, leading potentially to circular arguments. The main distinguishing features are usually defined as: narrow openings to the regular individual cells in contrast to the wide opening of the commercial units; the lack of interconnection between cells; and the proportions of the cells, usually long in relation to their width. One other important feature is the few and relatively narrow openings to the outside, which provide security for the goods stored there.

The difficulty comes with the interpretation put on the functioning of these buildings. The literary, legal, and epigraphic evidence from Rome makes it clear that *horrea* were not just concerned with storage but with distribution, and the same was presumably true for Ostia (*cf.* Rickman 1980, 141–2). Of the sixteen excavated buildings variously interpreted as *horrea*, only three (I.viii.2, II.ix.7 and II.ii.7) have been clearly proven to have been mainly for the storage of grain, and then only from the second century AD (Rickman 1971, 293–7), although Hermansen (1982, 227–35) would add at least two more (I.viii.1 and V.xii.1), if on tenuous grounds. The recent geophysical survey has identified ten more possible *horrea*, mostly in the area around the river harbour, but details must await further publication (Heinzelmann 2002, 112–4, taf. IV.2). On the other hand, we have already had reason to question the attribution of the so-called *horrea* by the Laurentine gate (V.i.2), which is likely to have been a market, while the '*mercato*' at III.i.7 seems to have begun life as '*horrea*'. Half the cells were converted into '*tabernae*' only in the second century by widening the openings, the rest of which were left narrow as the cells continued to be used for storage. In both cases, storage and retail appear to have existed side by side, and the simple label '*horrea*' or '*mercato*' disguises a more complex situation.

One possible method of analysis for identifying different functions or modes of operation in these buildings is to look at the proportion of space allotted to access and circulation compared to the amount of covered storage space; the other is to look at the arrangement of that space. The usual typological categorisation of *horrea* is as courtyard, corridor, or back-to-back arrangements. The standard theory is that the open courts of early buildings like the mid-first century AD *Horrea di Hortensio* (V.xii.1) were designed to facilitate the movement of goods (Figure 3.6c), but were considered too greedy of space under the changed conditions following the opening of Portus, leading to the open areas being reduced in size in second century structures such as the *Piccolo Mercato* (Rickman 1971, 77–8). This, it is argued, led ultimately to the creation of the back-to-back *horrea* of the later Antonine period. The recent geophysics at both Ostia (Heinzelmann 2001, 2002) and Portus (Keay *et al.*, forthcoming) however have given a different slant to this, as Portus has no virtually courtyard horrea, and Ostia very few back-to-back. This suggests that the difference is functional, and that the courtyard may have a specific role to play.

The proportion of open to closed space for the courtyard horrea of Ostia is given in Figure 3.7. One immediate problem in presenting this data comes with what to do with internal porticoes. If these formed part of the open circulation space, they should be treated as a covered extension of the courts, but this is not always the case. In the *Piccolo Mercato* the openings between the court arcades were blocked at a very early stage, to judge from their construction technique, while in the case of the grain *horrea* I.vii.2, the walls between the pillars are an integral part of the original construction. The same may have happened in the *Grande Horrea* in one of its early phases, as indicated by remains of *opus reticulatum* curtain walls, as it certainly did later (*cf.* Rickman 1971, 52–3). In these cases, therefore, the porticoes have been added to the storage area rather than to the open space. The situation may possibly be paralleled with the '*intercolumnia*' included in the lease notice for the private *horrea* of Q. Tineius Sacerdos in Rome, where these areas seem to have formed part of the storage rather than the circulation system (*CIL* vi.33860, discussed by Rickman 1971, 197–8). For comparison, I have included the ratio of open court including porticoes to total area for the *Horrea Galbana* and the *Horrea Lolliana* in Rome, as far as this can be ascertained from the Marble Plan (Fragments 24a & c, 25).

OPEN SPACE IN COURTYARD HORREA

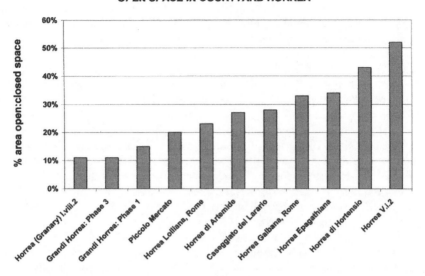

Figure 3.7 *Chart showing proportion of open to closed space in courtyard horrea*

OPEN SPACES IN CORRIDOR HORREA AND STREETS

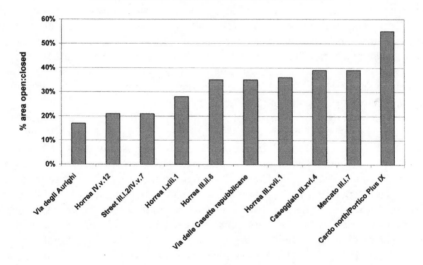

Figure 3.8 *Chart showing proportion of open to closed space in corridor horrea, bazaars and streets*

The resulting figures for open circulation area as a percentage of total area range from 11% to 52%, with a cluster in the 20s and low 30s including the late Republican *Horrea Galbana* and *Horrea Lolliana* at Rome, which runs counter to the accepted pattern of a reduction over time in the size of courts. In fact, the two buildings with the lowest percentage of open space are both securely identified grain *horrea*, rather contradicting the argument that the space is needed for manoeuvring bulk goods; given that the most likely way of transporting grain was by men carrying sacks, this should not have really been necessary anyway. It also suggests that public access may have been particularly limited, with the only movement the operation of storing and removing the grain for trans-shipment to Rome, or to the bakeries of Ostia for local consumption. In contrast, the courtyard *horrea* in the 20–30% range have a percentage of circulation space to total area comparable to that of the simple corridor *horrea* without courts, to most of the corridor bazaars, and to sections of streets flanked by rows of *tabernae* or even back-to-back *horrea* (Figure 3.8).

This is what might be expected if the same kind of access and circulation patterns were required in what we think of as storage buildings as in what are usually labelled markets or bazaars; and as with these fundamentally retail premises, the act of enclosure both provides security and allows for the frequenters to be static and cut-off from other street activities. It is interesting that the *Horrea Galbana* in Rome, where we have perhaps the clearest epigraphic evidence for retail or other commercial activity by private individuals in state-owned *horrea* (Rickman 1971, 173–6), is part of this group. The visibility of access of most of the *horrea* also puts them in the same category as markets or bazaars. Many had entrances located on major thoroughfares and enriched with columnar decoration, while the *Piccolo Mercato*, like the nearby *Caseggiato del Larario*, allowed through passage when open between its two equally elaborate entrances. In the case of the small *horrea* III.ii.6 the aedicular doorway was designed to be seen from a distance by those approaching from the street opposite, and the view through the main doors leads the eye to the central space with a *lararium* niche as a focal point (Figure 3.9). This contrasts with the location and access of the four groups of *dolia defossa* (I.iv.5, III.xiv.3, V.xi.5, and north-west of the *Horrea dei Mensores*), where giant storage jars embedded up to their necks in the ground were used as deposits for bulk foodstuffs. All were in walled courts set at the back of buildings with very limited access, and any associated *tabernae* could only be reached through a series of rooms. The deposit on the *Via di Annio* has a high level opening on the street which would make consignments to or from a cart easy, but this is a discreetly anonymous opening on a minor street.

One group of buildings which stand out from the rest are the two with exceptionally large amounts of open space, well beyond the standard: the *Horrea di Hortensio* and the partly excavated '*horrea*' just inside the *Porta Laurentina*, already possibly identified as a livestock and produce market (Figure 3.6b & c). Although the large court of the *Horrea di Hortensio* is usually seen as just a 'normal' early feature, it occupies a relatively much larger space than the courts of the late Republican *Horrea Lolliana* (43% v. 23% open space), and even than the *Horrea Galbana* (33% open space) if the remains and ground plan preserved on the Marble Plan do indeed represent *horrea* and not barracks (Gros 1996, 467). Furthermore, the central court was never subdivided nor built into despite its long life, extending possibly into the fifth century AD (Calza 1953, 153). This suggests that the court had a specific function, vital to the identity and use of the building. One possibility is suggested by the small shrine which was the only intrusive element in the circulation space, fitted into the portico probably in the early third century AD. In the mosaic inscription the donor of the *sacellum* and associated altar is identified as L. Hortensius Heraclida, a captain of the Roman fleet at Misenum (AE 1953, 262; Le Gall 1953, 233 and note 8). The gift is an *ex voto* and the location suggests that Hortensius had at the time either been stationed in Ostia or was visiting there on whatever occasion had given rise to the original vow. While religious dedications are not uncommon from *horrea*,

Figure 3.9 *View of I.ii.6 from street (Photo: author)*

where the evidence is sufficient to tell, all were either dedicated to the *genius* of the specific *horrea* or to Hercules, the protector of trade and merchants, or made by staff of the *horrea* and close associates (Rickman 1971, 312–5). While it cannot be proved, it seems reasonable therefore to posit a specific link through Hortensius between the *horrea* and the fleet, or at least with shipping. The large open space in turn would suggest storage or manoeuvring space for bulky and/or long items – ship timbers, ropes and sails all come to mind.

Auctions
As well as sheltering produce and other markets, any of the venues already discussed could also have been suitable places to house auctions, but recognising this in the archaeological record is difficult. The one space at Ostia which can almost certainly be associated with selling by auction – the *Forum Vinarium* – is known entirely from inscriptions and its location has never been identified with any certainty, although efforts have been made (Coarelli 1996). The epigraphic evidence however gives some idea of its form. A certain C. Septimius Quietus, a wine auctioneer, made a dedication to the 'genius of the most splendid body of wine importers and merchants', and from another inscription it is clear that these had their base at the '*quadriga*' – a statue base or an arch? – of the *Forum Vinarium*, which also contained a temple (Coarelli 1996, 106). The name and contents suggest a large, formal open space dedicated to the sale of an important commodity, rather than any kind of building with separate storage cells, of the type represented by the so-called '*Foro di Porta Marina*'. Nevertheless, what was being auctioned at the *Forum Vinarium* was presumably bulk imported wine being sold to a variety of purchasers, who might be large households, Ostian retailers, middlemen buying for local markets outside Ostia, buyers from Rome, or merchants or ships' masters seeking cargo for an outward voyage. The wine in question may have been held in ships docked in the river harbour (which may have required the buyer then to find storage space at Ostia for his purchases), or in temporary storage at Ostia, but not, it would seem, in the *Forum Vinarium* itself.

Such a separation of storage and selling points was not necessarily the norm. It can be argued that the *Horrea Epagathiana*, the only building in Ostia we know to have been called *horrea*, were specifically designed to facilitate auction (Figure 3.10a). The almost domestic

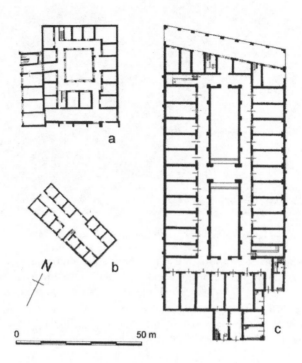

Figure 3.10 *Plans of a) Horrea Epagathiana; b) Horrea III.ii.6; c) Piccolo Mercato (Drawing: author) (after Calza 1953)*

nature of the architecture has long been noted. The sequence of entrance passage, mosaic decorated court, and large open-fronted room, which Packer (1971, 17) goes so far as to call the '*tablinum*', is suggestive of some Pompeian and Ostian *domus*, and the richly decorative façade and niches add to a sense of status. The wide doorway and side service entrances leading from the portico and storage rooms make it clear that this '*tablinum*' was not for storage. It could easily however function as a setting for sale – possibly by auction – to a select clientele, and if we wanted to attach a functional label, this would work as an *atrium auctionarium*. It is interesting to compare this space with the similar sized *Caseggiato del Larario*, which is clearly a group of commercial units but has no discrete focal space. One is retail, the other is concerned not simply with storage, but with a different way of selling the goods it stores. An earlier version of the *Horrea Epagathiana* arrangement may be found in the corridor *horrea* III.ii.6 (Figure 3.10b). It is distinguished by a fine entrance and the arrangement of internal space to create a central focal point emphasised by a niche, where extra storage space could easily have been inserted if the idea was to maximise storage space. Here again there is a direct view to this focus from the main entrance, as if to attract the passer-by to whatever is happening within. The space is admittedly small, but proportionately similar to the *Horrea Epagathiana*.

Providing a place for auction may also explain the unusual arrangement of the *Piccolo Mercato* (Figure 3.10c). The pillars of the porticoed courts were linked by curtain walls to form a corridor, with formal access to the courts limited to openings in the short ends of the courts near to the two entrances. In addition, the large piers between the two courts were linked by low arches only 2.3m high at the centre, suggesting service access only. This central section is the only part of the courts to have gutters implying it had a different form of roofing, most likely a shed roof of some sort. This can thus probably be reconstructed as a pavilion, open formally to the two courts and informally or for service to the long passages which give access to the storage cells. Such a feature could have provided a focus for auctions, with goods – perhaps samples – brought out for inspection in the courts or on wooden platforms under the pavilion, where the auctioneer could also have been located.

Auctioneering is one of those activities which made a mark on Roman urban life and helped to shape its character. It was not just confined to Rome and Ostia, as the *atria auctionaria* of Superaequum and the wax tablets of Pompeii's wealthy auctioneer, Caecilius Jucundus (Andreau 1974) show. But even at Ostia, arguably the best preserved commercial cityscape in the Roman world, finding clear archaeological evidence for this has proved difficult.

Conclusions

The commercial landscape at Ostia in the second century AD has proved to be compounded of overlapping and intersecting arenas of potential activity serving the varying needs of different sectors of the fluid and heterogeneous population. Despite the limitations of the archaeological evidence for the precise nature of goods sold or traded, the general patterns of activity are clear. Complexity and potential for multi-functionality have emerged as key characteristics of many commercial spaces, rather than the simple dichotomy of *taberna* : *horrea*, of selling versus storage. Patterns of distribution are equally varied, marked by differential degrees of visibility and variable control of access requiring different degrees of local or specialised knowledge to navigate. Individual *tabernae* on major thoroughfares provided fixed outlets for goods and services to passing trade, groups of units with variable degrees of controlled access served local neighbourhoods or specialised markets, flexible locations like *loggias* were provided for periodic markets, and multi-functional storage, sale and auction facilities catered to the wholesale trade and middlemen. Underlying all of this is the role of the individual entrepreneur and businessman as a key factor in the functioning and prosperity of the city (*cf.* Paterson 1998), as a balance to the better-known picture of state control and interference.

Acknowledgements

I am indebted to Dott.ssa Anna Gallina Zevi, Soprintendente di Ostia, for kind permission to study the standing remains and to access archival material, and to Dott.ssa Jane Shepherd and her staff in the Ostia archives. The research was supported by grants from the Arts and Humanities Research Board, the British Academy, and the British School at Rome. Thanks are due to Michael Heinzelmann, Axel Gering, Martin Millett and Michael MacKinnon for advanced access to unpublished papers, and to Jim Coulton and members of the Oxford Ancient Architecture Discussion Group and Ardle MacMahon and participants in the Durham symposium for helpful comments on earlier versions of this paper. Any errors which remain are my own.

Bibliography

Andreau, J. 1974. 'Les Affaires de Monsieur Jucundus', *Collection de l'École Française de Rome* 19. École Française de Rome, Rome.

Brenk, B. & Pensabene, P. 1998/99. 'Christliche Basilika oder christliche "Domus der Tigriniani"?', *Boreas* 21/22: 271–99

Calza G. 1953. *Scavi di Ostia I. Topografia generale*. Poligrafico dello Stato, Rome.

Coarelli, F. 1996. 'Il *forum vinarium* di Ostia: un'ipotesi di localizzazione', in Gallina Zevi, A. & Claridge, A. (eds) *'Roman Ostia' Revisited: archaeological and historical papers in memory of Russell Meiggs*. British School at Rome, London: 105–13

DeLaine, J. 2002. 'Building activity in Ostia in the second century AD', in Bruun, C. & Gallina Zevi, A. (eds) 'Ostia e Portus nelle loro relazioni con Roma', *Acta Instituti Romani Finlandiae* 27: 41–101

de Ruyt, C. 1983. *Macellum: marché alimentaire des Romains*. Publications d'histoire de l'art et d'archéologie de l'Université Catholique de Louvain 35, Louvain-la-Neuve.

de Ruyt, C. 2001. 'Les foulons, artisans des textiles et blanchisseurs', in Descoeudres, J-P. (ed.) *Ostia: port et porte de la Rome antique*. Musée d'art et d'histoire, Genève: 186–91

Frayn, J.M. 1993. *Markets and Fairs in Roman Italy: their social and economic importance from the second century BC to the third century AD*. Clarendon Press, Oxford.

Gering, A. 2001. 'Habiter à Osite: la fonction et l'histoire de l'espace "privé"', in Descoeudres, J-P. (ed.) *Ostia: port et porte de la Rome antique*. Musée d'art et d'histoire, Genève: 199–211

Gering, A. 2002. 'Die "Case a Giardino" in Ostia – ein unerfüllter Architektentraum? Von der geplanten Funktion zum Nutzungswandel und Nachleben einer Luxuswohnanlage', *Mitteilungen des Deutsches Archäologisches Institut. Römische Abteilung* 109, 109–40.

Girri, G. 1956. *La Taberna nel Quadro Urbanistico e Sociale di Ostia*. L'Erma di Bretschneider, Rome.

Gros, P. 1996. *L'architecture Romaine du début du IIIe siècle av. J.-C. à la fin du Haut-Empire. I. Les Monuments publics*. Picard, Paris.

Heinzelmann, M. 2001. 'Ostia. Ein urbanistisches Forschungsprojekt in den unausgegrabenen Bereichen des Stadtgebietes. Vorbericht zur 3. Grabungskampagne 2000', *Mitteilungen des Deutsches Archäologisches Institut. Römische Abteilung* 108: 313–28

Heinzelmann, M. 2002. 'Bauboom und urbanistische Defizite – zur städtebaulichen Entwicklung Ostias im 2. Jh.', in Bruun, C. & Gallina Zevi, A. (eds) 'Ostia e Portus nelle loro relazioni con Roma', *Acta Instituti Romani Finlandiae* 27: 103–21

Heinzelmann, M. & Martin, A. 2002. 'River port, *navalia* and harbour temple at Ostia: new results of a DAI-AAR Project', *JRA* 15: 5–19

Hermansen, G. 1982. *Ostia: aspects of Roman city life*. University of Alberta Press, Edmonton.

Howgego, C. 1992. 'The supply and use of money in the Roman world, 200 BC-AD 300', *JRS* 82: 1–31

Keay, S., Millett, M., Paroli, L., Patterson, H. & Strutt, K. Forthcoming. *Portus: an archaeological survey of the port of Imperial Rome*.

Kockel, V. 2000. 'Ausgrabungen der Universität Augsburg im sog. Macellum von Ostia', *Mededelingen van het Nederlands Instituut te Rome. Antiquity* 58 (1999) [2000]: 22–4

Kockel, V. 2001. 'Ostie: images de la ville', in J.-P. Descoeudres (ed.) *Ostia: port et porte de la Rome antique*. Musée d'art et d'histoire, Genève: 81–90

Laurence, R. 1994. *Roman Pompeii: space and society*. Routledge, London.

Leach, E.W. 1997. 'Oecus on Ibycus: investigating the vocabulary of the Roman house', in Bon, S.E. & Jones, J. (eds) *Sequence and Space in Pompeii*. Oxbow, Oxford: 50–72

Le Gall, J. 1953. *Le Tibre: Fleuve de Rome dans l'antiquité*. Publications de l'Institut d'Art et d'Archéologie de l'Université de Paris 1, Presses Universitaires de France, Paris.

Ling, R. 1990. 'A stranger in town: finding the way in an ancient city', *Greece and Rome* 37: 204–14

Loane, H.J. 1938. *Industry and Commerce of the City of Rome (50 BC-200 AD)*. John Hopkins University Studies in Historical and Political Science Series 56 no. 2, Johns Hopkins Press, Baltimore.

MacKeith, M. 1986. *The History and Conservation of Shopping Arcades*. Mansell, London & New York.

Maitland, B. 1985. *Shopping Malls: planning and design*. Construction Press, London.

Meiggs, R. 1973. (2nd edn) *Roman Ostia*. Oxford University Press, Oxford.

Mols, S.T.A.M. 2000. 'La vita privata attraverso lo studio delle decorazioni parietali', *Mededelingen van het Nederlands Instituut te Rome, Antiquity* 58 (1999) [2000]: 165–73

Packer, J.E. 1971. *The Insulae of Imperial Ostia*. Memoirs of the American Academy in Rome 31, Rome.

Paterson, J. 1998. 'Trade and traders in the Roman world: Scale, structure and organisation', in Parkins, H. & Smith, C. (eds) *Trade, Traders and the Ancient City*. Routledge, London: 149–67

Pavolini, C. 1991. *La vita quotidiana a Ostia*. Laterza, Roma-Bari.

Pavolini, C. 1996. 'Mercato ostiense e mercato romano: alcuni contesti ceramici a confronto', in Gallina Zevi, A. & Claridge, A. (eds) *'Roman Ostia' Revisited: Archaeological and historical papers in memory of Russell Meiggs*. British School at Rome, London: 223–42

Ricciardi, M.A. & Scrinari, V.S.M. 1996. *La civiltá dell'acqua in Ostia Antica*. Fratelli Palombari Editori, Roma.

Rickman, G. 1971. *Roman Granaries and Store Buildings*. Cambridge University Press, Cambridge.

Rickman, G. 1980. *The Corn Supply of Ancient Rome*. Clarendon Press, Oxford.

Riggsby, A.M. 1997. 'Public and private in Roman culture: The case of the *cubiculum*', *JRA* 10: 36–56

Spurza, J. 2000. 'The building history of the Palazzo Imperiale at Ostia: Evolution of an insula on the banks of the Tiber River', *Mededelingen van het Nederlands Instituut te Rome, Antiquity* 58 (1999) [2000]: 129–42

Temin, P. 2001. 'A market economy in the early Roman empire', *JRS* 91: 169–81

4

The shops and workshops of Roman Britain

Ardle Mac Mahon

The towns and settlements of Roman Britain have produced a rich variety of building types and many of these structures have been interpreted as *tabernae* (shops or workshops). Generally, when the buildings of Roman communities are considered, the concentration is usually on the more prestigious structures, such as public buildings. These buildings are important, but they account for only a small part of the built up area in any settlement. *Tabernae* were a feature of every type of settlement, large or small, official and unofficial, and as such their existence must be seen as an essential, rather than a marginal, feature in the social and cultural life of Roman Britain.

There has been a steady development in our understanding of *tabernae* from the earliest excavations in the late nineteenth century to the present day. However, it is surprising that despite the scholarly work that has been carried out on Roman Britain in the past a systematic study of shops and workshops has not been produced with the exception of a posthumously published paper by Richmond entitled 'Industry in Roman Britain' (1966, 76–86). This provides a summary of the *tabernae*, or more particularly workshops, excavated up to that time and attempts to place *tabernae* into their contemporary framework, emphasising the similarity in function of the *tabernae* in Roman Britain to those found in Italy. This paper builds upon the work of Richmond and brings together some general observations on the shops and workshops of Roman Britain.

Building layout

It goes without saying that the archaeological remains of Roman Britain cannot compare with the spectacular ruins that have survived in Pompeii and Herculaneum in terms of scale, height and preservation. However, sufficient evidence survives in the form of ground plans to demonstrate that there was a great diversity of structural types in Britain from simple single roomed buildings, to multi-roomed *tabernae*, to *tabernae* that were attached to large complex domestic buildings. As such, the ground layout of a *taberna* is the most useful interpretative tool to examine the development of *tabernae* in the major settlements of Roman Britain.

The plans of the early *tabernae* seem to have been relatively simple in form and are one of the most common types of structure that can be seen during the Roman settlement of Britain. In their apparently simplest configuration, *tabernae* consist of utilitarian, relatively long, narrow, rectangular plots, set perpendicular to the street. These are often known as 'strip-houses' or 'strip-buildings' and are an urban feature known throughout the empire (Stambaugh 1988, 174). *Tabernae* could comprise a single room, but more usually, they were initially composed of two rooms. The layout of the internal divisions of *tabernae* almost habitually follow a pre-set pattern with the room or rooms that were closest to the street used as a shop or workshop, with the chambers behind functioning as living or store areas (Todd 1970, 121; Wacher 1995, 66–7). This characteristic of *tabernae* in Italy led Boëthius to term this form of architecture as 'shop-houses' or '*taberna*-houses' (Boëthius 1934, 164). The twofold function of *tabernae* also existed in Roman Britain, and probably contributed greatly to the evolution of a form of architecture consisting of a long narrow rectangular building. This sequence sometimes becomes somewhat distorted with later developments but, as was practical, the front

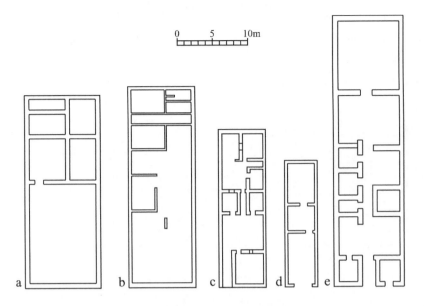

Figure 4.1 *Comparison of strip-buildings: a. IX.BIII, Silchester; b. Watling Court, London; c. Casa dell'Ara Laterizia (III.17), Herculaneum; d. I.xi.3, Pompeii; e. II.viii.5, Pompeii (Drawing: author)*

of the building continued to be utilised for selling and/or manufacture.

A distinction should be drawn between strip-buildings in Italy, more particularly in Pompeii and Herculaneum, and those found elsewhere. In Britain these strip-buildings are usually freestanding structures that do not share a party wall with a neighbouring structure or structures. Similar freestanding buildings are a rarity in Italy (Perring 2002, 55) where the remains of *tabernae* were more often incorporated into large blocks of buildings or *insulae*. Within the *insulae* of Pompeii and Herculaneum examples of long narrow independent building sharing party walls can be found such as I.xi.3 (Pugliese Carratelli 1990b, 519) and I.xii.9 (Pugliese Carratelli 1991, 784–93) in Pompeii, and the *Casa dell'Ara Laterizia* (III.17) (de Kind 1998, 127–30) and *Casa del Papiro Dipinto* (IV.8–9) (de Kind 1998, 151–4) in Herculaneum. Although the contrast between strip-buildings in Italy and Roman Britain should be borne in mind the emphasis in this paper is upon the design characteristics of *tabernae* rather than the specifics of design form (Figure 4.1).

Not all *tabernae* in Britain were freestanding independent buildings. Some shops and workshops were certainly built as part of a block, with *tabernae*, and possibly domestic dwellings, divided by party walls. The best known example of this is *insula* xiv at Verulamium (Figure 4.2; Frere 1972) but other instances were found in *insula* v at Cirencester (Holbrook 1998, 189–210) and London's Fenchurch Street (Philp 1977, 14–5; Merrifield 1983, 48–9). Buildings of a similar form have also been excavated in Gaul at Bliesbruck (Rorison 2001, 209), Malain (Rorison 2001, 135) and 'La Villasse' area of Vaison-la-Romaine (Bromwich 1993, 235). How common this building form is throughout the empire is uncertain. As such, the *tabernae* more common to Italy should perhaps not be seen in complete contrast to those found in the north-western provinces, but as *tabernae* in a more evolved and complex form,

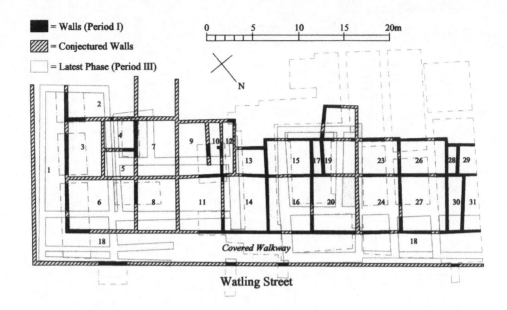

Figure 4.2 Verulamium insula xiv (Drawing: author) (after Frere 1972)

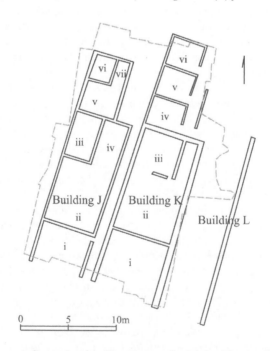

Figure 4.3 Newgate Street, London (Drawing: author) (after Perring & Roskams 1991)

in a more highly developed urban and economic environment.

Within the framework of the 'strip-building', variations and additions to building plans of *tabernae* were common after initial construction. It can be assumed that in most cases, that once a building is occupied and utilised, the changing patterns of use continually alters the original design so that it conforms to the needs of the inhabitants rather than the ideals of the 'architect' or builder (Locock 1994, 7). Initially, the early *taberna* façades and lengths were of similar spans and appear to demonstrate a level of economic comparability between the retailers and craftsmen. Any variations between neighbouring buildings are often marginal.

The later addition of appendages to the rear of premises was a common practice and one seen in many towns. There were many different configurations and these must balance the advantage of the increase in floor space and the potential disruption to natural light especially if neighbouring buildings were constructed close by. The likely loss of light was sometimes solved by an extension that did not take up the full width of the building, as in Newgate Street, London (Figure 4.3), and in Houses VIIIs (Ashby, Hudd & Martin 1902, 147–51) and XIXn at Caerwent (Ashby, Hudd & King 1910, 11–3). This occurrence increased the square footage of the house and used the site efficiently. The addition or extra living space may represent increased social ambition and the growth of personal prosperity, and is well indicated in London by the introduction of 'reception quarters' to structures that had previously seemed entirely functional (Perring 1987, 150). While the narrowness of lots close to the centre of settlements restricted the overall size of buildings, at the same time, these still served as a tool for individual expression through the choice of arrangement to the rear of structures.

These additions suggest owner-occupation of *tabernae* and represent a differentiation in the proportion of accumulated profit and of available capital to invest in construction and improvements. The circumstances of this can be observed in the enlargement of premises but is most explicit in the procurement of adjacent property. This was almost certainly the case in Wroxeter, *insula* viii, site VI. The area was initially composed of three *tabernae* that were later amalgamated into a more substantial building (Figure 4.4; Bushe-Fox 1916, 4–20; Walthew 1975, 191–2). As a consequence of these acquisitions the shopkeeper was able to make a more comfortable-sized home. This was also a frequent occurrence at Caerwent where the later Houses XVs, XVIs (Figure 4.5; Ashby, Hudd & King 1911, 421–34) and XVIIIn were composed of three distinct structures (Figure 4.6; Ashby, Hudd & King 1910, 7–11). The fully evolved form of House XXVIn was the result of the incorporation of two strip-buildings (Dunning 1948, 94; Nash-Williams 1948, 56–7). The amalgamation of neighbouring property can also be noted in Italy. The *Grande Taberna* IV.12–13, 15–16, in Herculaneum takes up the area of two of the original property lots merged into a single unit (de Kind 1998, 159–60). It can be argued that the development of a building into neighbouring property indicates the prosperity of one shopkeeper over another and the commercial success of the location (Mac Mahon 2003, 33). Retaining a location, rather then moving elsewhere, would have been important for a business that had expended a great deal of effort building up its customer base which could easily be lost through relocation (Mac Mahon 2003, 144). Few individuals would be willing to change the location of their establishment unless they were forced, economically or physically. Thus individuals wishing to expand their business will follow the pattern of developing their own site and then expand into the adjacent site. It is possible that less successful retailers and craftsmen moved to another settlement or relocated to another location within the town. As such, the amalgamation of properties should not simply be seen as indicative of the gradual decline of the urban population.

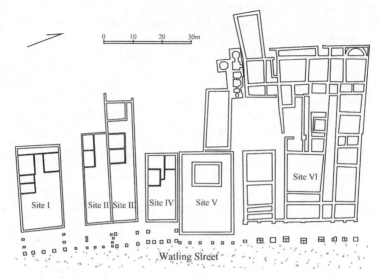

Figure 4.4 *Insula viii at Wroxeter (Drawing: author) (after Bushe-Fox 1913; 1914; 1916)*

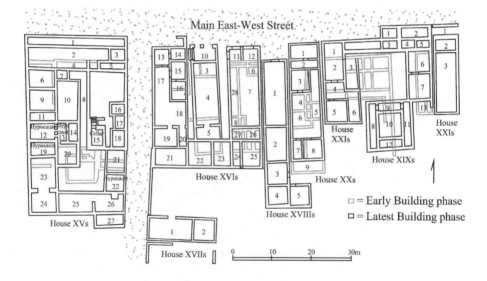

Figure 4.5 *Buildings south-west of the forum, Caerwent (Drawing: author) (Ashby, Hudd & King 1911)*

The ownership and/or control of *tabernae* appears to have been even more complex when the *taberna* was part of a more substantial building. In Building 20, a courtyard house in Colchester, two of the four rooms fronting onto the street were workshops (Crummy 1984, 62–3; Wacher 1989, 113; Perring 2002, 195). The possible courtyard house, Building 113, retained

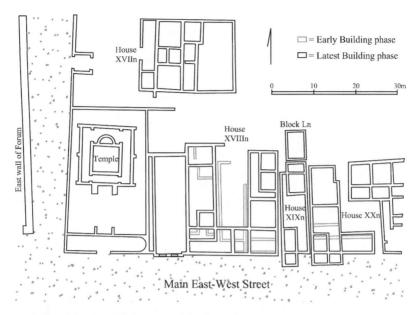

Figure 4.6 *Temple and buildings west of the forum, Caerwent (Drawing: author) (after Ashby, Hudd & King 1910)*

its connection with commerce by having a workshop next to the street and a high-quality mosaic in the next room (Crummy 1992, 79–82; Wacher 1995, 125). The rooms on the frontage of Building 16 and the succeeding Building 19 were also used as workshops (Crummy 1984, 50–4). Building 70, on the Middleborough site, was a substantial building with rooms arranged on at least three sides of a courtyard house, some of which appear to have been *tabernae* (Crummy 1984, 159). *Tabernae* fronting what appear to be large residential buildings can also be noted in other towns in Roman Britain.

A number of the rooms of Building xxviii.2 in Verulamium appear to have been dedicated to retailing or manufacture (Frere 1958, 9–12; 1983a, 246–7). It has been suggested that two rooms in the southern range of Building xxvii.2 served as shops (Frere 1983a, 214; Niblett 2001, 96). Rooms 2 and 3 that fronted House xiv.1 at Silchester were probably used as shops (Hope & Fox 1896, 221). Similarly, in House ii.2 rooms 3, 7 and 8 were given over to retailing (Fox 1892, 276). In the eastern part of a small town house (ix.3) in Silchester is a partially detached chamber which has been interpreted as a shop. The room cannot be entered from the main house and is further separated from the rest of House 3 by a corridor (Figure 4.7; Fox 1885, 444–5). It would seem that the *taberna* was a later addition to the original town house (pers. comm. Michael Fulford).

House XIIs in Caerwent demonstrates the complex relationship that could exist between *tabernae* and élite dwellings. However, it should be noted that this building has in the past been commonly identified as a *mansio* rather than a dwelling, but more recent consideration of the evidence does not fully support the early interpretation (Wacher 1995, 382). Rooms 3 and 4 of House XIIs were entered from the front rather than through the main house. While room 3 was independent, room 4 communicated with the main structure. Furthermore, rooms 11 and 12, although part of House XIIs, were independent of the main building, and had easy access to the

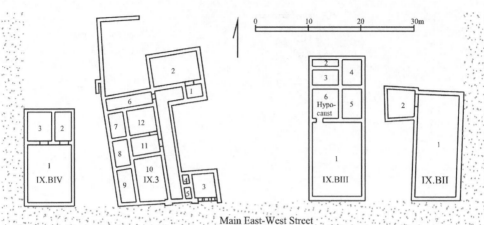

Figure 4.7 Strip-buildings in *insula* ix, Silchester (Drawing: author) (*after Fox 1895*)

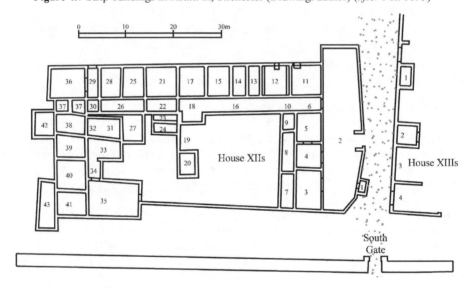

Figure 4.8 *Large courtyard House XIIs or mansio, Caerwent (Drawing: author) (after Ashby 1905)*

main street (Ashby 1905, 299–300). House XIIs is particularly interesting as it appears to present an example of an élite building that had *tabernae* that were part of the main building with access to the dwelling and, at the same time, had *tabernae* that were fully independent (Figure 4.8).

These structures would seem to indicate that there was a tendency, similar to that seen in Pompeii, to open *tabernae* along the street fronts in existing dwellings at the expense of front rooms. Examples in Pompeii can be seen in the *Casa di Sallustio* (VI.ii.4) that had six *tabernae* framing the door (Richardson 1988, 108) and the *Casa del Fauno* (VI.xii.2,5) which had five shops in the façade (Richardson 1988, 116). *Tabernae* fronting a main house have also been found in other regions of the empire. For example in France, the *Maison au Dauphin* in Vaison-la-Romaine (McKay 1975, 162–3), in Château-Roussillon one of the three Julio-Claudian houses seems to have had an entrance between two shops (Bromwich 1993, 70) and at Viénne, the *Maison au Vestibule à Colonnes* and the *Maison des Dieux Océan* had *tabernae* in the frontage (Desbat 1994, 110–11, 118 & 150). The *Casa dos Repuxos* at Conimbriga, Portugal (Meyer 1999, 117 fn. 67) and the *Haus vor dem Südportal des Kölnes Domes* in Cologne, Germany, were fronted by *tabernae* (McKay 1975, 177–8). More further afield, shops fronting élite dwellings can be seen in the *Maison du dallage* at Thamusida (Callu *et al.* 1970, 283–4) and the *Maison à la Disciplina* at Volubilis, Morocco (Rebuffat 1973–1975, 329–31) and in Algeria in the *Palais dit de Gordian* (Thouvenot 1958, 22–4) and the *Villa du Bord de Mar* in Tipasa (Blas de Roblès & Sintes 2003, 56).

If Roman Britain followed the paradigm that appears to have existed in other parts of the empire, then the shops probably remained the property of the original owner from whose house the *tabernae* had been developed. The *tabernae* with access to the larger dwelling may have been run by the owner or through the agency of a trusted freedperson or slave. Those that do not have access to the main house could have been leased to retailers either connected to or independent of the house owner (Ling 1983, 54). Naturally, this is a simplistic view of a complex commercial world, as some *tabernae* in Pompeii, which were originally connected to the principal building, were subsequently isolated, while others that were originally independent gained access. Presumably this reflects the changing relationship between the house and *taberna*. How common the occurrence of *tabernae* in front of large dwellings in Roman Britain is as yet not clear, and seems to be confined to the principal towns. Despite this, as Jongman points out in Pompeii, the proportion of *tabernae* that are an integral part of what are believed to be élite houses is sufficient to show that street fronts were presumably valuable enough to convert into shops and workshops (Jongman 1991, 178). The same economic considerations may also have been in the minds of the owners of the élite dwellings in Roman Britain.

This brief discussion on the ownership of *tabernae* is relatively basic and is a consequence of the lack of evidence for property ownership in Roman Britain in general. This being said, the study of *taberna* plans and the relationship of *tabernae* to larger more sophisticated buildings do allow some speculation on the nature of ownership. What is apparent is that the shops and workshops of Roman Britain emulate the patterns that can be observed in other parts of the empire. In general, it is clear that a complex and sophisticated social, commercial and economic environment existed in Roman Britain between *tabernae*, élite dwellings and towns.

Doorways

Tabernae throughout the empire seem to have had characteristic features and one shared by nearly all was their type of doorway. Doorways belonging to *tabernae,* with their wide entrances opening onto the street, were one of the most distinctive features of the Roman street. It should also be noted that a wide doorway, although very common in *tabernae*, was not always necessary. Some must have had quite ordinary doorways at their entrance, and were similar in width to a doorway in a domestic dwelling.

In Roman Britain the typical wide *taberna* doorway is indicated by the presence of long stone thresholds, or, as in most cases, the absence of front wall trenches. Despite this, there is rarely much evidence to show exactly the type of door that was used to shut off this large exposed area.

Figure 4.9 *Example of shop shutters is use at the National Korean Folk Village in Gyeonggi-do Province, Korea. Note also temporary canopy. (Photo: author)*

In Pompeii and Herculaneum a groove running along the stone threshold parallel to the street was used to hold vertical wooden shutters used to close the place of business at night (Packer 1971, 21; Bakker 1994, 80). Although reasonably rare similar finds have been discovered in Roman Britain. One of the best known examples in Roman Britain is the masonry threshold of a late second century *taberna* at Housesteads. Two massive stone slabs, which were cut with a groove, formed the western front end of a building close to the fort (Birley, Charlton & Hedley 1932, 228 & 231; Crow 1995, 76; 2004, 76). However, the groove is not continuous, nor as clearly defined as the Italian examples. A threshold with a slot found below House XIIIs, in Caerwent (Ashby 1905, 308) may have been used to support wooden planks for a shutter (Figure 4.9). Another sill at Caerwent, although broken survived to a length of 1.5m, had a groove, which according to Ward, would have received a wooden sheath about 0.05m thick (1911, 269–70). Alternatively, the slot may have been used to support a shutter, as there is no bolt or pivot-hole. Parts of a grooved threshold were found at Catterick (Burnham & Wacher 1990, 18, 45–5 & 114–5; Wilson 2002a, 103–4). More recently, an example of a *taberna* threshold was uncovered in the western corner of *insula* V in Cirencester (Holbrook 1998, 230).

At the extreme west of the 1912–13 excavations at Kenchester two well built structures were discovered. The larger of the two is roughly 10.5m square, and is divided into two equal parts by a wall. The entrance was on the longer western side, where there was a grooved stone threshold about 2.7m in length. The groove makes up approximately two-thirds of the threshold length and ends abruptly (Jack 1916, 28 + plate 25). At the time, the excavators could not imagine the form of door that covered this doorway. This is perhaps one of the most complete examples of a grooved stone threshold to be found in Roman Britain. However, it should be pointed out that the entrance to a *taberna* was normally located at the narrower end of a building. Although this does not by itself mitigate the possibility that this was a *taberna*, it is equally possible that this structure was a storehouse. Slotted thresholds such as those found in *tabernae* were also common in the warehouse buildings of Italy (Rickman 1980, 94–5).

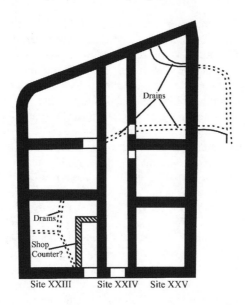

Figure 4.10 *'Butcher's shop' Vindolanda (Drawing: author) (after Birley 1977)*

The existence of a great many buildings with wide open frontages without stone sills would suggest that a many *tabernae* in Roman Britain had wooden thresholds that have now been lost. Of great interest to this belief is the preserved timber threshold from the Regis House warehouse found in London. The structure was initially used as a warehouse, but was later converted into *tabernae*. The frontage of the building incorporated a narrow vertical sided gully that was used to support removable timber shutters. This evidence is further substantiated by traces of timber planking found in the threshold groove (Bateman & Milne 1983, 222; Brigham *et al.* 1996, 38; Schofield & Malt 1996, 11).

Counters
A striking and visually imposing feature of the *tabernae* in Pompeii and Herculaneum is the shop counter. The surviving Italian examples were solid and constructed of cement, brick or rubble (Paoli 1975, 66). Although counters can be found in many *tabernae*, a selling counter was not a necessary prerequisite for many trades to carry out business. In fact, there are many *tabernae* in Pompeii that are void of a selling platform. While there is every reason to suspect that the open-fronted strip-structures of Roman Britain were used as *tabernae*, no clearly identifiable counters have been discovered in Britain.

A masonry counter was believed to have been found during the emergency excavation at the Greta Bridge *vicus* (Wilson 1975, 235). However, the subsequent excavation and re-examination of the related evidence has shown that there is no case for the existence of any masonry counter. In fact, the counter foundations were later interpreted as part of a porch (Casey & Hoffmann 1998, 122–5 & fig. 8).

The presence of a masonry counter has also been suggested at Vindolanda. The front room of Site xxiii contained a narrow wall to the left of the door that has been described as the base for a counter (Birley 1977, 40). However, the wall is thin and is not as wide as the Italian masonry counters, making it impractical for use as a serving counter (Figure 4.10). Although the wall is L-shaped it does not follow the usual pattern where the main counter fronts the street and the counter arm continues into the shop floor. Moreover, the entrance into the shop is small, and if this were a counter it would restrict those entering the shop to the area enclosed by the reputed counter. The position of Italian *taberna* counters at the shop frontage may restrict access to the shop but they were not used to enclose customers to parts of the shop floor (Mac Mahon 2003, 83). It is more likely that this feature is the foundation for a wall, and that the space contained a stairway that gave access to a separate apartment in an upper floor (pers. comm. Janet Delaine).

Dobinson makes an interesting suggestion for the purpose of two third century independent foundations found in the front room of xiv.6 (1.95m by 0.55m) and the back room of xiv.7 (2.1m by 0.6m) in Verulamium. Broadly based on their position within the structures, and counter measurements found in taverns in Ostia, and in particular the House of the Mills (2.2m by 0.84m) (see Hermansen 1981, 127–8), Dobinson believes that these were the bases for bar counters (1993, 171). However, this does not explain their depth of 0.9m, which seems excessive to support a shop counter which did not require such foundations. Given the near complete absence of evidence for counters in Roman Britain, it is likely that Frere's original suggestion, that they carried domestic shrines or supported stairs, is more plausible (Frere 1972, 101).

The most substantial remains for a possible counter were reported during the 1894 excavation of *insula* ix at Silchester. A layer of tiles, based on a masonry rubble foundation, occupied the entrance to room 3 of House iii (Figure 4.7). The excavator felt that this feature was similar in construct to counters belonging to the medieval period (Fox 1895, 445). *Insula* ix is currently being re-excavated and the feature may be reinterpreted, but at present this example stands alone as the only possible evidence for what is perhaps a substantial masonry counter found in Roman Britain. Given its uniqueness, its purpose as a shop counter seems doubtful.

A counter facing the street is generally accepted as one of the normal prerequisites for a *taberna*. This is clear from Italian examples, where many of the *tabernae* revealed by excavation provide little more than a counter that opened onto the street (Frayn 1993, 6). Counters are often depicted on reliefs from the north-west provinces but there is little physical evidence for their existence. Thus, while there is insufficiently evidence for the existence of masonry or stone counters in Roman Britain, there is no reason to doubt that counters were not common in another material. Indeed, it may be suspected that the counters depicted on reliefs were composed of timber. Although less well known, wooden counters have been discovered in Herculaneum and Pompeii. A partially excavated shop on the north side of the *Decumanus Maximus* in Herculaneum has a wooden bar counter (Hermansen 1982, 186), and wooden counters were uncovered in the spacious *caupona* II.ii.3 (Della Corte 1925, 73) and in I.vi.9 (Pugliese Carratelli 1990a, 352) in Pompeii but nothing remains of them. On the other hand, selling platforms in Roman Britain may have been similar to temporary stalls, such as that depicted on the relief of the Ostian vegetable vendor (Zimmer 1982, 222).

There may be some indications for the existence of such counters at Verulamium *insula* xiv. For example, the postholes located about 0.3m from the frontage in some of the *tabernae* may originally have supported a counter of some form (Frere 1972, fig. 8). In the covered walkway in front of Room 7 postholes were also discovered and these may have supported a counter or stall under the portico (Frere 1972, 42). At the forum in Wroxeter a number of grooves were found cut through the mouldings of some of the column bases that supported the eastern colonnade that fronted shops facing Watling Street (MacDonald 1930, abb 49). Their purpose is unclear but it is known that porticoes were used to sell merchandise, and these apertures may have supported some form of stall (Atkinson 1942, 64, 127–8). Alternately, and perhaps more likely, the grooves may have been used to fix railings or a balustrade, as would the finds of similar grooves in the column bases surrounding the temple of Apollo in Pompeii (Atkinson 1942, 63–4) and in Basilica 3 at Sabratha, Libya (Bonacasa Carra 1991, 165 & fig. 60, 64), would indicate. It is quite possible that selling tables may have been placed against the railing and other stock may have been hung from railings in nets as seems to have been the case in Wroxeter (discussed below).

Covered walkways

An interesting feature in Roman Britain is that many of the buildings had a covering to shelter the area in front of the *taberna*. This could be in the form of roof in front of a single *taberna* or in the more complex form of a covered walkway linking several *tabernae* together. Caerwent offers the best example of the individual approach to *taberna* frontages paralleled in Pompeii (Jashemski 1973, 40). The middle and eastern *tabernae* of House XVIs had solid sheltered walkways placed in front of them that were entered through the front and sides (Ashby, Hudd & King 1911, 429). In front of House XVIIIs, there were two bases that possibly carried columns or posts for a veranda (Figure 4.5; Ashby, Hudd & King 1911, 435). Bases in front of XVIIIn could have carried a porch or awning (Figure 4.6; Ashby, Hudd, & King 1910, 8). While shelters fronted neighbouring buildings along the main east-west street in Caerwent, they were not linked together, and would not have offered a continuous ambulatory for a customer to walk from *taberna* to *taberna*. At Caerleon, Bear House Field, of the six buildings excavated in 1954, the shop-frontages of two of the buildings had shelters in a similar form to those found at Caerwent (Anon. 1955, 122). This was also the method used in front of *tabernae* in the Walheim *vicus*, in Germany (Carroll 2001, 56). In cases were supports for a shelter in front of *tabernae* have not been found, especially those that where not built right up to the street frontage, it is possible that some form of canopy may have been built over the doorway on corbels, as in Pompeii and Herculaneum (Mac Mahon 2003, 104). Alternatively, for which there would be few archaeological traces, shelter could be offered in the form of a simple canopy that was supported by poles when the *taberna* was open for business and removed when the *taberna* was closed (See Figure 4.9).

The continuous colonnade linking the *tabernae* at Verulamium is perhaps one of the most remarkable features of the shop planning at *insula* xiv. Due to the absence of post-holes and the presence of a sleeper-beam, Frere has argued that the colonnade was composed of a number of evenly spaced posts with a wooden balustrade (Figure 4.2). A corresponding portico on the opposite side of the street, fronting what may have been similar buildings, was also uncovered. This suggests that Watling Street was flanked by two parallel covered walkways (Frere 1959, 3–8; Wacher 1995, 221). The absence of tiles at Verulamium suggests that a simple thatched or shingle roof covered the portico (Frere 1972, 14–5, 41, 77). A continuous colonnade, initially of wood and then of stone, appears to have existed in front of the *tabernae* along the side of *insula* viii at Wroxeter (Figure 4.4; Bushe-Fox 1913, 11–8). Similar mortised stones to those found in Wroxeter, used to support the early timber veranda, were also found alone the main east-west street at Kenchester (Jack 1916, 24 + plates 2, 11 & 56; 1926, 14–5, 23–7 + plates 1, 12 & 20). These porticoes were obviously important architectural features as they continued, with modifications, through the history of the respective sites.

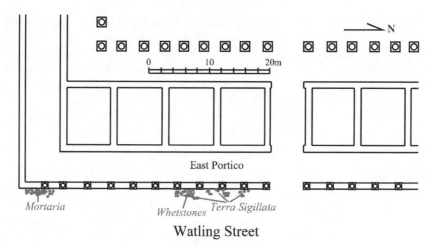

East Portico

Mortaria   Whetstones   Terra Sigillata

Watling Street

Figure 4.11 Eastern portico of the Wroxeter Forum (Drawing: author) (after Atkinson 1942)

Colchester has also provided examples of covered pedestrian walkways along many of its streets (Wacher 1962, 9; Crummy 1992, 32 fig. 3.7). *Insulae* ii, vi and v in Cirencester were flanked by covered walkways, and these complement that of the forum basilica (Wacher 1962, 9; Holbrook 1998, 192, 196 & 204–7). London has provides several examples of covered walkways such as at Courage Brewery and Park Street (Dillon, Jackson & Jones 1991, 258), *insula* v at 1 Poultry (Burch *et al.* 1997, 135) and Fenchurch Street (Philp 1977, 14–5; Marsden 1980, 22–3; 1987, 3 & 71; Merrifield 1983, 48). An interesting aspect of this brief examination of covered areas in front of *tabernae*, is that there seems to be a contrast between the size of the settlement and the type of covered walkways adopted, with the larger towns opting for continuous porticoes linking *taberna* and the smaller settlements choosing a more individualistic approach. This may be indicative of the wealth available to the settlement, the motivation of certain individuals or that of the civic authorities and the level of local control.

These covering were not simply designed to shelter pedestrians and customers or as architectural embellishments. Some form of covering in front of a *taberna* had a very practical function for the shopkeeper and this is well illustrated by the finds discovered in the portico of the Wroxeter forum. During one market day in AD 160–75 a fire started amongst the shops that fronted Watling Steet, which overwhelmed the stalls that had been set up in the Eastern Portico (Figure 4.11). One dealer lost more than 200 decorated and plain *terra sigillata* vessels. Amongst the nests of *terra sigillata* there were about a hundred Kentish whetstones, possibly belonging to an ironmonger or as a sideline for the merchant selling the *terra sigillata*. At the southern end of the portico a crate of *mortaria* were also recovered. Some were in an upright position, while others were bottom up, which may be consistent with the suggestion that they had fallen into that position from a stall placed between the columns of the portico (Atkinson 1942, 65, 127–8; Wacher 1995, 367). All the evidence seems to demonstrate that these products had been offered for sale under, and sheltered by, the covered walkway (White & Barker 1998, 89). A shelter in front of a *taberna* would have offered protection to the wide-open doorway, but its primary purpose for the shopkeeper was to enable the merchant to emerge from the confines of the *taberna*, increase workspace inside the *taberna*, expose more stock for sale and to carry out trade on the street side. Essentially, porticoes and colonnades were designed for the organisation of vehicular and pedestrian traffic routes around and leading to buildings. It separated pedestrians from traffic, and allowed customers to stop and study goods and services offered by shopkeepers. As such, not only did porticoes add to the architectural diversity of any settlement they further enhance the commercial environment of the towns of Roman Britain (Mac Mahon 2003, 106–12).

The use of space
Many of the *tabernae* in Britain were of the strip-building variety, but many of these structures must also have been the dwellings of people who worked the surrounding land or who were not associated with retailing or craft *per se* (Todd 1970, 120–1; Burnham & Wacher 1990, 46). The identification of structures as *tabernae* cannot be readily based upon form alone and must be further supported by features and artefacts that can be associated with *tabernae*. While many crafts and trades must have been practised in *tabernae*, it is frequently difficult to determine specifically what these practices were. As census returns, or any other form of official enumeration, are non-existent and tombstones naming specific occupations are rare in Roman Britain, knowledge of the economic activity of any settlement is primarily based on those industries that have left discernible traces on the ground. As a consequence, the focus will always be towards those industries that have left clear traces such as those that required a large amount of heat and supplies, produced a great amount of waste, or required a distinctive building or fixture (Schofield & Vince 1994, 118). Those *tabernae* that dealt solely in retail activity probably needed little in the way of fixtures and fittings to ply their trade, even if such fittings had survived. Despite these limitations, there is a continually growing corpus of evidence that confirms the industrial and commercial activity of these buildings.

In general manufacturing can be divided into two types, those that required high temperatures and those that did not. Examples of the former are production involving fired clay, metal and glass, and of the latter, are those that used materials such as wood, bone, textiles and leather (Cool 2002, 1). Pottery production is possibly the most clearly recognisable industry because, unlike metal-working or glass-working, the waste materials cannot be recycled. However, as pottery production is largely located outside urban areas it will not be discussed here.

Of the urban artisan industries, metal-working is perhaps the most easily identifiable in the archaeological record, and can be found on almost every Roman settlement in Britain. Evidence for metal-working frequently comes in the form of furnaces, hearths, scrap metals, crucibles, traces of trays, moulds and waste materials. The furnace was an essential piece of equipment in any manufactory that used a great deal of heat such as in metal and glass-working. Its significance is evident, as it would have been the largest item in the workshop and often the most costly in terms of construction, time and running costs (Cable 1997, 315; Sim & Ridge 2002, 49). Hearths and furnaces are common features of the type of structures under discussion and indicate the organisation and importance of metal-working. It seems that forging was carried out in open hearths which could have been a simple bowl furnace or were possibly raised to a convenient height above the ground. These would have been used for heating the blooms when they were prepared and consolidated by hammering and were not smith's furnaces in the normal sense (Manning 1976, 143–4). Pictorial evidence outside Roman Britain from the *Casa dei Vettii* (VI.xv.1) in Pompeii, the Catacomb of Domatilla in Rome and Aquileia suggest that a raised box type 'enclosed' hearth could also have been used (Manning 1976, 143; Sim & Ridge 2002, 57 & 125). However, the evidence for raised hearths in Roman Britain is limited, and the remains in the archaeological record will probably consist only of the brick or masonry base the purpose of which may not be obvious (Manning 1976, 144).

Large and substantial hearths were found in the buildings of Fenchurch (Frere 1989, 306) and Newgate Street in London (Perring & Roskams 1991, 97–9), implying an industrial function. It is likely that these were used in the production of goods sold at the frontage (Perring & Roskams 1991, 13). At Newgate Street a tile-based hearth with a semi-circular open front survived to a height of about 0.4m in Building J (Perring & Roskams 1991, 98). Large amounts of slag containing evidence of iron-working and smithing were also found on the site (Perring & Roskams 1991, 10 & 101).

Sapperton in Lincolnshire, although a small town, contained buildings that typify many of the distinctive features of these workshops. In this case, Building 2A was significant as its front room had traces of two sub-divisions. Between these were two substantial hearths producing chisels, knives and other iron objects. It is unclear whether this division occurred because of the manufacturing process, or because these were the separate workstations of two craftspeople. This division illustrates a degree of complexity, in that this large front room could be divided and utilised for different purposes (Simmons 1976, 5–11; 1985, 18; 1995, 162–4).

Verulamium provides a good example of artisans occupied with metal-working. In *insula* xiv there were strong traces of metal-working especially in copper (Frere 1972, 18–9; Niblett 2001, 64). The site contained crucibles and scrap waste but perhaps the most interesting find were the remains of trays containing copper alloy waste. Similar trays have been found in Building VII.2 at Catterick (Burnham & Wacher 1990, 115; Wilson 2002a, 93; 2002b, 34 & 164), Building A at Caerleon (Zienkiewicz 1993, 54–6), Building A in Exeter (Bidwell 1980, 31–4) and at the site of Bishophill Senior in York (Cool 2002, 4). It is thought that these trays were placed under, or at the end of a workbench, to trap the waste from lathe-turning, engraving or filing bronze for re-smelting later (Frere 1972, 18). One of the most interesting features of the strip-buildings in *insula* viii in Wroxeter was the number of furnaces containing traces of non-ferrous metal-working (Richmond 1966, 76). Precious metal-working was also carried out in Britain and some good examples have been found in London (see Hall this volume, 132–33).

Secondary glass production, rather than glass making, has been commonly reported on a number of sites in Roman Britain (see also Price this volume). Despite the considerable amount of glass finds, the information concerning the design and workings of glasshouses during the Roman period is lacking (Cool & Price 1995, 226). It would seem that the majority of glass produced in Britain was worked from cullet and waste (Price & Cool 1991, 27; Price 2002, 87). The most regular indications of glass-working are furnaces, crucibles and fragments of glass waste. Traces of glass-working are more difficult to find as under normal conditions waste was collected and re-melted.

A glass workshop is known to have existed in the Regis House warehouse. In one of the bays, a section of the timber flooring was removed and a glass furnace inserted. Manufacturing wastes included glass moils, droplets, trimmings and cullet. Other associated finds included imported blue 'raw glass', window glass, faïence melon beads, glass *tesserae* and a finger ring. It is possible that the workshop fabricated twisted glass stirring rods for mixing medicines and cosmetics, and small blown bottles (Brigham & Watson 1998, 45). Alternatively the twisted material may be from the production of handled vessels (Price & Cool 1991, 25). In normal practice crucibles, were used to melt glass but larger quantities of glass could be melted in a 'tank furnace'. Part of a furnace was found at Moorgate in London (Maloney & de Moulins

1990, 69; see also Hall this volume, 133) and a complete example was found at Caistor-by-Norwich (Atkinson 1930, 109–10). The wider context of Caistor-by-Norwich furnace is difficult to interpret, as it was located close to an extensive establishment that resembled a house rather than a workshop and their association is unclear (Atkinson 1930, 106–24). Although glass melting was certainly carried out at the site, the purpose is not known, as there is an absence of evidence for the blowing of glass vessels (Price & Cool 1991, 24–6).

The quantities of meat bones that have been found on Romano-British urban sites indicate that the consumption of meat was extensive. A series of pits found in the south-west of *insula* ii at Cirencester were almost completely filled with cut and sawn animal bones, which suggests that they were associated with the preparation and sale of joints of meat. These may imply the presence of butcher's shops or a meat market (Wacher 1995, 306–7; Holbrook 1998, 184–7). Similar pits containing animal bones were found in the western and southern porticoes of the *macellum* at Wroxeter. They are thought to have represented booths purveying food, possibly even hinting at 'sausage' manufacture in the portico (Rankov 1982, 358; Frere 1983b, 303). There can be no doubt as to the existence of butchers, not only from the evidence of leather and bone-working industries, but more importantly from the method by which bones were cut during the preparation of the carcasses (Maltby 1979, 40). Butcher's equipment such as flesh and meat hooks have also been uncovered at London, Silchester and Verulamium, while knives and cleavers are common discoveries (Manning 1972, 174–6; 1985, 105–13).

The leather industry is a by-product of butchery and was closely associated with the supply of meat. Trade in leather can be divided into two categories, the processing of hides into leather and the production of leather items (van Driel-Murray 2002, 109). The industrial process of tanning required specialised equipment, and in the absence of material evidence, it is difficult to identify the types of troughs, tanks and ovens that were used (Serjeantson & Waldron 1989, 135). A possible case of tanning was found in the western yard of xxxiv.1 at Silchester. In this open space there was an oak lined tank that measured 19m in length and 1 to 1.5m in breath (Hope 1907, 446–9; Boon 1974, 291). On the site of the Baths Basilica at Wroxeter a series of tanks with interconnecting channels, which may have been used in the tanning process, were found between buildings I-IV (White & Barker 1998, 56). Large wood-lined tanks and channels have been found in the upper Walbrook valley just inside the later city wall. These were connected to leather-working, as is evident by the large deposits of leather (Lees & Woodger 1990, 18; Perring 1991, 51).

The premises of cobblers and other leatherworkers are equally difficult to identify. Most of the evidence for the leather industry comes in the form of rubbish dumps of leather scraps. These must be carefully evaluated, as worn out shoes and other leather products show that leather goods were available, they merely indicate evidence of refuse, not manufacture. It is the finds of leather off-cuts that are significant, as they will remain in a workshop as the products were sold and dispersed (van Driel-Murray 2002, 110). A 'leather pit', dated to the Antonine period, from Alcester, provides a good example of this. The deposit of leather off-cuts and general domestic rubbish must represent the sweepings from a leather-workshop (Osborne 1971, 164) and may have been associated with a near-by timber building (Mahany 1994, 14, 149 & 159). A simple building, located between the Bath gate and the amphitheatre at Cirencester, had a furnace and more than 2,000 hobnails scattered about the floor, suggesting its use as a shoemaker's workshop (Wilson 1975, 273). In general, shoemaking off-cuts are so common in Roman Britain that it is safe to assume that almost any settlement could support at least one shoemaker (van Driel-Murray 2002, 117–9).

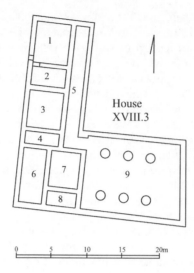

Figure 4.12 '*Bakery' or Mill from Silchester (Drawing: author) (after Hope & Fox 1898)*

Bread was an essential part of every Roman's diet. Although there were large numbers of bakeries in Pompeii (Frayn 1993, 60) and Banasa, in Morocco (MacKendrick 1980, 295), there is less evidence for the production of bread in the *tabernae* of Roman Britain. As grain, flour and bread are organic the lack of evidence is understandable. Furthermore, it is also quite possible that a great deal of baking was carried out on a domestic level. Despite this, building xviii.3 in Silchester is thought to have been devoted to flour milling on a commercial scale (Figure 4.12). A series of three circular masonry platforms on either side of a long walled area may have been used to support large hourglass shaped querns, similar to those found in Italy. Alternatively, they may have held querns of the common discoidal shape. The chambers to the west may have been used to store grain or to make and sell bread (Hope & Fox 1898, 113–20; Boon 1974, 289). Milling and baking must have occurred in every town in Britain. Several perfect millstones were found in one of the back rooms of House XXs in Caerwent (Ashby, Hudd & King 1911, 437–8). Block Ln, also at Caerwent, is a single roomed structure that contained both a lower and upper millstone (Ashby, Hudd & King 1910, 13–4). Indications for the production of flour and the making of bread have also been discovered in London (see also Hall this volume, 140).

As pointed out above, the evidence for *tabernae* which dealt solely in retailing rather than production is more difficult to uncover unless the commodities they sold survive in the archaeological record, such as pottery or glass. Part of one such *taberna*, dating from the mid first century, was discovered at Colchester, located in the south-west corner of *insula* xix (see also Price this volume, 179–80). The general impression gained from the deposit is that *terra sigillata* had been piled on the floor, or a lower shelf, with the glass vessels placed on a shelf above. During a fire the shelves collapsed, and glass had then melted and dripped over the broken sherds below until finally the whole building collapsed, enveloping the merchandise (Hull 1958, 152–8; Rhodes 1989, 53). What makes this find exceptionally interesting is that this *taberna*, if indeed it was a shop, did not specialise in any particular type of ceramics, but had a range of wares, and this may have implications for other commercial premises that sold more perishable goods. In general, it does not seem to have been unusual for pottery shops to sell glass, as was also the case in a building discovered in Castleford (Cool 1998, 360; see also Price this volume, 180).

Another shop in Colchester, which sold pottery, was discovered on the opposite side of the street in *insula* xxviii (Wacher 1995, 120). Various foodstuffs were also found, implying that provisions including figs, barley, lentils, horsebean, spelt, stone-pine and coriander may have been sold alongside the pottery (Hull 1958, 198–202; Rhodes 1989, 53). Pottery shops have also been interpreted in Corbridge (Haverfield 1911, 112–7; Birley 1935, 17–8) and in *insula* xiv at Verulamium (Frere 1972, 28; Rhodes 1989, 54).

An important function of many *tabernae* buildings was to provide living quarters to contain domestic activities. In general, the location of domestic spaces, such as kitchens and bedrooms, is less predictable in small structures than in larger Roman buildings (Clarke 1991, 25). Even in single roomed dwellings, some demarcation must have existed between zones but this is often impossible to distinguish. It is only when there is more than one room that a distinction between room functions can be more readily observed. The contrasting rôle of rooms to the rear of a *taberna* to that of the frontage is often made clear by differences in their decoration. Decoration can be seen to reflect the relative social and economic growth of individual *tabernae* but it also illustrates the designated purpose of a room. The introduction of mosaics, frescoes and other decorative features is significant, as it is assumed they would not have been placed where they would potentially be exposed to damage, as in a work area. In Wolvesey Palace, at Winchester, the front room of a strip-building had a chalk floor, whitewashed walls and contained an oven and a series of hearths. This sparsely decorated room contrasted with the more elaborate decoration of the room behind which had a floor of *opus signinum* and walls painted green, red, and black with yellow and red stripes (Biddle 1968, 281–2). This exact contrast can be clearly seen at Sapperton. While the workroom had a stone-flagged floor, the room to the rear had a mortar floor and painted plaster walls (Simmons 1976, 5–11; 1995, 162–4).

Conclusion

It is the belief behind this paper that *tabernae* were an essential and integral component of the urban environment. They would have been a very visible, familiar and active part of urban life. With their open fronts, goods on display and commercial activities that spread onto the street, they must have left as much an impression of urbanisation as monumental structures. The *taberna* itself was a dynamic organism that changed and developed to suit the needs of its occupants. It is obvious from material finds that a great diversity of goods were produced and sold in *tabernae*. A thriving and competitive retailing community existed in the major settlements of Roman Britain and this is clearly illustrated by the existence of *tabernae*. It is also clear that the urban retail trade had developed sufficiently in Roman Britain to acquire an organised and regular character that can be identified. In conclusion, the importance of *tabernae* in Romano-British society cannot be overestimated and deserve closer study.

Acknowledgements
I would like to thank Jennifer Price (University of Durham) for her many helpful comments and suggestions during the early drafts of this paper. Any mistakes and omissions are purely my own.

Bibliography

Anon. 1955. 'Roman Britain in 1954: sites explored', *JRS* 45: 280–335

Ashby, T. 1905. 'Excavations at Caerwent, Monmouthshire, on the site of the Romano-British city of Venta Silurum, in the year 1904', *Archaeologia* 59(2): 289–310

Ashby, T., Hudd, A.E. & King, F. 1910. 'Excavations at Caerwent, Monmouthshire, on the site of the Romano-British city of Venta Silurum, in the year 1908', *Archaeologia* 62(1): 1–20

Ashby, T., Hudd, A.E. & King, F. 1911. 'Excavations at Caerwent, Monmouthshire, on the site of the Romano-British city of Venta Silurum, in the years 1909 and 1910', *Archaeologia* 62(2): 405–48

Ashby, T. Hudd, A.E. & Martin, A.T. 1902. 'Excavations at Caerwent, Monmouthshire, on the site of the Romano-British city of Venta Silurum, in the year 1901', *Archaeologia* 58(1): 119–52

Atkinson, D. 1930. 'Caistor excavations 1929', *NA* 24: 93–139

Atkinson, D. 1942. *Report on the Excavation at Wroxeter 1923–1924.* Oxford University Press, Oxford.

Bakker, J.T. 1994. *Living and Working with the Gods: studies of evidence for private religion and its material environment in the city of Ostia 100–500AD.* Gieben, Amsterdam.

Bateman, N. & Milne, G. 1983. 'A Roman harbour in London', *Britannia* 14: 207–26

Biddle, M. 1968. 'Excavations at Winchester 1967: sixth interim report', *AntJ* 48: 250–84

Bidwell, P.T. 1980. *Roman Exeter: fortress and town.* Exeter Museums, Exeter.

Birley, E. 1935. *Corbridge Roman Station (corstopitum).* His Majesty's Stationary Office, London.

Birley, E., Charlton, J. & Hedley, W.P. 1932. 'Excavations at Housesteads in 1931', *AA* 9: 222–37

Birley, R. 1977. *Vindolanda: a Roman frontier post on Hadrian's Wall.* Thames & Hudson, London.

Blas de Roblès, J-M. & Sintes, C. 2003. *Sites et Monuments Antiques de l'Algerie.* SECUM, Edisud, Aix-en-Provence.

Boëthius, A. 1934. 'Remarks on the development of domestic architecture in Rome', *AJA* 38: 158–70

Bonacasa Carra, R.M. 1991. 'Il complesso paleocristiano a Nord del Teatro di Sabratha', *QAL* 14: 115–214

Boon, G.C. 1974. *Silchester: the Roman town of Calleva.* David & Charles, London.

Brigham, T. & Watson, B. 1998. 'Regis House: the Romans erect their port', *CA* 158: 44–7

Brigham, T., Watson, B., Tyers, I. & Bartkowiak, R. 1996. 'Current Archaeological work at Regis House in the city of London (part 1)', *LA* 8.2: 31–8

Bromwich, J. 1993. *The Roman remains of Southern France.* Routledge, London.

Burch, M., Hill, J., Jones, S., Lees, D., Rawson, P. & Treveil, P. 1997. 'No. 1 Poultry', *LA* 8.5: 127–35

Burnham, B.C. & Wacher, J.S. 1990. *The 'Small Towns' of Roman Britain.* Batsford, London.

Bushe-Fox, J.P. 1913. *Excavations on the Site of the Roman Town at Wroxeter, Shropshire 1912.* Society of Antiquaries Research Report, Oxford.

Bushe-Fox, J.P. 1914. *Second report on the excavations on the site of the Roman town at Wroxeter, Shropshire 1913.* Society of Antiquaries Research Report, Oxford.

Bushe-Fox, J.P. 1916. *Third Report on the Excavations on the Site of the Roman Town at Wroxeter, Shropshire 1914.* Society of Antiquaries Research Report, Oxford.

Cable, M. 1997. 'The operation of wood fired glass melting furnaces', in McCray, P. (ed) *The Prehistory and History of Glassmaking Technology.* American Ceramic Society, Ohio: 315–30

Callu, J.-P., Morel, J.-P., Rebuffat, R. & Hallier, G. 1970. *Thamusida II: fouilles du Service des antiquités du Maroc.* École française de Rome. Mélanges d'archéologie et d'histoire. Supplements 2, Paris.

Carroll, M. 2001. *Romans, Celts and Germans: the German provinces of Rome.* Tempus, Gloucestershire.

Casey, P.J. & Hoffmann, B. 1998. 'Rescue excavations in the *vicus* of the fort at Greta Bridge, Co. Durham', *Britannia* 38: 111–83

Clarke, J.R. 1991. *The Houses of Roman Italy 100 B.C.-A.D. 250.* University of California, Berkeley & London.

Cool, H.E.M. 2002. 'Craft and industry in Roman York', in Price, J. & Wilson, P. (eds) *Aspects of Industry in Roman Yorkshire and the North.* Oxbow, Oxford: 1–12

Cool, H.E.M. 1998. 'Life in Roman Castleford', in Cool, H.E.M. & Philo, C. (eds) *Roman Castleford: excavations 1974–85 Volume 1: The Small Finds*. Yorkshire Archaeology 4. West Yorkshire Archaeology Service, Wakefield: 355–73

Cool, H.E.M. & Price, J. 1995. *Colchester Archaeological Report 8: Roman vessel glass from excavations in Colchester, 1971–85*. Colchester Archaeological Trust, Colchester.

Crow, J. 1995. *Housesteads*. English Heritage, Batsford, London.

Crow, J. 2004. *Housesteads: a fort and garrision on Hardrian's wall*. Tempus, Gloucestershire.

Crummy, P. 1984. *Colchester Archaeological Report 3: excavations at Lion Walk, Balkerne Lane, and Middleborough, Colchester, Essex*. Colchester Archaeological Trust, Colchester.

Crummy, P. 1992. *Colchester Archaeological Report 6: excavations at Culver Street, the Gilberd School, and other sites in Colchester 1971–85*. Colchester Archaeological Trust, Colchester.

de Kind, R.E.L.B. 1998. *House in Herculaneum: a new view on the town planning and the building of insulae III and IV*. Gieben, Amsterdam.

Della Corte, M. 1925. *Pompeji: the new excavations. Houses and inhabitants*. Valle di Pompeii, Tipografica di F. Sicignano.

Desbat, A. 1994. *La Maison des Dieux Océan à Saint-Romain-En-Gal (Rhône)*. 55e Supplement a Gallia, CNRS, Paris.

Dillon, J., Jackson, S. & Jones, M. 1991. 'Excavations at the Courage Brewery and Park Street 1984–1990', *London Archaeologist* 6.16: 255–62

Dobinson, C.S. 1993. *Studies in Romano-British Urban Structures: a consideration of aspects of planning, building stock and internal structure of the major towns of Roman Britain*. Unpublished PhD thesis, University of Cambridge.

Dunning, G.C. 1948. 'Excavations at Caerwent', *AC* 100: 93–5

Fox, G.E. 1892. 'Excavations on the site of the Roman city of Silchester, Hants, in 1891', *Archaeologia* 53(1): 263–88

Fox, G.E. 1895. 'Excavations on the site of the Roman city of Silchester, Hants, in 1894', *Archaeologia* 54(2): 439–94

Frayn, J.M. 1993. *Markets and Fairs in Roman Italy: their social and economic importance from the second century BC to the third century AD*. Clarendon Press, Oxford.

Frere, S.S. 1958. 'Excavations at Verulamium, 1957: third interim report', *AntJ* 38: 1–14

Frere, S.S. 1959. 'Excavations at Verulamium, 1958: fourth interim report', *AntJ* 39: 1–18

Frere, S.S. 1972. *Verulamium Excavations: volume 1*. Reports of the Research Committee of the Society of Antiquaries of London, London.

Frere, S.S. 1983a. Verulamium excavations: *volume II*. Reports of the Research Committee of the Society of Antiquaries of London, London.

Frere, S.S. 1983b. 'Roman Britain in 1982: sites explored', *Britannia* 14: 280–335

Frere, S.S. 1989. 'Roman Britain in 1988: sites explored', *Britannia* 20: 257–326

Haverfield, F. 1911. 'The Corbridge "pottery shop" and other notes on Samian Ware', *Proceedings of the Society of Antiquaries London* 23: 112–21

Hermansen, G. 1982. *Ostia: aspects of early Roman life*. University of Alberta, Edmonton.

Holbrook, N. 1998. *Cirencester: the Roman town defences, public buildings and shops*. Cotswold Archaeological Trust, Cirencester.

Hope, W.H. 1907. 'Excavations on the site of the Roman city at Silchester, Hants, in 1906', *Archaeologia* 60(2): 431–50

Hope, W.H. & Fox, G.E. 1896. 'Excavations on the site of the Roman city at Silchester, Hants, in 1895', *Archaeologia* 55(1): 215–55

Hope, W.H. & Fox, G.E. 1898. 'Excavations on the site of the Roman city at Silchester, Hants, in 1897', *Archaeologia* 56(1): 103–26

Hull, M.R. 1958. *Roman Colchester*. Society of Antiquaries, London.

Jack, G.H. 1916. *Excavations on the site of the Romano-British town of Magna, Kenchester, Herefordshire, during the years 1912–1913*. Report of the Research Committee of the Woolhope Club, Hereford.

Jack, G.H. 1926. *Excavations on the site of the Romano-British town of Magna, Kenchester, Herefordshire, during the years 1924–1925.* Report of the Research Committee of the Woolhope Club, Hereford.

Jashemski, W.F. 1973. 'The discovery of a large vineyard at Pompeii: University of Maryland excavation, 1970', *AJA* 77: 27–41

Jongman, W. 1991. *The Economy and Society of Pompeii.* Gieben, Netherlands.

Lees, D. & Woodger, A. 1990. *The Archaeology and History of 60 London Wall London.* Museum of London, London.

Ling, R. 1983. 'The *insula* of the Menander at Pompeii: Interim report', *Antiquity Journal* 63: 34–57

Locock, M. 1994. *Meaningful Architecture: social interpretations of buildings.* World Archaeological Series 9, Avebury, Hampshire.

MacDonald, G. 1930. 'Forschungen im Römischen Britannien 1914–1928', *Sonderabdruck aus dem 19. Neunzehnten Bericht der Römisch-germanischen Kommission* 1929. Frankfurt-am-Main: 1–85

MacKendrick, P. 1980. *The North African Stones Speak.* Croom Helm, London

Mac Mahon, A. 2003. *The Taberna Structures of Roman Britain.* BAR (British Series) 356, Oxford.

Mahany, C. 1994. *Roman Alcester: southern extramural area.* Council for British Archaeology, York.

Maloney, C. & de Moulins, D. 1990. *The Upper Walbrook Valley in the Roman Period.* Council for British Archaeology, London.

Maltby, M. 1979. *Faunal Studies on Urban Sites: the animal bones from Exeter 1971–1975.* University of Sheffield, Sheffield.

Manning, W.H. 1972. 'The iron objects', in Frere, S.S. (ed) *Verulamium Excavations: volume 1.* Reports of the Research Committee of the Society of Antiquaries of London, London: 163–95

Manning, W.H. 1976. 'Blacksmithing', in Strong, D.T. & Brown, D. (eds) *Roman Crafts.* Duckworths, London.

Manning, W.H. 1985. *Catalogue of Romano-British Iron Tools, Fittings and Weapons in British Museums.* British Museum, London.

Marsden, P. 1980. *Roman London.* Thames & Hudson, London.

Marsden, P. 1987. *The Roman Forum Site in London.* Museum of London, London.

McKay, A.G. 1975. *Houses, Villas and Palaces in the Roman World.* Thames & Hudson, London.

Merrifield, R. 1983. *London: city of the Romans.* Batsford, London.

Meyer, K.E. 1999. 'Axial peristyle houses in the western empire', *JRA* 12: 101–21

Nash-Williams, V.E. 1948. 'Excavations within the Roman town of *Venta Silurum* at Caerwent, Mon.', *BBCS* 13: 56–9

Niblett, R. 2001. *Verulamium: the Roman city of St Albans.* Tempus, Gloucestershire.

Osborne, P.J. 1971. 'Insect fauna from the Roman site, Alcester', *Britannia* 2: 156–65

Packer, J.E. 1971. *The Insulae of Imperial Ostia.* Memoirs of the American Academy in Rome 31, Rome.

Paoli, U.E. 1975. *Rome: its people, life and customs.* Longman, London.

Perring, D. 1987. 'Domestic buildings in Romano-British towns', in Schofield, J. & Leech, R. (eds) *Urban Archaeology in Britain.* Council for British Archaeology, London: 147–55

Perring, D. 1991. *Roman London.* Batsford, London.

Perring, D. 2002. *The Roman House in Britain.* Routledge, London.

Perring, D. & Roskams, S. 1991. *Early Development of Roman London West of the Walbrook.* Council for British Archaeology, London.

Philp, B.J. 1977. 'The Forum of Roman London', *Britannia* 8: 1–64

Price, J. 2002. 'Broken bottles and Quartz-sand: glass production in Yorkshire and the North in the Roman period', in Price, J. & Wilson, P. (eds) *Aspects of Industry in Roman Yorkshire and the North.* Oxbow, Oxford: 81–93

Price, J. & Cool, H.E.M. 1991. 'The evidence for the production of glass in Roman Britain', in Foy, D. & Sennequier, G. (eds) *Ateliers de Verriers de l'antiquité à la période pré-industrielle.* Association Française pour L'Archéologie de Verre, Rouen: 23–7

Pugliese Carratelli, G. 1990a. *Pompei: Pitture e Mosaici (Regio 1 Parte Prima).* Istituto della Enciclopedia Italiana, Roma.

Pugliese Carratelli, G. 1990b. *Pompei: Pitture e Mosaici (Regio 1 Parte Seconda).* Istituto della Enciclopedia Italiana, Roma.
Pugliese Carratelli, G. 1991. *Pompei: Pitture e Mosaici (Regiones II, III, V).* Istituto della Enciclopedia Italiana, Roma.
Rankov, N. 1982. 'Roman Britain in 1981: sites explored', *Britannia* 13: 328–4
Rebuffat, R. 1973–1975. 'La maison à la disciplina, à Volubilis', *BAM* 9: 329–45
Rhodes, M. 1989. 'Roman pottery lost *en route* from the kiln site to the user-a gazetteer', *JRPS* 2: 44–58
Richardson, L. 1988. *Pompeii: an architectural history.* Johns Hopkins University Press, Baltimore & London.
Richmond, I.A. 1966. 'Industry in Roman Britain', in Wacher, J.S. (ed) *The Civitas Capitals of Roman Britain.* Leicester University Press, Leicester: 76–86
Rickman, G. 1980. *The Corn Supply of Ancient Rome.* Clarendon Press, Oxford.
Risse, M. 2001. *Volubilis: eine römische Stadt in Marokko von der Frühzeit bis in die islamische Periode.* Verlag Philipp von Zabern, München.
Rorison, M. 2001. *Vici in Roman Gaul.* British Archaeological Report (International series) 933, Oxford.
Schofield, J. & Malt, D. 1996. *MoLAS 96: annual review.* Museum of London Archaeological Service, London.
Schofield, J. & Vince, A. 1994. *Medieval Towns.* Leicester University Press, London.
Serjeantson, D. & Waldron, T. 1989. *Diet and Crafts in Towns: the evidence of animal remains from the Roman to the Post-Medieval periods.* British Archaeological Report (British Series) 199.
Sim, D. & Ridge, I. 2002. *Iron for the Eagles: the iron industry of Roman Britain.* Tempus, Gloucestershire.
Simmons, B.B. 1976. 'Sapperton: an interim report', *LHA* 11: 5–11
Simmons, B.B. 1985. 'Sapperton', *AL* 1: 16–20
Simmons, B.B. 1995. 'Sapperton', in Brown, A.E. (ed) *Roman Small Towns in Eastern England and Beyond.* Oxbow Monograph 52, Oxford: 157–65
Stambaugh, J.E. 1988. *The Ancient Roman city.* John Hopkins University Press, Baltimore & London.
Thouvenot, R. 1958. *Maisons de Volubilis: le Palais dit de Gordien et la Maison à la Mosaïque de Vénus.* Service des antiquités du Maroc, Rabat.
Todd, M. 1970. 'The small towns of Roman Britain', *Britannia* 1: 114–30
van Driel-Murray, C. 2002. 'The leather trades in Roman Yorkshire and beyond', in Price, J. & Wilson, P. (eds) *Aspects of Industry in Roman Yorkshire and the North.* Oxbow, Oxford: 109–23
Wacher, J.S. 1962. 'Cirencester, 1961: second interim report', *AntJ* 42: 1–14
Wacher. J.S. 1989. 'Cities from the second-fourth century cities', in Todd, M. (ed) *Research on Roman Britain: 1960–89.* British Monograph Series II, Alan Sutton, Glouchester: 91–114
Wacher, J.S. 1995. *The Towns of Roman Britain.* Batsford, London.
Walthew, C.V. 1975. 'The town house and the villa house', *Britannia* 6: 189–205
Ward, J. 1911. *Romano-British Buildings and Earthworks.* Methuen. London.
White, R. & Barker, P. 1998. *Wroxeter: the life and death of a Roman city.* Tempus, Gloucestershire.
Wilson, D.R. 1975. 'Roman Britain in 1974: sites explored', *Britannia* 6: 220–85
Wilson, P.R. 2002a. *Cataractonium: Roman Catterick and its Hinterland: excavations and research, 1958–1997. Part I.* Council for British Archaeology, London.
Wilson, P.R. 2002b. *Cataractonium: Roman Catterick and its Hinterland: excavations and research, 1958–1997. Part II.* Council for British Archaeology, London.
Zienkiewicz, J.D. 1993. 'Excavations in the *Scamnum Tribunorum* at Caerleon: the Legionary Museum site 1983–5', *Britannia* 24: 27–140
Zimmer, G. 1982. *Römische Berufsdarstellungen.* Deutsches Archäologisches Institut, Mann, Berlin.

5

The *taberna* counters of Pompeii and Herculaneum

Ardle Mac Mahon

One of the most characteristic features of the *tabernae* of Pompeii and Herculaneum is the distinctive shop counter or *mensa*. The significance of this element is that in many cases the purpose of a building or room is unknown, and it is frequently through the existence of a *taberna* counter that a building gains its identity. As such, the selling counter has become an important diagnostic key for the identification of the function of the surrounding space. For example a *taberna* is often described as a 'tavern' if the counter within enclosed large earthenware vessels known as *dolia*. However, it is becoming increasingly clear that the function of many counters has been misinterpreted. There are vague references in the ancient sources to the type of furniture that could be found in taverns, for example Martial (V.70) mentions stools and chairs, but it is interesting that none of the sources mention a shop counter. This paper will briefly discuss the form and decoration of the shop counters of Pompeii and Herculaneum. The paper will also examine the interpretation of a specific counter type, those that contained *dolia*, to evaluate if these counters can so easily be associated with taverns, and to discover if the selling-platforms that enclosed *dolia* have become imbued with a meaning that they may not have possessed in antiquity. In general, the paper will discuss the use of counters within *tabernae* and the role of selling-platforms in retail.

The study of counters in Pompeii is important as the site illustrates the great diversity of counter types that existed in the Roman world. These selling-platforms might be a simple peninsula form, but were more usually L- or U-shaped (Figure 5.1). Other counter forms that existed, although seldom mentioned in the archaeological literature, are the back-bar/single-wall counter, the island counter, the V-shaped (VI.viii.8) or the more complex G-shaped counter (VII.ii.32–33). In general, the counters are similar in design to modern examples with a worktop above a counter base, and are about waist level in height. The surviving examples of shop counters in Pompeii and Herculaneum are solid and constructed of cement, brick or mortared rubble (Figure 5.2). Despite this some were poorly built and have been lost to decay

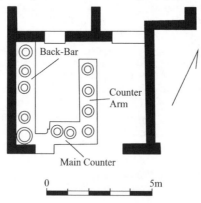

Figure 5.1 *U-shaped counter in the Caupona di Lucius Betutius Placidus (I.viii.8) in Pompeii (Drawing: author)*

70

Figure 5.2 A typical L-shaped shop counter from Pompeii (Photo: author)

and destruction (Paoli 1999, 66). It is also possible that many counters were composed of less durable materials, such as wood. The absence of counters in many *tabernae* would to some extent support this point and as a consequence some counter forms may have been lost. As such, the surviving examples must represent the selling-platforms of shopkeepers (*tabernarii*) or shop owners with access to greater funds to invest in more durable and permanent counters.

Shop counters were nearly always built against a wall, and step-formed shelves were placed at this end. The counter uncovered in the *Caupona di Euxinus* (I.xi.10–11) had three step shelves that were 15cm wide and 10cm deep (Jashemski 1973, 40). The four steps of VI.i.5 were 10cm in height. These steps presumably served to support different sorts of vessels and dishes or measures for liquids and food on sale (Packer 1978, 18; Parslow 1995, 112). A grave relief from Isola Sacra, now in the Museo Ostiense, confirms this function. The shelf arrangement can be seen over the *mensa* and drinking tumblers are shown on the top two shelves and a jar and flask on the lower one (Hermansen 1974, 175–6).

Many counters also possessed a stove or fireplace that was built into the end of the counter arm. The stove in the counter of the *Caupona di Euxinus* (I.xi.10–11) had a roof tile as a fire bed – 'a device used to ensure an especially hot fire' (Jashemski 1967, 37). In other cases, a stove was placed in the back-bar or elsewhere within the *taberna*. It can be assumed that the *tabernae* possessing stoves could serve hot food and/or drink to their customers.

Shop counters were predominantly located directly in or by the shop entrance, often blocking part of the doorway (Guhl & Koner 1994, 520). The counter would have been the location where goods could be displayed, and where much of the shopkeeper's equipment was used and stored when not in use, as the counter was also a worktop. This could have dire consequences as in the case of Verginius' efforts to save his daughter from the lustful advances of the *decemvir*, Appius.

> Permission being granted, he took the girl and her nurse aside to the shops near the shrine of Cloacina, now known as the 'New Shops', and there, snatching up a knife from a butcher, he plunged it into her breast, saying, 'Thus, my daughter, in the only way I can, I vindicate thy freedom (Livy 3.48.5–7).

It can be presumed that counters were placed in this location to deal with customers at the *taberna* entrance and that the majority of retailing activity was conducted at the entrance and

71

Figure 5.3 *The Caupona di Sotericus (I.xii.3) in Pompeii (Photo: author)*

not in the shop itself. A counter arm often continued into the shop and this would have allowed larger numbers of people to be dealt with at the same time, but more importantly created greater worktop space for the shopkeeper. In other *tabernae*, such as taverns and restaurants, the customer could enter the premises, sit down at a table and imbibe, in another room (Boissier 1905, 423; MacKenzie 1910, 29).

Decoration

Counters were often stuccoed and painted. The counter of I.xi.16 was unusual in that it was stuccoed, but was left unpainted. The front of the counter in the *Caupona di Euxinus* (I.xi.10–11) was plastered and painted red. This was further decorated with a single circular insert of variegated marble (Jashemski 1973, 40). The counter in II.x.13 was also painted red. This was a very simple form of decoration when compared to the counters that were painted with lavish and elaborate patterns. The frontage facing the street of the counter in II.i.1 was painted with coloured patterns in imitation of marble (Della Corte 1925, 37; Packer 1978, 47 & fn. 99), while the counter within the *taberna* was painted red with yellow garlands. The *Bottega del fruttivendolo Felix* (I.viii.1) had a magnificent counter. This was finely decorated with a trophy in the form of a shield that was embellished with the image of Medusa, flanked in the upper regions by the head of Pan on the left, a Gorgon on the right and two large vessels that stand in a floral display in the lower areas (Della Corte 1925, 27; Pugliese Carratelli 1990a, 793). The *mensa* of the *Caupona di Sotericus* (I.xii.3) was decorated in imitation of white tiles with a painted floral network (Figure 5.3), and inside the shop the counter was faced with depictions of birds, swans and a panther (Della Corte 1925, 43; Pugliese Carratelli 1990b, 704).

Perhaps the most ornately decorated counters were those covered with a veneer of irregularly shaped fragments of coloured marble (Figure 5.4). The work surface of the counter belonging to the *Caupona di Lucius Betutius Placidus* (I.viii.8) was covered in marble, as was the area facing the street frontage, which was further decorated with three coloured marble disks (Figure 5.5; Pugliese Carratelli 1990a, 804–5). The L-shaped *mensa* in IX.vii.24 also had a marble top and frontage (Pugliese Carratelli 1999, 871–2), and the top, front and side of the *taberna* counter in VII.ii.32–3 was covered in a veneer of marble (Pugliese Carratelli 1996, 720–1). In Herculaneum, the counter of the *Grande Taberna* (IV.15–16) was covered with polychrome marble fragments in a similar manner to that in Pompeii (Maiuri 1977, 57).

Figure 5.4 *A counter with a marble work surface from Pompeii (Photo: John Naylor)*

Figure 5.5 *The counter of the Caupona di Lucius Betutius Placidus (I.viii.8) (Photo: author)*

It is noteworthy that many of the surviving worktops from Ostia were also covered with marble slabs, such as the inn on the *via di Diana* (I.ii.5) and it has been argued that these counters date from the economic decline of the city in the third century when second-hand marble was easily acquired (Meiggs 1973, 428). However, the re-use of marble as counter decoration seems to have been a continuation of the custom that had existed long before in Pompeii and Herculaneum. It is possible that in Pompeii a great deal of broken marble may have been available after the earthquake of AD 62 from demolition and rebuilding. Indeed surviving indistinct fragments of lettering on some of the marbles belonging to counters of *tabernae* in the south of VI.i hint at their original use (pers. comm. Damian Robinson). Despite this the motive behind the use of marble on counters in a *taberna* must have been to make the *taberna* distinctive, display status or give the impression of status.

The re-use of marble to decorate shop counters should not simply be seen as economic expediency and/or *tabernarii* taking advantage of a cheap source of marble to embellish their counters. The use of solid surface materials on counters, such as marble, would demand someone familiar with the working properties of the material. Furthermore, accuracy in cutting

Figure 5.6 *Fresco from the tablinum of VII.iii.30 (after Gusman 1900)*

and co-ordination would be needed to place marble on a counter and accurate measurements would be at its most complex and expense if the countertop consisted of a single marble slab. The greater ease in fitting fragments may in some way explain why counters in Pompeii and Herculaneum were composed of marble fragments, even if re-using marble that may have been waste. It is probably likely that such counter decoration was carried out by specialists and would have been beyond the ability of the 'do-it-yourself' minded *tabernarius*. A counter embellished with a marble surface would have dramatically changed the *taberna* into a more luxurious environment.

In a study of the role of decoration within Pompeii, Wallace-Hadrill included twenty-nine decorated shops in his general research. He found that the decoration of *tabernae* fell well below that of private houses but what is of interest here is that in a sixth of the shops included in the study, the focus of embellishment was the decorated counter (1994, 155). Based on this small study it would seem that the counter itself was the main centre of attention, both physically and decoratively, in many *tabernae*.

The decoration and composition of shop counters would also be indicative of the economic resources available to the *tabernarius* in independently operated *tabernae*, or the resources that the shop-owner was willing to invest in client-operated businesses. Presumably a highly decorated *mensa* would have been relatively more expensive than a plain wooden counter. A fresco from the *tablinum* of VII.iii.30 is the only surviving illustration of a wooden counter in Pompeii (Figure 5.6). The counter is long and of simple construction, with horizontal bare timber planks held together by nails and vertical wooden beams (Ciarallo & de Carolis 1999, 134–5). Admittedly this is a lone example, and some wooden counters may have been quite ornate, but it does illustrate the point being made here. The first *tabernae* to adopt marble decoration would have appeared very lavish and unique, but as time progressed, and as more *tabernae* contained marble covered counters, this increased proliferation would have removed much of the vestiges of luxury and distinction associated with these *mensae*.

The counters in VI.i appear late in the sequence of the site, within a relatively short space of time, and are the final structural features added before the eruption in AD 79 (pers. comm. Damian Robinson). The adoption and decoration of *mensae* seems to indicate that shopkeepers actively competed with each other and that counter decoration was related to fashion, identity and status, and that shopkeepers followed trends in retail display. There appears to have been a general trend towards more decoration on counters and many of the most highly embellished counters belong to the latest period. Decorated counters must have played an active part in attracting customers but just as importantly the counter is making a statement of the social and economic position, or aspiration, of the shopkeeper or shop owner and the type of custom they wished to attract.

Shop counters in focus

The use of counters in retail has a number of advantages. It allows for the visual presentation of services, goods and food. Especially in the case of the latter, counters offered a hygienic means of dealing with foodstuff by making it possible for the customer to see at a glance the quality of non-staple goods available on a particular day (Frayn 1993, 101–2). Those counters with masonry worktops would have been particularly suitable for retailing meat and fish, as they offered a solid and durable work-surface for cutting and cleaning. However, masonry counters could not be used to chop flesh without damaging the cleaver, therefore a wooden chopping board or substantial wooden counter must have been used in those *tabernae* that dealt with meat. Large volumes of dry goods, such as grain and spices, are more likely to have been sold from sacks, jars, *dolia* and other containers. The surviving counters were far too high for these products to be practically displayed, as the customer would naturally have wished to carefully inspect and handle the goods. This is exactly what can be seen on a Bordeaux relief, which shows a customer testing grain by placing her hand into a sack of cereal (Espérandieu 1911, no. 1097; Higounet 1971, 80–1 relief 70; Frayn 1993, 106–7).

The most obvious purpose of the *taberna* counter was as a selling-platform and for the display of merchandise. As mentioned above, in the majority of *tabernae* the counter was located at the shop frontage and this meant that the most of the stock was probably placed on and behind the counter, and that the retailer was completely in control of the merchandise. This arrangement can be seen on the fresco in VII.iii.30. The customer did not have, nor were they given, the opportunity to see and compare the entire range of goods available, without the knowledge of the retailer (Figure 5.6). This did not mean that customers did not have the opportunity to handle goods displayed on the counter, as is apparent from the words of Horace. He mentions that 'no shop, nor stall, holds my books, from which the sweaty hands of the vulgar may soil' (1.4.71–4). Furthermore, Pliny's mention of bird droppings falling on the stock of shoes in front of a *taberna* belonging to a cobbler near the *Forum Romanum* indicates that stock was openly displayed (*Historia Naturalis* 10.121).

It is clear that in numerous *tabernae*, the shop counter was the most significant feature within the shop, and a great deal of expense and effort was put into their design and composition. Shop counters were broadly similar in function, as selling platforms, but closer examination shows that they were very different in design and composition. Thus, it can be presumed that they were custom made to the shopkeeper's specifications and reflect their specific use within the *taberna*. This belief would seem to be supported by the recent evaluation of the *tabernae* in *insula* VI.i in Pompeii. Changes were noted to some of the counters in the *insula* and this would suggest that counters were adapted to meet the changing requirements of the particular property (pers. comm. Damain Robinson).

The shape, height and depth of a counter presumably reflected the most appropriate form for the smooth running of the *taberna*. In determining the optimum dimensions for a counter in modern bars and restaurants reference has to be made to the representative body measurements of the intended users (Lawson 1994, 82–3). By analogy, the Pompeian counter dimensions were probably such that the *tabernarius* did not have to reach too high or too low or to stretch too far for objects or tools. At the same time the counter must have offered sufficient area to place or rest objects so that they would remain stable on the countertop. This is important, as the top must have been used as working, preparation and service space as well as for display. It can thus be presumed that the length of the counter was related to the nature and concentration of use.

It is probable that *tabernarii* or customers did not sit at the counter, even in those *tabernae* that are thought to serve food and/or drink. People seated at a counter take up more space than those that may be standing. Furthermore, there is less 'economy of space' than tables, since customers seating at a counter are normally only located on one side. In the design of modern bars and restaurants at least 0.45m is required (not including knee space of 0.3–0.5m or access space behind any seats) from the counter frontage by those seated at a counter (Lawson 1994, 82–5). It can be assumed that a similar space requirement would have been needed in the ancient world. The counters in Pompeii and Herculaneum are often placed at the shop frontage and any customers seated at the counter would obstruct people passing or from entering the *taberna*. Even space for possible seating by the counter arm is limited. People seated at a counter tend to spend more time at the counter while they consume their purchases. This will cause further obstructions to customer flow within the *taberna*, especially in those that the counter arm extended into the shop floor, and also take up precious preparation space on the countertop, increasing the likelihood that customers did not sit at the counter.

To sit comfortably at a counter, especially if one is eating or drinking, knee space is required below the countertop. In modern counters the higher the counter top the less knee space is required in the form of a counter recess or overhang. For example in a counter that is 0.75m in height, approximately 0.5m of knee space is needed, and in a counter that is 1.0m in height, 0.3m of clear knee space is required for each seated customer (Lawson 1994, 84–5). None of the counters in Pompeii or Herculaneum were designed to take into account this practical requirement. The assumption that patrons did not sit at shop counters is confirmed by depictions of *tabernae* that show individuals standing against the shop counter such as is illustrated on a fresco from the *tablinum* of VII.iii.30, mentioned above (Figure 5.6; Ward-Perkins & Claridge 1976, 54; Ciarallo & de Carolis 1999, 134–5), and a *taberna* sign of a poultry seller found in the *Via della Foce* in Ostia (Kampen 1981, 52–9 & fig. 28; 1982, 63; Veyne 1987, 123).

Furthermore, for the shopkeeper to serve customers from a seated position from behind a counter would be difficult without knee space. Again this is consistent with the surviving depictions of shopkeepers that show the *tabernarius* dealing with customers standing upright. The only cases where salespersons are shown seated is when they conduct business from behind a table as in the case of the shoe seller depicted on the lower panel of the fresco that flanked the entrance of the *Officina coactiliaria di Verecundus* (IX.vii.5–7) in Pompeii (Maiuri 1929, 99–100; Pugliese Carratelli 1999, 774–8) or on the relief of a vegetable seller from Ostia (Zimmer 1982, 222). These tables were wooden but it is interesting that *taberna* VII.i.41 had a stone table with tufa legs and a marble top located at the threshold (Pugliese Carratelli 1996, 460–1). This is a unique find of an alternative selling-platform within Pompeii, although similar, but more ornate, stone tables exist in market places in North Africa at Djemila and Timgad in Algeria (Albertini 1937, facing pages 32 & 33; Blas de Roblès 2003, 100) and Lepcis Magna in

Figure 5.7 *A tavern scene from the Caupona della via de Mercurio (VI.x.1), room b, south wall Pompeii (Photo: author)*

Libya (Degrassi 1951, 67; de Ruyt 1983, 318–9). Needless to say a chair or stool behind the counter would have been useful for the shopkeeper to rest during lulls in business and when not dealing directly with customers.

It is unlikely that customers stood at tavern counters for prolonged periods of time to eat or drink. The average height of a counter in a modern bar is about 0.99–1.08m to allow the customer comfortable elbowroom while standing at the counter (Lawson 1994, 82–3). The counters in Pompeii and Herculaneum are below that height. For example the masonry counter in the *Caupona di Euxinus* (I.xi.10–11) is 0.85m in height (Jashemski 1973, 40), that in VI.i.5 is 0.88m and the counter in the Bar of Pheobus (VI.i.17) is 0.95m in height (pers. comm. Damian Robinson). The counters of II.xvi.15 and VII.ii.39 are 0.72m high and that of VI.xvi.33 is 0.82m. In fact, customers shown in tavern scenes are seated at stools around a table away from the serving counter, as in the depiction from Isola Sacra (Hermansen 1974, 175–6; Meiggs 1973, pl. XXVIB). In depictions on frescos from the *Caupona della via de Mercurio* (VI.x.1) and the *Caupona di Salvius* (VI.xiv.36) from Pompeii, show customers served at their table or even standing by a waitress (Figure 5.7; Pugliese Carratelli 1993, 1005–19; Pugliese Carratelli 1994, 366–71). Space was probably at a premium in most *tabernae*, and *mensae* appear to take up a large proportion of the limited shop floor area, and any accommodation that was provided for customers within a *taberna* was probably in another room.

In general, it appears that the counters of Pompeii and Herculaneum seem to have been designed for the benefit of those employed in the *taberna* and are closer in height to modern examples in which the most comfortable working height for someone working behind a counter is 0.6–0.9m (Lawson 1994, 82–3). The counter creates a separation between service staff and customers, which increases speed and efficiency on the work floor. This may suggest that business was somewhat brisk with little interchange between staff and customers but this was probably no more so than in a modern shop. From a social point of view the use of counters actually increases social contact between customers and servers (Lawson 1994, 246). The counter was wide enough for people to stand out of the way of other customers, if they

Figure 5.8 A counter with dolia in Taberna IV.15–16 Herculaneum (Photo: Shaun Loader)

wished to examine goods at their leisure. The shopkeeper, if taking a very passive role, may only have interfered when a question was asked or a sale was about to be made. From the point of view of the customer the separation created by the counter offered a psychological barrier for the customer from overly forward retail staff and activities within the *taberna*, which increased the likelihood of buyers approaching the shop.

It is clear that counters were an important part of retailing but a large number of the *tabernae* in Pompeii do not appear to have possessed a counter. Of the ninety or so *tabernae* of varying types and sizes recognised in *Regio* I in Pompeii, just over thirty possess shop counters. While there is no evidence for the existence of masonry or stone counters in many *tabernae*, there is no reason to doubt that a large number had wooden counters that has not survived, as in the case of I.vi.9 (Pugliese Carratelli 1990a, 352). A partially excavated shop on the north side of the *Decumanus Maximus* in Herculaneum had a wooden shop counter blocking most of the wide *taberna* door (Hermansen 1982, 186). Further evidence for the existence of wooden counters is the above mentioned fresco from the *tablinum* of VII.iii.30 in Pompeii (Figure 5.6; Ward-Perkins & Claridge 1976, 54; Ciarallo & de Carolis 1999, 134–5). Counters constructed of timber may have been quite common in *tabernae* but it should be accepted that some *tabernae* may never have required a counter, or a counter of the form described above, to carry out business. All the counters in VI.i were preceded by ground level cooking platforms. This would suggest that these properties had a long history as cooked food, and possibly drink, retail outlets before the adoption of counters late in the sequence of the site (pers. comm. Damian Robinson). This further implies that counters were not essential to carry out trade, but that late in the history of the site, the shopkeepers or shop owners in VI.i felt that they were necessary. This must indicate that there was a change in the approach and psychology of retailing in Pompeii and Herculaneum.

Specialist counters

While many of the Pompeian counters were similar in form to contemporary examples, as flat-topped serving counters, others were more elaborate and reflected a specific function, such as those interpreted as belonging to taverns. Many of the *taberna* counters found in Pompeii and

Herculaneum encased large convex bodied earthenware jars known as *dolia* (Figure 5.8; Dyer 1867, 302; MacKenzie 1910, 28). Given the size of *dolia* it can be presumed that *dolia* were not inserted into a counter, but that counters were built around the vessels. The number of counters in which the sides of *dolia* appear to bulge out from the front and/or back of counters gives this assumption additional credence. Furthermore, those counters that have sufficiently disintegrated often show the flat bottom to *dolia* resting on the shop floor. This would again support the belief that counters were custom made for each *taberna* and reflect the particular retail use of that establishment.

The largest *taberna* in Herculaneum, IV.15–16, across from the entrance to the *Palaestra* had a counter with eight large *dolia* (Figure 5.8; Deiss 1985, 117; 1995, 97) as did II.6–7 (Budetta 1989, 264). In contrast IV.10–11 had only one *dolium* (de Kind 1998, 155). *Taberna* counters with *dolia* are frequently used as evidence to identify 'taverns', or more particularly, *thermopolii* or *cauponae* (Adam 1994, 321; Paoli 1999, 88). A *thermopolium* was a restaurant selling hot drinks. This is a word that is frequently used in modern literature but as a term it is not common in Latin vocabulary (Stambaugh 1988, 365 note 10). A *caupona* was an establishment that offered food, drink and board (Stambaugh 1988, 208). As the archaeological record is often insufficiently sensitive to distinguish between subtle variations in the use of a particular *taberna* the generic term 'tavern' shall be used in this paper to describe any establishment that sold wine.

Dolia were very versatile containers and were used to contain and store a great diversity of foodstuffs such as grain (Cato *De Re Rustica*, 11) and pickled vegetables (Columella 12.56.3). It is frequently stated that the *dolia* in *taberna* counters were used to hold wine that was served to customers (*e.g.* Boissier 1905, 423). In addition, Tanzer mentions that they not only held wine, but also hot stews (1939, 42). The assumption that *dolia* found in *taberna* counters contained any form of liquid would seem problematic. The rationale behind such doubts is the porous nature of the *dolium* fabric and the fact that *dolia* would have required some form of treatment if they were to contain liquids of any sort (Packer 1978, 47).

If wine, or any other non-viscous fluid, were to be carried it was essential to seal the porous earthenware container with an impermeable membrane of some form. The normal method used to waterproof unglazed porous earthenware containers in antiquity was to coat the inside, and sometimes the outside of the vessel in resin, or its prepared version pitch (Callender 1965, 45; White 1975, 145; Koehler 1986, 50; Formenti & Duthel 1996, 84). Pitch played an important part in the production and distribution of wine. It was almost taken for granted that any container in which wine was stored, particularly if it was to travel, must be thoroughly coated with pitch to make it watertight (Meiggs 1982, 468; Guhl & Koner 1994, 459). In contrast to *dolia*, the use of amphorae as containers has been relatively well evaluated in modern literature, and as such the properties of amphorae offer a suitable model to discuss the use of *dolia*. Amphorae are well know to have been used to contain and transport wine and like *dolia* were porous (Callender 1965, 42). The use of pitch as a lining for amphorae in the ancient world has been confirmed by the results of chemical analysis on a wide variety of transport amphorae from different periods (Peacock & Williams 1986, 49; Curtis 2001, 380).

Even before transportation, to complete the fermentation process, wine was poured into large earthenware vats whose interior was carefully lined with pitch (Ramsay 1894, 492). Both Cato (*De Re Rustica* 23) and Pliny (*Historia Naturalis* 14.120–1) state that when preparations were made for the vine harvest it was essential to see that all containers were pitched. Columella describes the process in full and states that large and small storage jars should be

Figure 5.9 *A view of counter dolia in Pompeii from above (Photo: John Naylor)*

treated with pitch some forty days before the vintage was decanted into them. He also describes the complex pitching process for *dolia* sunk into the earth (Columella 12.18.5–7). Although the pitching of vessels for the storage of liquids was widely practised, it would have been difficult to carry out the former process in *dolia* fixed into a counter. Even if the earthenware jars were coated before they became part of a shop counter, the pitch layers would probably have to be renewed after frequent use. Such an operation would have been very labour-intensive. None of the *dolia* contained in the counters of Pompeii and Herculaneum are reported to have been treated in this fashion. However, it could be argued that the resin has been absorbed into the fabric of the *dolia* and show few outwards traces of its use. It will only be through some form of chemical analysis that the absence or application of pitch will be determined.

The large size and wide mouths of *dolia* would mean that if they contained wine it would quickly sour, unless large amounts were consumed daily (Figure 5.9; Packer 1978, 47). Macrobius mentions the difficulty in keeping wine from going off, even in full containers (7.12.15). This is confirmed by Pliny, who also says that wine exposed to the air rapidly deteriorated (*Historia Naturalis* 14.133–135). If wine is not sealed properly, bacteria in the air produces an acid that quickly spoils it (Curtis 2001, 380). The distinctive wide-open mouths of *dolia* have a pronounced lip for the fitting of a lid (White 1975, 145). Lids covering *dolia* were found in the *Caupona di Sotericus* (I.xii.3) (Pugliese Carratelli 1990b, 709) and lids were used to seal the storage *dolia* found at the *Villa Regina* at Boscoreale (Borgongino & Stefani 2002, 193). Many *dolia* must have had lids to protect their contents, but it is unlikely that they would have by themselves created a continuous airtight seal needed to store wine. Horace mentions that corks used to seal amphorae were covered with pitch (Horace *Carmina* 3.8.10; Curtis 2001, 380). Wood and terracotta stoppers were also used in amphorae (Callender 1965, 42; Koehler 1986, 52–3; Peacock & Williams 1986. 50). Regardless of the material that was used to cover the mouth of a *dolium*, the edge of the lid would have had to be copiously smeared with resin to form a firm seal, and this seal would be lost through constant use.

Fixed vessels within counters appear to be inconvenient for the storage and distribution of wine on account of the great difficulty involved in cleaning such a *dolium* out. This is not just a modern hygiene concern, as Columella mentions that wine vats must be carefully cleaned and washed with seawater, or failing that fresh-water, before use (11.2.71 & 12.18.3). In Macrobius we are told that the wine in the lowest third of the jar is turbid, and of inferior flavour, as it is mixed with sediment and dregs (*Saturnalia* 7.12.14). Earthenware vessels continuously re-used, without cleaning, would have contained many impurities and this must have been to the detrimental quality of the wine. Although it is argued that the vineyards of Pompeii were designed for intensive viticulture to produce the maximum yield of low-price wine (Purcell 1985, 13), may Romans were probably concerned with the quality of what they drank. The slave of Marcius Antonius' friend carefully tasted the wine in a wine shop, and even asked for wine that was more choice and expensive before any was bought, as this was to be used in entertaining (Plutarch *Caius Marius* 44.1). Even a Roman with dubious tastes, such as Trimalchio, appreciated drinking from glass vessels as they had no odour and did not spoil the flavour of the wine (Patronius *Satyricon* 50). Although Trimalchio is making a comparison with Corinthian bronze ware, is does show that there may have been some general interest in the quality of the wine that was drunk, and the effect that the container may have on this quality, a point that is confirmed by the discussion in Macrobius's *Saturnalia* (7.12.13–16). There would be little point in advertising different types of wine available, as on the front of VI.14 (Pagano 1986, 209–15; Guadagno 1993, 88 & 96) and another *taberna* on the opposite side of the Decumanus Maximus at the crossing of Cardo V in Herculaneum (Pagano 1989, 268) and on the entrance to VII.ii.44/45 in Pompeii (CIL iv.1679; Cooley & Cooley 2004, 162) if the wine was to be spoilt by its container.

> Hedone says, 'You can drink here for one *as*, if you give two, you will drink better; if you give four, you will drink Falernian (CIL iv.1679)

It is unlikely that anyone would pay more for wine that tasted the same as the very cheapest variety. The availability of speciality wines from outside Pompeii is also attested by finds on amphorae (Jashemski 1979, 223).

If a counter *dolium* was intended to hold liquids, some form of drainage might be expected at their bases to aid the cleaning operation, which would have been important when continuously used for serving wine. The use of a drain in a counter can be seen in the official counter for the quantification of standard measures set up in the market place at Pompeii (Maiuri 1966, 38; de Ruyt 1983, 321; Ciarallo & de Carolis 1999, 225). This was located at VII.viii.31, in a prominent place in the western colonnade at the edge of the forum close to the Temple of Apollo. The marble counter was set up to measure liquid or possibly dry provisions, but what is of significance is that at the bottom of each container a hole had been cut so that the substance being measured could be easily removed from the measuring socket. Bungs or stoppers must have been placed at the bottom of each container to seal the substances while they were being measured and then taken out to return the commodity (de Vos & de Vos 1982, 48–9). In contrast, nothing in the form of drainage has been found in the counter *dolia* of Pompeii or Herculaneum (Packer 1978, 48). The size, problems of storage and cleaning, and the greater chance of deterioration of wine inevitably militate against the storage and selling of wine from counter *dolia*.

Regrettably nothing has been found in any of the counter *dolia* of Pompeii to indicate the type of merchandise that *dolia* may have contained. For this we must turn to Herculaneum where the unique preservation of the site has preserved many items and details that have been lost in Pompeii, including the contents of counter *dolia*. Here the finds support the assumption that counter *dolia* were not used as receptacles for liquids but for vegetables and dry foodstuffs such as grain, nuts and dried fruit. *Dolia* were one of the most suitable containers to display such substances, and would have provided the cool dry environment, required for storing such items (Packer 1978, 48).

In IV.10–11, an L-shaped counter contained a single *dolium*, and within the *dolium* insect infested carbonised grain was found. Grain was found elsewhere in the shop and it can be presumed that cereal products were the principal merchandise of the *taberna* (Maiuri 1977, 56; Wallace-Hadrill 1994, 201; de Kind 1998, 155–6). The counter *dolia* belonging to the *Grande Taberna* (IV.15–16) contained preserved cereals and vegetables (Maiuri 1977, 57; Wallace-Hadrill 1994, 201; de Kind 1998, 162). A similar find was discovered in the *taberna* counter *dolia* of V.10 (Maiuri 1977, 45). In other *tabernae*, *dolia* were not found in counters but placed elsewhere within the premises and these too seem to have held dry provisions. In the *dolia* of the *taberna* at *Insula Orientalis* II.13 grain, chickpeas and broad beans were discovered (Hermansen 1974, 169; 1982, 202; Maiuri 1977, 57; Meyer 1988, 189). Beans, cereals and chickpeas were found in the *dolia* of V.6 (Hermansen 1974, 169). It is apparent that the *tabernae* that possess counters with *dolia* sold food and that *dolia* within *tabernae* did not contain liquids. It is clear that the interpretation of a structure as a 'tavern' based purely upon the presence of counter *dolia* is not sustainable.

It seems that wine was usually served straight from the amphora and that amphorae were kept at a height in a horizontal position to ease the process of decanting. This allows the liquid to flow in one clear motion, otherwise it is difficult to debouch the liquid under control from an amphora (Koehler 1986, 66). This is demonstrated in a fresco from the *Casa dei Vettii* (VI.xv.1) from Pompeii in which a cupid is depicted decanting wine into a cup from an amphora that is held in a horizontal position (Tanzer 1939, 37; Callender 1965, 43; de Franciscis *et al.* 1991, fig. 60; Pugliese Carratelli 1994, 563). This practice is also paralleled in reliefs from outside Italy that depict barrels, which may have contained wine or beer. Barrels are shown lying on their sides and tapped to decant the liquid, such as on a relief from Sens (Espérandieu 1911, 18 cat. 2780) and on a relief in the Museo Nacional de Arte Romana, Mérida in Spain (Antonio & Antonio 1949, 254).

The surviving amphora racks from Herculaneum were suspended from the joists of the floor above, and attached to the walls. Semi-circular notches were cut in the horizontal boards of the rack to support the amphora necks. These racks held amphorae in a horizontal position and have been found in *tabernae* at V.6, VI.12 and *Insula Orientals* II.9. The partially preserved rack in the *taberna* in *Insula Orientals* II.9 may originally have supported twenty-four amphorae (Mols 1999, 62, 134 & 200–4). The frequent finds of socket holes in the walls of *tabernae* in Pompeii indicate that racks, or at least shelves, were also a common feature in this town. It is interesting that the *tabernae* in which racks have been preserved often do not contain counters with inset *dolia*. The exact nature of business carried out in these premises in Herculaneum is not known. It is likely that they were involved in the distribution of fluids, such as oil or wine, but the manner in which this was carried out is unclear. It is clear that taverns sold wine for consumption off-site from Plutarch's account of the slave buying wine for his master to entertain the orator Marcius Antonius (Plutarch *Caius Marius* 44.1). Small establishments with these features may have sold wine or oil directly to customers, while larger businesses will have had the capacity to sell wine for consumption off-site as well as on-site.

This does not of course mean that the *tabernae* that contain counter *dolia* did not sell wine as well as food. It is clear from the literary sources as well as depictions from wall

Figure 5.10 Tavern scene from the *Caupona della via de Mercurio* (VI.x.1) in Pompeii (Photo: author)

paintings that different types of food were sold in taverns (Suetonius *Tiberius*, 34; Suetonius *Nero*, 16; Cassius Dio 60.6.6–7, 62.14.2, 65.10.3). In the *Caupona della via de Mercurio* (VI.x.1) in Pompeii, there are paintings that show patrons seated at a table being served by a young boy, while various victuals, sausages, dried fruits and cheeses hang over their heads from hooks (Figure 5.10; Packer 1978, 48; Adam 1994, 321).

Although small, *taberna* V.6 in Herculaneum is likely to have been a food and wine shop as it contained racks and a *dolium* containing cereal but it did not offer space for customers to relax and enjoy their purchase. The *taberna* also possessed a stove which when found contained charcoal. This may have been used to cook foods such as soup or porridge and/or to heat wine for customers (Deiss 1985, 132; 1995, 90–1). In contrast, *taberna* IV.17 offered a backroom with couches on the three side walls for customers to sit and relax. This was clearly part of the *taberna* as the floor surface in both the shop and backroom was of plain *signinum*. Although Martial (V.70) describes taverns as stool ridden, it is likely that some *taverns* many have possessed a *triclinium* for their customers to drink and possibly eat in some comfort. This is confirmed by a sign advertising a *triclinium* in the *Caupona e hospitium di Sittius* (VII.i.44–5) in Pompeii (CIL iv.807; Stambaugh 1989, 181–2; Pugliese Carratelli 1996, 462–4). Amphorae were found within *Taberna* IV.17 and traces of shelves above the couches in the backroom may have supported amphorae. Furthermore, the counter was positioned in such as manner, away from the doorway and against the southern wall, to allow easy access to the back room. Finds of nuts indicate that food and drink may have been sold in this *taberna* (Maiuri 1977, 59; Deiss 1985, 119; 1995, 98; de Kind 1998, 165–7).

It is likely that the *Caupona di Euxinus* (I.xi.10–11) in Pompeii was a form of tavern. In this case, the L-shaped counter possessed two *dolia* (Jashemski 1973, 40) but based on the evidence from Herculaneum these must have contained substances other than liquid. The counter also contained a stove for cooking food and/or heating wine. It is clear that wine was also sold from the *taberna* as is evident from the finds of amphorae within, and the vineyard behind. Some of the amphorae were inscribed with the name, address and occupation of the innkeeper – 'At Pompeii, near the amphitheatre, to the copo Euxinus' (AE 1967 86d; Cooley & Cooley 2004, 162). It seems that wine shops offered their customers a choice of wine, and sold not only products they produced themselves, but also the produce of neighbouring vineyards and other regions. Holes in the west wall behind the counter may have been for shelves (Jashemski 1967, 37) or even amphorae racks (de Felice 2001, 203).

The tavern or wine shop at I.ix.11 could be considered to be a low-grade establishment given its modest decoration and location at the end of an *insula* away from the via dell'Abbondanza. In its latest phase a L-shaped counter, decorated by fragments of coloured marble, was constructed and behind the counter were two service rooms. I.ix.11 was clearly a wine shop as is evident by the number of amphorae found in the rear garden and the adjoining atrium next door in I.ix.12. The counter does not enclose any *dolium* but what is particularly significant is the variety of wine that may have been sold in the *taberna*. The amphorae found in the vicinity, contained Italian, Aegean, African, Iberian and Gallic wine (Fulford 1998, 62–8; Timby 2004, 384–8). This shows that even in a low-grade tavern a variety of wines, from disparate parts of the Mediterranean, were available to its customers. It is noteworthy the absence of local wines, which may have been for household consumption, and this may have implications for the *Caupona di Euxinus* (I.xi.10–11).

The *Caupona di Salvius* (VI.xiv.36) which is located on the *via de Mercurio* consisted of three rooms. In the front room was an L-shaped counter with two inset *dolia*. The strongest evidence for the use of this establishment as a tavern was found in one of the rooms to the rear. This contained four frescos painted on the walls (de Felice 2001, 253). The panels depict the lively scenes of a typical tavern from people greeting each other, customers sitting at a table served by a girl, two customers playing dice and the innkeeper ejecting two fighting customers (Ward-Perkins & Claridge 1976, 227; Pugliese Carratelli 1994, 366–71).

Panels showing tavern scenes can also be found in a rear room of the *Caupona della via de Mercurio* (VI.x.1). The paintings illustrate a wine delivery, a waitress serving wine to a standing customer and patrons seated at a table being served by a young boy (de Felice 2001, 248). In one of the frescos a customer makes a request for 'another cup of Setian!' (CIL iv.1292). Setian was a well known wine from a town in Latium at the foot of the hills bordering the Pontine Marshes (Mau 1899, 395–6). In the large front room is a L-shaped counter with a flat serving top (Packer 1978, 48; Pugliese Carratelli 1993, 1005–19; Adam 1994, 321). The absence of inset *dolia* is interesting, indicating that this tavern did not offer the types of foodstuff normally sold from *dolia*. However, it is quite possible that other types of food were sold as is suggested by one of the panels in the room behind (Figure 5.10).

It is apparent that the identification of an establishment as a 'tavern' based purely upon the existence of a counter with *dolia* is not sustainable. These *dolia* were used to contain foodstuffs and there must have been many *tabernae* that possessed these specialised counters that had nothing to do with the sale of wine. Furthermore, there must have been many *tabernae* that were involved in the retailing of beverages that did not possess counters with *dolia*. Of course numerous taverns must have offered some form of sustenance to their patrons and some of these did contain counters with *dolia*. It is only the existence of evidence such as frescos and items associated with the distribution and preparation of wine for sale that a tavern can be suggested. For example, Hermansen emphasises the significance of finds of mortars. Savoury and peppered wines, known as *conditum* or *piperatum*, appealed to the Roman palate and mortars were needed to grind pepper and must have been standard equipment in taverns

(Hermansen 1974, 178). It is evident that the distribution of food, wine and other products in Pompeii and Herculaneum is complex and that shop counters had an important part to play in this significant and fascinating retail system.

Conclusion

One of the most important components of the *tabernae* in Pompeii and Herculaneum was the selling-platform. The location of *taberna* counters at the threshold seems to indicate that the majority of retailing activity took place around the counter and at the doorway. There are indications that in some *tabernae*, customers were catered for inside the establishment, but this was probably restricted to taverns and restaurants where people could both eat and imbibe. On the whole, the limited space in *tabernae* seems to confirm that selling took place at the threshold. The surviving remains show that counters served not only as general selling-platforms but that many had a specific function that has frequently been misinterpreted. The counters that held *dolia* were used in *tabernae* in which food items such as dried fruit, vegetables and grain were sold, rather than wine. However, this does not mean that *tabernae* containing such counters were not involved in the retail of beverages. The important point is that counter *dolia* do not appear to have been used to store liquids and that the identification of a 'tavern' cannot be based solely upon the existence of such counters. It is only with additional supportive evidence, such as wine racks, wall paintings and items associated with the serving and consumption of wine, that the existence of a tavern maybe suggested. In fact, the taverns with counter *dolia* would probably have provided both food and wine to customers as is indicated in the literary evidence. It is clear from this brief discussion on *taberna* counters in Pompeii and Herculaneum that a great deal is still to be learnt concerning retailing during the Roman period and that *taberna* counters warrant further detailed study. To take this study forward the form, decoration and chronology of the shop counters of Pompeii and Herculaneum need to be catalogued and evaluated. However, counters should not be studied in isolation but researched in relation to the related *taberna*, and the material culture associated with the retail outlet. Once this has been achieved the contribution of fixed-point retailing to the economic and social environment of Pompeii and Herculaneum can be more fully appreciated.

Acknowledgments

I would like to thank Jennifer Price (University of Durham) and Damian Robinson (University of Oxford) for their many helpful comments and insightful suggestions during the early drafts of this paper. I am especially grateful to Damian for providing information on Insula VI.i in Pompeii. Any mistakes and omissions are purely my own. I am also grateful to John Naylor and Shaun Loader for the use of Figures 8.4, 8.7 and 8.8.

Bibliography

Adam, J.-P. 1994. *Roman Building: materials and techniques*. Routledge, London.

Albertini, E. 1937. *L'Afrique Romaine*. Brochure publiée sous les auspices du Gouvernement Général de l'Algerie, Alger.

Antonio, G. & Antonio, B. 1949. *Esculturas Romanas de España y Portugal*. Consego Superior de Investigaciones Cientifices, Madrid.

Blas de Roblès, J.-M. 2003. *Sites et Monuments antiques de l'Algérie*. SECUM, Edisud, Aix-en-Provence, Paris.

Boissier, G. 1905. *Rome and Pompeii: archaeological rambles*. Unwin, London.

Borgongino, M. & Stefani, C. 2001–2. 'Intorno alla data dell'eruzione del 79 d.C.', *RSP* 12–13: 177–215

Budetta, T. 1989. 'Attività dell'Ufficio Scavi: 1988–1989', *RSP* 3: 264–8

Callender, M.H. 1965. *Roman Amphorae*. Oxford University Press, London.

Ciarallo, A. & de Carolis, E. 1999. *Pompeii: life in a Roman town*. Electa, Milan.

Cooley, A. & Cooley, G.L. 2004. *Pompeii: a sourcebook*. Routledge, London.

Curtis, R.I. 2001. *Ancient Food Technology*. Brill, Leiden.

de Franciscis, A., Schefold, K., Laidlaw, A., Strocka, V.M., Cerulli Irelli, G., Pappalardo, U., Simon, E., Peters, W., de Caro, S., Zevi, F. & Aoyagi, M. 1991. *La Pittura di Pompei*. Jaca Book, Milano

Degrassi, N. 1951. 'Il mercato Romano di Leptis Magna: Parte I', *QAL* 2: 27–70

Deiss, J.J. 1985. *Herculaneum: Italy's buried treasure*. J. Paul Getty Museum, Malibu.

Deiss, J.J. 1995. *The Town of Herculaneum: a buried treasure-trove*. J. Paul Getty Museum, Malibu.

de Felice, J. 2001. *Roman Hospitality: the professional women of Pompeii*. Marco Polo Monographs 6, Shangri La Publications, Pennsylvania.

de Kind, R.E.L.B. 1998. *Houses in Herculaneum: a new view on the town planning and the building of insulae III and IV*. Gieben, Amsterdam.

Della Corte, M. 1925. *Pompeji: the new excavations. Houses and inhabitants*. Valle di Pompeii, Tipografica di F. Sicignano.

de Ruyt, C. 1983. *Macellum: marché alimentaire des Romains*. Institut Supérieur D'Archéologie et D'Histoire de l'Art Collège Érasme, Louvain-la-Neuve.

de Vos, A. & de Vos, M. 1982. *Pompei, Ercolano, Stabia*. Laterza, Roma.

Dyer, T.H. 1867. *Pompeii: Its history, buildings and antiquities*. Bell & Daldy, London.

Espérandieu, E. 1911. *Recueil Général des Bas-Reliefs de la Gaule Romaine*. Imprimerie Nationale, Paris.

Frayn, J.M. 1993. *Markets and Fairs in Roman Italy: their social and economic importance from the second century BC to the third century AD*. Clarendon Press, Oxford.

Fulford, M.G. 1998. 'Region 1, insula 9, the British project', in Berry, J. (ed.) *Unpeeling Pompeii*. Electra, Milan.

Guadagno, G. 1993. 'Ercolano. Eredità di cultua e nuovi dati', in *Ercolano 1738–1988: 250 anni di ricerca archeolofica*. L'Erma di Bretschneider: 73–98

Gusman, P. 1900. *Pompei: the city, its life and Art*. Heinemann, London.

Formenti, F. & Duthel, J.M. 1996. 'The analysis of wine and other organics inside amphoras of the Roman period', in McGovern, P.E., Fleming, S.J. & Katz, S.H. (eds) *The Origins and Ancient History of Wine*. Gordon & Breach, Amsterdam: 79–85

Guhl, E. & Koner, W. 1994. *The Romans: their life and customs*. Senate, Middlesex.

Hermansen, G. 1974. 'The Roman inns and the law: the inns of Ostia', in Evans, J.A.S. (ed.) *Polis and Imperium: studies in honour of Edward Togo Salmon*. Hakkert, Toronto: 167–82

Hermansen, G. 1982. *Ostia: aspects of early Roman life*. University of Alberta, Edmonton.

Higounet, M.C. 1971. *Bordeaux: 2000 ans d'histoire*. Musée d'Aquitaine, Bordeaux.

Jashemski, W.F. 1967. 'Caupona of Euxinus at Pompeii', *Archaeology* 20: 37–44

Jashemski, W.F. 1973. 'The discovery of a large vineyard at Pompeii: University of Maryland excavation, 1970', *AJA* 77: 27–41

Jashemski, W.F. 1979. 'The garden of Hercules at Pompeii (II.viii.6): the discovery of a commercial flower garden', *AJA* 83: 403–16

Kampen, N.B. 1981. *Image and Status: Roman working women in Ostia*. Mann, Berlin.

Kampen, N.B. 1982. 'Social status and gender in Roman art: the case of the saleswoman', in Broude, N. & Garrard, M.D. (eds) *Feminism and Art History: questioning the litany*. Harper & Row, New York: 62–77

Koehler, C.G. 1986. 'Handling of Greek transport amphoras', in Empereur, J.-Y. & Garlan, Y. (eds) *Recherches sur les Amphores Grecques*. Bulletin de Correspondance Hellénique, Supplément 13: 49–67

Lawson, F. 1994. *Restaurants, Clubs and Bars: planning, design and investment for food service facilities*. Butterworth Architecture, Oxford.

MacKenzie, W.M. 1910. *Pompeii*. A & C Black, London.

Maiuri, A. 1929. *Pompeii*. Instituto Geografico de Agostini, Roma.

Maiuri, A. 1966. *Pompeii*. Instituto Geografico de Agostini, Roma.

Maiuri, A. 1977. *Herculaneum*. Instituto Poligrafico Dello Stato, Roma.

Mau, A. 1899. *Pompeii: its life and art*. MacMillan, London.

Meyer, F.G. 1988. 'Food plants identified from carbonized remains at Pompeii and other Vesuvian sites', in Curtis, R.I. (ed.) *Studia Pompeiana & Classics in honor of Wilhelmina F. Jashemski*. Aristide D. Caratzas, New York: 183–230

Meiggs, R. 1973. *Roman Ostia*. Clarendon Press, Oxford.

Meiggs, R. 1982. *Trees and Timber in the Ancient Mediterranean World*. Oxford University Press, Oxford.

Mols, S.T.A.M. 1999. *Wooden Furniture in Herculaneum: form, technique and function*. Gieden, Amsterdam.

Packer, J.E. 1978. 'Inns at Pompeii: a short survey', *CP*4: 5–53

Pagano, M. 1986. 'Semo Sancus in una insegna di bottega a Ercolano', *CE* 16: 209–15

Pagano, M. 1989. 'Altra insegna di bottega da Ercolano', *RSP* 3: 268

Paoli, U.E. 1999. *Rome: its people, life and customs*. Longman, London.

Parslow, C.C. 1995. *Rediscovering Pompeii*. Cambridge University Press, Cambridge.

Peacock, D.P.S. & Williams, D.F. 1986. *Amphorae and the Roman Economy*. Longman, London.

Pugliese Carratelli, G. 1990a. *Pompei: Pitture e Mosaici* (Regio 1 Parte Prima). Istituto della Enciclopedia Italiana, Roma.

Pugliese Carratelli, G. 1990b. *Pompei: Pitture e Mosaici* (Regio 1 Parte Seconda). Istituto della Enciclopedia Italiana, Roma.

Pugliese Carratelli, G. 1993. *Pompei: Pitture e Mosaici* (Regio VI Parte I). Istituto della Enciclopedia Italiana, Roma.

Pugliese Carratelli, G. 1994. *Pompei: Pitture e Mosaici* (Regio VI Parte II). Istituto della Enciclopedia Italiana, Roma.

Pugliese Carratelli, G. 1996. *Pompei: Pitture e Mosaici* (Regio VI Parte III, Regio VII Parte I). Istituto della Enciclopedia Italiana, Roma.

Pugliese Carratelli, G. 1999. *Pompei: Pitture e Mosaici* (Regio IX Parte II). Istituto della Enciclopedia Italiana, Roma.

Purcell, N. 1985. 'Wine and wealth in ancient Italy', *JRS* 75: 1–19

Ramsay, W. 1894. *A Manual of Roman Antiquities*. Charles Griffin, London.

Tanzer, H.H. 1939. *The Common People of Pompeii*. John Hopkins University Press, Baltimore & London.

Stambaugh, J.E. 1989. *The Ancient Roman City*. John Hopkins University Press, Baltimore & London.

Timby, J. 2004. 'Amphorae from excavations at Pompeii by the University of Reading', Eiring, J. & Lund, J. (eds) *Transport Amphorae and Trade in the Eastern Mediterranean*. Monographs of the Danish Institute in Athens 5: 383–92

Veyne, P. 1987. *A History of Private Life: from pagan Rome to Byzantium*. Harvard University Press, Massachusetts & London.

Wallace-Hadrill, A. 1994. *Houses and Society in Pompeii and Herculaneum*. Princeton University Press, Princeton.

Ward-Perkins, J. & Claridge, A. 1976. *Pompeii AD 79*. Imperial Tobacco, Bristol.

White, K.D. 1975. *Farm Equipment of the Roman World*. Cambridge University Press, Cambridge.

Zimmer, G. 1982. *Römische Berufsdarstellungen*. Deutsches Archäologisches Institut, Mann, Berlin.

6

Re-thinking the social organisation of trade and industry in first century AD Pompeii

Damian Robinson

The social organisation of industry in the ancient city remains an area of scholarly debate and controversy. Nowhere perhaps is this more evident than in the often acrimonious interpretations of Pompeian trade and industry. Whether a particular interpretation aims at economic sophistication for the ancient city or an economically minimalist argument, the archaeological evidence from Pompeii has been routinely abused (*cf.* Jongman 1988, 158–86 commenting on Moeller 1976), mishandled (*cf.* Banaji 1989, 229–31 and Frier 1991, 243–7 in their reviews of Jongman 1988) or simply overlooked.

One of the most fundamental works on industry in Pompeii is by Moeller (1976). This is an unashamedly modernistic interpretation of a rationally organised textile industry, controlled by aristocratic 'boss fullers', producing material for an export market. While Moeller's identification of the archaeological remains of textile production has had a profound and lasting effect (*cf.* Laurence 1994, 57–61; D'Orazio & Martuscelli 1999, 92–4), his interpretation of the social aspects of this industry has been the subject of intense vitriol. Labelled as 'desperately pathetic' by Finley (1985, 195) and attacked over his careless use of the evidence and unwarranted conclusions by Jongman (1988, 158–70), Moeller's social theories pertaining to the nature of the industrial organisation of Pompeii have gained little favour. Such criticisms have concentrated mainly upon Moeller's interpretation of the Pompeian economy as being economically sophisticated and his explicit rejection of the consumer city paradigm championed by Finley, Jongman and others.[1]

This paper puts to one side the consumer city model and the debates surrounding its applicability to this particular ancient city in order to re-think the social aspects of the organisation of trade and industry. It takes a look at the archaeology of the town's buildings, their function and their location in order to come to an interpretation of the ownership patterns of its workshops. Was there any evidence for upper class participation in the urban economy? Was there a commercial 'bourgeoisie'?[2] Were there moral or ideological barriers to the participation of certain social classes in particular industries? These are questions that can be tackled directly through the archaeology of first century AD Pompeii.

Elites, trade and the apparent absence of an independent economic mercantile class

Moeller's 'fantasy of a Pompeii run by fuller bosses' (Wallace-Hadrill 1994, 119–20) has its intellectual roots in the works of Roman moralisers, such as Cicero (*De Officiis* 1.150–1), who

---

[1] See Finley (1985) for a full explanation of the 'consumer city' paradigm. The literature on the nature of the economy of the ancient city is large; see Engels (1990), Fentress (1990), Leveau (1984) and Wacher (1974) for alternative explanations of the economy of the ancient city; Jongman (1988) and Whittaker (1990 & 1995) for a strong defence of the paradigm; Mattingly (1997) on the limiting nature of this debate; see the contributions in Parkins & Smith (eds) (1998) and Mattingly & Salmon (eds) (2001) for further critiques of, and attempts to move beyond, the Consumer City Model.

[2] The term bourgeoisie is taken from Jongman (1988, 178–9) and is used with some hesitation due to its 'historical phrase-mongering' (Banji 1989, 231).

denigrated all those involved in small-scale urban trade and industry. When interpreting the final years of Pompeian social and economic life, Maiuri (*e.g.* 1960) was clearly influenced by such moralising works. He suggested that there was a major socio-economic transformation in the Vesuvian area, hastened by the earthquake of AD 62, which saw the decline of the old patricite with their wealth based solely in agricultural land, in favour of a new mercantile group of *nouveaux riches*.[3] This dichotomy between the traditional landed aristocracy and trade and the applicability of a Late Republican senatorial moralistic discourse to Imperial Pompeii and its upper class is questioned in the works of Wallace-Hadrill (1994, 118–41), Parkins (1997) and Mouritsen (2001). These authors no longer emphasise the divisions within Pompeian society based upon wealth and social class, rather they highlight the role of patronage and the bonds between the elites and their clients that would have brought the upper classes into regular contact with the commercial world. This new paradigm focuses upon the role of the upper class household, which would have included a portfolio of urban economic establishments and workers. The ownership of rental workshops and properties were intended to enhance the individual wealth of the large household, to support political activities in the city and to supply the requirements of inheritance and dowry (Parkins 1997, 97–102). Parkins (1997), for example, uses the work of Pirson (1997; 1999) to demonstrate upper class participation in trade by selecting the example of the *Insula Arriana Polliana* (VI.vi), in the years around AD 79 (*cf.* Franklin 2001, 95), with its aristocratic owner *Gnaeus Alleius Nigidius Maius*, rental inscription (CIL iv.138) and range of shops and workshops. Here the shop (VI.vi.22) interconnecting with the main aristocratic house in the *Insula*, the *Casa di Pansa* (VI.vi.1), is regarded as having been run by a slave belonging to the household (*cf.* Fiorelli 1875, 106 reprinted in Pappalardo 2001, 55–6), while the other self-contained *tabernae* were leased out (Pirson 1997, 167–73).

While the new elites and trade paradigm proposed by Wallace-Hadrill (1994, 118–41) and others has taken us several steps further in our interpretations of the social organisation of trade and industry in Pompeii, it largely ignores the economic role of the lower social classes. It is almost as if the pendulum has swung entirely in the opposite direction from the interpretations of Maiuri; whereas once the elites did not participate in trade, now all economic activity would appear to come under their auspices (*cf.* Mouritsen 2001). In the rush to emphasise the scale of upper class economic activity, the presence of any potential independent mercantile group has been largely forgotten. Again this ignores the fact that there were fortunes to be made by the economic lower classes. Mouritsen (1997, 80–1), for example, suggests that the city was naturally prosperous and had a high rate of social mobility, with twenty one percent of the magistrates of late Pompeii being of servile origin. Such a high rate of social mobility, in effect, demonstrates that there was some sort of relatively affluent economic 'middle class' in Pompeii. Consequently this paper will attempt to explore the balance between the extent of economic activity dominated by the Pompeian aristocracy and the role played by the group of independent commercialists.

Moral or ideological barriers to participation in trade and industry
The shops and workshops surrounding the *Insula Arriana Polliana* reveal that a close association with trade and industry proved to be no barrier for its owner, *Gnaeus Alleius Nigidius Maius*, who achieved outstanding political success in Pompeii (*cf.* van Buren 1947).

---

[3] *cf.* Wallace-Hadrill 1994, 122–3 for a more detailed deconstruction of this model of Pompeian society.

The Roman legal Digests also show no disapproval of shops, except houses of ill repute such as bars (*poppina*) or gambling dens (Digest 47.10.26). Such an exception is intriguing. Wallace-Hadrill (1995), for example, suggests that the urban landscape is symbolically charged with contrasting areas of virtue and vice and that bars were deliberately excluded from certain areas of the city by official action.[4] He cites the absence of bars from the stretch of the *Via dell'Abbondanza* linking the main forum with the triangular forum as an act of official moral purification of this road (Wallace-Hadrill 1995, 46–7). Such an ideological cleansing would have been done under the auspices of the Pompeian *ordo*, which was comprised of members of Pompeii's upper class. If there were such ideological and moralistic objections to bars and other such houses of ill repute (*cf.* Laurence 1994, 72–5) does this also suggest that the Pompeian upper classes would themselves refrain from investing in this type of economic activity? Certainly the shops associated with the *Insula Arriana Polliana* had nothing to do with such morally dubious industries (*cf.* Eschebach *et al.* 1993, 173–6), but was this more to do with the economic choices of the freedmen and tenants of *Gnaeus Alleius Nigidius Maius* or a reflection of a widespread upper class economic ideology and mirrored in other upper class properties in the city?

This paper will consequently study different kinds of urban trade and industry to examine whether the Pompeian aristocracy operated in all spheres of the economy, or whether moral and ideological categorisations did indeed help to shape their commercial portfolios. A morally derived avoidance of certain forms of trade and industry would have important implications for the presence (or absence) of any group of independent commercialists. Such a group may well have been unencumbered by upper class ideologies and therefore were free to operate within a morally dubious commercial sphere. Alternatively, the participation of a significant proportion of the Pompeian upper classes in morally dubious trades, such as the hospitality industry, may well demonstrate that such notions of upper class morality, which have been derived from the aristocratic literature of Rome, hold no place within Pompeian society.

Methodology
For Moeller (1976, 1) the manufacture and distribution of woollen cloth was the main industry in Pompeii, but it was not the only one. Hopkins (1978, 72), for example, counts some eighty-five trades present in Pompeii, while the concordance of Eschebach *et al.* (1993) reveal over a hundred different types of shops, workshops and industrial units. To put textile production into perspective quantitatively it is possible to discern the function of over 450 trading establishments (Robinson 1999, appendix), of which only thirty are securely identified as textile workshops; just over six percent of the total number. Consequently Moeller's assertion of the primacy of the textile industry can be seen to be unfounded. This highlights the danger of drawing large-scale socio-economic conclusions from a limited sample. In order to try and obviate this problem this paper will re-analyse the social organisation of the textile industry in conjunction with two other archaeologically visible trades: baking and the hospitality industry. Together these case studies will allow a wider examination of urban production and retail and enable us to re-think the place of such industries within Pompeian society.

Wallace-Hadrill (1994, 66–72) demonstrated the effectiveness of quantifiable studies to give information on general trends within the Pompeian dataset. Such a methodology avoids the well-trodden path to a few scattered 'representative' properties and too much anecdotal

---

[4] See McGinn (2002, 30–2) for arguments against the applicability of this model to Pompeii.

conjecture. As part of a larger study every completely excavated property in the city was analysed and categorised according to its size, function and architecture, from which it was possible to interpret the relative social class of the property (Robinson 1997).[5] Subsequently, where a 'shop' or industrial unit could be identified, by either a wide shop doorway or the archaeologically observable traces of industrial facilities, its function was pursued in the standard reference sources, such as the specialist studies of bakeries (Mayeske 1972; 1979), bars, inns (Kleberg 1957; Ruddell 1964; DeFelice 2001), and the textile industry (Moeller 1976; Jongman 1988) and cross referenced with the concordance of Eschebach *et al.* (1993) and the properties visited, where possible. Finally, the structural relationship between a commercial property and those surrounding it was assessed. From this the potential economic dependence or independence of the commercial property was inferred and the potential patterns of dependency were assessed.[6] Together these three analytical avenues allow the ownership patterns of workshops to be considered, from which it will be possible to offer an interpretation of the extent of upper class participation in the urban economy and to assess the presence (or absence) of an independent group of commercialists.

It should be acknowledged, however, that the archaeological evidence has its limitations. Foremost among these is the realisation that the interpretation of economic function from the surviving archaeological evidence is by no means straightforward (*cf.* Allison 1992, 1999; Berry 1997). The choice of bakeries, bars and inns and textile facilities was deliberate as these properties have been the subject of specialist study and also have a high archaeological visibility. Nevertheless Jongman (1989, 167–9) has cast doubt on the actual function of the class of properties referred to by Moeller (1974, 13 and subsequently by the majority of authors, *e.g.* Laurence 1994, 60–1) as scouring plants. The literary evidence suggests that scouring was undertaken in specialist industrial facilities in heated cauldrons (Pliny *Historia Naturalis* 29.10.35–38). Such heated cauldrons, together with a ready supply of water and benches on which to clean the fleeces are all located in Moeller's scouring plants. In the absence of a creditable alternative type of industrial facility at which scouring could have taken place, it is proposed that Moeller was probably correct in his identification of scouring plants. Equally, there are some difficulties in knowing whether a particular bar was just a bar, or whether it provided lodgings for the night, or indeed the services of its staff as prostitutes (*cf.* Laurence 1994, 78; McGinn 2002, 11–3). Did this make it a bar, an inn, a brothel or all three? Often the archaeological evidence is simply not subtle enough to differentiate adequately between structurally similar properties that may have had rather blurred functional boundaries. In any study such as this, however, decisions must be taken to assign properties to particular categories and while the precise economic function of an individual property may be questioned, the strength of a quantitative study such as this one lies in the general patterns observable within the data.

In this analysis the convention has been to treat 'any discrete physical unit that is inaccessible from a neighbouring unit' (Wallace-Hadrill 1994, 103) as a single property. Consequently the small *fullonica* (I.x.6) adjacent to the *Casa del Menandro* (I.x.4) is treated as

---

[5] This methodology is a developed form of that initially proposed by Wallace-Hadrill (1994, 80–2, fig. 4.11).

[6] This methodology is a simplified form of that initially proposed by Grassner (1986, *tafel* 1–11) and is supplemented by the observations of Pirson (1997; 1999) pertaining to the ownership patterns of the *Insula Arriana Pollina*.

an independent property, even though it was probably under the legal ownership of the *Casa del Menandro* (Ling 1997, 250). Here we see the difference between what may well have been a single unit of ownership, but multiple units of habitation (*cf.* Wallace-Hadrill 1994, 105). It is often inferred that shops connected to another property via a doorway would have been operated directly by the householder, perhaps by a slave or a freedman, whereas shops separated, perhaps by a blocked doorway, from the household, would have been run by a tenant paying rent to the household (Pirson 1997, 163–73; Parkins 1997, 103–6). Although as Ling (1997, 250) points out there are also other possibilities, for example, a shop separated from the main body of a household could have been operated by the owner of the house through an agent or manager (*institor* – Digest 14.3). From the archaeological record, however, we simply cannot tell whether the operator of the bakery on the south-west corner of the *Insula Arriana Polliana* (VI.vi.17), for example, was a slave, freedman, or free-born. Nevertheless, given the presence of the rental inscription from the *insula* (CIL iv.138) and the close structural relationship between this property and the larger adjacent *Casa di Pansa*, we can speculate that there would have been some form of dependence relationship between the two. Consequently the intention here is to concentrate on the structural relationships between properties and any dependence relationships that can be inferred from them, while asking only appropriate questions of the archaeological record (*cf.* Allison 2001, 181).

While there are certainly interpretative difficulties to be faced in this kind of quantitative survey, they are not insurmountable. As the study of the *Insula Arriana Polliana* demonstrates (Pirson 1997; 1999; Parkins 1997), social and economic relationships can be inferred from the archaeology and it is from a quantified dataset, such as that amassed for this study, that the structuring principles that define the social and economic life of Pompeii can be brought out. It is to the three case studies of trade and industry in the city that we now turn.

The textile industry

From the material remains of the textile workshops, Moeller proposed the following sequence of processes for the production of woollen textiles in Pompeii (1976, 11–24): scouring to wash the wool in the grease to remove the natural and unnatural dirt; dyeing to colour the raw wool; combing, spinning and weaving to remove the knots and tangles from the loose wool and then interlace warp and weft threads to create pieces of cloth; fulling to clean the wool further, to shrink the cloth and to close up the weave. Although Moeller proposed that each stage in the production process took place in its own archaeologically distinctive type of workshop, this paper only uses scouring plants, dye works and fulleries, as there are doubts about Moeller's (1976, 16–8) identification of spinning and weaving 'factories'.[7]

The relative social class of each textile workshop was assessed through a combination of the size of the property and the presence or absence of socially significant reception rooms (Table 6.1). Class 4 properties, for example, have a large ground area, with atrium(s), peristyle(s) and other reception rooms. They were most likely the houses of Pompeii's richest

---

[7] The spinning and weaving 'factories' identified by Moeller (1974, 16–8) have not been included in this analysis. Spinning and weaving clearly took place in the city, as loom weights and spindle whorls are a common find in Pompeian houses (Allison 1992, 221). It is unlikely, however, that the properties identified by Moeller were 'factories' (Jongman 1988, 164–5). It is more likely that spinning and weaving would have been an occupation of every household rather than a specialist activity. The largely unexcavated dye works at IX.vii.2 and the fullonica at IX.xiii.5 identified by Moeller (1976, 39 & 51) were also not included in this analysis, which has only looked at complete workshops.

Social Class	Number	Percentage
1	12	40
2	12	40
3	6	20
4	0	0

Table 6.1: The social class profile of the properties of the textile industry

Economic Property Type	Number	Percentage
A	0	0
B	13	43
C	1	3
D	8	27
E	8	27

Table 6.2: The economic property type profile of the textile industry

and most important citizens and are illustrated by the *Casa di Pansa* and its owner *Gnaeus Alleius Nigidius Maius*. There are only forty-two properties of this type in Pompeii and it is this class of dwelling that are referred to throughout this paper as the homes of Pompeii's upper social class. At the other socio-economic extreme, Class 1 properties have few rooms, a small ground area and no status architecture and are best represented as the small properties that surround the *Casa di Pansa* in the *Insula Arriana Polliana*.

Textile production in Pompeii was generally concentrated in small workshops, with eighty percent of them located in properties of the lowest two socio-economic classes (Table 6.1). If it was assumed that each workshop was owner-occupied these results could be used to infer that the Pompeian textile industry was entirely in the hands of the lower social classes. From such an assumption it would be relatively easy to return to the former ideas championed by Maiuri regarding the antipathy of the urban aristocracy towards the world of industrial production. Yet such an interpretation ignores the possibility that urban production may take place under the control of the upper classes without it being physically located inside their properties.

The *Insula Arriana Polliana*, for example, suggests that commercial properties adjacent to larger upper class houses may have been under the control of the larger property (Parkins 1997; Pirson 1997; 1999, 23–47). Such a dependent relationship between a big house and an adjacent commercial property is also observable in the case of the *Casa del Menandro* (I.x.4) and its neighbouring *fullonica* (I.x.6). Here Ling (1997, 145, 250–1) suggests that the fullery was under the control of the owners of the *Casa del Menandro*. Another example of an upper class property being heavily involved in textile production can be seen in the nearby *Casa del Citarista* (I.iv.25). This is one of the grandest properties in the city, with entrances on both the *Via dell'Abbondanza* and the *Via Stabiana*, both of which were flanked by a textile workshop: a scouring plant (I.iv.26) and a small *fullonica* (I.iv.7). In both of these examples, the commercial workshops were effectively 'carved out' from the main bodies of the *Casa del Menandro* and the *Casa del Citarista* and may represent active investment in the textile industry by their upper class owners. Not only did separate workshops need to be created, but they also required the provision of the necessary industrial facilities, namely tanks, vats, a ready supply of water, and also a staff of trained slaves or freedmen.

The emerging pattern of small workshops adjacent to upper class properties suggests a certain amount of aristocratic participation in the textile industry. Table 6.2 investigates this

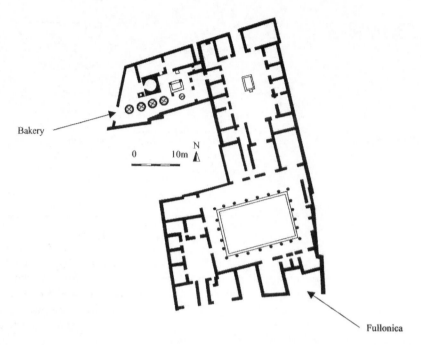

Bakery

0   10m   N

Figure 6.1 *The bakery in the Casa di Popidius Priscus (VII.ii.20.22) and the adjacent small fullonica (VII.ii.41)*

situation further by examining observable structural dependence relationships between larger properties but which do not have linking doorways, the small *fullonica* (I.x.6) adjacent to the *Casa del Menandro* illustrates this. Type C properties have large industrial quarters spatially separated, but interconnecting with, a large domestic residence, for example, the *Casa di Popidius Propiscus* (VII.ii.20.22) (Figure 6.1). Types D and E are increasingly larger, separate economic units with rooms set aside for both accommodation and industry. In the first three types (A-C) the shops and workshops are taken to have an observable structural and hence dependent relationship with a larger domestic dwelling. The final two types (D and E) have no archaeologically recoverable dependent relationships and are regarded as the homes and workshops of independent craftsmen.

The economic property type profile in Table 6.2 indicates that the textile industry is generally located in small-scale workshops. Forty-three percent of the industry, however, was located in small workshops adjacent to larger properties, the vast majority of which (ninety-two percent of the Type B workshops) are the homes of Pompeii's upper social class. Effectively the industry is kept at arms length, outside the homes of the upper classes, yet it was a lucrative and necessary aspect of the economic portfolio of its owners. For example, V.i.4 and V.i.5 are the two smallest dye works in Pompeii and probably operated together as a pair. They are sandwiched between the twin *fauces* of the *Casa del Toro* (V.i.3.7) and it is likely that either a slave or a freedman ran the dye workshops on behalf of the aristocratic house (Figure 6.2). The analysis has demonstrated that some of the richest and most powerful people in Pompeii were prepared to invest in all areas of the industry; roughly a third of all dye works and scouring plants and half of the fulleries are located adjacent to aristocratic properties.

N

0   10m ⬆

Dye workshops
(V.i.4 and V.i.5)

Figure 6.2 *The twin dye workshops (V.i.4 and 5) adjacent to the Casa del Toro (V.i.3.7)*

Approximately fifty-seven percent of textile workshops were located in properties that do not have any obvious dependent relationship with a nearby property. Consequently, although there was an obvious upper class participation in the textile industry they were secondary to independent producers, both in terms of the size of the total group and hence also probably in terms of the quantity of production. The dye workshop at VII.xiv.5 is a good example of the upper end of this socio-economic group. It is the largest dye works in Pompeii and its occupier presumably earned enough from its dyeing activities both to own or rent a property of some size and to completely decorate the accommodation area of the house in the latest Pompeian Fourth Style (Figure 6.3). The numbers of tanks and dye vats in this property are roughly equal to those located between the twin *fauces* of the *Casa del Toro*. Yet where the profits from the workshops at V.i.4 and V.i.5 were channelled back into the *Casa del Toro*, they were sufficient for the owner of VII.xiv.5 to live relatively comfortably. The workshop inside VII.xiv.5 is located at the rear of this property and is effectively hidden from the casual viewer looking into the house from the front door. While the removal of the workshop from the living area is a common feature in larger properties, it would give the impression to a viewing public that the owner of the property was engaged in a toil-free life through disguising the extent of the owner's participation in industry.

The analysis would tend to suggest that there was both a group of producers under the control of Pompeii's wealthiest families and another social group who operated outside of this control. We now turn to the second of our case studies to see whether these inferences can be supported by another form of industrial production.

The baking industry
In Pompeii, the workshops, equipment and occasionally their carbonised products are all

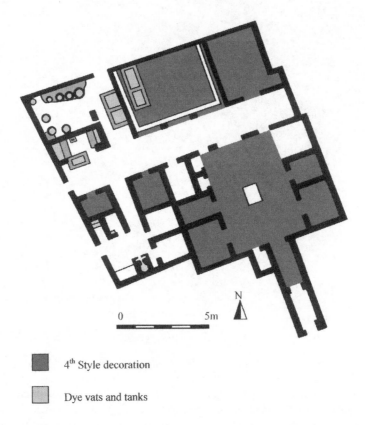

4th Style decoration

Dye vats and tanks

Figure 6.3 The dye workshop at VII.xiv.5 and the location of its fourth style decoration

available for an examination of the city's baking industry. Commercial bakeries are identified in the archaeological record through the presence of elaborate ovens (Mayeske 1979, 40–1). These are often associated with large rotary mills (Moritz 1958; Peacock 1980; 1986; 1989), although some of the smaller bakeries did without these. Thirty-three commercial bread or pastry workshops can be identified in the material remains of Pompeii (Mayeske 1979, 43).

The epigraphic evidence demonstrates that Pompeian consumers were able to purchase a whole range of different kinds of breads and pastries. Scratched into the wall of an inn (IX.vii.24–25) is a grocery list that lists bread fourteen times (CIL iv.5380). Three types of bread are mentioned, *pane, pane puero, pane cibar,* which indicates that bread could be bought in different qualities, shapes and sizes. There were also specialist pastry bakers (Mayeske 1979, 40) and moulded cakes were also made as offerings to the gods. Indeed, some Pompeian graffiti tells us that such offering cakes could be purchased from *Verecunnus* (CIL iv.1768) and *Pudens* (CIL iv.1769) near to the Temple of Venus.

Unlike the textile industry, where the participation of the upper social classes had to be inferred, there is direct evidence for the industrial production of bread inside some of the grandest houses in Pompeii. For example, the bakery in the *Casa del Labirinto* (VI.xi.9–10) (Strocka 1991, 95) would have been too large for household production alone and was involved in the manufacture of bread on an 'industrial' scale (Mayeske 1979, 45). Although this property does not have an attached shop, the products from the bakery could easily have been traded from a stall in the forum or indeed from a shop run by either a slave or a freedman elsewhere in the city. The bakery was built after the earthquake of AD 62, which led Strocka to infer a change of ownership and the potential social downgrading of the property (Strocka 1991, 134–5). The bakery, however, would undoubtedly have been a financial asset and should be regarded as part of the economic portfolio of the upper class owners of the *Casa del Labirinto*, rather than simply an indicator of the social downgrading of the property or its owners. In fact such facilities were rather commonplace in the houses of Pompeii's upper classes and appear in five other aristocratic properties,[8] such as the *Casa di Popidius Priscus* (VII.ii.20.22) (Figure 6.1).

Clearly the location of commercial bakeries inside the homes of Pompeii's upper social class demonstrates their active participation in this form of industrial production, but to what extent did this socio-economic group control the entire baking industry? Table 6.3 breaks down the social class profile of the properties in which the baking industry was located. It demonstrates that although there was an amount of upper class participation, this only accounted for twenty percent of all bakeries and that the majority of them were located inside properties of a lower social class.

Social Class	Number	Percentage
1	4	11
2	19	58
3	4	11
4	6	20

Table 6.3: The social class profile of the properties of baking industry

The two bakeries in the *Insula Arriana Polliana*, for example, would fall into the lowest two social classes (Robinson 1999, figure 7). Nevertheless, their lowly social status belies their likely dependent relationship with the owner of the *Insula, Gnaeus Alleius Nigidius Maius*. Consequently every bakery's relationship to its neighbours was assessed to see whether it was under the economic and social domination of a secondary, larger property, or whether it could be classed as being independent. The results of this analysis are presented in Table 6.4.

Economic Property Type	Number	Percentage
A	0	0
B	5	15
C	8	25
D	11	33
E	9	27

Table 6.4: The economic property type profile of the baking industry

---

[8] The presence of bakeries in upper class properties is contrary to the views of Wallace-Hadrill (1994, 139) who suggests that bakeries were not attached to aristocratic houses. This assertion is directly related to his sample of the city, however, which did not include the upper class properties at VII.ii.20.22 *Casa dei Marmi*, VII.xv.1–2.15 *Casa di Marinaio*, VIII.iv.14–16.22–23.30 *Domus Cornelia*, IX.i.22.29 *Casa del Parnasso* and IX.iii.5.10–12 *Casa delle Suonatrici*.

The profile of the economic property types involved in the baking industry is highly revealing. Whereas Table 6.3 would appear to suggest that the upper two social classes controlled approximately a third of the baking industry, this figure increases slightly to forty percent when the obvious structural dependence relationships are taken into account (*i.e.* dependent properties A-C). This leaves approximately sixty percent of bakeries, however, in the hands of independent craftsmen and it can be suggested that while it would appear to be socially or morally acceptable to locate a commercial bakery inside an upper class property, this particular social class did not necessarily dominate bread production.

The social or perhaps moral codes that made it acceptable for a bakery to be located inside the upper class house and at the same time relegated textile workshops to separate properties adjacent to the *fauces* are intriguing. Does this represent some form of moral categorisation of certain industries? Was it acceptable for the upper classes to invest in all forms of economic activity and to advertise or disguise the extent of their participation through the location of their investment in relation to their house? Or was economic investment in certain industries encouraged or discouraged by prevailing social or ideological factors? These themes are investigated further in the final case study, which deals with the hospitality industry.

The hospitality industry
In Roman literature bars and inns are often thought of as places of ill repute, their customers were the morally bankrupt (Juvenal *Satire* 8.171) and that the principles of their owners not that much better (Martial *Epigrams* 3.57). Yet there are also similar literary invectives against the participation of the upper classes in trade and industry (Cicero *On Duties* 1.151) and as we have seen this did not appear to restrict the participation of the Pompeian upper classes in either the baking or textile industries. Consequently this case study will analyse whether the Pompeian upper classes regarded the ownership of bars and inns as simply another potential moneymaking enterprise, or whether there were indeed moral or ideological barriers to their participation in this form of industry.

The identification of bars and inns was based upon the concordances of Kleberg (1957), Ruddell (1964), Packer (1978), Eschebach *et al.* (1993) and DeFelice (2001). In the literature, such properties are ascribed a confusing array of Latin names: bars are often termed *popina*, *thermopolia* and *taberna*, while inns are known as *hospitia*, *caupona* and *stabula* (*cf.* Kleberg 1957, 26–44). Unfortunately the archaeological remains are not subtle enough to distinguish between potentially small differences in function and also how the establishments were perceived to operate at the time of their use. Consequently, here the properties have been categorised as either bars or inns in the full knowledge that there was undoubtedly an overlap in function between these two (ideal) types.

A typical Pompeian bar has a front room with a wide opening onto the street. This room usually has a stone or occasionally wooden counter, which is normally L-shaped, and faces out into the street to serve passing trade. Against the wall, at one end of the counter a series of small steps form shelves for the display or storage of goods. Most counters were furnished with some apparatus for heating food and warming wine. Often terracotta *dolia* were sunk into the counter for the storage of food. Behind the counter of many Pompeian bars there were often several rooms furnished with either tables, or benches, (*e.g.* I.ix.11–12). There are other forms of supporting evidence for the identification of bars, such as amphorae, bar-like wall paintings (*cf.* Kleberg 1957, 157–62, plates 11–20) and bar-like graffiti (*e.g.* CIL iv.8258 and 8259). The defining characteristic of the Pompeian inn was the presence of several, usually rather small,

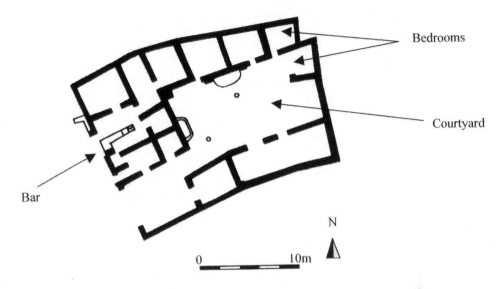

***Figure 6.4** A typical Pompeian inn (VI.i.2–4)*

bedrooms to provide over-night accommodation for guests. The guestrooms typically opened off a central open space. This was often a courtyard, where carts and travellers' animals may have been parked (Figure 6.4). Many inns also had bars attached to them, as well as dining facilities. In such cases the entire property was always categorised as an inn.

The location of economic properties adjacent to the *Casa di Pansa* in the *Insula Arriana Polliana* demonstrates the tendency of the Pompeian upper classes to maximise the economic potential of the space in and around their homes. It consequently follows that industries in which there was a significant amount of investment by the Pompeian upper classes would generally tend to be located close to their houses. The corollary of this would be than those industries without significant upper class investment would generally be located further from these houses. Such a relationship is illustrated in Table 6.5. Here the distance by road figures were measured between the front door of a workshop and the *fauces* of the nearest upper class house. The table shows that baking and textile workshops are located much closer to upper class properties than those premises associated with the hospitality industry. This observation is also supported by the straight-line distance figures, which measure the shortest distance between the economic property and its nearest upper class property. Here again the figures demonstrate a close relationship between the upper class house and the baking and textile industries and the distancing of the hospitality industry from the upper class house. Overall Table 6.5 tends to suggest that the upper classes did not have significant investments in the hospitality trade, or that any investments were not located close to their houses.

	Distance by road	Straight line distance
Baking	33	23
Textiles	43	23
Hospitality	63	35

***Table 6.5:** The average distance (in metres) between élite houses, industry and bars and inns*

The social profile of the hospitality industry is investigated in Table 6.6. This demonstrates that only one upper class house, the *Casa di Octavius Quartio* (II.ii.2), incorporated a bar within its boundaries and that the vast majority of bars and inns were located in smaller properties (Types 1 and 2).

Social Class	Number	Percentage
1	56	44
2	58	45
3	13	10
4	1	1

Table 6.6: The social class profile of bars and inns

Table 6.6 could be taken as further evidence to support the relative non-participation of the upper social orders in the hospitality industry. At this stage, however, a note of caution should be sounded, as Table 6.1 would also appear to demonstrate a similar social class profile for the textile industry. In this instance, however, the location of the industry in small workshops disguised the actual extent of upper class control over a large proportion of textile processing activities. The linkage between the upper class and the textile industry was identified on the basis of the identification of workshops that had been 'carved out' from the main body of larger domestic properties. Earlier, the fullery (I.x.6) next to the front door of the *Casa del Menandro* (I.x.4) was used as an example of the kind of structural relationship that can illustrate socio-economic dependencies between adjacent properties. In a similar way a small bar (I.x.13) was carved out from the stable area of *Casa del Menandro* (Ling 1997, 245) and may well have been operated by a slave or freedman of the large house. This would indicate that the aristocratic owner of the property *Q. Poppaeus*, a member of the *decurional* class and probably a *duovir* (Ling 1997, 142), had interests in the hospitality industry. In order to assess the extent of upper class investment in this particular industry, however, it is necessary to quantify the structural dependence relationships that can be inferred from all of the properties of the hospitality industry and those surrounding them (Table 6.7).

Economic Property Type	Number	Percentage
A	14	10
B	29	23
C	5	4
D	57	45
E	23	18

Table 6.7: The economic property type profile of bars and inns

The economic property type profile of the hospitality industry (Table 6.7) would suggest that this trade was largely in the hands of independent operators, with sixty-three percent of hospitality properties belonging to types D and E. This would suggest that the remaining forty-seven percent of hospitality properties might have been socio-economically dependent upon another dwelling. The baking industry also had a very similar proportion of independent to dependent properties and in this case it was suggested that upper class investment was significant. While it is certainly true that bars can be seen to be structurally dependent upon six Type 4 upper class houses, this should not be taken to suggest that upper class investment in this form of economic activity was as significant as that for the baking industry. For example, the average social class for the properties upon which the bakeries themselves were dependent was 3.6, compared to 3.8 for the textile industry but only 2.7 for the hospitality industry. Only eight percent of hospitality properties of Type A (1 out of 13) and twenty three percent of Type B properties (7 out of 30) were dependent upon an upper class house, compared to 92 percent of Type B (12 out of 13) textile and sixty percent of Type B (3 out of 5) baking workshops. Together these figures would tend to suggest that upper class participation in the hospitality industry was more limited.

In the introduction to this paper it was suggested that there could have been some moral or ideological reasons that may have restricted upper class participation in the hospitality industry. Such ideological or moral codes may also have sanctioned the location of bakeries inside upper class homes and textile workshops adjacent to their *fauces*. Where upper class properties did participate in the hospitality industry, however, it would appear that this participation was disguised by locating the hospitality property away from *fauces*. The bar (I.x.13) associated with the *Casa del Menandro*, for example, was located in the stable wing of the property and fronted onto a completely different street than the main entrance of the *Casa del Menandro*. Similarly, the bars (VI.xvi.2 and 40) that can be structurally associated with the *Casa degli Amorini Dorati* (VI.xvi.7) have their main entrances on different streets. In those cases where the entrances to the bar and the main house are on the same street, such as the *Casa del Citarista* (I.iv.25) and the *Casa delle Nozze di Ercole* (VI.ix.47), the bars are not located adjacent to the *fauces* but are at least one doorway removed from the front door. In all of these cases it would appear that there was a conscious desire on behalf of the owner to disguise their participation in the hospitality industry through the visual separation of the bar and their front door. Consequently, it can be suggested that the prevailing moral or ideological codes which saw upper class literary invective ranged against the hospitality industry and perhaps even the moral purification of certain Pompeian streets (Wallace-Hadrill 1995) similarly helped to channel economic investment into ideologically appropriate industries or ensure that any participation in an inappropriate industry was disguised.

Conclusions

The Pompeian upper classes appear to have invested in all areas of the urban economy. They possessed diverse portfolios of different kinds of urban economic properties. The owners of the *Casa del Menandro*, for example, would appear to have had invested in textile production, the hospitality industry and property rental, as well as having more 'traditional' interests in agriculture. Such archaeologically observable traces of economic participation are concentrated around the *Casa del Menandro*, a distribution pattern that is also paralleled around the *Insula Arriana Polliana* and around other upper class properties in the city. This helped to maximise the economic potential of elite urban landholdings. Indeed the presence of shops and workshops in the *Insula Arriana Polliana* can be traced back to the earliest period of the atrium complex of the *Casa di Pansa* in about 140–120 BC (de Albentiis 1989, 44–5). This illustrates the potentially long-standing relationship between the Pompeian upper social classes and the urban economy. The location of workshops in close proximity to the *domus* would also have created areas of social domination and political support for the upper class householder (*cf.* Mouritsen 1988, 52–7). Consequently, the owner of the *Insula Arriana Polliana, Gnaeus Alleius Nigidius Maius*, would have relied upon his clients surrounding his house to provide the kind of political support that helped him to ascend to the highest offices in the city (Robinson

1997, 143). Aside from the strictly economic contribution to the upper class household, shops and workshops could be given as part of an inheritance or dowry and may well have been used to cement social and political ties between families (Parkins 1997, 97–102). Highlighting the role of the patrician *domus* as a node in the exploitation and domination of neighbourhood space and their wider function within upper class society also demonstrates the duel role of a satellite network of such dependent properties. Shops and workshops were not simply economic units there to provide a ready supply of cash; they also had important social or political roles to play.

This study has only examined the archaeologically recoverable traces of potential dependence of economic properties upon the Pompeian upper classes, or their independence from them. It would be naïve, however, to think that aristocratic economic investments were only situated in properties adjacent to the upper class house. At the southern tip of *Insula* VI.i, for example, a group of four initially separate workshops were constructed as part of a single, coherent building programme (Jones & Robinson *forthcoming*). In their final form they comprised of two bars (VI.i.17 and 18.20), a metal smithy (VI.i.14–15.21) and an upstairs rental apartment (VI.i.16). The complex of workshops was under single ownership and the pattern of property speculation and a mixed portfolio of investments is reminiscent of that described earlier for the inhabitants of the *Casa del Menandro* (I.x.4). This may well suggest that the construction and subsequent operation of these properties was under the auspices of a wealthy family, although as there are no obvious structural relationships to associate this complex with any large house, it is difficult to be certain about this assumption. Consequently we must question the true extent of upper class participation in trade and industry and acknowledge the possibility that it may be greater than suggested here. For example, it has been suggested that upper class participation in the hospitality industry was limited and that where this investment did occur it tended to be located away from the front door of the aristocratic property with which it was associated. What better disguise, therefore, than to locate such an investment in another *insula* altogether? Although both of these examples are possibilities, they cannot be tested against the archaeological data set and consequently the amount of disguised upper class participation in the hospitality, or indeed any other, industry is unquantifiable. While we may infer an increased quantity of upper class participation, however, this should not be allowed to deflect attention away form the central point that trade and industry in Pompeii were not dominated by its upper class and that a group of independent commercialists existed who were also active in the urban economy.

Despite the attention given here to economic investments, it should not be taken that Pompeii had an entirely rational capitalist market economy. For example, upper class participation in certain industries appeared to be governed by a form of 'economic morality', that saw bakeries located inside upper class houses, textile workshops adjacent to their *fauces* and hospitality properties hidden away. Indeed this form of morality appears to have limited the extent of archaeologically visible upper class participation in the hospitality trade. Such a moral categorisation of industry consequently left areas of the urban economy open for exploitation by members of the lower social orders. Nevertheless, this should not be taken to suggest that there was a simple divergence between morally acceptable industries that were dominated by the upper classes and morally unacceptable industries dominated by the lower classes. On the contrary there was both upper and lower class commercialists active in all areas of this vibrant urban economy.

In the race to move away from previous (mis)interpretations of the Pompeian economy with its concentration on the economic impotence of the traditional land-owning aristocracy and the dynamic mercantilism of the freedmen, there has been a justifiable tendency to assert the economic dominance of the upper class. Yet this assertion of their supremacy has come at a price, the marginalisation of the role of the independent commercialists. It is hoped that the arguments contained in this paper have gone some way towards readdressing this imbalance and to present an interpretation of the social structure of the Pompeian economy that on the one hand stresses the role of the urban elites and emphasises their substantial investments in urban trade and industry, while at the same time demonstrating the presence of a large and successful group of independent commercialists. The Pompeian urban economy in the first century AD was a dynamic arena in which there were many opportunities to be exploited by the ambitious at all levels of society.

Acknowledgements
It is a pleasure to acknowledge the generous sponsors of this study, the University of Bradford, whose Research Studentship allowed me to undertake the initial research contained in this work and the British Academy, whose Postdoctoral Fellowship has allowed me to bring it to publication.

I would also like to acknowledge Simon Clarke, Barry Hobson, Heather Hopkins, Rick Jones, Jane Richardson and Astrid Schoonhoven for their comments and discussions of earlier drafts of this paper. I would also like to thank Ardle Mac Mahon and Jennifer Price, for inviting this contribution, even though I was unable to attend the original conference due to fieldwork commitments and for their editorial comments.

Bibliography
Allison, P. 1992. *The Distribution of Pompeian House Contents and its Significance.* PhD Dissertation, University of Sydney.
Allison, P. 1999. 'Labels for ladles: interpreting the material culture of Roman households', in Allison, P. (ed.) *The Archaeology of Household Activities.* Routledge, London: 57–77
Allison, P. 2001. 'Using the material and written sources: turn of the millennium approaches to Roman domestic space', *AJA* 105: 181–208
Banaji, J. 1989. 'The economy and society of Pompeii', *JRS* 79: 229–31
Berry, J. 1997. 'Household artefacts: towards a re-interpretation of Roman domestic space', in Laurence, R. & Wallace-Hadrill, A. (eds) *Domestic Space in the Roman World: Pompeii and Beyond.* JRA, Supplementary Series 22, Portsmouth: 183–95
D'Orazio, L. & Martuscelli, E. 1999. 'Textiles in Pompeii: technology, industry and commerce', in Ciarallo, A. & de Carolis, E. (eds) *Pompeii: life in a Roman town.* Electa, Milan: 92–4
de Albentiis, E. 1989. '"Indagini sull" *Insula Arriana Polliana* di Pompei', *Dialoghi di Archeologia Series* 3.7(1): 43–84
DeFelice, J. 2001. *Roman Hospitality: the professional women of Pompeii.* Marco Polo Monographs 6, Shangri La Publications, Pennsylvania.
Engels, D. 1990. *Roman Corinth: an alternative model for the classical city.* University of Chicago Press, London.
Eschebach, L., Müller-Trollius, J. & Eschebach, H. 1993. *Gebäudeverzeichnis und Stadtplan der Antiken Stadt Pompeji.* Böhlau Verlag GmbH & Cie, Köln.

Fentress, E.W.B. 1990. 'Sitifis – the economy of an inland city', in Ier siècle av. J.-C.-IVe siècle ap. J.-C. (eds) 'L'Afrique dans l'Occident Romain', *Collection de l'École Française de Rome* 134, École Française de Rome, Rome: 98–128

Finley, M. 1985. *The Ancient Economy* (2nd Edition). Penguin, London.

Fiorelli, G. 1875. *Descrizione di Pompei*. Tipografia Italiana, Napoli.

Franklin 2001 J. L. jr. *Pompeis Difficile Est – Studies in the Political Life of Imperial Pompeii*. The University of Michigan Press, Ann Arbor.

Frier, B. 1991. 'Pompeii's economy and society', *JRA* 4: 243–7

Grassner, V. 1986. *Die Kaufläden in Pompeii*. VWGÖ, Wein.

Hopkins, K. 1978. 'Economic growth and towns in Classical Antiquity', in Abrams, P. & Wrigley, E. (eds) *Towns in Societies: essays in economic history and historical sociology*. Cambridge University Press, Cambridge: 35–77

Jones, R. & Robinson, D. Forthcoming. 'The economic development of the Commercial Triangle (VI.i.14–18, 20–21)' Studi della Soprintendenza Archeologica di Pompei. L'Erma di Bretschneider, Roma

Jongman, W. 1988. *The Economy and Society of Pompeii*. Geiben, Amsterdam.

Kleberg, T. 1957. *Hôtels, Restaurants et Cabarets dans l'Antiquité Romaine*. Almquist & Wiksells Boktryckeri AB, Uppsala.

Laurence, R. 1994. *Roman Pompeii: space and society*. Routledge, London.

Leveau, P. 1984. 'Caesarea de Mauretaine – une Ville Romaine et ses Campagnes', *Collection de l'École Française de Rome* 70. École Française de Rome, Rome.

Ling, R. 1997. *The Insula of the Menander at Pompeii. Volume 1: the structures*. Clarendon Press, Oxford.

Maiuri, A. 1960. *Pompeii*. Instituto Geografico De Agostini, Novara.

Mattingly, D.J. 1997. 'Beyond belief? Drawing a line beneath the consumer city', in Perkins, H.M. (ed.) *Roman Urbanism Beyond the Consumer City*. Routledge, London: 210–8

Mattingly, D. & Salmon, J. (ed) 2001. *Economies beyond Agriculture in the Classical World*. Routledge, London.

Mayeske, B.J.B. 1972. *Bakeries, Bakers and Bread at Pompeii: a study in social and economic history*. PhD Dissertation, University of Maryland.

Mayeske, B.J.B. 1979. 'Bakers, bakeshops and bread: a social and economic history' in *Pompeii and the Vesuvian Landscape*. Archaeological Institute of America, Washington: 39–58

McGinn, T. 2002. 'Pompeian brothels and social history', in McGinn, T., Carafa, P., de Grummond, N., Bergmann, B. & Najberg, T. (eds) *Pompeian Brothels, Pompeii's ancient history, Mirrors and mysteries, Art and nature at Oplontis, and the Herculaneum 'Basilica'*. JRA, Supplementary Series 47, Portsmouth: 7–46

Moeller, W.O. 1976. *The Wool Trade of Ancient Pompeii*. Brill, Leiden.

Moritz, L.A. 1958. *Grain Mills and Flour in Classical Antiquity*. Clarendon Press, Oxford.

Mouritsen, H. 1988. *Elections, Magistrates and Municipal Élite. Studies in Pompeian Epigraphy*. Analecta Romana Instituti Danici 15. L'Erma di Bretschneider, Roma.

Mouritsen, H. 1997. 'Mobility and social change in Italian towns during the Principate', in Parkins, H. (ed.) *Roman Urbanism Beyond the Consumer City*. Routledge, London: 59–82

Mouritsen, H. 2001. 'Roman freedmen and the urban economy: Pompeii in the first century AD', in Senatore, F. (ed.) *Pompei tra Sorrento e Sarno – Atti del terzo e quarto ciclo di conferenze di geologica, storia e archeologia. Pompei, gennaio 1999 – maggio 2000*. Bardi Editore, Roma: 1–27

Packer, J. 1978. 'Inns at Pompeii: a short survey', *Chronache Pompeiane* 4: 5–53

Pappalardo, U. 2001. *La descrizione di Pompei per Giuseppe Fiorelli*. Massa Editore, Napoli.

Parkins, H. 1997. 'The "consumer city" domesticated? The Roman city in élite economic strategies', in Parkins, H. (ed.) *Roman Urbanism Beyond the Consumer City*. Routledge, London: 83–111

Parkins, H. & Smith, C. (ed) 1998. *Trade, Traders and the Ancient City*. Routledge, London.

Peacock, D.P.S. 1980. 'The Roman millstone trade: a petrological sketch', *WA* 12: 43–53

Peacock, D.P.S. 1986. 'The production of millstones near Orvieto, Umbria, Italy', *AntJ* 66: 45–51

Peacock, D.P.S. 1989. 'The mills of Pompeii', *Antiquity* 63: 205–14

Pirson, F. 1997. 'Rented accommodation at Pompeii: The evidence of the *Insula Arriana Polliana* VI.6', in Laurence, R. & Wallace-Hadrill, A. (eds) *Domestic Space in the Roman World: Pompeii and beyond*. Journal of Roman Archaeology, Supplementary Series 22. Portsmouth: 165–82

Pirson, F. 1999. *Mietwohnungen in Pompeji und Herkulaneum – Untersuchungen zur Architektur, zum Wohnen und zur Sozial- und Wirtschaftsgeschichte der Vesuvstädte*. Verlag Dr. Friedrich Pfeil, München.

Robinson, D. 1997. 'The social texture of Pompeii', in Bon, S.E. & Jones, R.F.J. (eds) *Sequence and Space in Pompeii*. Oxbow, Oxford: 135–44

Robinson, D. 1999. *The Shape of Space in Pompeii*. Unpublished PhD Dissertation, University of Bradford.

Ruddell, S. 1964. *The Inn, Restaurant and Tavern Business in Ancient Pompeii*. MA Dissertation, University of Maryland.

Strocka, V.M. 1991. *Casa del Labirinto (VI 11 8–10) Häuser in Pompeji 4*. Hirmer, Munich.

van Buren, A.W. 1947. 'Gnaeus Alleius Nigidius Maius of Pompeii', *AJP* 68: 382–93

Wacher, J. 1974. *The Towns of Roman Britain*. Batsford, London.

Wallace-Hadrill, A. 1994. *Houses and Society in Pompeii and Herculaneum*. Princeton University Press, Princeton.

Wallace-Hadrill, A. 1995. 'Public honour and private shame: The urban texture of Pompeii', in Cornell, T.J. & Lomas, K. (ed.) *Urban society in Roman Italy*. University College London Press, London: 39–62

Whittaker, C.R. 1990. 'The consumer city revisited: The vicus and the city', *JRA* 3: 110–8

Whittaker, C.R. 1995. 'Do theories of the ancient city matter?', in Cornell, T.J. & Lomas, K. (ed.) *Urban society in Roman Italy*. University College London Press, London: 9–26

Classical sources

Cicero *On Duties* translated by Griffin, M.T. & E.M. Atkins, E.M. 1998. Cambridge University Press, Cambridge.

Digest *The Digest of Justinian* edited by Watson, A. 1998. Pennsylvania University Press, Philadelphia.

Juvenal *The Sixteen Satires* translated by Green, P. 1974. Penguin, London.

Martial *Epigrams I* translated by. Ker, W.C.A. 1968. William Heinmann, London.

Pliny *Natural History Volume VIII, Libri XXVIII-XXXII* translated by Jones, W.H.S. 1963. William Heinmann, London.

7

Of lumberjacks and brick stamps: working with the Tiber as infrastructure

Shawn Graham

At a fundamental level, the growth of the City of Rome was dependent on Rome's ability to exploit successfully the resources of its immediate hinterland, the Tiber Valley (Figure 7.1). One of the most important industries to utilise the valley was the building industry, relying on (amongst other resources) the extensive clay deposits to provide bricks (*cf.* DeLaine 1995). Consider a city of over a million people, a city whose fabric was overwhelmingly made of brick-faced concrete. Calculate what it would take in manpower and in natural resources, to make, fire, and transport bricks to the building sites. Even as a thought-experiment, it is apparent that the logistics of the brick industry were immensely complicated. How *did* the brick get to Rome and elsewhere in the Tiber Valley, anyway? Did all individual brick makers have the same degree of access to the market, and if not, why not? What was the role of the Tiber in this regard? This paper is concerned with examining how the Tiber may have functioned as a piece of infrastructure for the brick industry, and what that implies for the economic geography of the valley during the first to third centuries AD. Understanding the Tiber in this way, combined with a novel use of brick stamp evidence, provides insight into the working lives of the individuals (men and women who range in status from humble slave to the Emperor himself) named on stamped bricks.

The Tiber as Infrastructure

To understand how the Tiber functions as a piece of infrastructure, we need to shift our perspective away from our customary two-dimensional cartographic point of view. We need to put ourselves on the water. Not long after the Second World War, Louise and Leicester Holland (1950) took a rubber raft down the Tiber river to explore the experience of the landscape from the point of view of those who would have worked on the river. They found that it was almost impossible for them to gain their bearings because the view from the river was hampered by vegetation along the shore. Elevated landmarks and the confluence of other streams became the markers by which they navigated. They were only able to keep track of where they were by noting the confluence of other streams and by sighting the occasional hills in the distance which played 'hide and seek' with them, coming into view and then disappearing again, as they meandered along the oxbow loops. We might easily imagine that these particular hills and confluences may have taken on a similar significance for the ancient boatmen. Such familiar 'companions' on any river journey may even have been named. These places, if they could be identified, might provide the evidence for understanding the usage of the river.

Some of these places might be where there are backwaters in the stream. When kayaking or canoeing for example the easiest place to bring one's boat ashore, and keep it there, if one is loading or unloading, is where there are backwaters. Backwaters can form where there is an object in the river, disrupting the flow; the current turns back on itself in the object's lee, creating a small pool. This pool is the backwater; a river pilot can use these contrasting currents to remain relatively motionless in relation to the river's banks. Other places where backwaters form are where there is a confluence of rivers, or where curves in the river bed send

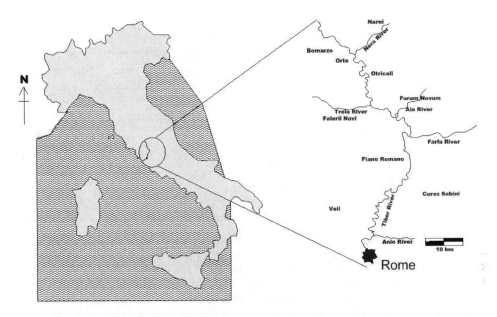

Figure 7.1 *Map of the Tiber Valley, Central Italy, indicating places mentioned in the text*

the current from one side of the river to the other (Gabler, Sayer & Wise 1999, 474). The obvious place therefore to look for ports, landings, and other evidence for how the river was used as infrastructure is at the backwaters behind bridge piles, or where other streams enter the Tiber, and also where bends in the stream send the current from one bank to another. For instance, the town of Otricoli (an olive-oil-exporting port also named in brick stamps CIL xv.1.389a, b) sat on such an inside bend, although the change in the channel's course since antiquity has placed Otricoli on the outside bend (underlining the importance of understanding changes in the river's course overtime). The port structures downstream from Rome in a bend of the river near Pietra di Papa, close to the suburb of EUR (Mocchegiani Carpano 1984, 34–5) also demonstrate the usage of the backwater phenomenon. There is also some evidence from geophysical survey at Forum Novum for what may be a small port facility on a bend of the river Aia (Gaffney, *et al.* 2001, 62). However, every backwater would not necessarily be used or would be suitable for a stopping place; the river pilot would need to know where the suitable ones were. Backwaters which could be located in reference to hill-tops or other landmarks (remembering the Hollands' experience of the Tiber) would be more likely to form part of a river pilot's mental map of stopping places.

Stopping places along the river might be indicated in brick stamps and other inscriptions. Brick stamps CIL xv.1.917,1227–1230; S. 325–326, S.328 record *a(b) pr(aedia) a pila herculis* (from the estate away from the pillar -of a bridge?- of Hercules), seemingly referring to an estate which sat in relation to a particular landmark, the Pila Herculis. The formula '*a pila...*' is not confined to brick stamps. CIL xi.4121 a+b are two inscriptions recovered from either ends of a bridge on the Nera, near modern Narni. It reads:

Shawn Graham

(a) A PILA SECUNDUM/ VIAM P L P [...]
(b) A PILA LO[...]/ NAR P LE[...]

These fragmentary inscriptions seem to act rather like milestones, giving spatial measurements calculated with reference to the piers of the bridge on which they were placed. The piers of this bridge, in being named, point to a role in the landscape beyond being merely part of a bridge. They are a 'place', or 'node' in a Favro-Lynch sense (Favro 1996, 13; Lynch 1960, 47, 72), part of the mental landscape of places where other things happen. For Favro, the naming of places orders the landscape in the same way the ancient orator used the mnemonic device of the 'house of memory'. In each 'room' in the house, the orator 'stores' the parts of his speech, to be remembered as he 'walks' through each room in turn (Favro 1996, 7). In the same way, the association of a 'place' in the landscape has become the 'organizational clues' which enabled an individual to successfully navigate the environment.

To judge by the Narni inscription, the Pila Herculis ought to be similarly a small port or settlement related to the piers of a particular bridge. (It may be in fact that the bridge referred to in the Narni inscription is the same place known in the sixth century as the 'Pile Augusto', the actual river port at Narni, below the city (Quilici 1986, 209)). Other *praedia/figlinae* (estates, brickyards) which are named in stamps using the preposition 'ab' include the *figlinae: ab Apollini* (CIL xv.1.2156), *ab Isis* (CIL xv.1.248–255), and *ab Neptuno* (CIL xv.1.355). Perhaps these bricks are referring to landmarks in the same way the *a pila* formula does.

Farmers ploughing their fields at Seripola (near Orte) in the 1970s uncovered the base of an altar dedicated to Isis; the subsequent rescue excavations conducted at the river port of Seripola (near Orte) during the construction of the Autostrade del Sole uncovered much evidence of a cult centre connected to Isis (Nardi 1980, 235–6). Temples and sanctuaries would make excellent landmarks while navigating on the river; the Temple of Venus for example above the so-called 'Sarno Baths' at Pompeii may have acted as a landmark for the river-port of Pompeii (pers. comm. Curti, E.), while at Ostia there is a temple at the river harbour, facing the mouth of the Tiber (Heinzelmann 2002) which probably served the same purpose. The cult centre of Isis at Seripola therefore might conceivably be connected to the tiles stamped *figlinae ab Isis*.

To argue that some *figlinae* might take their names from notable local landmarks, and being landmarks in their own right some stopping places along the river might be named after the *figlinae*, is not a circular argument. Rather, it points to the fact that *figlinae* were part of the landscape, and their presence helped create a coherent order to it (*cf.* Favro 1996, 7–13). There is an assumption that *figlinae* were on the banks of the Tiber itself, and so are now buried under metres of alluvium (*cf.* Quilici 1986, 213); this assumption seems to be based on the idea that bricks had to be shipped by water (*cf.* Steinby 1981, 239). Yet there are other sites accessible by water but high enough to have avoided the problems of Tiber flooding. Despite what the variability in the water regime in Central Italy would lead us to expect, there are indications that many lesser streams might have been suitable for trade and transportation (Laurence 1999, 109–14). Some of the tributaries of the Anio (especially the Fosso dell'Osa and the Fosso di Grotta Oscura, leading to the sources of the Gabine building stone) were canalized and fitted with locks. The locks would hold back the water until there was enough to float the boats, barges, or rafts to the main river; the same system was used on the upper Tiber above Orte (Quilici 1986, 210–11; Pliny *Historia Naturalis* 3.5.53). The nine-day cycle of holding back and releasing the water corresponds with the market-calendar, the *nundinae* (LeGall 1953, 124) and indicates that these locks were tied to the necessities of trade (and not, say, irrigation). This suggests that as long as there was access to some sort of stream, it was

108

fully possible for places distant from the Tiber and the Anio to float their produce to the major river highways

Cassiodorus (*Variae* 1.26) mentions a *tegularium* (brick warehouse) called the *Portus Licini* (still operating during Theodoric's reign, though known from second century brick stamps CIL xv.1.139,226,408a-d,630) from which it has been argued that *portus* in the context of brick stamps means a place where produce is brought together and then redistributed (Steinby 1981, 239). What sort of change in meaning there would be between the second and fifth centuries is not discussed. DeLaine (1997, 90) suggests that the *tegularium* meaning is secondary and originally such a place ought to be a harbour. Albertazzi *et al.* (1996, 368) have shown that some bricks with *Portus Licini* stamps are composed of material from the banks of the Tiber's tributary, the Aia, some way upstream from the Tiber itself. Similarly, the *Portus Parrae* (CIL xv.1.409–412, S.103–104) ought to be at the confluence of a river with the Tiber, but perhaps the *figlinae* proper are situated some distance up the lesser river. Mocchegiani Carpano (1984, 39) writes that these names could refer to particular stretches of docks and wharves and were named after nearby warehouses and other facilities. Perhaps these landing places are indeed named after certain *figlinae*, but the *figlinae* themselves do not necessarily need to be physically placed on the river itself. By indicating quite specifically where the bricks originate ('*ex figlinis...*') the text in brick stamps could be read backwards (as it were) to indicate the stopping places along the river, the points in the network where the river communicated with the outside world.

In *Portus Licini* stamps, *officinator* (brick-maker) names are never mentioned. Sub-types are distinguished by four distinct *signa* (a figurative device in the middle of the stamp): Mars (408a), Mercury (408b), Aries (408c), and Victoria (408d). In Steinby's chronology of brick stamps, she uses these *signa* to connect stamps from other *figlinae* where the *officinator* is named to the *Portus Licini* (1974, 73–4) on the grounds that a particular *signum* functions almost as a personal seal, and is therefore unique to the individual. Yet there are several examples of different individuals using the same *signa*, for example CIL xv.1.1106b, 968a, 1290a of Aprilis, St. Marcius Stator, and C. Nunnidius Fortunatus all use the head of a cow as a *signum,* which may exclude heraldry as a motivation for its use. Indeed in the year AD 123, the year when seemingly every stamp type carries a consular date, there are only about 40 distinct *signa* employed, not enough to give each individual working in the industry in this year his or her own unique mark. However (and there is a degree of uncertainty here), if *signa* do not necessarily correspond with named individual persons and we can connect the names of *figlinae* with the landing/unloading place, however, could *signa* refer to particular docks (the Mercury docks; the Victoria docks etc) or wharves at the *Portus Licini* complex?

The docks of Rome
There are indications in the topography of Rome that certain areas along the Tiber were in fact given over to the unloading of specific goods. Mocchegiani Carpano (1984, 39) gives as an example the area called '*ad ciconia nixas*' on the left bank of the Tiber in the Campus Martius which was linked to the *Portus Vinarius* and given over to the unloading of wine amphorae. Coarelli (2000, 375–8) argues that a certain portion of the Severan marble plan of Rome actually indicates a storage area for brick along the slopes of the little Aventine. The piece in question seems to indicate a large open structure, and carries the label 'NAVALEMFER' (reproduced in Carettoni *et al.* 1960, plate XV, fragment no.2), which is usually taken to indicate one of the lower *navalia* or shipyards (*navale inferius*). However, in Coarelli's view,

this label is very similar to the text on a stamped brick from Pannonia (CIL iii.11382) where '*navalia*' seems to be used in the same sense as *portus* in the *Portus Licini* stamps. He then suggests that this strange use of 'shipyard' is a colloquial expression equating brick yards, with their long rows of brick, with shipyards and the furrows made in the ground by the pulling up of ships onto dry land in the boat sheds. Coarelli notes that there is a second piece of the marble plan (reproduced in Carettoni *et al.* 1960, plate XLI, fragment no.201) which seems to indicate an open area with rows of she ds. He then re-interprets the label on the marble plan to read *Navale M(arci) Fer[ocis]*, a man known to history as Cn Pompeius Ferox Licinianus (consul suffect in AD 98), and connects the two pieces of the marble plan together. He concludes that here, on the marble plan, is the *Portus Licini* of brick stamps. Unfortunately, the fragments of the plan do not indicate how these structures communicate with the river. The structures Coarelli identifies could well be to do with the storage of brick and tile, which is an important identification.

It seems reasonable to argue then that the docks along the Tiber in Rome could be indicated by a particular name (in a way similar to how Ling 1990 suggests urban space could be organised) and that these docks could be given over to the trade in particular goods, as Mocchegiani Carpano (1984, 39) argues. Warehousing connected with brick has always been suspected (*cf.* Steinby 1974, 74) and Coarelli (2000, 375–8) may have discovered where at least one such complex was located. The example of the Port of London in the seventeenth to nineteenth centuries (Weinreb & Hibbert 1995, 235–7) may be taken as an indication of the dynamics of how all these pieces fit together. In the tidal reaches of the Thames, ocean-going vessels had to anchor in mid-stream, to be unloaded by lighters, which then took the goods to a variety of different docks. Piracy and smuggling took their toll as goods did not always reach their intended destination, and duties were lost. Queen Elizabeth I passed a law requiring that all goods were to be unloaded at a limited number of 'legal quays', ensuring that customs duties could be collected. As trade grew in proportion to the Empire, the various quays, wharves, and docks began to specialise in certain trade items. Over the eighteenth century limited docking facilities, congestion, inadequate warehousing, and theft began to have a serious effect on the efficiency and profitability of trade in the port. By the beginning of the nineteenth century, to address these problems private companies had obtained charters to open new docking and warehousing facilities, including the East India docks, the West India docks, St Katharine's docks, and the Surrey Quays. These charters enabled them to obtain long-term monopolies in certain goods. Rum and hardwood were unloaded at the West India docks, softwood was unloaded at the Surrey Quays, sugar and rubber were unloaded at St Katherine's. The private docks took a percentage of the value of all the cargoes which passed through, making docking and warehousing a particularly lucrative business. However, not just the dock complexes themselves were named, but also individual docks and even the staircases which lead from the embankment to the water's edge – names like 'Goat Stairs'; 'Three Cranes Wharf'; Limehouse Dock'; 'Elephant Stairs'; 'Puddle Dock' (Place names in Rotherhithe, 2002).

With regard to the brick trade, the scale of the trade in the second century and the continual demand for building materials in Rome ought to have contributed significantly to congestion on the Tiber. Congestion was a significant problem for eighteenth century London, when that city had a population nearing (if not surpassing) a million people (Weinreb & Hibbert 1995, 631). The Thames in London is a much wider river than the Tiber in Rome; if congestion on the Thames was a problem in the eighteenth century, it could well have been significant on the

Tiber in the second century (allowing for the fact that the sea-going vessels docked and were off-loaded into barges at Portus and Ostia). Similar physical constraints in one time and place may have given rise to similar solutions in another. In Antiquity, at Ostia and at Arles (France) taxes and duties were paid on goods when they were unloaded (Mocchegiani Carpano 1984, 52–3); this was also the case at Rome itself as is indicated by a partial inscription found near San Silvestro (CIL vi.1785, 31931). Mocchegiani Carpano suggests that the curator of the Tiber may have acted to a degree as a sort of 'harbour master' (1984, 39); if so, he may have played a role in collecting these duties, but more importantly (from the point of view of the dock owner) in deciding which docks would have the right to unload what product in the first place.

It may have been that, like in Georgian and Victorian London, warehouse owners could be the people who also owned the docks at which the goods for their warehouses were unloaded; alternatively, the docks might be owned by a person connected to the warehouse owner by ties of patronage. It is not all that far-fetched to suppose that a warehouse owner in Rome might have specialised in providing storage space for brick. Warehouse contracts, specifying the type of good and the space in which it would be stored, are known from Puteoli (Rickman, 1980, 236–8). In this scenario, the *Portus Licini* (with its four different stamp *signa*) might well indeed be identified with those structures identified by Coarelli (2000, 375–8), but the docks serving the complex may have been operated by four distinct individuals. Because the docks specialised in particular goods (perhaps brick needs special ramps, pulleys, cranes to unload) brick makers might have long-standing arrangements for their bricks to go to these particular docks. The *signa* could therefore be incorporated into a stamp because the destination in Rome for each consignment would already be known.

Perhaps there is some more archaeological evidence for a brick-related installation along the river, if these arguments are correct. Near the Campus Martius, the 'Tor di Nona' is a 96m long mole which jutted into the Tiber and had a temple at its end (Quilici 1986, 202). The temple had capitals decorated with the skin of a wild beast, either a panther or a lion (pers. comm. Delaine, J.), Panther skins are an attribute of Bacchus, while lion skins are an attribute of Hercules. Both Hercules and Bacchus appear in *signa* (Hercules: CIL xv.1.156, 214–6, 241, 324–5, 686, 715, 768, 772, 1247, 1497 *Figlinae: Domitianae, Favorianae, Genianae, Marcianae, Voconianae*; Bacchus: *CIL* xv.1.126, 382 *Figlinae: Caninianae, Oceanae Minores*). The construction of this mole is Augustan in date, and was later incorporated into the Hadrianic embankment (Quilici 1986, 202). The *figlinae* date from the mid first century through to the reign of Commodus (Steinby 1974, 29, 34–5, 37, 41–45, 61–6, 69–71). If we imagine that the docks would also take their names from landmarks or other prominent features, then it is a small matter to connect the *signa* of Hercules or Bacchus with the temple at the end of this mole. Perhaps the Tor di Nona is one of our putative specialised docks, dealing exclusively with the produce of these *figlinae*.

Effective Parallels for the Brick Industry
During the eighteenth and nineteenth centuries at the Port of London, certain named docks were given over to the trade of particular commodities, a practice that resulted out of the logistical complexities of conducting worldwide trade from a narrow river port (Port of London Authority 2002). Perhaps on the Tiber we are viewing a similar solution to a similar problem. There are other parallels which may aid our understanding of the use of the Tiber as infrastructure.

Discussions of brick stamping usually refer to other categories of stamped materials in the Roman world, usually *fistulae*, *amphorae*, and *terra-sigillata* (*cf.* the variety of papers in Harris (ed.) 1993). Comparing brick stamps to these other classes of material seems to treat the stamp itself as an entity entirely unrelated to the material on which it is found. The similarity between up-market pottery such as *terra-sigillata* and common brick has not been demonstrated to the point that we are able to equate the meaning/purpose of one with the other. Besides which, Darvill and McWhirr (1984, 240–1) in their discussion of the economic organisation of the Romano-British brick industry, have a good point when they draw attention to the fact that the dynamics of a heavy industry will be quite different from those of a light industry, simply by virtue of how the product is sold in batches rather than in individual units; they draw a direct parallel with mining and timbering. Comparisons to those sorts of activities would be more appropriate.

Stamps have been found in fact on other building materials, although this is not widely known or recognised. In 1868 a chunk of bitumen was recovered in the contrada Pignatara (Lettomanoppello) in Abruzzo with a rectangular stamp reading: [...]ALONI C(aii) F(ilii) ARN(iensis) SAGITTAE (Agostini & Pellegrini 1996, 57–8). In England, a stamped squared-timber has been recently recovered from the Thames foreshore. Dendrochronology dates the felling of the timber to around AD 63. The investigators record that the stamp mentions just a single name- TRAEGAUG or perhaps TRAECAUC (Brigham *et al.* 1996, 36). They have interpreted this as the stamp of a Thracian auxiliary unit, but the initial letter in the branded stamp is very unclear, with only the bottom of the stem of the letter being preserved. Alternatively the stamp could be read as PRAECAUG or (ex) PRAE(dis) C(aesaris) AUG(ustus), a formula similar to that found on Tiber valley bricks. If this is correct, and assuming that these timbers were floated downstream, then they may have been cut from an imperial estate belonging to Nero somewhere in the Thames valley watershed. There is another connection between brick and timber for according to Collingwood and Wright (1992, 26) the earliest stamped tiles found in Britain were the products of 'an imperial tilery of Nero's reign near Silchester' (RIB 2.5 2482).

Timbers stamped with full Roman nomenclature have also been discovered *in situ* in the foundations of the circus of Arles at the mouth of the Rhone (pers. comm. Feugere, M. 2000). A direct connection between brick and timber can be illustrated by the activities of the Roman Army in Britain. Stamped brick displaying the legend of the legion involved are well known (Peacock 1979, 8). In 1983 at Annetwell Street in Carlisle in a second century AD context, there was found a wooden bung for a barrel. This bung had been cut from a piece of wood which had previously been branded: [...] LEG [...]/[...]EG XX [...] or *Leg(io) XX [V(aleria) V(ictrix)]* (RIB 2.4 2442.11). This is the same formula used in military-stamped bricks in Roman Britain. In all of these examples, the key points are the shapes, standardised abbreviations, the clear indication of origin, and the indication of the end user (*e.g. Legio XX*). These timber stamps and the bitumen stamp are closer relatives to brick stamps than to the pottery which informs most models of stamping practice, and therefore the mechanics of these trades ought to be more directly relevant for our understanding of the brick industry.

Given these similarities between brick stamping and timber branding, an understanding of timbering practices could help us understand how the brick industry worked. The standard reference is Meiggs 1982, but his time-scale is so broad that it does not deal in much detail with the period in which we are interested. However, there are only about 75 generations which separate modern from ancient practice (Adam 1984, 109 note 151) and fewer than six of those

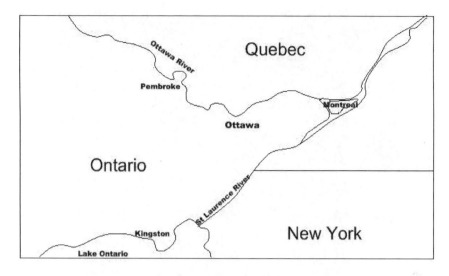

Figure 7.2 *Map of the Ottawa Valley, Eastern Canada*

have been industrialised. Until the advent of mechanisation, the logistics of exploiting primary resources are largely similar to ancient practice (*cf.* DeLaine 1997, 105–7). Ethnographic comparison with well-documented though importantly non-mechanised timbering practices in nineteenth century Canada provides an appropriate model for a riverine economy of the same scale and level of development as the ancient brick industry (*cf.* Dyson 1992, 16; 1979 where he argues for the suitability of colonial North America as a effective parallel for the Roman world).

The Ottawa Valley Timber Industry in the nineteenth century
The Ottawa River in Eastern Canada (Figure 7.2) was used as a conduit for trade and as an integral piece of infrastructure by Europeans for nearly two hundred years. The Ottawa valley was rich in stands of tall white pine, and this material was heavily in demand by the Royal Navy for shipbuilding, but also by American homebuilders. The appearance, flourishing, and decline of the timber industry (in the form which relied on the Ottawa to get the timber to market) happened quite quickly. From one operator to hundreds in the space of twenty years, the industry organised itself without the imposition of formal government regulation. It experienced rapid consolidation in the hands of powerful well-connected men.

Little capital was needed for a man to get started in the trade. Since the actual trade was largely seasonal it complemented the agricultural calendar (initially forming an important aspect of a farm's income). In its early days there was a huge number of small producers in the forest. Profits could be considerable (Carlisle & Cheliak 1984, 20–3). However, poor communication with the main markets meant that the lumberjacks, the men whose livelihood was made through the cutting down of timber, could not accurately predict demand. Consequently there were repeated cycles of over-supply and price collapse (Reid 1990, xlvii). These shocks drove out the many small independent operators leaving a reduced number of men who had the considerable capital, credit, and market information to be able to absorb the frequent crises. Consolidation took place in two forms. In the first, the larger operators

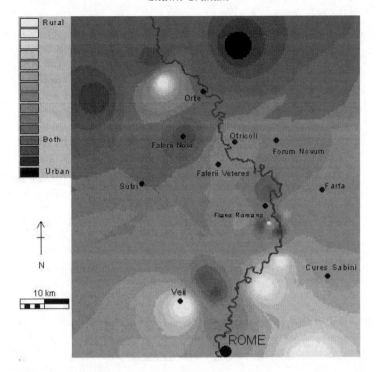

***Figure** 7.3 Economic geography of the Tiber Valley in the Julio-Claudian period, based on the index values constructed for brick stamp types found at sites throughout the Valley. Brick makers whose production runs of a particular stamp type are oriented towards the Rome market are interpreted as having had access to the infrastructure which made in possible to market in Rome. For those whose production runs were not so oriented, they are interpreted as having been excluded from that infrastructure.*

subcontracted or provided financial backing to the smaller firms, which shifted the risk of transportation and the potential non-sale of goods to the timber barons (or larger operators) whose social and political contacts and clout considerably reduced that risk. In the second form, the larger firms simply continued to expand their operations at all levels, buying out their competitors (Reid 1990, lxiv).

Ownership of the logs was indicated in two ways. In the first, a heavy hammer with a particular pattern on the end was driven against the end of the log. The resulting imprint would be taken up by the grain of the wood and remained legible even if damaged (thus guarding against theft). In the second, a simpler mark would be scribed into the bark to be visible while the log was in the water (Hughson & Bond 1987, 88, 104). As the trade became more complex, so too did the uses of these stamps. At waterfalls and severe rapids the rafts were broken up into smaller units and run down the timber slide one unit at a time, bypassing the obstruction. The owners of the slides were able to charge a toll on the other operators for the logs that went through, based on close attention to the stamps (Theilheimer 1984, 33). By the 1860s the timber barons had banded together and formed a co-operative venture for the improvement of navigation and commerce on the Ottawa. The company undertook to build the necessary infrastructure on the river, the towing of logs over flat water, and the like. The stamps on the

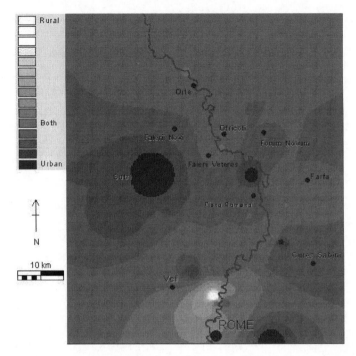

Figure 7.4 *Economic geography of the Tiber Valley in the Flavian period, based on the index values constructed for brick stamp types found at sites throughout the Valley. Brick makers whose production runs of a particular stamp type are oriented towards the Rome market are interpreted as having had access to the infrastructure which made in possible to market in Rome. For those whose production runs were not so oriented, they are interpreted as having been excluded from that infrastructure.*

logs formed the basis of payment for the services offered by the company (Hughson & Bond 1987, 107–8). The stamps also served in the measurement of wood volume and later on, taxation by the government. As the trade became more complex and the timberers were farther and farther afield, some lumbermen used different stamps to indicate timber cut in different watersheds, and to indicate at which sawmill that particular log was to be cut (Stiell 1984, 33). This informal but complex system, it will be noted, came about without the intervention of any legal body.

In 1870, at the behest of the largest timbermen the Canadian Parliament passed a law that required each log to be stamped according to a mark already registered with the Government. Registration entailed recording the mark, a description of it, serial number, and the name and address of the operator. Over 2000 different stamp types are known, formed from ligatures of the operator's initials, to depictions of animals, to quite abstract shapes (Stiell 1984, 33).

Implications for the Roman Brick Industry in the Tiber valley
The crucial points of comparison are that:
    - originally the trade was part of regular, seasonal farming activities
    - low start up costs, combined with the inability to predict production or demand, created repeated cycles of over-supply and price-collapse

– uncertainty and crises drove the tendency towards consolidation into the hands of the large operators

– the cheaper the price of the product, and the further the distance from point of sale, more improvements were necessary to bring that product to market

– large operators banded together for the improvement of the river, giving them the concomitant right to charge others for the use of these improvements

– stamps were used for ownership, indication of destination, indication of origin, calculation of volume shipped, taxation and tolls

– stamps developed informally in response to the difficulties of shipping on the river: their codification in law happened later and was at the behest of the large operators, likely to their advantage

On a basic level, putting a mark on something is about control, about differentiating it from something else. The dynamics of the Ottawa Valley timber industry were tied not only to seasonal fluctuations in demand and poor communications, but also to the need to control access to the infrastructure which made it possible to use the river. Stamps developed in complexity in response to this need. With regard to rivers in general, the lesson is that not everybody has equal access to the river or its infrastructure, and in this fashion, river transport is much different to that by road. Whereas a road can transform the 'space-economy' of a region, making places closer together by shortening travel time (*cf.* Laurence 2001, 596, 598), a river requires an *intermediary*, a port. Consequently, a river's role in the 'space-economy' is much more complex. Along the Tiber, the indication of access points implied by *figlinae* names suggests a limited number of places where the Tiber could be joined. Whoever controlled the ports, controlled the river. The Tiber therefore may not have merely facilitated trade but rather enabled the *social control* of trade in a way that roads could not. In the distribution network for brick which connected the hinterland to the city, the river offered a short-cut into the heart of the city which was not available to all.

Markets and access
The Tiber is not a very large river, in terms of the actual area available for shipping. Wheat, oil, wine, fruit and vegetables, wood, and stone were all shipped down the river. This picture of the middle Tiber, from Orte to Rome, is of a very busy stream. In such crowded conditions, our ethnographic parallel suggests that the stamps on brick could serve like the timber stamps in the easy identification of cargoes and, when compared against shipping contracts, the destination of those cargoes, primarily warehouses. On the Tiber, the year AD 123 is perhaps the most frequent date occurring in brick stamps. It has been suggested that some sort of order was issued by the government that year (Bloch 1959, 237), which if true seems analogous to the formal stamping law passed by Parliament. On the Ottawa, it was the largest operators who felt the need for a new law to regulate a customary practice according to *their* rules and so requested the state to legislate the industry (many of the timber barons being members of Parliament, this was not unduly difficult). By having all timbers stamped and the marks registered, unauthorised production could be curbed and the proper calculation of tolls and taxation effected. On the Tiber, the Domitii *familia* were the largest brick producers in 123; in that year the urban prefect was Annius Verus, the father-in-law of Domitia Lucilla, *domina* (or mistress) of the estate. One role of stamping may be to control shipping and access to the Tiber and its associated infrastructure.

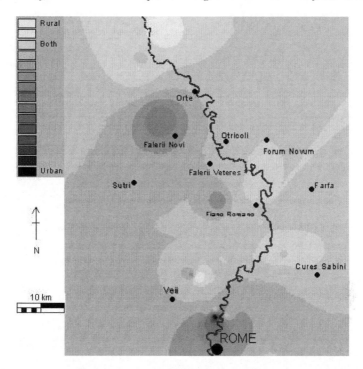

Figure 7.5 *Economic geography of the Tiber Valley in the period from Nerva to Hadrian, based on the index values constructed for brick stamp types found at sites throughout the Valley. Brick makers whose production runs of a particular stamp type are oriented towards the Rome market are interpreted as having had access to the infrastructure which made in possible to market in Rome. For those whose production runs were not so oriented, they are interpreted as having been excluded from that infrastructure.*

The occurrence of stamped brick types in the Tiber Valley compared to the City of Rome can be used to investigate this differential access to the river infrastructure. If an assemblage of stamped bricks at a given site consists of the kind of stamp types which are usually found only in Rome, then for this site one could argue that the person paying for the construction had access to the distribution networks usually centred on Rome. This site can be imagined as having a high degree of integration with the city, a little piece of the city in the surrounding countryside. Conversely, if these stamp types are usually found not in Rome, then that site may be thought of as being excluded from the urban distribution networks. A simple index was developed by tabulating for each stamp type the number of examples found in the Valley (the Valley frequency), and the number found in Rome (the Rome frequency) as recorded in CIL xv.1. The Valley frequency was divided by the Rome frequency, and the results were standardised so that a number greater than one demonstrated a production run excluded from urban distribution networks, while a number less than -1 indicates production geared towards the Rome market. Results which ranged between -1 and +1, were taken to mean production equally able to access urban and rural networks. The index is constructed from 523 examples of stamped bricks found in the Tiber Valley (Filippi & Stanco, unpublished catalogue); there are over 2000 examples of the same types recorded in Rome (CIL xv.1).

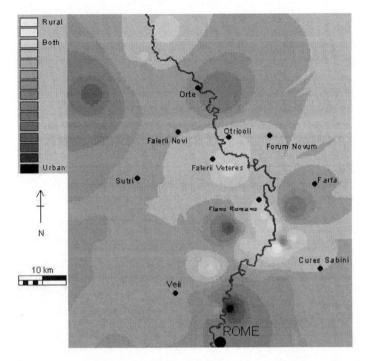

Figure 7.6 *Economic geography of the Tiber Valley in the period from Antoninus-Pius to Commodus, based on the index values constructed for brick stamp types found at sites throughout the Valley. Brick makers whose production runs of a particular stamp type are oriented towards the Rome market are interpreted as having had access to the infrastructure which made in possible to market in Rome. For those whose production runs were not so oriented, they are interpreted as having been excluded from that infrastructure.*

This series of maps (Figures 7.3–8) link the distribution of each stamp type found in the Tiber Valley to their degree of participation in the rural or urban networks. The zones are based on the index value for each stamped brick at a site, and were plotted using the GIS programme ARCVIEW. These maps give us a sense of the degree to which various parts of the hinterland were integrated with the City from the point of view of consumption, or even ideology (the desire to use the same materials as used in Rome). Functionalist economists would argue that integration with Rome depends on how close an area is to Rome, but that is clearly not the case. The situation is much more complex, and changes overtime. During the Julio-Claudian period, there are only a few sites which have access to materials for which the primary market was Rome (Figure 7.3). There is quite a bit of variability between the Julio-Claudian and Flavian periods, with most places in the Valley having access to urban distribution networks (but with quite an opposite pattern nearest the city) (Figure 7.4). Over the next hundred years (Figures 7.5 & 7.6) the situation settles to a state where during the Severans (Figure 7.7) only a few pockets build with the same materials as in Rome. In late antiquity (Figure 7.8), there is suddenly much more variety than once there was; it is almost a return to conditions prevailing in the Julio-Claudian period. Note in these maps firstly the gradual blurring of the rural/urban networks, and secondly the close proximity to Rome of areas which are completed excluded from urban production. Finally, there is the opposite situation as well, where places quite

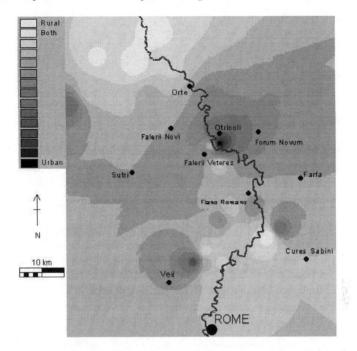

Figure 7.7 *Economic geography of the Tiber Valley in the Severan period, based on the index values constructed for brick stamp types found at sites throughout the Valley. Brick makers whose production runs of a particular stamp type are oriented towards the Rome market are interpreted as having had access to the infrastructure which made in possible to market in Rome. For those whose production runs were not so oriented, they are interpreted as having been excluded from that infrastructure.*

distant from Rome are building with the same materials as at Rome. Forum Novum, the subject of recent work by the British School at Rome (Gaffney, *et al.* 2001), is quite a stable site, neither predominantly rural nor urban until late antiquity, when suddenly it is using the same material as in Rome. This pattern might be explained with reference to the early medieval period, with the establishment of Forum Novum as the papal cathedral centre for the Sabines (on the history of Forum Novum *cf.* Gaffney, *et al.* 2001, 59–60).

Stamped bricks made by at least thirty different slaves of the Domitii appear in the Tiber valley, but their production alternates between Rome (urban networks) and the Valley (rural networks) at different stages in their careers. For example, the slave Trophimus Agathobuli first appears in the Tiber valley stamps in about AD 93/4, with Cn Domitius Tullus as *dominus*. This stamp (CIL xv.1.1002) appears in a Rome zone. As time passed, Tullus died and his daughter Domitia Lucilla inherited his estate. The next stamp of Trophimus Agathobuli (CIL xv.1.263) dates to shortly before AD 115, with Lucilla as *domina*, and the production run with this stamp demonstrates an equal weighting between Roman and Tiber valley production. After his manumission in AD 115, Trophimus Agathobuli appears again, but this time his production (stamp CIL xv.1.1108) is decidedly tilted towards rural production. A slave belonging to Trophimus Agathobuli also appears at this time, and his production (stamps CIL xv.1.1118a-b) is similarly positioned (on the history of the slaves of the Domitii, see Steinby 1974, 47–58).

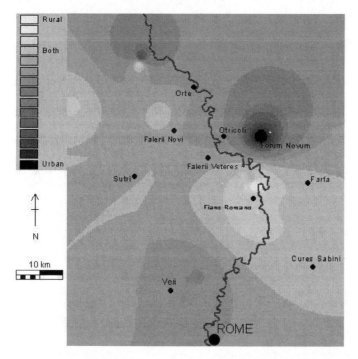

Figure 7.8 *Economic geography of the Tiber Valley in the Diocletianic period, based on the index values constructed for brick stamp types found at sites throughout the Valley. Brick makers whose production runs of a particular stamp type are oriented towards the Rome market are interpreted as having had access to the infrastructure which made in possible to market in Rome. For those whose production runs were not so oriented, they are interpreted as having been excluded from that infrastructure.*

For this example at least it is as if access to the major market is controlled by the important landowners (eventually the Domitii produced an Emperor, Marcus Aurelius). While their slave, the output of Trophimus Agathobuli, enriched them and so those bricks went to the market where they could command the best prices *i.e.* Rome. Alternatively, while a slave, he had access to the transportation network and warehousing facilities that made it economic to market in Rome. Then, as a slave of a new mistress, for whatever reason, the main market was slowly denied to him. Finally, as a freedman, while occasionally getting product to Rome, he and his slaves were largely unable to get major market access, his outfit being too small or lacking the resources to transport a very heavy, very bulky material the distance, or perhaps locked out by the dominance of the few and the powerful (*cf.* Wallace-Hadrill 1989, 73). Figure 7.9 plots the course of the careers of two other individuals based on the stamp indicators. It is noteworthy that Trophimus' contemporary, Aprilis Agathobuli, has a career that runs almost the opposite of Trophimus, suggesting that he was much better at the political game. The career of C. Nunnidius Fortunatus ends at a high level in the index, suggesting a fair degree of success at accessing the distribution networks, a success we could lay at the feet of Asinia Quadratilla, his *domina* who was also the granddaughter of the patron of Ostia at the end of the first century Q. Asinius Marcellus (Setälä 1977, 71–2).

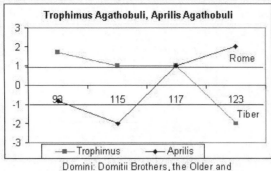

Domini: Domitii Brothers, the Older and
Younger Lucillae

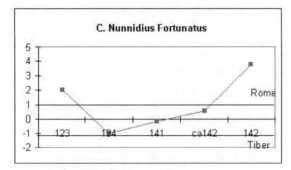

Domina: Q. Asinia Quadratilla

Figure 7.9 *Three career histories. For each stamp type a particular brick maker made, an index value can be calculated, determining the relative degree of access to the urban or rural markets (the same index on which Figures 7.3–8 are based). Career histories can then be plotted, and compared.*

Questions of market access apply also to the *figlinae* as a whole. Recently, a production site of the *gens* Domitii has been located near Bomarzo (north of Orte) (pers comm. G. Filippi). The identification of the two kilns as belonging to the Domitii is partly based on the finds of brick stamp wasters, but also on the recovery of a boundary stone explicitly naming the brothers Domitii. The index constructed for the stamps from the one kiln indicate a production split between Rome and the Tiber valley except in the period from Nerva to Hadrian, when its production shifted dramatically towards Rome (Figure 7.10). The other kiln was similar in that its production was split between Rome and the Tiber valley, but in the Antonine period, production became centred to a large degree on the Valley.

Conclusion

In this paper I have indicated some of the ways the Tiber may have functioned as infrastructure in the brick industry. This industry, since it is so obviously connected with the landed estates of the élite (and therefore the sources of their political and social legitimacy), may be taken as an indicator for larger economic patterns, and therefore it has a wider significance. Not all

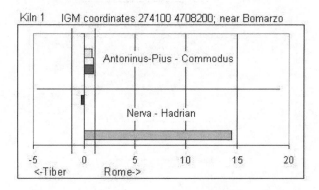

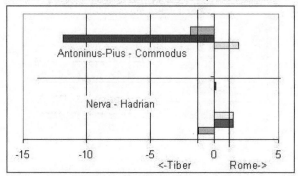

Figure 7.10 *Two kiln histories. As for individuals, so too for production sites. All of the stamped brick recovered from a production site (each type represented here by a horizontal bar) can be used to create an index value by period, indicating to which market producers using a particular kiln had access.*

individuals working in the brick industry had access to the infrastructure which enabled supply to Rome. Mapping the index of relative use of different stamp types in the hinterland compared to the city enables us to develop a picture of the changing economic geography of the Tiber valley. The evidence of brick stamps can also illuminate the relative fortunes of individual producers, and the marketing strategies of different *figlinae*. The stamping index suggests that some *domini*, or their agents, took active steps to control the trade. This control manifested itself in the countryside by limiting some areas to materials which were produced locally while others could obtain the same materials as were used in the City itself. With the Tiber as the main transportation artery for the brick industry (*cf.* Steinby 1981), the control of access points, such as port structures and other infrastructure, may account for these changing economic and geographic patterns.

Acknowledgements
This study contributes to the British School at Rome's Tiber Valley Project (Patterson and Millett 1998); an earlier version of this paper was presented at the 4th Tiber Valley Workshop. My thanks to Filippi, G., Stanco, E., Patterson, H., Laurence, R., Haughton, B. and DeLaine, J.; errors are of course my own. This research was supported by the Social Sciences and Humanities Research Council of Canada, and the Overseas Research Studentship Scheme administered by the Committee of Vice-Chancellors and Principals of the Universities of the UK.

Bibliography
Adam, J.-P. 1984. *La Construction Romaine: materiaux et techniques.* Grands Manuels Pircard, Paris.
Agostini, S. & Pelligrini, W. 1996. 'Altre Risorse della Maiella: testimonianze di archeologia industriale', in Staffa, A.R. (ed.) *La Presenza dell'Uomo sulla Maiella: Archeologia e paesaggio storico. Guida alla Sezione Archeologica del Museo Paolo Barrasso Centro Visitatori della Riserva naturale Valle dell'Orfento.* Ministero delle Risorse Agricole, Alimentari e Forestali, Corpo Forestale dello Stato Pescara, Regione Abruzzo; Ministero per I Beni Culturali e Ambientali, Soprintendenza Archeologica dell'Abruzzo Chieti, Parco Nazionale della Maiella, Caramanico Terme (PE): 57–8
Albertazzi, A., Failla, A., Filippi, G & Turci, G. 1996. 'Analisi archeometriche di laterizi bollati di eta romana: un esempio dalla Sabina', in *Museologia Scientifica* 13. supplemento, Atti 10 Congresso A.N.M.S. Bologna: 347–72
Bloch, H. 1959. 'The Serapeum of Ostia and the Brick-Stamps of 123. A New Landmark in the History of Roman Architecture', *AJA* 63: 225–40
Brigham, T., Watson, B., Tyers, I. & Bartkowiak, R. 1996. 'Current Archaeological Work at Regis House in the City of London (Part I)', *LA* 8.2: 31–8
Carettoni, G., Colini, A., Cozza, L. & Gatti, G. eds. 1960. *La pianta marmorea di Roma antica. Forma urbis Romae.* Comune di Roma, Rome.
Carlisle, J.A. & Cheliak, L. 1984. 'The Heyday of Valley Logging', in *Ottawa Valley Forestry: 1984 forestry capital of Canada.* Ottawa Valley Forestry Capital Promotion Society, Petawawa Ontario: 20–3
Coarelli, F. 2000. 'Discussions, sous la presidence de J.-M. Pesez', in Boucheron, P., Broise, H. & Thebert, Y. (eds). *La Brique Antique et Medievale.* École Française de Rome, Rome: 371–81
Collingwood, R. & Wright, R. 1993. *The Roman Inscriptions of Britain Volume 2: Instrumentum Domesticum,* fascicule 5. Frere, S.S. & Tomlin, & R.S.O. (eds) Alan Sutton, Stroud, Glos.
Darvill, T. & McWhirr, A. 1984. 'Brick and tile production in Roman Britain: models of economic organisation', *WA* 15: 239–61
DeLaine, J. 1995. 'The supply of building materials to the City of Rome', in Christie, N. (ed.) *Settlement and Economy in Italy 1500 BC–AD 1500: Papers of the Fifth Conference of Italian Archaeology.* Oxbow, Oxford: 555–62
DeLaine, J. 1997. *The Baths of Caracalla: a Study in the design, construction, and economics of large-scale building projects in imperial Rome.* JRA, Supplementary Series 25, Portsmouth, Rhode Island.
Dyson, S.L. 1979. 'New methods and models in the study of Roman town-country systems', *Ancient World* 2: 91–5
Dyson, S.L. 1992. *Community and Society in Roman Italy.* Johns Hopkins University Press, Baltimore.
Favro, D.G. 1996. *The Urban Image of Augustan Rome.* Cambridge University Press, Cambridge & New York.
Filippi, G. & Stanco, E. (unpublished) Toponomastica ed epigrafia della produzione laterizia nella Valle del Tevere: l'Umbria e la Sabina tra *Narnia* e *Nomentum*; L'Etruria tra *Horta* e *Lucus Feroniae.*
Frere, S.S. & Tomlin, R.S.O. 1992. *Roman Inscriptions of Britain* (Vol 2, fasc 4). Gloucester, Sutton.
Gabler, R., Sayer, R. & Wise, D. 1999. *Essentials of Physical Geography.* Harcourt Brace, Orlando.

Gaffney, V., Patterson, H. & Roberts, P. 2001. 'Forum Novum-Vescovio: studying urbanism in the Tiber valley', *JRA* 14: 59–79

Harris, W.V. 1993. *The Inscribed Economy: production and distribution in the Roman Empire in the light of instrumentum domesticum*. JRA, Supplementary Series 6, Portsmouth, Rhode Island.

Heinzelmann, M. 2002. 'Latest Results from Ostia' *http://www.dainst.org/index.php?id=2901&session Language=en* accessed on March 28 2002

Holland, L. & Holland, L. 1950. 'Down the Tiber on a Raft', *Archaeology* 3.2: 87–94

Hughson, J.W. & Bond, C.C.J. 1987. *Hurling Down the Pine*. Historical Society of the Gatineau, Chelsea, Quebec.

Laurence, R. 1999. The Roads of Roman Italy: mobility and cultural change. Routledge, London.

Laurence, R. 2001. 'Roman Italy's Urban Revolution', in Lo Cascio, E. & Marino, A.S. (eds) *Modalità insediative e strutture agrarie nell'Italia meridionale in età romana*. Edipuglia, Bari: 593–611

LeGall, J. 1953. *Le Tibre, fleuve de Rome dans l'antiquité*. Publications de l'Institut d'Art et d'Archéologie de l'Université de Paris 1, Presses Universitaires de France, Paris.

Ling, R. 1990. 'A Stranger in Town: Finding the Way in an Ancient City', *Greece & Rome* 37.2: 204–214

Lynch, K. 1960. *The Image of the City*. Massachusetts Institute of Technology & Harvard University Press, Cambridge MA.

Meiggs, R. 1982. *Trees and Timber in the Ancient Mediterranean World*. Clarendon Press, Oxford.

Mocchegiani Carpano, C. 1984. 'Il Tevere, archeologia e commercio', *Bollettino di Numismatica* 2–3: 21–83

Nardi, G. 1980. *Le antichità di Orte: esame del territorio e dei materiali archeologici*. Consiglio nazionale delle ricerche, Centro di studio per l'archeologia etrusco-italica, Roma.

Patterson, H. & Millett, M. 1998. 'The Tiber Valley Project', *PBSR* 66: 1–20

Peacock, D.P.S. 1979. 'An Ethnoarchaeological Approach to the Study of Roman Bricks and Tiles', in McWhirr, A. (ed.) *Roman Brick and Tile: studies in manufacture, distribution and use in the western Empire*. BAR (British Series) 68, Oxford: 5–11

Place Names in Rotherhithe. 2002. *http://www.bathspa.ac.uk/greenwood/lplaces.html* Accessed Aug. 28 2002

Port of London Authority. 2002. 'The History of The Port of London up to the Advent of the Port of London Authority' *http://www.portoflondon.co.uk/display_fixedpage.cfm?id=238&site=leisure* Accessed on Aug. 28 2002

Quilici, L. 1986. 'Il Tevere e l'aniene come vie d'acqua a monte di Roma in età imperiale', *Archeologia Laziale* 7.2: 198–217

Reid, R.M. 1990. *The Upper Ottawa Valley to 1855*. Carleton University Press, Ottawa.

Rickman, G. 1980. *The Corn Supply of Ancient Rome*. Clarendon Press, Oxford.

Setälä, P. 1977. 'Private Domini in Roman Brick Stamps of the Empire: A historical and prosopographical study of landowners in the district of Rome', *Annales Academiae Scientiarum Fennicae, Dissertationes Humanarum Litterarum* 10. Suomalainen tiedeakatemia, Helsinki.

Steinby, E.M. 1974. 'La cronologia delle "figlinae" doliari urbane dalla fine dell'età repubblicana fino all'inizio dell III secolo', *Bullettino della Commissione Archeologica Comunale di Roma*, 84: 7–132

Steinby, E.M. 1981. 'La diffusione dell'opus doliare urbano', in Giardina, A. & Schiabone, A. (eds) *Merci, Mercati e Scambi nel Mediterraneo* 2: 237–45

Stiell, W. 1984. 'Timber Marks', in *Ottawa Valley Forestry: 1984 forestry capital of Canada*. Ottawa Valley Forestry Capital Promotion Society, Petawawa Ontario: 33

Theilheimer, I. 1984. 'Timber on the Move: From River Drive to Overdrive', in *Ottawa Valley Forestry: 1984 forestry capital of Canada*. Ottawa Valley Forestry Capital Promotion Society, Petawawa Ontario: 30–2

Wallace-Hadrill, A. 1989. 'Patronage in Roman society: from Republic to Empire', in Wallace-Hadrill, A. (ed.) *Patronage in Ancient Society*. Routledge, London & New York: 63–88

Weinreb, B. & Hibbert, C. 1995. *The London Encyclopaedia*. Macmillan, London.

124

8

The shopkeepers and craft-workers of Roman London

Jenny Hall

Roman London was in many ways typical of the other towns of the province of Britannia. London had the normal trading activities of a town, and craft-workers to produce the necessities for everyday existence. It was, however, different in other respects both as the capital of a province, with spheres of activity controlled by state officials, and as a bustling port with a waterfront area likely to have its own specialised crafts and industries. When the town underwent rapid expansion in the mid to late first century, a large workforce of clerks, craftsmen and labourers, was required to sustain this economic growth. All these Roman Londoners and their families needed somewhere to live in the rapidly expanding town. The majority were probably native Britons drawn to work in the new town, hopeful of making their fortunes. Many of these would have made up the working classes, although specialist craftsmen may have been brought to London from abroad, commissioned for specific works.

Most of the buildings of early Roman London consisted of properties built as long strip-buildings with narrow frontages. Such buildings were common, lining the main road that ran east to west through the northern settlement and to the south, abutting the main road leading to the bridgehead. These narrow structures were probably divided between commercial areas with shops and bars to the front and workshops, stores and residential quarters to the rear. Recent work in London has shown that these timber-framed buildings were made from prefabricated frames of squared oak timbers as base and wall plates. The walls varied between mud brick and wattle-and-daub, either keyed to take plaster or sometimes with additional external timber planking. The stud timbers were either exposed internally or rendered over. They had beaten earth or timber floors and thatched or planked roofs. Without any foundations, bar the timber base-plate, many of these buildings only lasted five to ten years before needing to be replaced due to rising damp. The most likely occupants of these Mediterranean-style buildings were the craft-workers and shopkeepers of the town.

In 2000, *High Street Londinium*, a temporary exhibition held at the Museum of London, attempted to recreate three of these buildings with their shops and workshops, based on the archaeological evidence found at 1 Poultry in 1994 (Hall & Swain 2000; Figure 8.1). Although the excavations at Poultry, and the subsequent exhibition, formed a framework for this paper, the evidence for manufacturing activities in all areas of Roman London, north and south of the river Thames is reviewed in this paper. For the exhibition, the houses reconstructed were identified as a baker's premises, a carpenter's house and a merchant's shop. At Poultry over seventy timber buildings were excavated spanning some 350 years (Map 8.1.1; Rowsome 2000). Many were timber-framed strip-buildings separated by narrow alleyways, with walls preserved up to half a metre in height in the damp conditions. From the site evidence, it was possible to reproduce the exact ground plans and the relationship of one building to another. However, to be able to recreate such buildings in their entirety, it was necessary to look at other London evidence where a considerable number of re-used building timbers have been found on several sites and these have added technical detail to the study of domestic Roman carpentry (Goodburn 1991, 182–204), windows (Rowsome 2000, 34) and window heights (Brigham 2001, 84).

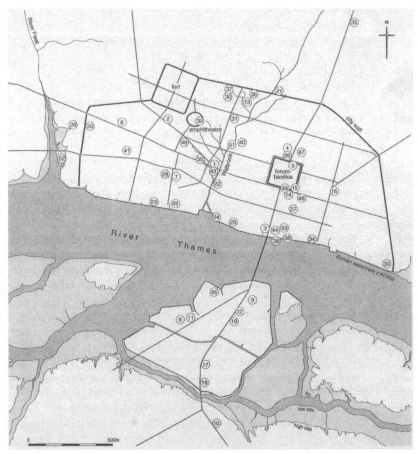

Map 8.1 *Map of Roman London showing the location of sites mentioned in text*

Key to sites and site codes
1. 1 Poultry (ONE94); **2.** 10 Gresham Street (GSM97); **3.** Regis House, King William Street (KWS94); **4.** 7–11 Bishopsgate (ETA89); **5.** Leadenhall Court (LCT84); **6.** 76–81 Newgate Street (GPO75); **7.** Watling Court (WAT78); **8.** Park Street (CO88); **9.** Toppings Wharf (TW70); **10.** Arcadia Buildings, Great Dover Street (AB78); **11.** Courage's Brewery (COSE84); **12.** Borough High Street Ticket Hall (BGH95); **13.** 15–35 Copthall Avenue (KEY83); **14.** 5–12 Fenchurch Street (FEN83); **15.** 21 Lime Street (LME01); **16.** 60 & 63 Fenchurch Street (FNE01); **17.** 106–114 Borough High Street(106BHS73); **18.** 207–211 Borough High Street (207BHS72); **19.** 1–7 St Thomas Street (1STS74); **20.** Central Criminal Court. Old Bailey (GM131); **21.** 85 London Wall (BLM87); **22.** Bucklersbury House, Walbrook (GM157/WFG44/45); **23.** Dominant House, 85 Queen Victoria Street (DMT88); **24.** Cannon Street Station (LYD88); **25.** Suffolk House, 154–156 Upper Thames Street (SUF94); **26.** 62–64 Cornhill (CIL86); **27.** 23–29 Eastcheap (EST83); **28.** Watling House, Watling Street (GM213); **29.** 19–25 Old Bailey (OBT88); **30**. 55–61 Moorgate (MGT87); **31.** Northgate House (MRG95)/20–28 Moorgate (GM119); **32.** Guildhall Yard (GAG87); **33** Inmost Ward, Tower of London; **34.** 84 St Dunstan's Hill (GM163); **35.** Norton Folgate (NRT85); **36.** 60 London Wall (LOW88); **37.** 2–3 Cross Keys Court (OPT81); **38.** Billingsgate Buildings, 101–110 Lower Thames Street (TR74); **39.** New Fresh Wharf (NFW74); **40.** Bank of England (GM257); **41.** St Paul's Cathedral; **42.** Sugar Loaf Court, Garlick Hill (SLO82); **43.** Bucklersbury (BUC87); **44.** Pudding Lane (PDN81); **45.** Winchester Palace (WP83); **46.** 30 Gresham Street (GHT00); **47.** 1–7 Whittington Avenue (WIV88); **48.** Plantation Place, Fenchurch Street (FER97); **49.** 168 Fenchurch Street (GM297); **50.** 72–80 Cheapside (CID90); **51.** Princes Street; **52.** Fleet valley (VAL88); **53.** Peninsular House, Lower Thames Street (PEN79)

By the end of the first century, with perhaps more money and pretentions, some of the strip-buildings included reception areas with painted walls and mortar floors. A timber-framed house excavated at 10 Gresham Street showed a central room with plastered walls and a small mosaic panel with geometric design set in a wide red tessellated border (Map 8.1.2; MoLAS 2002, 32). In the third century, stone-built townhouses replaced these buildings or, as was the case at Poultry, the timber frontages remained with stone extensions to the rear (Rowsome 2000, 42–5), although timber and clay-walled buildings continued in some parts of the town.

These strip-buildings varied in layout, some were double-fronted with central corridors that led from front to back. Entry was from the main wooden boardwalk of the street and the corridors led through the houses to the backyards, which served as rubbish and waste food dumps. Other houses were constructed with three or more rooms, one behind the other, with long corridors running down the side of the buildings. Where the front room consisted of a shop, there were rarely front walls but wooden sills laid out to take removable wooden shutters. Some houses had outhouses in the backyard where the inhabitants would have kept livestock. Where space was at a premium in the centre of town, the houses were separated by narrow alleys, sharing eavesdrips from the roofs and with covered drains that led into larger roadside drains (Rowsome 2000, 26). Most houses were probably single storeyed but some may have had upper floors or utilised the roof space. Others had small cellars where buildings on slopes were terraced to form half-cellars, such as a timber-framed example at Regis House (Map 8.1.3; Brigham & Watson in preparation). A cellar of a late first to early second-century timber-framed structure, excavated at 7–11 Bishopsgate, was reached by a flight of stairs cut into the natural surface (Map 8.1.4; Sankey, forthcoming). Many of the craft-workers would have had family members helping them in construction and their work and these families would have lived in close proximity to each other (Hall & Swain 2000).

Some buildings may have been rented out to several tenants. Behind the early Flavian forum, at Leadenhall Court, narrow single-storey buildings included rooms with small domestic hearths which could have been simple one-room lodgings (Map 8.1.5; Milne 1992, 77). Similar rooms existed behind a strip-building at 76–81 Newgate Street (Map 8.1.6; Figure 8.2) and a better built late first-century building with shallow foundations at Watling Court (Map 8.1.7) may have been divided into apartments (Perring & Roskams 1991, 104–5). Some houses may not have had hearths, indicating that those lodging there had to rely on local hostelries for hot food or the local bakers for cooking their meals. Most houses had rooms with hearths of semi-circular mud brick and plaster structures built against walls or as hollows in the floor. At Poultry, the central room of one of the houses had a hearth, reconstructed in the *High Street Londinium* exhibition, constructed as a hollow in the brickearth floor with a tiled surface beside it, which acted as an adjacent hot-plate, while another hollow was full of food waste. In the corner of the same living room, a greyware pot had been set into the floor for use as a toilet.

Roman London is able to demonstrate that it was well-placed to deliver the various craft outlets and retail facilities needed in a thriving and commercially-orientated town in the first and second centuries. Small-scale workshops continued to be spread throughout the expanding and contracting settlement, north and south of the river and were integral with domestic buildings. While excavations in the central part of the town revealed Roman-style buildings indicating an element of Romanisation, native-style circular structures were also found on the outskirts of the new community. At several sites in the City at 76–81 Newgate Street (Perring & Roskams 1991, 101) and 10 Gresham Street (Ayre in preparation) and at Park Street (Map 8.1.8) and Toppings Wharf (Map 8.1.9) in Southwark (Cowan 2000, 15), circular structures

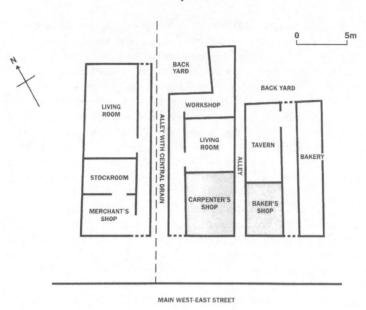

Figure 8.1 *The strip buildings, as laid out at 1 Poultry and reconstructed in High Street Londinium: Building 1 (left), a merchant's shop destroyed in AD60/61; Building 2 (centre), a carpenter's house destroyed by fire in AD100; Building 3 (right), a baker's premises and tavern destroyed by fire in AD100*

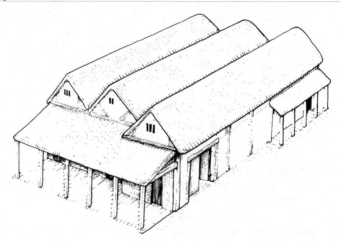

Figure 8.2 *Timber-frame strip buildings fronting onto the main road through Londinium, based on excavations at Newgate Street, London (Reconstruction by Nick Griffiths)*

may have been associated with workshops or open work areas and indicate that some of Roman London's craft-workers must have been indigenous. At 10 Gresham Street, workers were recycling Roman glass (white, dark blue and blue) to produce blue and white native-style

Figure 8.3 *Reconstructed tavern from the High Street Londinium exhibition*

glass beads in the period AD 50–70 (pers. comm. Angela Wardle). At Toppings Wharf, early metal-working debris and later hearths were possibly associated with metal-working (Sheldon 1974, 92–4). Metal-working debris and an Iron-Age form of crucible from Arcadia Buildings in Southwark is thought to be native rather than Roman in origin (Map 8.1.10; Dean 1980, 369).

The evidence for craft-working in Roman London is threefold. Firstly, the site of hearths and workshops indicate where crafts were being practised, pinpointing areas where craft-workers may have congregated together for specific requirements of their trade or industry. Secondly, the material discarded from any craft provides strong evidence that those practical skills must have been practised in London and finally, the tools used by the workers may indicate the craft-worker as a consumer or as the manufacturer of tools supplied to the trade.

The debris from working metals produces the most obvious evidence of workshops and perhaps the clearest indicator has come from a series of excavations on the site of Courage's Brewery, Southwark. The metal-working evidence indicated a service industry, fulfilling the needs of those living on the north island of Southwark (Map 8.1.11; Cowan, forthcoming). On three of the sites, clay and timber houses and less substantial structures had been used for craft production, predominantly metal-working in this industrial area for more than three hundred years. There was evidence for both iron-smithing and copper-alloy working workshops, beginning firstly as open area small-scale iron-smithing, then as metal-working hearths, protected by insubstantial timber-frame shelters. In the early third century, more substantial workshops were constructed with a clear distinction between domestic and workshop buildings. In total, seventy-four hearths were found during the excavations of the workshops with three types of clay-lined hearth found: surface hearths for smithing; bowl hearths (open pits) for iron-smithing or for casting copper alloy and bowl hearths with an open or closed

Figure 8.4 *A hearth set into the floor of the living room of the carpenter's house in High Street Londinium*

superstructure, perhaps used for smelting ores. A great number of the hearths were associated with the production of metal objects either by iron-smithing or by processes of copper-alloy working, annealing or melting, although there was no indication of the range of products (Hammer forthcoming).

In the pre-Boudican period, there were other iron smithies in operation just south of the river, found during excavations at Borough High Street Ticket Hall. A blacksmith's workshop on the same site was later added to the front of some domestic rooms and was perhaps built with a more substantial floor to support the forge and anvil (Map 8.1.12; Drummond-Murray & Thompson 2002, 28). At 15–35 Copthall Avenue in the City, a number of complex hearths, ovens and scorched brickearth floors, confined to one half of the building, suggested that industrial activity was carried out with the other half perhaps used as domestic quarters (Map 8.1.13; Maloney 1990, x). At 5–12 Fenchurch Street, just south of the forum, iron-working took place before the Boudican fire and probably, also on a small scale, in workshops abutting a Flavian hall (Map 8.1.14; Hammer 1987, 6–12) and at 21 Lime Street, in an area of the forum during the second century, metal-smelting slag was found in a shallow pit (Map 8.1.15; MoLAS field project report 2003).

Evidence for mixed iron and copper-alloy working is widespread with crucible fragments occurring in small numbers on most Roman London sites. In the City at 76–81 Newgate Street, there was evidence for small-scale mixed metal-working in first and early second-century buildings (Perring & Roskams 1991, 101). At 60 & 63 Fenchurch Street a series of eight small industrial buildings were associated with both smelting and smithing in the early second century (Map 8.1.16; Wessex Archaeology website 2003). In Southwark, copper-alloy casting and iron-working residues were recorded along the main Roman road at 106–114 (Map 8.1.17)

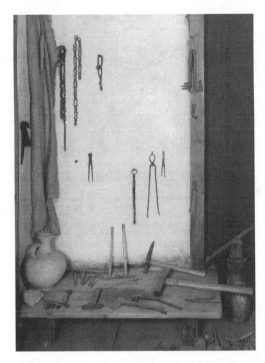

Figure 8.5 *An ironworker's bench and anvil. (Museum of London display)*

and 207–211 Borough High Street (Map 8.1.18; Schwab 1978, 190; Feretti & Graham 1978, 79). A crucible with beads of copper and bronze in the slag on its inner surface was found in 1–7 St Thomas Street (Map 8.1.19) and a bronze bar for working came from Borough High Street (Merrifield 1983, 102).

Although metal-working must have been a legitimate industry (Figure 8.5), there are aspects that could be regarded as either criminal or at least unofficial. Cast coins produced in terracotta moulds have been found on two sites in London. Two moulds for making *denarii* were found with a genuine silver *denarius* of AD 213–217, hidden in rubbish under the stairway of a tower in the city wall at Old Bailey (Map 8.1.20; Merrifield 1983, 160–2). At 85 London Wall over 700 terracotta moulds were found, thrown into the city ditch (Map 8.1.21; Boon 1988, 125–6). These moulds had been stacked into columns and the columns coated in clay to produce a container, similar in form to that shown in Boon (1988, 125–6, fig. 4). Molten metal was poured in and the containers broken open to retrieve the coins. Some of the coins being copied were silver *denarii* spanning the period AD 200–244, using copper with significant levels of zinc and tin. Other moulds were found for copying copper-alloy coins of the mid-third century that used copper with only small traces of zinc and lead. These mid-third century coins were being copied at a time when small change was in short supply and so devalued as to make their value almost worthless. There was, however, no evidence as to where this forging was being practised.

During the Roman period the major industry for producing wrought iron was centred on Sussex and Kent. London was, therefore, an obvious centre for the working of such semi-forged iron into saleable merchandise. In London, numerous tools have all been found in an

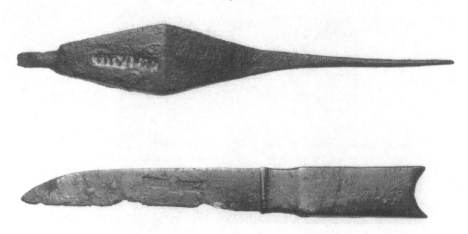

Figure 8.6 *Tools stamped with makers' marks*

excellent state of preservation in the waterlogged layers of the Walbrook stream that ran through the centre of the Roman town. Their presence, mainly from the Bucklersbury House site (Map 8.1.22), has been discussed by Merrifield (1983, 100; 1995, 27–44). Such tools included chisels, gouges, awls and foot-rules, the tools of woodworkers; the tongs, punches, hammers, an anvil, a large furnace bar, the tools of metalworkers; various types of spatulae, the tools of plasterers; lewising-tools and trowels of masons and builders and a wide variety of Knives. Some knives and tools were stamped with makers' names, some names occurring more than once (Collingwood & Wright 1991, 58–62). Four examples of knives made by the cutler Basilis or Basilius with a very distinctive personalised logo have come from different sites in the City (RIB 2428.5–8) with a fifth found more recently at 1 Poultry (pers. comm. Angela Wardle) and Olundus (RIB 2428.14) also made knives. Aprilis (RIB 2428.2) and Martialis (RIB 2428.12–13) stamped their chisels, Titulus, a leatherworker's iron awl (RIB 2428.16) and Bonosus (RIB 2428.9) and Reginus (RIB 2428.15), iron styli (Figure 8.6). They may all have been local toolmakers.

The working of tin and lead alloys in the Walbrook area is suggested by a number of domestic and tableware items (Jones 1983, 49–59) and by assorted waste (Beagrie 1989, 189). From Dominant House in Queen Victoria Street (Map 8.1.23), a stackable stone mould was for the production of lead-alloy bowls and another mould from Cannon Street Station (Map 8.1.24) was for the production of metal vessels with decorative rims (pers. comm. Jackie Keilly). Lead ingots were found buried under the floor of a Flavian waterfront warehouse at Regis House (Brigham 1998, 27–9), while lead-alloy ingots of forth century date, were found in the nineteenth century (Collingwood & Wright 1990, 68–70, RIB 2406.1–10) in the Thames at Battersea and another two more recently on the foreshore (Tomlin & Hassall 1998, 438) in the same area. Thus, the raw materials were travelling through London and would have been available to the London metalworkers.

There were also craft-workers working precious metals. Crucibles for refining gold were found in late Flavian pits under Cannon Street Station near Suffolk Lane (Marsden 1975, 9–12) and more recently at the adjacent site of Suffolk House (Map 8.1.25; Brigham 2001, 116–20). The gold-working material from both sites provided evidence for stages in gold processing; for the cupellation of gold in small crucibles; the process of gold parting in larger vessels, a

Figure 8.7 *A glassworking workshop (Reconstruction by Derek Lucas)*

refining process that separated gold from the other metals and the melting of gold in crucibles before being made into ingots. Crucibles, sealed with strips of clay stamped with lions and boars, ensured that no gold was accidentally lost during the refining process (Marsden 1975, 100–2). In St Thomas Street, Southwark (Sheldon 1978, 31) traces of gold on crucible fragments and a possible segment of blow-pipe were found. There is no direct evidence for work in other precious metals except at 15–35 Copthall Avenue where three out of five crucibles found were probably used for melting debased silver. Another crucible had been used for refining small quantities of silver, while the final crucible had been used for melting gold (Maloney 1990, 84). A broken crucible containing liquid mercury for soldering, found resting on a hearth set in the floor of a building at 62–64 Cornhill, suggests decorative gold smithing (Map 8.1.26; Schofield & Maloney 1998, 225).

As goldsmiths were operating in the Cannon Street and Cornhill areas, Henig (1984, 14) has suggested that perhaps the area south of the centre, towards the river was the enclave of craft-workers in luxury products. Associated with such working, the workshops of the gemcutters might have been sited near to the goldsmiths' workshops. A cache of four intaglios from Eastcheap (Map 8.1.27; Henig 1984, 11–5) may be evidence for a specialist foreign *gemmarius* resident in London. Engraved and unmounted, they were found under the floor of a timber building destroyed in the Boudican fire. A second-century gem workshop may have also operated at 1–7 St Thomas Street in Southwark where a shaped but unfinished carnelian may have been from the stock of a gemcutter (Dennis 1978, 402–3).

Evidence of glass-working, consisting of glass-coated burnt clay and waste glass, has been recorded in several areas of the town. The evidence was brought together and discussed by Shepherd and Heyworth (1991, 13–22). Shepherd identified five areas at different dates. Pre-

Figure 8.8 *Leatherworkers cutting out leather and making shoes (Reconstruction by Derek Lucas)*

Flavian glass debris at Watling House/Watling Street suggested that early workshops existed nearby (Map 8.1.28; Shepherd 1986, 141–3). More recently, on the waterfront at Regis House a first-century warehouse bay was used as a glass workshop (Figure 8.7). The workshop included a short succession of small furnaces and considerable quantities of waste and broken products (Brigham 1989, 27 & note 7). Late first century glass-working debris was found at 19–25 Old Bailey (Map 8.1.29) but most evidence is centred in the northern part of the town in the second century. At 15–35 Copthall Avenue, in the upper Walbrook, a substantial quantity of residual furnace-lining was found in late first to early second century levels (Maloney 1990, 82) and at 55–61 Moorgate, part of a glass-working kiln or tank furnace, dated to AD 140–160 (Map 8.1.30; Schofield & Maloney 1998, 252–3). Recent finds at Northgate House, Moorgate (Map 8.1.31) have revealed further tank furnaces of different construction, blowing waste and waste vessels (cullet) collected for recycling, dating to the early second century (pers. comm. Jackie Keilly). To the east of the amphitheatre at Guildhall Yard very extensive dumps of early second-century cullet were found (Map 8.1.32; Bateman 1997, 67 & note 86) with evidence of glassblowing waste but no workshop. At the Inmost Ward/Tower of London (Map 8.1.33) and 84 St Dunstans Hill (Map 8.1.34) two dumps of glass-working debris of late second or third century date were recorded while a third-century dump was found beyond the city wall at Norton Folgate (Map 8.1.35; Shepherd & Heyworth 1991, 15). Shepherd concluded that the glass-working evidence showed that the manufacturing processes were located on the peripheries of the town or on low quality land alongside other crafts and industries. Furthermore, it would appear that there was only one glass workshop active at any one time.

Whether these were permanent establishments or temporary, perhaps seasonal, sites is still open to debate (pers. comm. John Shepherd).

Although the evidence for Roman London's workshops is limited to metal or glass-working processes, other craft workshops must have also existed. Many would have formed part of domestic buildings where their identification is made more difficult. Often, it is only the discarded material that may help to identify the workplace. The carpenter's house from 1 Poultry and reconstructed in *High Street Londinium*, for example, was suggested by the quantity of wooden off-cuts in the room to the rear of the house, rather than by any tools (Figure 8.4; Rowsome 2000, 28). That room had been enlarged with a later lean-to extension perhaps to provide more room for the workshop. Unfortunately, there were no tools left behind when the house was destroyed by fire in the Hadrianic period.

Leather-working which was clearly one of Roman London's most important industries. Access to a good water supply must have attracted leather-workers' workshops to the area of the Walbrook stream. Vast quantities of dumped leather from reclamation dumps, from all over the whole Walbrook area, suggest that leather workshops were situated close-by in the first and second centuries (Figure 8.8). At Bucklersbury House skins were found pegged out on a hut floor, indicating tanning (Grimes 1968, 97). At 60 London Wall in the upper Walbrook valley, wood-lined tanks and channels may also have been used for tanning, fulling and dyeing (Map 8.1.36; Lees & Woodger 1990, 18) and due to the use of urine for the tanning process, perhaps such workshops were sited away from normal habitation because of odious smells.

The evidence for one aspect of leather-working, that of shoe-making, has been found in quantity. Pieces of leather and incomplete shoes and cobblers' tools were found at 60 London Wall and nearby pits may have been used for processing hides to prepare them for cutting out into shoes (Lees & Woodger 1990, 17–8). At 2–3 Cross Keys Court, hundreds of leather off-cuts survived, probably waste from shoemaking, indicate that a workshop lay nearby (Map 8.1.37; Maloney 1990, 82). Numerous leather-working tools, awls and punches have been found in the Walbrook (Manning 1985, 39–41 and Museum of London, unpublished). Dumped waterfront material, at both Billingsgate Buildings (Map 8.1.38; Jones 1980, 99–128) and St Magnus House/New Fresh Wharf (Map 8.1.39; Miller *et al* 1986, 218–26), has produced further evidence for shoes. Other leather products such as briefcases from Poultry (pers. comm. Carol van Driel Murray) and other Walbrook sites and furniture with leather covers would have been made and purchased locally. Small leather off-cuts displayed tanners' marks and various pieces of leather had names incised or stamped motifs (Collingwood & Wright 1992, 28–42) and it is possible that Liber (RIB 2445.7), Burdonius (RIB 2445.22), Lucius Ursius (RIB 2445.32), Sammius (RIB 2445.35) and Verus (RIB 2445.39) were local leatherworkers.

Evidence for large-scale textile production in London is uncertain. However, spindles of wood and bone and spindle whorls of ceramic, bone and stone are common on many sites. Iron shears for trimming fleeces have been found in the Walbrook and iron wool combs at 5–12 Fenchurch Street and elsewhere (Museum of London, unpublished). A large clay-lined wooden tank found at Poultry may have been part of a fulling and dyeing mill where spun cloth was sent for treatment (Rowsome 2000, 29). The discovery of bone weaving tablets supports the local production of braids with evidence for tablet weaving in London as early as the late first century AD. A rectangular tablet, heavily worn around its four holes came from a building at 5–12 Fenchurch Street and two triangular bone tablets came from the Bank of England (Map 8.1.40). From the wear patterns, it has been possible to discern that they had been used for weaving (Pritchard 1994, 157–61).

Figure 8.9 *Carpenters at work (Reconstruction by Derek Lucas)*

Evidence for the craft of bone-working, a by-product of the butchery trade, is shown by small amounts of worked bone occurring on many sites and not in specific areas of the town, except in the upper Walbrook area. At Cross Keys Court, numbers of adult cattle scapulae (29 worked and a further 46 sawn fragments) were recovered which had been cut to remove flat plates from the blades, not only for mounts and inserts (Maloney 1990, 82) but also for triangular weaving tablets where further evidence of an unfinished weaving tablet and one that had broken during manufacture was found associated with the off-cuts (Pritchard 1994, 157). Waste from pin or needle production was found in Fenchurch Street as well as possible weaving tablet and die production (Brigham & Bluer in preparation). Antler-working was carried out on the Courage's Brewery site in Southwark where combs and knife handles were being made (Cowan 2000, 18). Another by-product of the butchery trade was found at 60 London Wall where a large number of chopped and broken bones were found, suggesting fat or oil extraction or glue manufacture (Lees & Woodger 1990, 32).

It seems likely that there was a pottery industry along the north side of Newgate Street where temporary pottery kilns were set up on the fringes of the city. Several Flavian kilns were recorded behind the ribbon development along the east-west road (Marsden 1969, 39–44) and kilns, recorded by John Conyers and found during the construction of St Paul's Cathedral in 1672 (Map 8.1.41), were probably part of this group. Pottery and 'wasters' from a Neronian kiln found at Sugar Loaf Court/Garlick Hill may have been operated by Caius Albucius, an immigrant potter from Lyons or western Switzerland (Map 8.1.42; Davies *et al* 1994, 29–34). Deposits of coarseware wasters at 20–28 Moorgate in 1936 suggested kilns in the Moorgate

Figure 8.10 *A mosaicist's workshop (Reconstruction by Paul Sharp)*

area (Marsh & Tyers 1976, 228) and two circular kilns uncovered nearby at Northgate House in 1999, were contemporary with the glass furnaces, discussed above. Here potters, including Lucius, Valentinus and Maximus, were making a wide range of mainly mica-dusted vessels, including lamps, lids, bowls and dishes in the early second century (MoLAS 2002, 55). Much of London's pottery in the first and second centuries, however, was supplied from kilns outside London at Brockley Hill and Highgate Woods or imported from abroad so any local kilns must have been for relatively small-scale production only.

Construction sites must have been a common feature of town life. Although the public buildings were built on a grand scale, many of the domestic houses were small and densely packed in need of constant repair and replacement. The timber remains of the houses themselves and the numerous tools found in the Walbrook stream provide evidence of the building trade. The prefabricated timber-framed domestic structures have been discussed above but other buildings were constructed using split logs, a native construction technique (Lees & Woodger 1990, 20). Such buildings would have required teams of woodworkers and carpenters and it seems likely that two groups of carpenters were working in London, one of local craftsmen and the other of foreign itinerant workmen introducing Mediterranean techniques in the first century (Figure 8.9).

Other woodworkers were busy in the town, providing many items of smaller-scale wooden articles such as fencing, furniture, dough troughs and boxes. A possible furniture-maker's shop may have existed at Bucklersbury, near Poultry (Map 8.1.43; Rowsome 2000, 26). On the waterfront at Pudding Lane, off-cuts of wooden barrels may indicate refashioning into smaller artefacts in the first and early second century (Map 8.1.44; Milne 1985, 27). Other wood-working industries on the waterfront may have included shipbuilding and ship repair. Although no such evidence has been found, a writing tablet from London refers to shipbuilding (Merrifield 1983, 99).

Figure 2.11 *The merchant's shop from the High Street Londinium exhibition*

Plastering and decorating would also have been important crafts, since even the humblest of dwellings were plastered inside and out. The tools of plasterers have been found in the Walbrook (Manning 1985, 31–2 and Museum of London, unpublished) and evidence for a paint pot in Park Street, Southwark (MacKenna & Ling 1991, 171 note 23). The vast majority of painted work was basic and mainly consisted of simple panel designs but fine decorated wall paintings provide evidence for highly-skilled wall painters. The paintings executed in the second-century bath-house at Winchester Palace in Southwark (Map 8.1.45; MacKenna & Ling 1991, 159–71), comparable with examples from towns such as Pompeii and Cologne, and the tantalising figural fragments from dumped building material in 30 Gresham Street (Map 8.1.46; MoLAS 2002, 31) indicate specialist workers, possibly from abroad in the second century.

Other craftsmen were needed for creating the floors of the richer houses and public buildings. A mosaic floor from Watling Court reflected the mid-first century tradition popular in Italy and was undoubtedly laid by Gaulish or Italian workers (Perring & Roskams 1991, 92). A quantity of small, apparently unused *tesserae*, were found in a late first-century warehouse at Regis House may represent the stock of a mosaic worker (Brigham & Watson in preparation). Quantities of loose *tesserae*, found in a building at Whittington Avenue (Map 8.1.47; Schofield & Maloney 1998, 287–8), adjacent to the forum and at nearby Plantation Place/Fenchurch Street (Map 8.1.48; MoLAS 2001, 26–7), may be the stock-piles of mosaic workers. Mosaic schools may have operated in London in the late first to early second centuries and again in the mid to late third century (Figure 8.10; Jones 1988, 10–11).

The tile-making industry, in part, was probably under state control and was one of the responsibilities of the procurator. The distribution of procuratorial tiles, stamped PPBR or similar, was densely concentrated in London itself and mainly confined to London's major public buildings (Collingwood & Wright 1993, 29–33). Publicly controlled tile-makers kept up a plentiful supply for the intensive building programme that was taking place in London. A study of the Roman tiles from London indicates that the tiles were probably made in kilns scattered around London but their sites are as yet unlocated (Betts 1995, 207–29). Some tiles show evidence of workers' signatures as they were probably paid piece-rate in the yards for the

Figure 8.12 *Wooden troughs from the baker's premises, reconstructed in the High Street Londinium exhibition*

number of tiles made each day. One tile cites tile-maker, Austalis, for worker absenteeism (Collingwood & Wright 1993, 138, RIB 2491.147). Private tile-makers were also supplying the building trade and the two Decimi were probably freedmen who made tiles locally in their own tile kilns (Collingwood & Wright 1993, 60–1, RIB 2489.13 A-E).

Evidence for the shopkeepers of Roman London is harder to define. Little is left in the shops to show what goods were being sold. A shop at 1 Poultry, destroyed in the Boudican fire and reconstructed in *High Street Londinium*, however, indicated the shop of a merchant selling a variety of goods (Figure 8.11; Map 8.1.1). The archaeological evidence showed that the shop had been stocked with South Gaulish samian bowls and Central Gaulish green glazed vessels. The fire had caused the newly-constructed shop's wooden shelves to collapse and wooden and bone spoons were found on the floor mixed with wooden beads and imported spices (Rowsome 2000, 22). The contents of the shop must have meant a sizable capital outlay for the shopkeeper. The building consisted of a long strip-building with the shop fronting the road, with no front wall and probable wooden shutters. It had been constructed as a timber-frame building with plastered over wattle and daub walls. Behind the shop lay two further rooms with a corridor running from front to back on the eastern side. The central room had acted as the storeroom and stacks of bowls were found lying on the floor of the room. The back room had an unusual feature in that a well had been sunk into the floor. Normally wells were sited in backyards, in open areas for public use or were of a size to warrant a machine-operated bucket chain as at 30 Gresham Street (Blair 2002, 509–16).

Shopkeeper's premises ranged along the town's roads and in the waterfront area. As successive waterfronts extended into the river, so some of the earlier stone warehouses were modified to become shops (Milne 1985, 30) in the mid to late second century. At 60 & 63 Fenchurch Street an early second century timber-framed building fronting onto the road had a line of large amphorae set into the floor of the front room (Wessex Archaeology website 2003). There is abundant evidence, however, for milling, baking and butchery in the town and bakeries have been found throughout the City and Southwark. In Southwark, after the

Boudican destruction, a butcher's shop and a bakery were constructed at Borough High Street and the bakery may also have served as a granary (Drummond-Murray & Thompson 2002, 28–31). In the area around the forum, grain deposits (burnt in the Boudican revolt) and three late first century tiled bread ovens were found at 168 Fenchurch Street (Map 8.1.49; Philp 1977, 17) and more recently at 60 & 63 Fenchurch Street (Wessex Archaeology website 2003). Flavian grain deposits were also found near the waterfront at Regis House (Brigham & Watson in preparation).

The bakery from 1 Poultry, reconstructed for *High Street Londinium,* fronted onto the main road and had shutters that opened onto the street (Figure 8.12; Map 8.1.1). The building was double-fronted with a central corridor. It was timber-framed with mud brick infills for the walls. No evidence for hearths was found internally but a hearth had been built into the outside wall of the building in the back yard and there may have been an insubstantial awning to protect it from the elements. The discarded remains of two wooden troughs for kneading dough were found and quantities of bran on the floors indicated the fine sieving of flour (Rowsome 2000, 27).

Adjacent to the original building at Poultry was a domed double-oven (Rowsome 2000, 27) and nearby, over 1000 fragments of lava quernstone and donkey mills were found reused as paving around a water tank (Rowsome 2000, 30). Millstones, querns and burnt grain were also found due west in the Cheapside area, in buildings destroyed in the Boudican fire (Map 8.1.50; Hill & Woodger 1999, 52; Shepherd 1987, 31–3). This whole area must have been devoted to milling and flour production, as a large part of a donkey mill was also found in the Walbrook in Princes Street in 1928 (Map 8.1.51; Merrifield 1965, 240–1 & pl. 106). The canalisation of the lower Walbrook and a large millstone of German lava may indicate the site of a watermill (Marsden 1980, 72). An early second century building on an eyot adjacent to the east bank of the River Fleet outside the town, may also have been a water-mill (Map 8.1.52; Schofield & Maloney 1998, 284). These various milling establishments must have produced large quantities of flour in order to supply the town.

Near the waterfronts in the City and Southwark, timber tanks, possibly used for the production of fish sauce and an amphora containing a residue of locally-produced fish sauce (Milne 1985, 87) indicate a small-scale fish-processing industry. At Peninsular House, a quayside deposit contained a high concentration of many thousands of young herring and sprats, all local fish perhaps being used in the production of fish sauce in the late third or early fourth century (Map 8.1.53; Bateman & Lockyer 1982, 204–7). Very large quantities of oysters were found at Pudding Lane and Regis House where there were thick layers of shells. These may have been processed for local consumption but it seems likely that they were also shipped further afield (Milne 1985, 91–5).

Conclusion

There is, therefore, a substantial body of evidence for large-scale manufacturing activities in certain areas of the town and the town can be divided into residential, commercial and industrial areas of activity (Perring 1991, 94). As most of the surviving evidence is of first and second century date, often due to preservation of organic materials in the Walbrook valley, it is difficult to be certain whether many of the crafts and industries continued until the end of Roman occupation. Perring points out that the later second century is demonstrably a turning point in the provincial economy (1991, 84–9). The town, following its massive expansion in the late first and early second centuries and dependence on imported goods, contracted and changed in character over the third and fourth centuries with more of a regard for provincial self-sufficiency. In the third century, wealthier houses were rebuilt in stone but the working classes still continued to live in the same style timber-frame houses of the earlier periods. Buildings in large areas of the town, however, were dismantled and left as open areas. While a smaller urban population needed less commodities and, as a consequence, less tradesmen and workers to serve its needs, the upgrading of the houses required specialist craftsmen to produce wall paintings and mosaic floors.

Early activities may have been affected by the town's rapid expansion and moved out to remain beyond the town's boundaries. In the northern settlement, large areas of industrial activity lay to the west and north of the main area of habitation. There were Flavian pottery kilns to the west in the Newgate Street area and second century kilns at Moorgate. The Moorgate kilns competed with the more rural production centres at Brockley Hill and Highgate Woods. They, in their turn, ceased production in the late second century and pottery was later being supplied to London from Oxford and Surrey.

The major activities of glass and leather-working were sited to the north in the Moorgate area, centred around the upper reaches of the Walbrook stream in the City, where large early second century cullet dumps for recycling glass and vast quantities of first and second century leather shoes and working waste have been found. This may suggest some water may have been needed in the manufacturing process or that those particular craftsmen were the first to make use of what was a damp and undesirable area for housing. When the Walbrook silted up in the third century, the area was taken over and redeveloped for domestic housing. Leather-working areas may have moved to where water was still available while the third century shoes found in waterfront dumps provide proof that shoes were still being manufactured in London. This whole area, therefore, may have acted as an industrial corridor separating the town from the military zone of the fort in the second century (pers. comm. John Shepherd).

Perring suggests that in the later Roman period, most larger-scale manufacturing centres were rural in order to avoid the increasing burden of taxation of urban facilities (1991, 89). This could well apply to the areas in the north of the town. On the other hand, the large-scale metal-working industries in Southwark were sited away from the main settlement and hearths and workshops continued in the area for over three hundred years. Although evidence for small-scale working continued throughout the whole settlement, indicating that various craftsmen perhaps acquired the raw or semi-worked materials to work up for their own purposes, the large manufacturing areas appear to have disappeared as little evidence for their continuation has been found.

Acknowledgements
An important summary on the state of knowledge of Roman London was drawn together by Perring & Brigham (2000, 138–43) and this overview makes due acknowledgement here to that work. However, an overview such as this can only be made possible by the continuing work on excavations in London and by all those involved in post-excavation artefactual research and it has not always been possible to include all the evidence. My special thanks go to Jackie Keily and Angela Wardle of the Museum of London Specialist Services and John Shepherd of the London Archaeological Archive and Research Centre both for information prior to publication but especially for their advice and comments on the contents of this paper.

Bibliography
Ayre, J. in preparation. Excavations at 10 Gresham Street, London.
Bateman, N. & Lockyer, A. 1982. 'The sauce of the Thames', *London Archaeologist* 4.8: 204–7
Bateman, N.C.W. 1997. 'The London amphitheatre excavations 1987–1996', *Britannia* 28: 51–86
Beagrie, N. 1989. 'The Romano-British Pewter Industry', *Britannia* 20: 169–91
Betts, I. 1995. 'Procuratorial tile stamps from London', *Britannia* 26: 207–29
Blair, I. 2002. 'Roman London's waterworks', *Current Archaeology* 180: 509–16
Boon, G. 1988. 'Counterfeit coins in Roman Britain', in Casey, J. & Reece, R. (eds) *Coins and the Archaeologist*. Batsford, London
Brigham, T. 1989. 'The Port of Roman London', in Watson, B. (ed) *Roman London: recent archaeological work*. Journal of Roman Archaeology Supplementary Series 24, Portsmouth: 23–34
Brigham, T. 2001. *Roman and Medieval Townhouses on the London Waterfront*. Museum of London Archaeology Service Monograph 9, London.
Brigham, T. & Bluer, R. in preparation. *Excavations at Lloyds Registry, Fenchurch Street, London.*
Brigham, T. & Watson, B. in preparation. *Excavations at Regis House, City of London, 1994–1996.*
Collingwood, R.G. & Wright, R.P. 1990. *The Roman Inscriptions of Britain* (Vol. 2 Fasc. 1). Gloucester, Sutton: 68–70
Collingwood, R.G. & Wright, R.P. 1991. *The Roman Inscriptions of Britain* (Vol. 2 Fasc. 3). Gloucester, Sutton: 58–62
Collingwood, R.G. & Wright, R.P. 1992. *The Roman Inscriptions of Britain* (Vol. 2 Fasc. 4). Gloucester, Sutton: 28–42
Collingwood, R.G. & Wright, R.P. 1993. *The Roman Inscriptions of Britain* (Vol. 2 Fasc. 5). Gloucester, Sutton: 30–40, 60–1 and 138
Cowan, C. 2000. *Below Southwark: the archaeological story*. Southwark Council, London.
Cowan, C. forthcoming. *The Development of North-west Roman Southwark: excavations at Courage's Brewery, 1974–90*. Museum of London Archaeology Service Monograph Series, London.
Davies, B., Richardson, B. & Tomber, R. 1994. *A Dated Corpus of Early Roman Pottery from the City of London*. Council for British Archaeology, London.
Dean, M. 1980. 'Excavations at Arcadia Buildings, Southwark', *London Archaeologist* 3.14: 367–73
Dennis, G. 1978. '1–7 St Thomas Street', in *Southwark Excavations 1972–1974* (Vol. 2). London & Middlesex Archaeological Society & Surrey Archaeological Society Joint Publication 1: 291–422
Drummond-Murray, J. & Thompson, P. 2002. *Settlement in Roman Southwark: archaeological excavations (1991–8) for the London Underground Limited Jubilee Line Extension Project*. Museum of London Archaeology Service Monograph Series 12, London.
Feretti, E. & Graham, A. 1978. '210–211 Borough High Street', in *Southwark Excavations 1972–1974* (Vol. 2). London & Middlesex Archaeology Society & Surrey Archaeological Society Joint Publication 1: 53–176
Goodburn, D. 1991. 'A Roman timber-framed building tradition', *Archaeological Journal* 148: 182–204
Grimes, W.F. 1968. *The Excavation of Roman and Mediaeval London*. Routledge & Kegan Paul, London
Hall, J. & Swain, H. 2000. *High Street Londinium*. Museum of London, London.
Hammer, F. 1987. 'A Roman basilical hall and associated buildings at Fenchurch Street', *Archaeology Today* 89: 6–12
Hammer, F. forthcoming. *Industry in North-west Roman Southwark: excavations at Courage's Brewery 1984–8*. Museum of London Archaeology Service Monograph Series, London.
Henig, M. 1984. 'A cache of roman intaglios from Eastcheap, City of London', *Transactions London & Middlesex Archaeological Society* 35: 11–15
Hill, J. & Woodger, A. 1999. *Excavations at 72–75 Cheapside/ 83–93 Queen Street City of London*. Museum of London Archaeology Service Archaeology Studies Series 2, London.
Jones, D.M. 1980. *Excavations at Billingsgate Buildings 'Triangle', Lower Thames Street, 1974*. London & Middlesex Archaeological Society Special Paper 4, London.

Jones, C.E.E. 1983. 'A review of Roman Lead-alloy Material Recovered from the Walbrook Valley in the City of London', *Transactions London & Middlesex Archaeological Society* 34: 49–59

Jones, C.E.E. 1988. *Roman Mosaics*. Museum of London, London.

Lees, D. & Woodger, A. 1990. *The Archaeology and History of 60 London Wall London EC2*. Museum of London, London.

MacKenna, S.A. & Ling, R. 1991. 'Wall paintings from the Winchester Palace site, Southwark', *Britannia* 22: 159–71

Maloney, C. 1990. *The Upper Walbrook Valley in the Roman Period*. Council for British Archaeology, London.

Manning W.H. 1985. *Catalogue of the Romano-British Iron Tools, Fittings and Weapons in the British Museum*. British Museum, London.

Marsden, P. 1969. 'The Roman pottery industry of London', *Transactions London & Middlesex Archaeology Society* 22 part 2: 39–44

Marsden, P. 1975. 'The excavation of a Roman palace site in London, 1961–1978', *Transactions London & Middlesex Archaeology Society* 26: 1–102

Marsden, P. 1980. *Roman London*. Thames & Hudson, London.

Marsh, G. & Tyers, P. 1976. 'Roman pottery from the City of London', *Transactions London & Middlesex Archaeology Society* 27: 228–44

Merrifield, R. 1965. *The Roman City of London*. Benn, London.

Merrifield, R. 1983. *London City of the Romans*. Batsford, London.

Merrifield, R. 1995. 'Roman metalwork from the Walbrook – rubbish, ritual or redundancy?', *Transactions London & Middlesex Archaeology Society* 46: 27–44

Miller, L., Schofield, J. & Rhodes, M. 1986. *The Roman Quay at St Magnus House, London: Excavations at New Fresh Wharf, Lower Thames Street, London 1974–78*. London & Middlesex Archaeology Society Special Paper 8, London

Milne, G. 1985. *The Port of Roman London*. Batsford, London.

Milne, G. 1992. *From Roman Basilica to Medieval Market: archaeology in action in the City of London*. HMSO, London.

MoLAS 2001. *Annual review for 2000*. Museum of London Archaeology Service, London.

MoLAS 2002. *Annual review for 2001*. Museum of London Archaeology Service, London.

Perring, D. 1991. *Roman London*. Seaby, London.

Perring, D. & Brigham, T. 2000. 'Londinium and its hinterland: The Roman period' in *The Archaeology of Greater London*. Museum of London, London: 119–70

Perring, D. & Roskams, S. 1991. *Early Development of Roman London West of the Walbrook*. Council for British Archaeology, London.

Philp, B.J. 1977. 'The forum of Roman London: excavations of 1968–9', *Britannia* 8: 1–64

Pritchard, F. 1994. 'Weaving Tablets from Roman London', in Jaacks, G. & Tidow, K. (eds) *Archaeological Textiles*. Textilsymposium Neuminster (NESAT V): 157–61

Rowsome, P. 2000. *Heart of the City*. Museum of London, London.

Sankey, D. forthcoming. *Roman, Medieval and Later Development at 7 Bishopsgate, London EC2*.

Schofield, J. & Maloney, C. 1998. *Archaeology in the City of London 1907–1991: a guide to the records of excavations by the Museum of London and its predecessors*. Museum of London Archaeological Gazetteer Series 1, London.

Schwab, I. 1978. '106–114 Borough High Street', in *Southwark Excavations 1972–1974*. London & Middlesex Archaeological Society & Surrey Archaeological Society Joint Publication 1: 177–220

Sheldon, H.L. 1974. 'Excavations at Toppings and Sun Wharves, Southwark, 1970–72', *Transactions London & Middlesex Archaeological Society* 25: 1–116

Sheldon, H.L. 1978. 'The 1972–74 excavations: their contribution to Southwark's history', in *Southwark Excavations 1972–1974*. London & Middlesex Archaeological Society & Surrey Archaeological Society Joint Publication 1: 11–49

Shepherd, J.D. 1986. 'The Roman features at Gateway House and Watling House, Watling Street, City of London (1954)', *Transactions London & Middlesex Archaeological Society* 37: 125–44

Shepherd, J.D. 1987. 'The pre-urban and Roman topography in the King Street and Cheapside areas of the City of London', *Transactions London & Middlesex Archaeological Society* 38: 11–60

Shepherd, J. & Heyworth, M. 1991. 'Le travail du verre dans Londres Romain (Londinium): un etat de la question', in Foy, D. & Sennequier, G. (eds) *Ateliers de Verriers de l'antiquité à la période pré-industrielle.* Association Française pour l'Archéologie du Verre, Rouen.

Tomlin, R. & Hassall, M. 1998. 'Inscriptions', *Britannia* 29: 438–9

9

Pottery in urban Romano-British life

Jeremy Evans

This paper intends to look at the use of pottery in urban Romano-British contexts and to offer some general comments on Romano-British urban manufacture, consumption and retailing of ceramics.

The first obvious point worth making, although the author has little good quantitative evidence to back it up, is that urban pottery use in Roman Britain is not like urban pottery use in the core of the classical world, around the Mediterranean, and particularly unlike that in the eastern Mediterranean and the Near East. Ceramics are much more ubiquitous and the types of vessels used are quite different.

In part the difference in the scale of pottery use may be accounted for by the massively larger quantities of amphorae in Mediterranean assemblages, but even if these are excluded quantities of pottery vessels are still several orders of magnitude larger on Mediterranean sites. Taphonomic factors may also be cited to explain these differences. Certainly in the eastern Mediterranean pottery seems to have been used as hard-core in many deposits, suggesting domestic waste was rapidly removed from domestic contexts, sorted and the ceramic element re-cycled for this purpose. Given the hot summer climate, and the comparatively low quantities of animal bone from such contexts, this seems probable (and also implies that most pottery particularly in eastern Mediterranean cities comes from contexts divorced from where it was originally used). However, it still seems highly probable that ceramic use was much more intense in the Mediterranean than in the north-west provinces.

Mediterranean ceramic use also encompassed wide use of functional types very rarely found in Roman Britain, along with the near absence of some types commonly found in Britain and elsewhere in the north-west provinces. Thus *mortaria*, often seen in the north-west provinces as an archetypical Roman type, are often almost completely absent from Mediterranean assemblages (Hartley 1998), whilst casseroles, and their accompanying braziers, are a very frequent type in the south and east Mediterranean provinces but are barely found in the north-west provinces, except for occasional examples such as ones used by the African units deployed in northern Britain (Swan 1992).

Thus, ceramic use varies considerably, even in an urban context, across the Empire and the interpretations offered here for a Romano-British context are not necessarily valid elsewhere.

What is urban?

For the purposes of this examination all nucleated settlements which do not appear to have been primarily involved in agriculture or to be solely military are regarded as 'urban'. This means that 'urban' includes 'public towns' and 'small towns', but not nucleated rural sites, that is villages such as Catsgore (Leech 1982). The position of military *vici* and supply centres will be discussed further below.

Urban manufacture

There is quite a lot of evidence for the production of ceramics at urban centres. *Prima facie* this would seem economically rational since the urban population would provide a consistent and concentrated market in its own right, as well as, potentially, providing markets from which products could be distributed throughout its economic hinterland. The former seems reasonably true, but the latter proves to have some major exceptions. In what for ease of use will be described as the 'highland zone' there are a number of towns which, at least in ceramic terms, and probably in many others to judge by the finds assemblages from sites in their 'hinterlands', do not appear to have had an economic hinterland.

Places such as Wroxeter, which supported a local pottery industry, seem to have had precious little of a rural market to judge by the very low quantities of ceramics from rural sites in its vicinity (Gaffney *et al.* forthcoming; White & Gaffney 2003). Similarly Catterick, despite supporting a series of local pottery industries from the first to the fourth centuries, seems to have had virtually no rural market for ceramics in the first to mid third centuries, and a fairly weak one even after that (Evans forthcoming a). Most ceramics produced here, which were marketed beyond the town itself, seem to have travelled north to military sites or the town/*vicus* at Piercebridge. Other 'urban' sites of a similar nature might include Corbridge and Carlisle. The functioning of these towns does demonstrate that an urban market alone is capable of supporting a small pottery industry – although whether such potters were employed full-time at the craft or merely using it as a supplement to another meagre living is uncertain.

Urban based industries were sometimes fairly large in scale, of which the best example may be Colchester, with an industry that included large scale mortaria production, and colour-coated roughcast beakers. The mortaria can be found across the north (Tyers 1996, fig. 111) as can be seen by the distribution of second century Colchester mortaria stamps and the mortaria themselves. Colchester also briefly produced samian ware, although it does not appear to have been made in large quantities, nor to have travelled so far as the mortaria (Tyers 1996, fig. 102).

Although urban-based pottery industries were fairly common, rural-based ones were more so. This particularly becomes the case in the later Roman period, where, particularly from the mid third century onwards, a small series of rural industries grow to dominate pottery supply on a regional scale, generally as fineware and specialist producers, but also, in some cases, as coarseware suppliers (for the former see the Oxfordshire (Young 1977) and New Forest (Fulford 1974) industries and for the latter see Alice Holt (Lyne & Jefferies 1979), Crambeck (Evans 1989) and Harrold (Brown 1994; Evans 2001, fig. 7.55). This trend is by no means universal and there were large-scale rural-based industries from the first century onwards, such as Black Burnished Category 1 (hereafter BB1) at Poole Harbour (Sunter & Woodward 1987; Farrar 1973; Williams 1977) and Severn Valley wares (Webster 1976), and fairly large-scale urban industries did occur in the late Roman period, as at Swanpool near Lincoln (Webster & Booth 1947).

Millett (1990, fig. 52) published an interesting study by Saunders (1986) plotting the distance of pottery kiln from urban sites by period from data in Swan (1984) which nicely demonstrated the trend to ruralization of pottery production through the Romano-British period. The reasons for this are not clear. Given the requirements for potting, access to firewood or charcoal was certainly important and in an urban location this would be in competition with urban demand for fuel, which may have made this raw material more expensive in an urban context, particularly as land near urban centres became more intensively used. However, to set against this, there is evidence suggesting declining urban populations in the 'public towns' if not the 'small towns' in the later Roman period.

In the fourth century there is also the possibility that the *collatio lustralis* tax may have been a negative influence. The *collatio lustralis* (Jones 1964, 431–2) was levied on all urban tradesmen and was regarded as a particularly harsh burden. However, this could only apply to 'civitas capitals' and other formal towns as there is no evidence that most 'small towns' ever rose above the status of *vici* and they should therefore technically not be liable to urban taxation. It is also the case that pottery manufacture was widely regarded in the ancient world as an agricultural activity, and it was acceptable for senators to own such a business without being tainted by 'trade', so that it is quite possible that potting would not be an occupation which brought liability to the *collatio* anyway. It is also worth pointing out that even if the *collatio* is relevant, it was imposed at a single point in time, whereas the ruralization of pottery production looks much more like a long-running process rather than the result of a single administrative action.

Given that there seems to be little evidence for urban marketing as a mechanism for the distribution of coarse pottery (see below), proximity to raw materials and other rural settlements may have favoured rural locations.

Urban retailing

There are two sets of evidence for urban retailing of ceramics, direct evidence from a limited number of 'pottery shop' deposits and evidence from the distribution of various types suggesting the use of urban markets.

Pottery shops

'Pottery shop' deposits have been largely discussed within the very useful gazetteer produced by Rhodes (1989) for north-west Europe. One common feature to all the Romano-British pottery shop deposits is the presence of quantities of unworn samian ware. This is variously associated with flagons, *mortaria*, lamps Lyons ware, Central Gaulish glazed ware, BB1 and occasionally coarsewares. At several sites pottery is associated with glassware, and at one of the Colchester 'pottery shops' and at the recently excavated shop at No 1, Poultry in London (pers. comm. Louise Rayner at the Study Group for Roman Pottery in Liverpool, 2001; see also Hall this volume, 139) spices were associated with pots.

It is worth noting that all known 'pottery shops' date to the first or second centuries AD and no later Roman examples have ever been found. It would seem that without samian ware 'pottery shops' ceased to function as separate entities. It is also important that all pottery from then, except for a few coarseware vessels from Corbridge, consists of finewares (samian and early colour-coats or glazed wares), 'specialist wares', *mortaria* and flagons, or BB1. Thus 'pottery shops' show evidence of urban retailing of pottery, but only of a specialist subset of pottery, mainly samian, BB1 and specialist wares. Given the association of glassware with pottery at some 'pottery shops', Price and Cool's (1991) review of Romano-British glass production is of interest. They note that all eleven known production sites have been discovered by accident and that nearly 30% have been found on pottery kiln sites. At none of these sites was there evidence of primary glass production, rather than the recycling of cullet. Price and Cool (1991) suggest that many of the small-scale glass production sites may have been associated with potting, using the same distribution networks and receiving cullet back from them. It is very much of note that the three pottery kiln sites with associated glassworking all produced 'specialist wares', which are known to have been distributed through 'pottery shops' and it seems quite likely that these may also have acted as purchasers of cullet. Cool (pers. comm.) also notes that there are some hints that glassware from pottery shops tends to include some of the finer material, both at the Colchester pottery shop (Cool 1996, 52–62) and at Castleford, which includes unusual purple jugs.

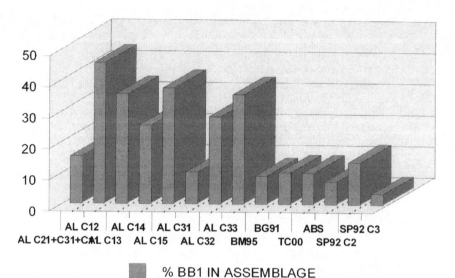

Figure 9.1 Proportions of BB1 in assemblages at Alcester and on nearby rural sites

Distributional evidence

Apart from 'pottery shop' deposits distributional evidence can be found for the urban marketing of some pottery types. Evidence of the proportion of samian ware from different types of site has been assembled by Willis (1998, tables 1 and 2). This clearly demonstrates generally much higher levels of samian ware on urban (and military) sites than on rural ones. This, and the 'pottery shop' evidence combined makes a very strong case for the urban marketing of samian wares, at least partly through specialist 'pottery shops' and demonstrates that there is a separate civilian marketing structure for samian wares which is not directly reliant on military supply (*contra* Middleton 1979).

Given the convergence of 'pottery shop' and distributional evidence for the urban marketing of samian ware the distributional evidence for the urban marketing of other pottery types is strengthened.

Figure 9.1 shows the levels of BB1 in assemblages from third century groups at Gas House Lane, Alcester, Warwickshire, and BB1 levels from a series of predominantly later Roman groups from rural sites in the Arrow Valley to the south of the town (and therefore slightly closer to the source of BB1). There is a clear and marked difference between the urban assemblages and those from the rural sites, with generally much higher urban levels. A similar point might be made of BB1 levels in north Warwickshire and Leicester, with Leicester producing 20% (by maximum vessel count) of BB1 from the Hadrianic-early Antonine group at Bath Lane site 1 (Clamp 1985, 42, table 1) and 6.3% from a Hadrianic-early Antonine group from the West Bridge area (Pollard 1994, 78, table 8.II) compared with 1.4% from Bubbenhall (Evans forthcoming b), 0.1% and 0.6% from Princethorpe (Cutler & Evans 1998) and 0.6% from Ling Hall (Evans forthcoming c), all rural sites in north Warwickshire well to the south of Leicester.

A further sequence of BB1 data from a variety of second century sites is available from

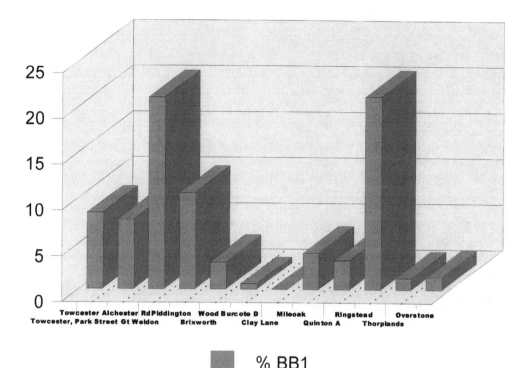

Figure 9.2 *Northamptonshire sites BB1 levels (data after Griffiths 1989)*

Northamptonshire (Griffiths 1989). These are plotted on Figure 9.2. Again high levels generally come from the urban sites at Towcester, although higher levels are found on two rural villas, Great Weldon and Piddington, and the apparently basic level rural site at Ringstead (the assemblage from the latter, however, also appears to be of high-status in terms of finewares – see Figure 9.4 below).

Fulford and Allen also recognise difficulties in seeing fall-offs in BB1 distribution on a small scale, although they are clearly visible at a large scale, and the effects of urban marketing are likely to largely account for this. They recognise the importance of the road system and urban marketing with 'comparatively higher ratios from forts and both major and minor urban communities, but patchy representation from rural settlements' (Fulford & Allen 1996, 267). It seems clear that quantitative studies of BB1 need to take account both of chronological change and site type.

It might be worth noting that the north-western distribution of BB1, whatever the case around the Severn estuary, could not be related to the distribution of salt supplies, since these were copiously available from local sources such as Middlewich and did not need to be brought from Dorset.

Thus distributional evidence tends to suggest, like the contents of 'pottery shops', that BB1 was subject to urban marketing in southern England, and that this continued into the later Roman period.

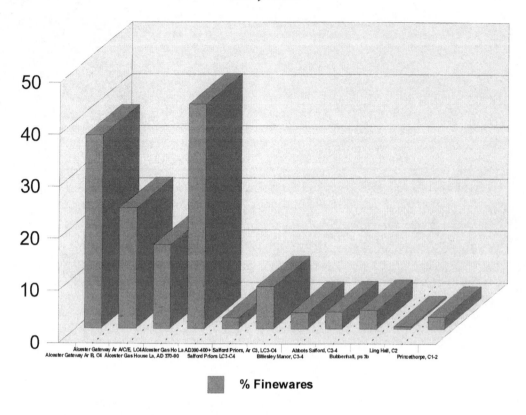

% Finewares

Figure 9.3 *Proportions of finewares from Alcester and Warwickshire rural sites*

Figure 9.3 shows late Roman fineware levels from sites in the Roman small town at Alcester, Warwickshire, and rural sites in the Arrow Valley to its south (after Evans 2001, fig. 10). It is clear that the urban fineware levels (basically Oxfordshire, Nene Valley and South-West Brown-slipped wares) are considerably higher than those from the rural sites. Similarly, Figure 9.4 shows the proportions of finewares from second century sites in Northamptonshire (data from Griffiths 1989) where again the urban levels from Towcester are much higher than any of the rural sites (although again the morphologically basic level site at Ringstead stands out as having an anomalously high level of finewares for such a site).

Hodder (1974a, fig. 8) also conducted a major study of later Roman fineware levels from sites in the south-west, again concluding that 'finer wares were only found in large percentages (20 to 25 percent) in the towns and in sites on or near the roads'. Booth (1991) conducted a similar study in Warwickshire examining levels of finewares and specialist wares combined, this again demonstrated higher levels from urban sites and low ones from rural sites. Using the same method (Booth forthcoming a) he has also examined sites in Oxfordshire in the early and later Roman periods. Fine and specialist ware levels are very different in the two periods, as might be expected given the rise of the Oxfordshire industry, but again in both periods the basic pattern of higher urban levels and lower rural ones is clear.

Thus in the case of both BB1 and finewares distributional evidence for urban marketing would seem to suggest urban marketing in the second century, as the 'pottery shop' evidence

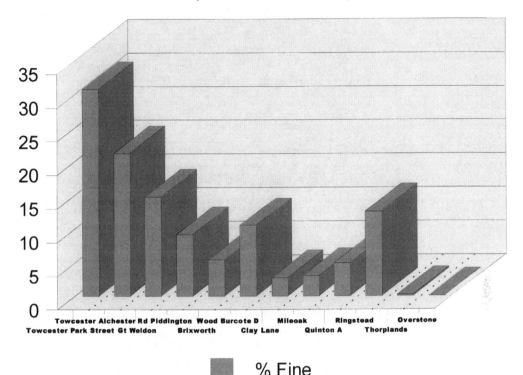

35
30
25
20
15
10
5
0

Towcester Alchester Rd Piddington Wood Burcote D   Mileoak   Ringstead   Overstone
Towcester Park Street Gt Weldon   Brixworth   Clay Lane   Quinton A   Thorplands

■ % Fine

Figure 9.4 *Northants sites fineware levels (data after Griffiths 1989)*

also does, and that this continued until the end of the Roman period.

One other coarseware type for which there is some evidence of urban marketing is late Roman Southern shell-Tempered ware from Harrold. Figure 9.5 shows levels of this from Alcester and Arrow Valley rural sites. As can be seen, the urban levels of this are much higher than those from the rural sites, although the rural site groups tend to extend over greater date ranges and thus would be expected anyway to have lower levels.

However, evidence for the urban marketing of pottery coarsewares, excepting BB1 and shell-tempered wares in the very late fourth century, is slight. Figure 9.6 shows Severn Valley ware levels from Gas House Lane, Alcester and various rural sites in the Arrow Valley to the south of the town. As can easily be seen, urban levels of Severn valley wares at Alcester tend to fall consistently below those of the rural sites.

Hodder offers two case studies which seem to suggest urban marketing of coarsewares, in the distribution of Savernake ware, around Mildenhall (Hodder 1974a, fig. 1) and the distribution of Malvernian Metamorphic tempered ware (Hodder 1974a, fig. 5). In the case of Savernake ware the distribution around Mildenhall looks fairly convincing, but the kiln sites are fairly close to the town and a distribution centred on them, but also using the road network, as the distribution clearly demonstrates, would look very similar. The best reason to accept urban marketing in this case is the very high figure from the town of Mildenhall itself. Unfortunately this figure comes from a late first century well (Annable 1966). Well deposits are often of rather unusual functional composition, being dominated by vessels used for

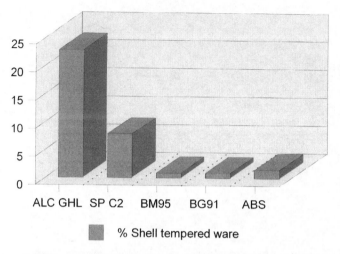

Figure 9.5 *Alcester and Arrow Valley rural sites levels of shell-tempered wares*

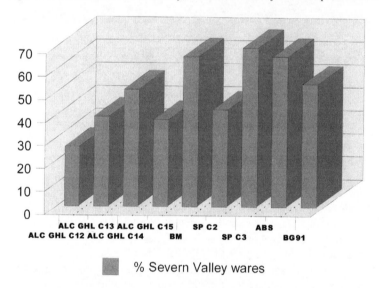

Figure 9.6 *Severn valley ware levels at Alcester and Arrow Valley rural sites*

drawing water, and generally jar dominated (Evans 1993). This is turn often leads to the fabric composition of such deposits being unrepresentative of the site as a whole, because fabrics providing jar forms are over-represented. This would be important here since Savernake ware are predominantly in jar forms (Hodder 1974b).

Table 9.1 shows the functional composition of the Mildenhall well deposit from the illustrated vessels and the samian listed as rimsherds (this would seem to be reasonably accurate since there are 69 rimsherds in a total assemblage listed by Hodder (1974b) as 666 sherds, a ratio of about 1 rimsherd in 10 which seems fairly usual).

The data in Table 9.1 show the well deposit is not massively jar dominated like some well deposits, however, its jar levels are still very high for an urban assemblage. If the data from Table 9.1 were plotted against other rural and urban sites in the region, as in Evans (2001) figure 5, they clearly group with rural site assemblages in the region, not urban ones. Thus, the Mildenhall well deposit is unlikely to have the typical composition of an urban assemblage from Mildenhall, and is likely to have an assemblage which over-represents Savernake wares. Hodder himself (1979) noted that 'the marketing hypothesis for Savernake ware has always had difficulties explaining the westward bias in the distribution' and went on to argue that 'this lop-sidedness may occur because of some social boundary to the east'. The presence of this putative boundary, however, would not in itself, rule out the marketing of Savernake ware from Mildenhall.

Flagons	Constricted-necked jars	Jars	Beakers	Bowls	Dishes	Lids	N
2.9	2.9	55.1	10.2	15.9	11.5	1.5	69 rims

Table 9.1

Hodder's other example, the distribution of Malvernian metamorphic tempered ware (Hodder 1974a, fig. 5) begins to look much more doubtful as more modern data are added to his map (Figure 9.7), with a dog-leg shape of high value sites which run north-south along the Severn, west by road to Kenchester, with the road probably passing close to the kiln site, and east from the Severn along the river Avon. Thus, the distribution seems to reflect river and road transport corridors, but urban marketing is certainly not clear.

The apparent lack of urban marketing amongst coarsewares particularly seems to beg the question of whether their distribution is embedded in social relations (Hodder 1979), and if so how much and at what period. If it is assumed that most later Iron Age exchange was embedded in social relations then it seems unlikely that this was swept away at the conquest. Apart from anything else, much of the province remained under the administration of client rulers at the conquest. Returning to ceramics, it is notoriously difficult to establish the date of the conquest in the south-east precisely because there is virtually no change at this date: 'Belgic' wares dominate assemblages with finewares consisting of *Terra Rubra, Terra Nigra* and their local copies and imported or local copies of Gallic whiteware flagons. These assemblages in Britain are often regarded as typical late Iron Age assemblages, but this, of course, is deeply deceptive in that they are really typically Gallo-Roman (Stead & Rigby 1989, 201; Creighton 2000). Contemporaneously, in the south-west there is a Durotrigian tradition in Dorset (from which the BB1 industry sprang) and Severn Valley wares in the Severn Valley, the latter including much of the 'Belgic' range, accompanied by a widespread vegetable tempered storage jar (Warwickshire Museum fabric R31) and Malvernian Palaeozoic Limestone Tempered ware. It is not coincidental that on most rural sites occupied from before the conquest samian ware is absent at this period, as it is something which has an urban based distribution system. These assemblages are very close to those in northern Gaul, including the shortage of early samian ware.

Just how 'Gallo-Roman' assemblages from early *oppida* were is given some indication by Evans (2001, fig. 9), which shows they had much higher levels of drinking vessels than any of the early Roman cities (London, Verulamium and Colchester) and were similar in this to rural sites in the Aisne Valley.

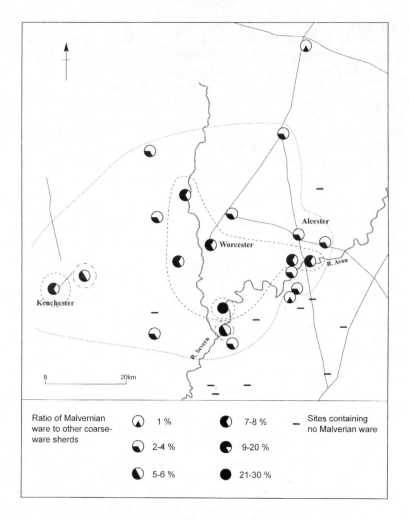

Figure 9.7 *Distribution of Malvernian metamorphic tempered ware*

It is often comparatively unremarked that there is a major change in Roman rural pottery assemblages from around the decade *c*AD60/70. *Terra Nigra* ceases to be used on rural sites around AD 60. This is not because it ceased to be produced, or even that it ceased to be imported into Britain, for late *Terra Nigra* is found on Romano-British military sites in to the Flavian period (Rigby 1977; Tyers 1996, fig. 204). It is only in the Flavian period that South Gaulish samian ware penetrates in any quantity onto non-military sites in the countryside. This is clear, although comparatively unremarked, in Millett's study of samian ware distribution in West Sussex (Millett 1980, 62–3). It is similarly clear on rural sites in Cambridgeshire (Willis forthcoming) and Warwickshire, and Willis (1998, 91–2) notes that the pattern appears to hold generally in Britain and northern France. Cool (pers. comm.) also draws the author's attention to the expansion in glassware distribution in a similar manner to samian at much the same date, following a minute level of glass ware use in the pre-conquest period.

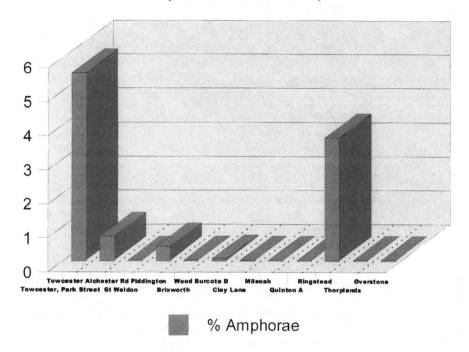

Figure 9.8 Northamptonshire sites; levels of amphorae (data after Griffiths 1989)

Along with the appearance of samian goes the large scale disappearance of 'Belgic wares', Malvernian Palaeozoic Limestone Tempered ware, and the rise of what in Britain tend to be termed 'Romanised' greywares. It may be of note that Iron Age coinage also seems to cease circulation' around this time (Haselgrove 1987). What seems to really take place here is a change in the model of 'Romanization' from the pre and post conquest 'Gallo-Roman' to the more eclectic style, which draws more from the elements found in military supply and that developing in 'urban' centres.

The major material changes in the Flavian period, together with the ending of 'client kingdoms' and the consequent imposition of cash taxes would tend to suggest that rural sites could no longer evade the need to sell goods to raise money to pay taxes. This, in itself, does not require that market transactions take place in urban centres, but given quite large immigrant communities in urban centres, coming from other parts of the Empire where market based transactions were the norm, it is difficult to see these as being other than market based transactions. That the urban fineware type of choice, samian ware, along with glassware, starts to appear in some quantity on rural sites from this time on seems more than coincidental. Of course the level of market based transactions to those which are socially embedded can vary. Creighton (1992) rightly points to the comparatively low level of monetization in the second century AD, which might point to an economy quite largely 'embedded', but it seems doubtful whether high mediaeval economies had monetization levels even as high, yet these are regarded as market economies.

Millett (1990, 168–9) has regarded the *civitas* elite as controlling marketing, in an urban context, and keeping exchange embedded. However, whilst elites may have remained in place at the conquest it is far from clear that they survived unchanged through the first century, nor

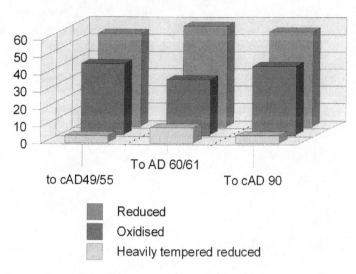

Figure 9.9 Colchester proportions of oxidised and reduced ware

would their putative control of urban centres have had much influence on the distribution of coarse pottery. It is also unclear how they might have controlled 'small towns' and there is also not much evidence of elite presences in towns in the earlier first century.

Hodder (1979) preferred to see most of the economy embedded until the later third century, when he and Reece (1979) both viewed the massive increase in the money supply, and the evidence that it was used even on basic level rural sites, as suggesting that a full-scale market economy was in operation. That an expansion of market-based transactions took place at this date in southern Britain at this time seems likely, but given the evidence of goods on rural sites which would have passed through market-based transactions in the second century, particularly the ubiquitous presence of Antonine samian, it would seem that the market economy was not inconsiderable, and that all 'Lowland Zone' rural sites participated in it to some extent, much earlier.

None of this is to preclude evidence of social constraints on the distributions of various types of goods: these in themselves are not evidence of embeddedness or a market-based economy. It is quite possible for one social group not to want to deal with members of another social group within a market economy and to operate preferentially with members of their own social group rather than 'strangers'. It is also quite possible for 'strangers' to be regarded differently, 'Roman' strangers might be regarded as of status, whilst strangers from groups to which 'we' were traditionally hostile might be regarded with enmity. Thus, hard boundaries in the transmission of goods from one area to another could easily persist within a world where market-based transactions were the norm.

Gregson (1982) in a stimulating paper argued that villa development largely indicated the growth of a market in land, a process which began after the conquest and 'seems to have been reasonably complete in the third century', that is that Hodder's and Reece's full monetization saw the completion of a free market in land, but that this had been developing from the first century.

Pottery as containers
One other aspect of urban retailing to which pottery contributes is in its use as containers for other commodities; that is, in the distribution of amphorae. In this case, the ceramics were merely the wrapping and their contents were the objects of interest to 'consumers'. Amphorae in Roman Britain were primarily supplied to military sites, as Carreras-Montfort has demonstrated well with the distribution of Dressel 20 amphora stamps (1994, fig. 28) following Collingwood and Myres (1937, 242). However, the non-military distribution of amphorae is very much an urban feature. Evans (2001, fig. 11) shows higher urban amphora levels than on basic level rural sites from various sites in the West Midlands, although some villa sites show near urban levels. Similarly Figure 9.8 (after data from Griffiths (1989)) shows urban amphorae levels from Towcester are generally much higher than levels from rural sites in Northamptonshire (yet again the site at Ringstead is anomalous, and a ritual or very high-status use for this site would seem likely).

Thus, unsurprisingly, there does seem to be good evidence that imported commodities, olive oil, wine, fish sauce, etc were distributed by urban retailing, and were primarily consumed on urban sites.

Urban consumption and the identity of urban communities
The urban model of pottery consumption in the early Roman period is of some interest. As noted above it has major differences from that on rural sites. In London (Davies *et al.* 1994) in pre-Boudiccan deposits samian comprises 77% of finewares, along with Lyons ware, Gallo-Belgic whitewares, Pompeian redware, micaceous wares and ring and dot beakers. Nearly all of these are types which might be found on military sites, but not on *oppida* or rural sites. Oxidised wares and whitewares also form a substantial element of the pre-Boudiccan assemblage, in contrast to rural sites, but as military sites tend to until the Hadrianic period. Locally produced pottery seems to come from a series of immigrant and indigenous potters. By the late Neronian period greywares dominate the assemblage as they continue to do thereafter, and samian ware levels decline from a very high level of 17% in the previous phase. Davies (*et al.* 1994) note by the Flavian period 'the early handmade products of the local kilns at Highgate Wood are still the most common but, even so, are greatly reduced. This shortfall is made up by a greater proportion of wheelmade Highgate C wares. Although occurring in small quantities, a similar transition from native to more Romanized types can be seen in the local sandy ware, with the latter more Romanized variant dominating in this phase'.

It is clear that not only is early pottery at London very different from assemblages on rural sites and *oppida*, with a samian dominated fineware assemblage, but that much is imported and possibly a majority is made by immigrant potters, although material in a 'Belgic' tradition is also used.

At Colchester Bidwell (1999, 490) notes that quantities of Gallo-Belgic imports 'reaching the fortress and early *colonia* were very small when compared with the finds at Sheepen', and that beaker Cam 113/119 'was an import which occurred in enormous numbers at Sheepen' and 'its extreme scarcity in the fortress and early *colonia* is not to be explained by the cessation of its manufacture shortly after the conquest, for the type occurs at Exeter and at Usk which are both fortresses founded in the reign of Nero'. This puzzle seems to be easily accounted for by the differences between *oppida* type assemblages and those of the new 'Roman' towns. Unfortunately it seems impossible to obtain from the report any of the basic quantified data to assess this numerically, which despite the provision of CD Rom the authors and editors seem to have omitted.

Figure 9.9 shows the proportions of oxidised wares and reduced wares from Colchester (after Bidwell 1999, table 8.1). As at London oxidised wares were important in the assemblage, in contrast with rural assemblages and those from *oppida*. Bidwell (1999, 493) also notes 'almost all the types in oxidised wares and many of those in the finer greywares were introduced by Continental potters following the conquest ... many of these types were current in the Rhineland, and one obvious origin for introducing the types at Colchester was the fortress at Novaesium'.

Both of these early urban examples make clear the obvious point that many potters associated with urban supply at the conquest were immigrants, although local products would also be used and these clearly adapted gradually to new demands. Early urban communities throughout the south would have had substantial immigrant elements, some probably citizens, and as such not so easily malleable by pre-existing elites. The *coloniae*, of course, were almost entirely immigrant at foundation, and sites such as Wroxeter and Exeter probably ought to be regarded as effectively the same. Similarly many towns formed at the location of early forts, and it is difficult not to see at least some population from the *vici* at these locations, where they owned property and businesses, remaining when military units moved on (*contra* Millett 1990, 74–5). Certainly in the case of towns like Wroxeter (see below for further discussion of similar northern towns) it is very difficult to understand why the army and all the *vicani* should have left, and a small subset of the Cornovii should have moved in and suddenly started using Romanized pottery and material culture, whilst all their fellow countrymen in the surrounding territory remained happily virtually aceramic (Gaffney *et al.* forthcoming). This Potemkin village explanation really does not seem preferable to accepting that much of the population of this town were immigrants, and many, *vicani*.

Thus, it is suggested that an amalgam of immigrants, military influence, and indigenous traditions formed early pottery use in Romano-British towns, and that this urban model did much to create Romano-British pottery traditions, in contrast to the preceding, so-called 'Belgic', Gallo-Roman tradition.

Tables 9.2–9.4 show a series of functional analyses from three southern urban sites, further data are available from London (Davies *et al.* 1994, fig. 148) for the first and second centuries, and Chelmsford (Going 1987, table 10) and there are the original sequences from Verulamium, Neatham and Chichester (Millett 1979, fig. 13). All are fairly consistent in their major trend, a gradual decline in jar levels with time and a rise in tablewares (dishes and bowls). This seems to represent a gradual diversification of pottery use from an Iron Age style jar dominated pattern to a more 'Romanized' tableware dominated assemblage, and this is something also seen, but to a lesser extent, on rural sites. Given the southern pattern that from early northern military associated towns, Catterick, York and Carlisle (Evans 1995, table 5.5) are curious. It is clear that most northern towns (with the exception of Brough-on-Humber) show a strikingly different pattern from the southern towns. They start with very low jar levels, and if anything these tend to rise with time, indeed they rise considerably from the later third century onwards. This latter phenomenon the author has discussed elsewhere (Evans 1993; Evans in prep a) and will not be considered much further here, but the meaning of the low jar and high tableware levels from the Flavian period and through the second century is of interest. These levels, like much of the rest of the composition of these assemblages, reflects those in contemporary forts. These urban and military assemblages have the functional composition from the start of a 'fully

Period	Flagons	Constricted-necked jars	Jars	Wide-mouthed jars	Beakers and cups	Tankards	Bowls	Dishes	Dish/bowl	Amphorae	Mortaria	Lids	Other	Indet	N
11	0	2.3	93.2	0	0	0	2.3	0	0	0	0	0	0	2.3	43
15/18	0	0	80.1	0	0	0	6.7	6.7	0	0	0	0	0	6.7	15
21	0.6	1.4	68.2	1.2	5.2	2.4	11.1	2.0	0.6	0.2	1.2	1.2	0.4	4.4	504
25	3.0	0	51.5	0	0	3.0	27.2	3.0	3.0	0	3.0	0	0	6.1	33
28	1.2	1.2	54.9	1.8	5.2	2.4	17.1	5.2	1.0	0	1.6	5.4	0.2	2.6	496
29	0	0	59.0	5.1	12.9	7.7	7.7	5.1	0	0	0	2.6	0	0	39
30	1.0	2.0	44.9	4.1	10.2	2.0	14.3	4.1	0	0	0	6.1	0	10.2	49
31	0	0	51.0	4.3	8.5	0	14.9	6.4	4.3	0	0	4.3	2.1	4.3	47
35	4.8	2.4	50.0	2.4	2.4	0	4.8	11.9	4.8	0	2.4	9.5	0	2.4	42
38/39	1.7	1.4	44.5	3.4	7.4	4.3	13.0	10.5	1.7	0	4.3	4.5	0	3.1	352
41	0	2.5	40.9	3.3	3.2	1.6	18.9	17.2	0	0	3.3	2.5	0	6.4	122
45	1.3	1.3	35.7	6.5	4.5	1.9	22.7	12.3	1.3	0.6	3.9	1.9	0	5.8	154
48	1.3	1.4	48.2	4.3	5.7	1.3	14.5	10.8	1.8	0	4.0	2.2	0.3	5.3	719
50	0.3	1.3	42.5	6.7	6.3	4.2	13.6	9.1	2.9	0	2.1	4.2	0.1	6.6	788
99	0.6	1.9	47.5	4.7	5.6	2.6	15.3	8.0	1.7	0.1	2.7	3.6	0.2	5.6	1353

Table 9.2 TD 81 Tiddington functional analysis by phase (after Booth forthcoming b) by minimum numbers of rims

Romanized' assemblage, in contrast to the gradual development in the southern towns – and as they eventually interact with local traditions in the area they begin to become 'less Romanized'. Indeed most northern Flavian-Trajanic urban assemblages, like those of the forts, can be immediately distinguished from contemporary rural assemblages, in areas where there are rural assemblages, simply by their colour, military and urban assemblages being chiefly oxidised and those from rural sites almost uniformly reduced. Similarly the types on these northern urban sites are interchangeable with those from local forts, and have little contribution from 'native' style producers.

A particularly striking case is York which produced its own oxidised wares and persevered in this tradition until the mid third century (perhaps significantly the point by which extra-provincial recruitment had ceased and the garrison had probably fallen), whilst the local countryside (and other northern towns and forts from the Hadrianic period) used almost exclusively reduced wares. York until the later third century remained a largely self-sufficient ceramic island (Monaghan 1997), making its own pots and importing material from other parts of the province and abroad, but using almost nothing from its local area, and exporting virtually none of its products to the local countryside, even to local rural sites a few miles away (although some York products are found on other military sites in the region, as at Binchester (Evans and Rátkai forthcoming a) and Malton (Bidwell & Croom 1997).

The obvious conclusion from this is that much of the population of these 'towns' is alien to the area. They are military associated settlements, like the *vici*, with populations associated with the army or coming from other areas of the province. Indeed for many of them they were probably alien islands of Latinity amongst a massively Cumric speaking rural population.

Vici

Vici superficially have many of the attributes of at least 'small towns' and it has been argued that they served the same purpose in relation to the countryside, and indeed this role is implicit in the suggestion that many southern towns developed from early *vici* (Webster 1966).

Evidence from the north of England tends to suggest that they might fulfil the above role, but that principally they served military communities with little, if any, role as centres serving local rural populations. *Vici* on Hadrian's Wall and in Cumbria and rural sites in those areas show this best (Evans forthcoming d; Evans forthcoming e). Here the *vici* have pottery supplies pretty well identical to those of the forts, although perhaps with rather fewer pieces of samian and amphora. By contrast, local rural sites are very close to being aceramic (Evans forthcoming e), quite often have sherds of local handmade fabrics in their assemblages (which do not appear at the *vici*) and often have rather different fabrics compositions from *vicus* site assemblages. This is not simply that rural sites failed to interact with the *vici* in terms of ceramics but obtained other goods from them. Nails are very scarce on rural sites, and small finds very few, glassware being usually limited to occasional bangles. There is no material evidence of any real level of interaction between local rural sites and *vici*, just as there is none with the frontier towns of Corbridge and Carlisle.

The *vicus* at Malton/Norton is a little different. In the Flavian-Trajanic period it does seem to have shown little interaction with local sites, but by the Antonine period local wares become well represented in the *vicus* (Bidwell & Croom 1997) and from perhaps the early third century, greywares produced at Norton found a market on local rural sites, as at Wharram (Evans forthcoming f). Thus Malton/Norton seems to have had a high level of interaction with local rural sites for much of the Roman period, and this would seem to correlate with the appearance

Period	Constricted-necked jars	Flagons	Jars	Wide-mouthed jars	Beakers and cups	Tankards	Bowls	Dishes	Dish/bowl	Amphorae	Mortaria	Lids	Other	Indet	N
ALC 72/2 C	-	6	44	-	0	11	28	0	0	6	0	6	0	0	18
ALC 72/2 D	-	0	88	-	4	0	0	4	0	0	0	4	0	0	24
ALC 72/2 E	-	11	41	-	0	15	22	7	0	0	4	0	0	0	27
ALC 72/2 F	-	4	29	-	3	8	31	22	0	0	3	2	0	0	154
ALC 72/2 G	-	0	37	-	0	3	20	40	0	0	0	0	0	0	30
AL23 7N C12	2	1	26	7	1	17	22	22	0	0	0	1	0	0	85
AL23 7N C13	4	2	24	7	1	12	32	14	0	0	2	2	0	0	140
AL23 7N C14	2	2	25	6	1	20	26	13	0	0	2	4	0	0	110
AL23 7N C15	5	0	21	0	5	16	19	26	0	0	5	3	0	0	38
AL23 T2 D	0	6	35	0	0	0	34	20	0	0	4	0	0	0	49

Table 9.3 Alcester composite functional sequence; Baromix (ALC 72/2 and Gas House Lane (AL23) sites (by minimum numbers of rims)

Phase	Storage jars %	Wide-mouthed jars %	Other jars %	Flagons %	Constructed necked jars %	Bowls %	Dishes %	Dish/bowl %	Beakers %	Tankards %	Lids %	Mortaria %	Amphorae %	Other %	n
2+ #	1.4	0	94.4	0	0	2.8	0	0	1.4	0	0	0	0	0	71
3	8.3	0	75.0	0	0	4.2	8.3	0	0	0	0	4.2	0	0	24
4	1.7	0	54.2	6.8	1.7	20.3	11.9	0	3.4	0	0	0	0	0	59
5	0.7	0	59.7	4.6	2.5	14.5	8.1	0	5.3	0	0	1.4	0.7	0	283
6	2.4	0.1	35.7	1.2	4.0	15.7	17.5	2.0	18.8	0	0.1	2.0	0.3	0.3	759
7	1.3	0.1	35.3	0.7	2.5	16.3	18.3	1.9	18.3	0	0.1	3.2	0.4	0.2	919
8	3.5	0.4	33.0	0.8	2.1	22.1	16.7	1.0	13.2	0.1	0.4	6.1	0.3	0.3	1564
9	4.8	0.6	30.8	1.0	2.4	25.9	16.3	0.3	10.6	0	0.2	6.1	0.4	0.4	1117

Table 9.4 Functional analysis of A421 Iron Age and Roman pottery by Period (by minimum numbers of rims) (# - All Iron Age material from the site)

of 'Romanized' material on many rural sites from the later second century (Evans 1995).

North-Western 'towns'

The ceramic evidence of one final group of 'towns' ought to be mentioned. These are the 'towns' of lowland Lancashire and Cheshire sometimes taken as just another group of small towns (pers. comm. Hanson). All these sites are located on King Street, and they consist of Walton-le-Dale, Wigan, Wilderspool and Middlewich. The pottery supplies at all these sites are fairly similar and all seem to have a clearly 'military-associated' supply, with high to very high levels of samian ware, and very high levels of amphorae. Cool (2001; pers. comm.) also points out that the glass assemblages from Middlewich and Wilderspool are both of military-associated, being 'dominated by bottle which suggest a military involvement as military assemblages of this period tend to show this feature to a much greater degree than contemporary urban civilian assemblages' (Cool 2001, 1).

The evidence from all the sites on King Street (Wild forthcoming) is that they first commence around AD 90, in contrast to the Pennine skirt road which links a series of sites with much earlier Flavian forts. Good dating evidence is available to this author for Walton-le-Dale (Evans & Rátkai forthcoming b), Wilderspool (Webster 1992, fig. 70) and Middlewich (Evans in prep b). All tend to have a weak late Flavian-Trajanic start, peak under Hadrian and run slowly down in the Antonine period, with a rapid decline in the first half of the third century, with only the occasional vessel of later date. This chronological pattern seems to be almost unique to these sites if they were regarded as 'urban'. Their second century pattern is common to many north-western forts, but most *vici* continue later, coming to an end towards the end of the third century or early in the fourth. The evidence from considerable modern excavations at Walton-le-Dale shows a series of large timber hall-like structures, associated with large numbers of hearths/furnaces. Wilderspool also produced many hearths/furnaces and again some large timber hall-like buildings. There are hints of similar buildings at Wigan and Middlewich. These are not standard *vicus* 'strip-buildings', being much larger and with little sign of domestic occupation. There is evidence of a pottery industry at Wilderspool and another at Walton, consisting in large part of potters who had migrated from Wilderspool (Evans & Rátkai forthcoming b).

The small finds from Walton are regarded as being of fairly low-status (pers. comm. C. Howard-Davis) and the animal bone from the northern site as very low status (pers. comm. S. Stallibrass). The evidence from Walton of large buildings associated with some form of production, furnaces, potting and little evidence of domestic accommodation, together with a pottery supply with very high levels of samian and amphorae, probably arriving in transshipment (for which there is evidence amongst the amphorae in relation to Ribchester), and very low-status food and small finds, does seem to point to servile production. It is also clear that all these sites on King Street belong in the same zone of military supply, and one which is different from that to Chester and Segontium (Evans & Rátkai forthcoming b; Evans forthcoming e).

Thus it is tempting to see all these sites on King Street, which are clearly linked in the same military supply zone, as being involved in production for army supply, quite possibly largely servile, perhaps by the leasing of plots at these centres to different *negotiatores* (*cf.* Swan 2000). One thing is certain, as with the northern *vici* these sites were not 'small towns' serving the local countryside, for rural sites north of the Mersey, and quite possibly those in Cheshire, outside the Wirral, were virtually aceramic, and produce virtually no Roman material culture.

Discussion

This paper has attempted a brief survey of trends in urban pottery supply, manufacture and use patterns, in the course of which it becomes clear that whilst there is good evidence for urban retailing of fine and specialist pottery types there is very little to confirm urban retailing of coarsewares, and the evidence would seem to suggest that it would be dangerous to assume this took place on a large scale. Another interesting area of debate, which looks like it may deserve further revisiting, is in the emergence of a market economy within the province, and the scale

of this and its time-scale. There has been a tendency either to assume that it took place rapidly at the conquest, or to accept the Hodder/Reece consensus (Hodder 1979; Reece 1979) on the later third century. This author suggests that the evidence would better fit a widespread establishment of market economics by the Flavian period, but with little evidence for this under Claudius or Nero. The level of exchange conducted in this manner relative to that in 'embedded' exchange may have been low in the Flavian period, but it encompassed a high proportion of sites in the 'Lowland zone'. Certainly by the Antonine period goods which are most likely to have been distributed by market exchange reached virtually every occupied rural site in the province, even those in the 'Highland zone', and this must suggest quite considerable levels of market exchange (which cash taxes would also require).

Looking at the 'ceramic identity' of urban assemblages reminds us of the obvious, that early urban communities had a significant population of extra-provincial origin, with quite a lot of influence from the Rhenish frontier. The tastes of this urban population had a major impact on the development of Romano-British traditions which largely replaced the Gallo-Roman tradition dominant in the south-east until the Flavian period.

Acknowledgements

The author would like to thank Paul Booth for generously providing data from Tiddington in advance of its publication. He would also like to thank Hilary Cool for reading and commenting on an earlier draft, needless to say any remaining errors are entirely the author's responsibility. Figure 9.7 is the work of Nigel Dodds.

Bibliography

Annable, F.K. 1966. 'A late first century well at Cunetio', *WANHM* 61: 9–24

Bidwell, P. & Croom, A. 1997. 'The coarse wares', in Wenham, L.P. & Heywood, B. (eds) *The 1968 to 1970 Excavations in the Vicus at Malton, North Yorkshire*. Yorkshire Archaeological Report 3, Leeds: 61–102

Bidwell, P. 1999. 'A survey of pottery production and supply at Colchester', in Symonds, R.P. & Wade, S. (eds) *Colchester Archaeological Report 10: Roman pottery from excavations in Colchester, 1971–86*. Colchester Archaeological Trust, Colchester: 468–500

Booth, P. 1991. 'Inter-site comparisons between pottery assemblages in Roman Warwickshire: ceramics indicators of site status', *JRPS* 4: 1–10

Booth, P. Forthcoming a. 'Quantifying status: some pottery data from the Upper Thames Valley', *JRPS*

Booth, P. Forthcoming b. 'Iron Age, Roman and Saxon pottery', in Palmer, N. (ed.) *Report on excavations at Tiddington, Warwickshire*.

Brown, A. 1994. 'A Romano-British shell-gritted pottery and tile manufacturing site at Harrold, Bedfordshire', *BA* 21: 19–107

Carreras-Montfort, C. 1994. 'Una reconstruccion del comercio en ceramicas: la red de transportes en Britannia: aplicaciones de modelos de simulacion en PASCAL y SPANS', *Cuadernos de Arqueologia* 7

Clamp, H. 1985. 'The late Iron Age and Romano-British pottery', in Clay, P. & Mellor, J.E. (eds) *Excavations in Bath Lane, Leicester*. Leicester Museums, Art Galleries and Record Service Archaeological Report No 10, Leicester: 41–58

Collingwood, R. & Myres, J.N.L. 1937. *Roman Britain and the English Settlements*. Clarendon Press, Oxford.

Cool, H. 1996. 'The Boudican Uprising and Glass Vessels from Colchester', *Expedition* 38: 52–62

Cool, H. 2001. *A Summary of the Middlewich Glass*. Unpublished assessment report for Giffords.

Creighton, J. 1992. *The Circulation of Roman Coinage from the first to the third century AD*. Unpublished PhD dissertation, University of Durham.

Creighton, J. 2000. *Coins and Power in late Iron Age Britain*. Cambridge University Press, Cambridge.

Cutler, J. & Evans, J. 1998. 'A section through the Fosse Way and the excavation of Romano-British features at Princethorpe, Warwickshire, 1994', *TBWAS* 102: 57–72

Davies, B., Richardson, B. & Tomber, R. 1994. *A Dated Corpus of Early Roman Pottery from the City of London*. Council for British Archaeology, London.

Evans, J. 1989. 'Crambeck: the development of a major northern pottery industry', in Wilson P.R. (ed.) *The Crambeck Roman pottery industry*. Yorkshire Archaeological Society, Roman Antiquities Section Monograph, Leeds: 43–90

Evans, J. 1993. 'Function and finewares in the Roman north', *JRPS* 6: 95–118

Evans, J. 1995. 'Reflections on later Iron Age and "native" Romano-British pottery in north-eastern England', in Vyner, B. (ed.) *Moorland Monuments*. Council for British Archaeology, London: 46–68

Evans, J. 2001. 'Material approaches to the identification of different Romano-British site types', in James, S. & Millett, M. (eds) *Britons and Romans: advancing an archaeological agenda*. Council for British Archaeology, London: 26–35

Evans, J. Forthcoming a. 'The pottery from Mourie Farm, Low Worsall', in Cottrell, T. & Cox, P. (eds) *Five Ancient Yorkshire Landscapes – The Iron Age and Romano-British archaeology of the BP Teesside to Saltend ethylene pipeline*, 1998–2000.

Evans, J. Forthcoming b. 'The Roman pottery from Bubbenhall', in Palmer, S. (ed.) 'Report on excavations at Bubbenhall, Warwickshire', *TBWAS*.

Evans, J. Forthcoming c. 'The Roman pottery from Ling Hall', in Palmer, S. (ed.) 'Report on excavations at Bubbenhall, Warwickshire', *TBWAS*.

Evans, J. Forthcoming d. '"Romanization", pottery and the rural economy in the North West', in Philpott, R. & Lupton, A. (eds) *Volume of Papers Resulting from the Liverpool North-Western Research Priorities Meeting*.

Evans, J. Forthcoming e. 'This small harvest: pottery from 'Highland zone' sites in north Wales and the North-West', *JRPS*.

Evans, J. in prep a. 'Fin de siècle: the road to the end of Roman Britain, possibly', *OJA*.

Evans, J. in prep b. *An assessment of the Middlewich Roman pottery*. Unpublished report for L-P Archaeology.

Evans, J. & Rátkai, S. Forthcoming a. 'The Binchester Roman pottery', in Ferris, I.M. & Jones, R.F.J. *Monograph on Excavations at Binchester 1978–1988*.

Evans, J. & Rátkai, S. Forthcoming b. 'The Roman pottery from Walton-le-Dale', in *English Heritage monograph on excavations at Walton-le-Dale, Lancs*.

Farrar, R.A.H. 1973. 'The techniques and sources of Romano-British Black-Burnished ware', in Detsicas, A. (ed.) *Current Research in Romano-British Coarse Pottery*. Council for British Archaeology, London: 67–103

Fulford, M.G. 1974. *New Forest Roman Pottery*. BAR (British Series) 17, Oxford.

Fulford, M.G. & Allen, J.R. 1996. 'The distribution of south-east Dorset Black Burnished Category 1 pottery in South-West Britain', *Britannia* 27: 223–82

Gaffney, V., White, R. & Buteaux, S. Forthcoming. *Wroxeter, the Cornovii and the urban process: Final report on the work on the Wroxeter Hinterland Project and the Wroxeter Hinterland Survey*, 1994–1999. Journal of Roman Archaeology, Supplementary Series, Portsmouth, Rhode Island.

Going, C. 1987. *The Mansio and other sites in the south-eastern sector of Caesaromagus: the Roman pottery*. Council for British Archaeology, London.

Gregson, M. 1982, 'The villa as private property', in Ray, K. (ed.) *Young Archaeologist: collected unpublished papers, contributions to archaeological thinking and practice*. Gregson, Clackton on Sea: 143–71

Griffiths, K. 1989. 'Marketing of Roman pottery in second-century Northamptonshire and the Milton Keynes area', *JRPS* 2: 66–76

Hartley, K.F. 1998. 'The incidence of stamped mortaria in the Roman empire, with special reference to imports to Britain', in Bird, J. (ed.) *Form and Fabric: studies in Rome's material past in honour of B.R. Hartley*. Oxbow, Oxford 199–217

Haselgrove, C. 1987. *Iron Age Coinage in south-east England: the archaeological context*. BAR (British Series) 174, Oxford.

Hodder, I.R. 1974a. 'Some marketing models for Romano-British coarse pottery', *Britannia* 5: 340–55

Hodder, I.R. 1974b. 'The distribution of Savernake ware', *WANHM* 69: 67–84

Hodder, I.R. 1979. 'Pre-Roman and Romano-British tribal economies', in Burnham, B.C. & Johnson, H.B. (ed.) *Invasion and Repose: The case of Roman Britain*. BAR (British Series) 73, Oxford: 189–96

Jones, A.H.M. 1964. *The Late Roman Empire 284–602: a social, economic and administrative survey*. Backwell, Oxford.

Leech, R. 1982. *Excavations at Catsgore, 1970–1973*. Western Archaeological Trust Excavation Monograph 2, Bristol.

Lyne, M.A.B. & Jefferies, R.S. 1979. *The Alice Holt/Farnham Roman pottery industry*. Council for British Archaeology, London.

Middleton, P. 1979. 'Army supply in Roman Gaul: an hypothesis for Roman Britain', in Burnham, B.C. & Johnson, H.B. (eds) *Invasion and Response: the case of Roman Britain*. BAR (British Series) 73, Oxford: 81–97

Millett, M. 1979. 'An approach to the functional interpretation of pottery', in Millett, M.J. (ed.) *Pottery and the Archaeologist*. Institute of Archaeology Occasional Publication 4, London: 35–47

Millett, M. 1980. 'Aspects of Romano-British pottery in West Sussex', *Sussex Archaeological Collections* 118: 57–68

Millett, M. 1990. *The Romanization of Britain: an essay in archaeological interpretation*. Cambridge University Press, Cambridge.

Monaghan, J. 1997. *Roman pottery from York*. York Archaeological Trust by the Council for British Archaeology, York.

Pollard, R. 1994. 'The late Iron Age and Roman pottery', in Clay, P. & Pollard, R. (eds) *Iron Age and Roman Occupation in the West Bridge Area, Leicester: excavations* 1962–1971. Leicestershire Museums Arts & Records Service, Leicester: 51–114

Price, J. & Cool, H.E.M. 1991. 'The evidence for the production of glass in Roman Britain', in Foy, D. & Sennequier, G. (eds) *Ateliers de Verriers de l'antiquité à la période pré-industrielle*. Association Française pour L'Archéologie de Verre, Rouen: 23–7

Reece, R. 1979. 'Roman monetary impact: addendum', in Burnham, B.C. & Johnson, H.B. (eds) *Invasion and Repose: The case of Roman Britain*. BAR (British Series) 73, Oxford: 216–17

Rhodes, M. 1989. 'Roman pottery lost en route from the kiln to the gazetteer', *JRPS* 2: 44–58

Rigby, V. 1977. 'The Gallo-Belgic pottery from Cirencester', in Dore, J. & Greene, K. (eds) *Roman Pottery Studies in Britain and Beyond*. BAR (International Series) 30, Oxford: 37–46

Saunders, L. 1986. *A Study of the Distribution of Romano-British Pottery Kilns with respect to Major Settlements of the Province*. Unpublished BSc dissertation, University of Durham.

Stead, I.M. & Rigby, V. 1989. *Verulamium: the King Harry Lane site*. English Heritage Archaeological Report 12, London.

Jeremy Evans

Sunter, N. & Woodward, P.J. 1987. *Romano-British Industries in Purbeck*. Dorset Natural History and Archaeological Society Monograph No 6, Dorchester.

Swan, V.G. 1984. *The Pottery Kilns of Roman Britain*. Her Majesties' Stationary Office, London.

Swan, V.G. 1992. 'Legio VI and its men: African Legionaries in Britain', *JRPS* 5: 1–34

Swan, V.G. 2000. 'Legio XX VV and tile production at Tarbock, Merseyside', *Britannia* 31: 55–68

Tyers, P. 1996. Roman Pottery in Britain. Batsford, London.

Webster, G. 1966. 'Forts and towns in early Roman Britain', in Wacher, J.S. (ed) *The Civitas Capitals of Roman Britain*. Leicester University Press, Leicester: 31–45

Webster, G. & Booth, N. 1947. 'A Romano-British pottery kiln at Swanpool, near Lincoln', *AntJ* 27: 61–79

Webster, P.V. 1976. 'Severn Valley ware: a preliminary study', *TBGAS* 94: 18–46

Webster, P.V. 1992. The coarse pottery', in Hinchliffe, J. & Williams, J.H. (eds) *Roman Warrington: Excavations at Wilderspool*. University of Manchester, Manchester: 42–77

White, R.H. & Gaffney, V.L. 2003. 'Resolving the Paradox: the work of the Wroxeter Hinterland Project', in Wilson, P.R. (ed) *The Archaeology of Roman Towns: Studies in Honour of Professor John S Wacher*. Oxbow, Oxford: 221–232

Wild, F. Forthcoming. 'The samian ware', in *English Heritage monograph on excavations at Walton-le-Dale, Lancs*.

Williams, D.F. 1977. 'The Romano-British black-burnished industry', in Peacock D.P.S. (ed.) *Pottery and Early Commerce*. Academic Press, London: 163–238

Willis, S.H. 1998. 'Samian pottery in Britain: exploring its distribution and archaeological potential', *AJ* 155: 82–133

Willis, S.H. Forthcoming. 'The samian ware', in Hinman, M. (ed.) *A Late Iron Age Farmstead and Romano-British Site at Haddon, Peterborough*. BAR (British Series), AFU monograph number 2, Oxford.

Young, C.J. 1977. *Oxfordshire Roman Pottery*. BAR (British Series) 43, Oxford.

10

Glass-working and glassworkers in cities and towns

Jennifer Price

Introduction

Glass held an unusual position among the manufactured goods of the Roman world as it was essentially novel, becoming widely used for everyday purposes only after the invention of glass blowing in the mid-first century BC. Small decorated core-formed containers, open sagged tablewares and moulded inlays were produced in different areas of the eastern Mediterranean region in the middle and late Hellenistic periods. Some of these reached cities and towns in the western Mediterranean region and further afield, but no substantial tradition of working and using vessel glass developed in Italy or the western provinces until the last years of the Roman Republic. At around this time, Roman literature began to include comments on the appearance and qualities of glass, and glass vessels appeared in wall-paintings in Rome and the Vesuvian towns (Naumann-Steckner 1991; 1999).

The surviving archaeological, textual and iconographic evidence shows that glass had many functions in the cities and towns of the Roman empire. The range of vessels included tablewares for displaying, serving and consuming liquids and solid foodstuffs, and household wares and containers for storing and transporting liquid and semi-liquid foodstuffs and cosmetic and medical preparations. It was also used to make items of jewellery, as well as counters and gaming pieces, figurines and elements of statues and many other objects. In addition, it frequently featured in public and private architectural schemes, for windows and for the decoration of floors, walls, vaults and furniture.

The reasons for adopting glass must have varied in different parts of the Roman world in the early imperial period. The population of cities and towns in the eastern and Mediterranean provinces were presented with a much wider choice of forms of a material with which they were already familiar, whereas using glass in new and peripheral provinces like Germany or Britain may have had symbolic appeal to elements of provincial society as a quintessentially Roman material. For example, glass vessels were scarcely present in Britain before the Claudian conquest (Price 1996), but in the decades after AD 43 they rapidly became available in the emerging civil settlements at Colchester (Cool & Price 1995, 211–3) and elsewhere.

Glass was not essential for any specific function; acceptable alternatives were usually available, but it was a versatile material which could be formed into many shapes and decorated in many styles. It could be opaque, brilliantly coloured or completely transparent and was sometimes made in imitation of more costly materials such as obsidian or chalcedony or rock-crystal. Glass vessels had some practical advantages over their ceramic or metal equivalents, both as transport and household vessels and as tablewares. The contents could be seen, the flavours of the contents were not absorbed into the fabric of the vessels so they could be washed and reused, and the vessels themselves had no taste and therefore did not contaminate the contents. In a well-known dining scene, Trimalchio noted that glass vessels, unlike Corinthian bronze vessels, did not taste and if they were not so fragile he would prefer them to gold (Petronius *Satyricon* 15.50).

In this paper, the extent of urban glass production will be examined through the evidence for glass-working sites, the artisans involved in production, the retail outlets, and the glass in circulation, using information from the eastern Mediterranean as well as from Italy and the western provinces (Maps 1–2).

Working glass in cities and towns
Scientific analyses demonstrate the homogeneity of the composition of most Roman glass, suggesting widespread use of a limited number of sources of raw materials. Primary production (*i.e.* making glass from the basic raw materials, which were sand, soda and lime) and secondary production (*i.e.* forming objects and vessels from glass already made) appear to have been two different and often physically separated processes, the glass made at the primary sites being transported to secondary workshops throughout the empire (summarised in Freestone *et al.* 2000, 66–7).[1]

Primary production sites with rectangular tank furnaces producing large amounts of glass have been recognised in Egypt, at Lake Maryut near Alexandria and Wadi Natrun, the source of much of the mineral soda in the ancient world (Nenna *et al.* 2000), and on the coast of Syria/Palestine between Apollonia and Akko (*Ptolemais*), close to the sand from the River Belus (Freestone *et al.* 2000). These sites, however, date from the sixth to seventh and later centuries, and analyses indicate that the glass they produced is unlikely to have been the source of the Roman glass in western Europe (Nenna *et al.* 2000, 105; Freestone *et al.* 2000, 72–4). The primary furnaces of the first to fifth centuries have yet to be identified, but a similar mode of separation between primary and secondary production is suggested by the presence of lumps of raw glass in ships wrecked in this period,[2] and at ports and coastal sites,[3] and by evidence that they were transported overland.[4]

The secondary workshops in or close to cities and towns depended on reliable supplies of glass to produce objects and vessels for their markets. Much of this presumably arrived as lumps of raw glass, though another important source was waste and recycled glass. Various categories of waste glass, such as moiles, twisted rods, drips and trails and lumps of furnace waste (Figure 10.1), were generated in the workshops, and broken vessel or window glass was collected as cullet for remelting.[5]

---

[1] Evidence for primary production not separate from secondary production has been recorded at York (Jackson *et al.* 1998; Cool *et al.* 1999) and in the Hambach Forest, west of Cologne (Wedepohl *et al.* 2003).
[2] Blue-green glass lumps weighing 100kg came from a late first-century wreck near Mljet, an island off the Croatian coast (Radić & Jurišic 1993, 122 fig. 7.2), and second to third and fourth to fifth century wrecks in southern France have produced lumps of colourless, pale greenish glass and yellowish green glass (Foy 2000, 149–50).
[3] As in Marseilles, the Gulf of Fos and Narbonne in southern France (Foy & Nenna 2001, 106–8).
[4] A third-century reference in the Babylonian Talmud mentions pack-animals transporting lumps of glass (cited in Weinberg 1988, 25 fn. 2).
[5] This material often survives in small amounts on working sites: *e.g.* the total amount of glass waste from the Romano-British workshops at Leicester, Mancetter and Wroxeter weighed 0.5kg, 1.0kg and 1.2kg respectively (Price & Cool 1991, 25–27, table 1). More substantial quantities have also been recorded, as in the mid first-century workshop at Avenches in Switzerland which produced more than 10kg of raw glass, waste and cullet (Amrein 2001, 17–40), and very large deposits have sometimes been found in pits; *e.g.* 33kg of waste and cullet came from a late first- or early second-century pit in Saintes,

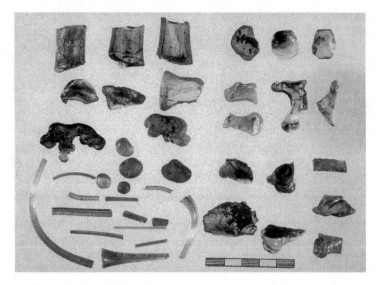

Figure 10.1 *Waste glass and cullet from Mancetter, Warwickshire and Wroxeter, Shropshire (photo: University of Leeds Photographic Service)*

The transport of cullet by sea is attested,[6] but most waste glass and cullet was probably collected from the urban population in the vicinity of the workshops. Martial (*Epigrams* 1.41.1–5) and Statius (*Silvae* 1.6.70–74) note the practice of collecting broken glass in exchange for sulphur in Rome in the late first century (Leon 1941; Whitehouse 1999, 78–9), and similar activities presumably also took place in towns throughout the Roman world.[7]

There is some textual and epigraphic evidence for glass workshops in urban settlements. For example, an early fourth-century inscription mentioned a *clivus vitriarius* in Puteoli in Campania (Dessau 1892, 269 no. 1224b), and some of the evidence for glass-working in Rome has come from similar sources. The earliest is Strabo, writing in the Augustan period, who noted that many inventions in glass production in the city produced various colours and facilitated production (*Geography* 16.2.25), and two fourth-century catalogues of the structures and topographic features of the city, the *Notitia* and the *Curiosum Urbis Romae*, refer to a *vicus vitrarius* in Regio I between the Aventine and the Caelian hills (Nordh 1949, 73), probably situated along the first section of the Via Appia between Porta Capena and the Baths of Caracalla Steinby 1999, 200). In addition, glass-working on the right bank of the River Tiber is assumed from Martial's account of a pedlar from that area who traded sulphur matches for broken glass (*Epigrams* 1.41.1–5).

---

south-west France (Amrein & Hochuli-Gysel 2000, 92–3) and 55 kilos of similar material came from an early-second century pit at Guildhall Yard, London (Pérez-Sala Rodés 2001, 66).

[6] A wooden cask containing a large quantity of broken square bottles, plates, beakers and other glass vessels was part of the cargo of a second- or early third-century ship wrecked near Grado in north east Italy (Parker 1992, 197 no. 464; Giacobelli 1997)

[7] Archaeological evidence for this practice is difficult to recognise, though marked differences in the numbers and size of glass fragments found in urban settlements at different periods sometimes suggests episodes of deliberate collection.

Figure 10.2 *The furnace excavated at Mancetter (photo: K.F. Hartley)*

Many working sites, particularly in the western provinces, have been recognised through archaeological excavation or post-excavation analysis of finds; for example, there are now more than 70 in France and more than 20 in Britain (Foy & Sennequier 1991; Sternini 1995; Nenna 2000; Foy & Nenna 2001). The nature of the surviving evidence for the sites is variable, but evidence for furnaces has frequently been recorded .

Most furnaces are known only from their ground plans and substructures and there is limited information about the details of construction, though pieces of the upper parts sometimes survive.[8] They are generally circular with a single flue, and small in size, measuring between 0.4 and 1.0m in diameter (Figure 10.2).[9]

The glass-working structures represented on first-century pottery lamps from Asseria in Croatia (Abramić 1959), Voghenza, near Ferrara in north-east Italy (Baldoni 1987), and Školarice-Križišče in Slovenia (Figure 10.3; Lazar 2004, 26–7, 56 no. 25, fig. 15) and on an unprovenanced first- or second-century terracotta group in the British Museum (Figure 10.4; Price 1988) add further detail to the archaeological evidence. The lamps show a low, domed superstructure with a sloping platform on one side at the top and the terracotta group shows a tall, tapering superstructure; both have with firing and melting chambers.

---

[8] Part of the clay and tile domed roof of a mid first-century furnace was found at La Manutention site 3 (also known as Subsistances) at Quai Saint-Vincent in Lyons (Foy & Nenna 2001, 48–9; Becker & Monin 2003, 299–302 figs 4–6), and the brick, tile and stone Byzantine furnace at Bet She'an (*Scythopolis*) in Israel had firing and melting chambers, although the superstructure was completely destroyed (Gorin-Rosen 2000, 59–60)

[9] The diameters of furnaces 1 and 2 at La Manutention/Subsistances site 3 in Lyons were 0.9m and 0.6m (Foy & Nenna 2001, 48–9; Becker & Monin 2003, 299–302 figs 4–6), the four furnaces at Avenches were between 0.5m and 0.65m (Amrein 2001, 87), the late third-century furnace at Leicester was 0.6m and the second century furnace at Mancetter was initially 0.8m, later reduced by relining to 0.5 x 0.34m (Price 1998, 345).

Figure 10.3 *The furnace on the pottery lamp from Školarice-Križišče, Slovenia (photo: Tomaž Lauko)*

Comparatively little is known about the structure and layout of most urban workshops, though some, as at Avenches (Amrein 2001, 92–4), Besançon (Munier & Brkojewitisch 2003, 321–5 figs 2–4) and at Moorgate (Frere 1987, 463) and Regis House (MacMahon this volume, 62; Hall this volume, 132–3) in London, were sited in warehouses and other rectangular buildings. In some instances, as at Mancetter, a single circular furnace was relined several times, while Avenches and Lyons and other towns have produced evidence for groups of circular furnaces in close proximity, or, as in the first-century workshops at Besançon and Eigelstein in Cologne (Follmann-Schulz 1991, 35–6 fig. 4), for circular furnaces in association with rectangular structures (Figure 10.5). Workshops often appear to have functioned in rather confined spaces since new furnaces were constructed on top of earlier ones, though some may have operated more than one furnace at the same time.[10] The workshop at Avenches has been reconstructed to show three furnaces operating simultaneously (Amrein 2001, 92–4 fig. 96), and but evidence of this kind is comparatively rare.

Uniquely, a great deal is known about the layout of the Byzantine glass workshop at Bet She'an as the building was destroyed in an earthquake in the sixth-early seventh century, sealing the structures and deposits inside. The workshop had a central room with a courtyard to the south and a store-room to the north. The single furnace was sited at the entrance to the central room and two adjacent heaps of ash and olive pits were used to anneal the vessels. Lumps of glass and groups of finished vessels were found in the central room, and the

---

[10] This is observable in many urban glass workshops in the western provinces, as in furnaces 3 and 4 at Avenches (Amrein 2001, fig. 4), Besançon (Munier & Brkojewitsch 2003, figs 5–6), Eigelstein 14 and 35–37 in Cologne (Follmann-Schulz 1991, 35–6 fig. 4), and furnaces 1 and 2 at La Manutention/Subsistances no 3 at Lyons (Foy & Nenna 2001, 48 figs; Becker & Monin 2003), though not as yet in Britain.

Figure 10.4 The furnace on the unprovenanced terracotta group (photo: British Museum)

storeroom contained further groups of finished vessels, lumps of raw glass and cullet in pots and baskets or sacks, and materials for maintaining the furnace (Gorin-Rosen 2000, 59–60).

Although no information about leases or the conditions of operation for glass workshops has been found, the evidence of restricted working conditions mentioned above suggests that the available space was often limited. However, valuable information about a comparable craft activity has survived in papyrological records of short-term leases for potteries at Oxyrhynchus in Egypt (Cockle 1981). These include statements about provision of facilities, equipment and materials and the requirement that at the end of the term of the lease the pottery was to be returned to the lessor 'free from ash and sherds' (*i.e.* cleared and in a tidy state). Swan (1984, 50) has related this requirement to the systematic clearance of pottery sites in military *vici* in Britain on abandonment, where pits and ditches were filled, structures were dismantled and the area was levelled. Whether site clearance on exit was a general condition in leases for other craft and industrial activity is unknown, but such a requirement in leases for urban glass workshops might provide a context for the large deposits of glass waste and cullet buried in pits, as at Saintes (Amrein & Hochuli-Gysel 2000, 92–3), Guildhall Yard in London (Pérez-Sala Rodés 2001), and in the *canabae legionis* at Nijmegen (Isings 1980).

Location of workshops
Early glass workshops were set up away from the public and residential areas of towns and cities,[11] at the margins of the settlement and often close to rivers or main roads (Figure 10.6–8),

---

[11] As at Augst (Rütti 1991, 152–3), Avenches (Amrein 2001, 11–2), Besançon (Munier & Brkojewitisch 2003), Cologne (Fig. 11–7; Follmann-Schulz 1991, 35–6 fig. 2), London (Shepherd & Heyworth 1991, 14–5 figs 2, 4–5; Cleary 1996, 427), Lyons (Fig. 11.8; Foy & Nenna 2001, 42–3, 48–50; Becker & Monin 2003; Motte & Martin 2003) and elsewhere.

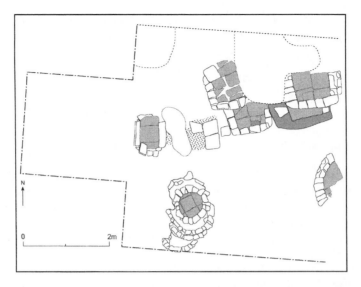

Figure 10.5 The glass-working site at Eigelstein 35/37, Cologne (after Follmann-Schulz 1991)

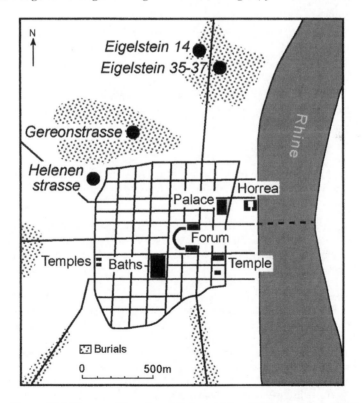

Figure 10.6 Glass-working sites at Cologne (after Follmann-Schulz 1991)

though in many cases the settled area subsequently expanded and engulfed them. Other craft processes, such as lime burning, metal smelting, pottery and tile making and tanning were also excluded from the central residential and public areas to minimise the risk of causing fires or damage to health through unpleasant fumes,[12] and in Britain and in other western provinces glass was often worked in close proximity to one or more of these activities.[13]

At later periods, glass workshops were often established within the walled areas of towns and cities, either close to the centre in public buildings or in areas which had gone out of residential use, or on the main thoroughfares. For example, the site of the late second- or early third-century furnace at La Vieille Monnaie in Lyons was originally a residential area (Foy & Nenna 2001, 52–3), the furnace at Leicester was constructed in the west colonnade of the city's market (Wacher 1978, pl. 30), and early fifth-century glassblowing debris has been found in the provincial forum at Tarragona in north-east Spain (Benet & Subias 1989, 343 nos 9.71–2, figs 188–9). These indications that urban life in the western provinces was breaking down are also recognisable elsewhere, as in Rome, where in the fifth century a glass furnace was built in the ruins of the Crypta Balbi, a public building in the Campus Martius (Sternini 1995, 183–4 fig. 258; Sagui 2000, 203–5).

The situation is rather different in the eastern provinces, where cities continued to function until the early seventh century, and glass production remained as part of the late Roman and Byzantine urban economy. For example, evidence for glass-working between the fourth or fifth century and the early seventh century has come from several cities in Israel. Production is attested in the area of the forum at Samaria-Sebaste (Crowfoot 1957, 404–5; Gorin-Rosen 2000, 58), in various parts of the city at Sepphoris (*Diocaesarea*) (Gorin-Rosen 2000, 57), and in a row of shops inside the north-east gate along the main street at Bet She'an (*Scythopolis*) (Mazor & Bar-Nathan 1998, 27–9; Gorin-Rosen 2000, 59–60). Similarly dated glass-working evidence has been recorded in Turkey, in the agora at Ephesus (pers. comm. Barbara Czurda-Ruth) and in the area of the synagogue and the baths complex at Sardis (von Saldern 1980, 95–7; Crawford 1990).

The glassworkers
In common with the majority of skilled artisans in the ancient world, little is known about the glassworkers as individuals. There are no detailed records of their activities and the names of

---

[12] Julian of Ascalon, probably writing in the sixth-early seventh century, said that workers in glass and iron should not carry out their business in the city, but if it was necessary, the workshops should be in remote and sparsely populated parts of the city, to prevent sickness and the destruction of property by fire (cited in Trowbridge 1930, 119).

[13] At Moorgate in London a second-century glass workshop was associated with metal-, bone- and leather-working (Shepherd & Heyworth 1991, 14), at Deansway, Worcester, a second- or early third-century workshop was associated with iron-working (Price 1998, 346) and at Leicester a third- or fourth-century workshop may have been associated with cupellation of silver (Price & Cool, 1991, 24). Links between glass and pottery production are also frequent. An undated furnace with a crucible containing glass was found in an area of pottery kilns outside Water Newton in Cambridgeshire (Artis 1828, pl. XXV, 4–5), a second-century and later glass furnace (Figure 10.2) was excavated by Kay Hartley among the pottery kilns outside Mancetter (Price & Cool 1991, 24 fig. 3; Price 2002, 85 fig. 6), and a burnt floor and glass production waste in a pit were found among the late first- or early second-century pottery kilns at Sheepen, Colchester (Price 1998, 344). Similar links have also been noted in other provinces, as at Quai St-Vincent in Lyons (Foy & Nenna 2001, 49; Becker & Monin 2003; Motte & Martin 2003).

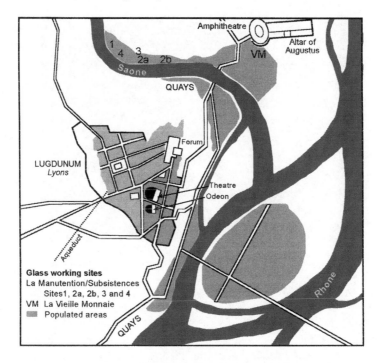

Figure 10.7 Glass-working sites at Lyons (after Foy & Nenna 2001)

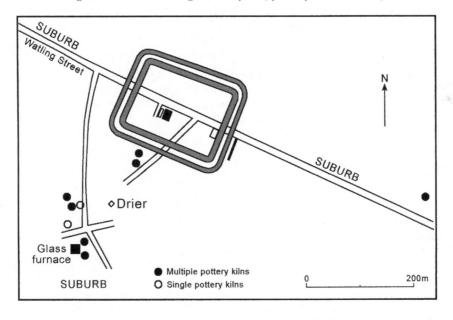

Figure 10.7 Glass-working and pottery production at Mancetter (after Burnham & Wacher 1990)

Figure 10.9 *Funerary monument in Lyons commemorating Julius Alexsander (photo: J. Price)*

most of them have not survived. Numerous written accounts mention Roman glassworkers,[14] but the names of these artisans were not recorded, presumably because they were not of interest to the writers or the readers.

The names of individual glassworkers generally occur either on their funerary monuments or on the glass vessels they made, though the pottery lamp from Asseria mentioned above bears the names of the two glassworkers (Abramić 1959). In general, funerary monuments provided few details about the workers other than their name, craft and age,[15] though their origins and affiliations were occasionally recorded. For example, Julius Alexsander, described as *opifex arti vitriae* (master in the art of glass), who died aged 75 years, five months and 13 days, and is commemorated on a third-century tombstone found in Lyons (Figure 10.9), was born in Africa and a citizen of Carthage (Foy & Sennequier 1989, 61–2 no. 8).

The information found on the glass vessels, many of which were mould-blown, is also largely confined to the name, though a place of origin is sometimes included. On early imperial mould-blown decorated tablewares the name is found within the design on the body (Figure 10.10),[16] while on mould-blown prismatic or cylindrical corrugated bottles the name is

---

[14] Such as Strabo, who wrote '…I heard in Alexandria from the glass workers…' (*Geography* 16.2.25), Seneca, who noted the glassblower '…who by his breath alone fashions glass into a thousand shapes…' (*Epistulae Morales* 14.90.29), and Petronius and Pliny who wrote about a glassworker who showed a glass vessel that did not break to the emperor Tiberius (*Satyricon* 51; *Natural History* 36.195).

[15] For example, brief epitaphs in Latin or Greek for glassworkers are known on tombstones in Cherchel, Salona, Sparta, Athens, Tyre and elsewhere (listed in Trowbridge 1930, 114–28; Foy & Nenna 2001, 67)

[16] Names on mould-blown tablewares, such as Aristeas (Calvi 1965), Aristeas the Cypriot (Constable-Maxwell 1979, 157–60, lot no. 280), Ennion (Figure 10.10; Harden 1935; Lehrer 1979; Price 1991; Barag 1996), Jason, Meges and Neikais (Harden 1935; Stern 1995), were generally in Greek characters. A few mould-blown tablewares have Latin names, such as C Caesius Bugaddus on African-head beakers (Price 1974).

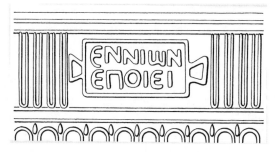

Figure 10.10 *ENNION in Greek characters on an unprovenanced mould-blown cup in Newark Museum, New Jersey (after Lehrer 1979)*

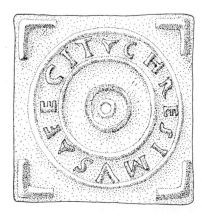

Figure 10.11 *CHRESIMUS.FECIT. in Latin characters on the base of a rectangular bottle from Usk, South Wales.*

included in the design on the base (Figure 10.11).[17] Names are much less common on free-blown vessels, but these were sometimes impressed into the end of the handles of drinking cups (Figure 10.12).[18]

---

[17] Most names on the bases of the mould-blown bottles produced in the western provinces were Latin or latinised. Names such as Sentia Secunda of Aquileia (Harden 1969, 49, 73 pl. IVB), Gn Asinius Martialis (Price 1981, 353–4 fig. 113.47; RIB 2.2, no. 2419.106–7), P Gessius Ampliatus (Scatozza-Horicht 1986, 76, fig. 12), Titianus Hyacinthus (Whitehouse 2003) or Chresimus (Figure 10.11; Price 1995, 186 no. 124, fig. 48, pl. xv; Hanel 1995, 246, 661 E147, taf. 155) are found on first- and second-century prismatic bottles, and Felix (Isings 1957, 107; Painter 1968, 62 no. 79), Frontinus (Chassaing 1961; Sennequier 1985, 169–82) and other names occur on second- to fourth-century cylindrical corrugated bottles. Names in Greek characters, such as Paulinos of Antioch, Magnos, Theodoros, Alexandros or Zosimos, have also been recorded on third- to fifth-century prismatic bottles, especially in the eastern Mediterranean (Barag 1987, 109–11; Jacobson 1992; Sternini 1994; Tek 2003)

[18] Names such as Ariston, Artas (Figure 10.12), Neikon and Philippos, sometimes in both Greek and Latin characters and sometimes giving Sidon as their place of origin, were impressed on the wings of folded handles of first-century cups. Many have been found in Rome (Fremersdorf 1938; Sagui *et al.* 1996, 218 fig. 3; Sagui 1998, 22–3 fig. 21) and elsewhere in the western provinces, though some are from

Figure 10.12 *ARTAS SIDON in Latin and Greek characters on the folded handle of a cup from Rome (after Fremersdorf 1938)*

There is little evidence to determine whether glass workers worked full time at their craft or combined seasonal glass-working with other activities, but there are some indications that craftsmen moved from place to place to produce glass for urban populations. Julius Alexsander, who died (and presumably worked) in Lyons was a native of Africa and a citizen of Carthage, and similar movements of craft skills in the early imperial period are implied by the addition of 'the Cypriot' or 'of Sidon' to the names on mould-blown and free-blown tablewares.

Regional patterns of production of glass vessels are recognisable from the middle of the first century onwards, and it is occasionally possible to identify a glass worker operating within a limited geographical area. For example, the name Amaranthus is found on several forms of first-century tablewares and containers in Burgundy and elsewhere in central France (Sennequier 1986; Cabart 2003, 162).

Some of the activities and organisations of urban glassworkers are recorded in legal documents, or in epigraphic and papyrological sources. In the early first century, glassworkers in Egypt were listed among the traders and artisans in the Tebtunis papyri (cited in Trowbridge 1930, 51 fn. 14), in the third century glassworkers were taxed by Alexander Severus (*SHA Aurelius Lampridius: Alexander Severus* 24.5) and glass from Egypt was taxed by Aurelian (*SHA Flavius Vopiscus: Divus Aurelianus* 45.1), while under Constantine in the early fourth century *vitrearii* (glassworkers) and *diatretarii* (cutters) were exempted from taxes to enable them to 'become more skilled and to train their sons' (*Codex Theodosianus* 13.4.2). Papyri from Oxyrhynchus in Egypt refer to a guild of glass workers in the city in the early fourth century (Bowman *et al.* 1977, 146 no. 3265; Coles *et al.* 1987, 113–5 no. 3742) and a guild of *specularii* (window glassmakers) is attested in Rome (CIL vi.2206). Further epigraphic references to *specularii* have been found in Rome, including a third- or fourth-century funerary inscription in the catacomb of Domitilla commemorating Sabinius Santias which includes a sketch of a window with nine panes (CIL vi.33911; Sternini 1995, 183 fig. 257).

Supplying glass in the city
After the middle of the first century, much of the glass used in towns and cities may not have travelled far from the workshop to the consumer, but some vessels, particularly pieces

---

the east Mediterranean, as at Corinth (Davidson 1952, 103 no. 650 fig. 10) and Mytilene (Price & Cottam 2000, 59 fig. 2.5).

involving exceptionally high standards of craftsmanship in their manufacture and decoration, are likely to have been produced in specialist workshops and distributed over longer distances, by water and on land. Vessels have been found in Mediterranean shipwrecks and port deposits,[19] and the movement of glass vessels by pack-animals is also attested in the Babylonian Talmud (cited in Weinberg 1988, 25 fn. 2).

Little is known about the cost of glass before the fourth century, the principal source of this information being the Edict of Maximum Prices, issued by Diocletian in AD 301. Fragments of the section on the prices for glass found in Aphrodisias between 1970 and 1972 refer to two different kinds of glass, Alexandrian and Judaean, and describe two categories of each, raw glass and undecorated vessels, and two categories of window glass, all of which were priced by weight. The inscription was studied by Barag (1987, 113–6) who argued that the names for the kinds of glass did not indicate that they were produced in Alexandria or Judaea. He interpreted these names as traditional trade-names for glass of different qualities, Judaean being the bluish green and greenish common glass and Alexandrian the colourless, high-quality glass. More recently, Stern (1999, 460–6) has used the Edict of Maximum Prices to calculate that the cost of a glass vessel was between 10 and 20 times more than the cost of a pottery vessel of equivalent capacity, and that the cost of one or two vessels of average size of Judaean glass, or one of Alexandrian glass, was equivalent to daily wage of an unskilled labourer. She has also pointed out that the listed maximum prices for glass appeared to be very low and that the price differential between the raw glass and the finished vessels, allowing for the loss of up to 40–45% of the glass during the production processes,[20] would have made it difficult for glassblowers to earn a living and may have driven utilitarian vessel glass out of the market.

Retail outlets for glass in towns and cities
Information about the arrangements for retailing glass is sparse. Generally, it is not known whether glass was sold from shops, or stalls in the town markets, or from the workshops, or whether the glassworkers doubled as retailers or supplied glass to order, or whether retail outlets specialised in glass or stocked glass with other goods. In discussing glass vessels as merchandise, there is a distinction between tablewares which were produced for sale in their own right and containers for other products. The latter group – bottles, flasks jars, pots and unguent bottles – were intended to hold a wide variety of liquid and semi-liquid preparations, and were presumably made for the use of other trades and professions, such as food suppliers, perfume and unguent makers, or pharmacists and doctors.

Links between glassworkers and frankincense dealers are suggested in the epigraphic reference to 'the quarter of the glassworkers, also known as the quarter of the incense dealers' in Puteoli (Dessau 1892, 269 no. 1224b), and there is an indication of connections between glass vessels and perfume production at Pompeii. During the excavation of the large garden

---

[19] For example off the coast of south-eastern France, the cargo in an Augustan wreck at La Tradelière included 200–300 ribbed and plain sagged glass bowls stacked in piles in boxes and separated by layers of vegetable matter (Feugère & Leyge 1989; Foy & Nenna 2001, 105), and the cargo of a late second-third century wreck at Embiez-Ouest included colourless drinking vessels packed in groups of five (Foy & Nenna 2001, 110–1). First-century port deposits are known from Pisa in Italy (Stiaffini 2000) and Narbonne (Feugère 1992) and a late second- to third-century deposit has been found in London (Shepherd 1986).
[20] Based on her practical experience as a glassworker.

attached to house II.viii.6, thought to have been a commercial flower garden producing flowers for the perfume industry, an exceptional number of fragments of small glass unguent bottles and some almost complete specimens were found, and a large number of similar unguent bottles came from a room within the house (Jashemski 1979, 407, 410, pl. 58 fig. 7).

Glass containers also appear to have been used for medical preparations from the early empire onwards. Small glass vessels have sometimes been found in the tombs of doctors (*e.g.* Künzl 1982, figs 66, 70–2, 74, 88), and textual references also refer to the use of glass containers. For example, Scribonius Largus, writing in the Claudian period,[21] specified glass vessels as suitable for containing liquid, honey-like, dry gummy and waxy medical preparations (see Taborelli 1996 for discussion of this text).

Shops selling glass
The interpretation of the precise functions of retail outlets in Roman towns and cities is usually problematic as diagnostic evidence is only likely to survive when commercial activity came to an abrupt halt as a result of an unforeseen disaster. Nonetheless, a few structures have been interpreted as storerooms or shops selling glass in the early empire and in the fourth and later centuries.

The earliest was found in the *colonia* at Cosa, about 100km north of Rome, where between AD 40 and 45, the north-west wall of the forum-basilica collapsed on an adjacent building, demolishing several rooms at the rear of the annexe to the *atrium publicum*. The rooms in this building had wide doorways facing the forum or the surrounding streetsand were probably shops rented by the town to tradesmen (Grose 1974; Brown *et al.* 1993, 135–7, 241). The annexe housed two *tabernae* with several rooms, and a back room (22,II) destroyed by the collapse of the wall produced two coins, more than 200 Arretine, thin-walled and coarse ware pottery vessels, 12 amphorae, more than 40 pottery lamps, 76 glass vessels, mostly tablewares, and a range of other objects. The pottery and glass were chronologically contemporary, most pieces being well-preserved with little signs of use, indicating that they were probably assembled only shortly before the room was destroyed, and the deposit has been interpreted as stock in the storeroom of a shop (Grose 1974).

Soon after this time, a building on the main street in *insula* XIX in the *colonia* at Colchester was destroyed by fire and a deposit containing hundreds of South Gaulish samian vessels, some colour-coated pottery and a large quantity of glass, mostly completely melted, was sealed by the collapse of the walls (Hull 1958, 153–4, no. 127; Harden 1958; see also Mac Mahon this volume, 64). This was identified as a store or shop, in which the pottery vessels appeared to have been stacked in piles on the floor or a low shelf with the glass vessels above them on a higher shelf. As the glass had dripped over the pottery, fused together, or melted into lumps during the fire, the vessel forms cannot be discussed in detail but they appear to have been mainly tablewares and probably imported from Italy or southern Gaul. The precise date of destruction of the Colchester shop is uncertain; Millett (1987, 102–6) has argued that on the evidence of the stamps on the samian this could have been around AD 50–55, while Crummy (1997, 82) favours AD 60/61, the date of the Boudican destruction of the *colonia*. It is noteworthy that the Cosa and Colchester deposits have produced glass tablewares as stock in association with pottery tablewares. Both these retail outlets functioned at a time when glass

---

[21] Sconocchia, S. 1983. *Scribonii Largi, Compositiones*. Leipzig, Teubner

vessels were probably not being locally produced, and they appear to have stocked categories of goods likely to appeal to the same urban markets.

Glass vessels may also have been associated with pottery in some later retail outlets in civil settlements in Britain, though this is less certain as deposits sealed within buildings have not been found. For example, a building on the main road in the *vicus* at Castleford, West Yorkshire, has been identified as a pottery shop (Dickinson & Hartley 2000, 36–55; Rush 2000, 149, 158 fig. 82; Hartley, 2000). It was destroyed by fire around AD 140–50 and approximately 600 burnt Central Gaulish samian vessels, plus a large quantity of other burnt pottery vessels, principally *mortaria* and Black Burnished wares, were subsequently used as levelling material in the surrounding area. Considerable quantities of glass fragments distorted by heat were found in association with the pottery, suggesting that the shop may also have dealt in glass vessels (Cool 1998a, 8; 1998b, 355, 360).

By contrast, the Flavian and later deposits interpreted as shops or storerooms in the Mediterranean world appear to have contained only glass vessels and objects, though there is some uncertainty about this as information about other materials in the deposits is not always available. The *taberna* on the north-east side of the *decumanus maximus* to the west of *cardo* IV at Herculaneum destroyed in the eruption of Vesuvius in AD 79 contained a wooden crate with 46 or 47 glass vessels packed in straw. Of these, 35 were tablewares and 11 or 12 were probably containers (de Franciscis 1963; Scatozza Höricht 1986, cat. nos 2341–2376). The commercial context of the find is uncertain as finds on the floor or shelves of the *taberna* have not been recorded, and the deposit raises some questions about retailing glass vessels. It is noteworthy that several forms of apparently empty containers were packed in the same consignment as tableware vessels, and that single examples of some forms were present as well as sets of nearly identical vessels. The name on the base of the square bottle, P Gessius Ampliatus, has been noted elsewhere in Campania (see fn. 16), and much of the glass was probably produced in local workshops, although there is no evidence that P Gessius Ampliatus made the other vessels in the packing case (*contra* Scatozza Höricht 1986, 22; 1991, 77).

Further instances of glass vessels packed in cases have been recorded in Karanis, a town in the Fayoum in Egypt (Wainwright 1924; Harden 1936). Seventy pieces of fourth-century glass, almost all in perfect condition, were found in ten elaborately decorated wooden boxes some of which were repaired. The position and context of the find were not recorded, but the size of the find, the presence of locks on the boxes, and the straw packing in one box caused Wainwright (1924) to interpret the deposit as the stock of a dealer, perhaps a glass merchant, rather than as the contents of a private house. Harden (1936, 34–8), however, pointed out that more than half of the complete glass vessels found at Karanis came from comparable groups or hoards. He listed 13 deposits found in large pottery vessels, wooden boxes, palm-leaf baskets, niches in walls, or pits in the floors, sometimes with other household objects, and argued that they contained tablewares used by the inhabitants of the town in the fourth century. It is therefore necessary to view this deposit with some caution, since storing glass in containers was apparently a late Roman domestic or ritual, rather than commercial, practice at Karanis.

At Sardis, a row of more than thirty shops is known at the back of the south colonnade of a large public building complex containing the baths, gymnasium and synagogue (von Saldern 1980, 35–97; Crawford 1990). Most of the shops produced some glass, and two (E 12–13) contained exceptional quantities of vessel and window glass fragments. These shops appear to have been used either to store stock or broken glass for recycling, or, more probably, to sell

Figure 10.13 *Glass vessels in a taberna; from a catacomb at Sousse, Tunisia (after Foy & Nenna 2001)*

ordinary and locally produced glass vessels, including goblets, bottles, flasks and lamps and window panes. The shops are not closely dated, but they appear to have functioned from around AD 400 until they were destroyed by fire in the early seventh century, and the range of glass forms is broadly comparable with the Bet She'an finds (see below).

The position of the sixth- or early seventh-century glass workshop at Bet She'an among other shops on a main thoroughfare and the finds in it suggest that it may also have functioned as a retail outlet, though we must wait for the final report for a definitive interpretation. Vessels of similar form were grouped together and neatly stacked in piles on shelves, in niches in the walls and in baskets on the floor in the central room and the storeroom. The range of forms was limited to three kinds of everyday table and household wares (drinking vessels, flasks and jugs), plus bowl-shaped lamps with stems and rectangular and circular window panes, and these were probably supplied to customers within the city, since similar forms have been found in churches and tombs nearby (Gorin-Rosen 2000, 59–60).

Glass use in urban contexts
In examining the evidence for working and supplying glass in towns and cities, some uses of glass tablewares and containers have also been mentioned, as has the relationship of glass containers to other urban crafts such as food preparation, medicine and perfume making. Archaeology and writings are the principal sources of information for considering the functions of glass vessels, but iconographic evidence in mosaics, wall decoration and funerary monuments are also valuable for showing how both tablewares and containers were used and treated in everyday life.

Glass was sometimes included in tavern scenes, as in a wall painting from a catacomb at Sousse in Tunisia (Figure 10.13) where drinking vessels were arrayed on the counter and shelves of a *taberna* (Foy & Nenna 2001, 185, fig.). Similar vessels occurred in other drinking

M·VAL·CELERINVS
PAPIRIA·ASTIGI
CIVIS·AGRIPPINE
VETER·LEG·X·G·P·F
VIVOS·FE·CIT·SIBI
E·T·MARCIAE·PRO
CVLAE·VXORI

Figure 10.14 *Tombstone of M. Valerius Celerinus in Cologne, showing a bottle on the floor beside the table (after Kisa 1908)*

and dining scenes, as did glass containers. In the dining scenes on some funerary monuments in the Rhineland (Figure 10.14), prismatic and cylindrical bottles were placed on the floor close to dining tables.[22] The Neumagen bottles were enclosed in woven, presumably wickerwork, or solid, presumably wooden, cases, and bottles with similar casing are shown on a mosaic from El Djem and a in wall-painting from Carthage (Foy & Nenna 2001, 114, figs), suggesting that protection of this kind may have been common for household bottles.[23] It is also apparent that other glass containers were protected in daily use, although the casings have survived only in dry conditions.[24] Glass tablewares were also carefully looked after within dwellings, as in the cupboards at Pompeii and Herculaneum, and the various containers, wall niches and pits at Karanis, and additional packaging was employed to safeguard personal items on journeys. For the most part the journeys were completed and the packaging has not survived, but a neatly wrapped and bulky package of palm fibres tied with a palm fibre cord

[22] As at Neumagen on the River Moselle (von Massow 1932, 197–8 nos 260, 261a-b, pl. 50) and at Cologne, on the tombstone of Marcus Valerius Celerinus, (Figure 10.14) a veteran of the Tenth legion who was a native of Astigi in Spain and a citizen of Cologne (Kisa 1908, 89, 237, 324, fig. 14). At Simpelfeld, the household effects in the scenes carved inside the sarcophagus included cylindrical and square bottles standing on a low bench (Holwerda 1933; Liversidge 1955, 65–6, pls 68–9).

[23] Wooden carrying cases containing bottles are known at Pompeii (Kisa 1908, 89 fig. 15), and corded and basketwork impressions, perhaps from casing, have been noted in the melted surface of a cylindrical bottle from Rocester in Staffordshire (Cool 1996, 108, 117 no. 36 fig. 41.21, pls 13–14). In addition, many bottles have vertical scratches on their sides, presumably from being lifted in and out of closely fitting cases.

[24] In Egypt, the body and neck of flasks and unguent bottles were often protected by fixed papyrus or palm-frond wrappings (Edgar 1905, 54 nos 32.655–62, pl. VIII; Foy & Nenna 2001, 115 no. 135), and it is likely that, using different wrapping materials, this practice also occurred in other parts of the Roman world.

protecting three colourless plates left in the Cave of the Letters in the Judaean Desert in Israel in the second quarter of the second century (Yadin 1963, 41, 101, 105–10, figs 39–40 pls 29.66/1, pl. 30.66/2–4) shows the care that was taken of treasured household possessions.

As already explained, vessel glass accounted for only part of the glass consumed in cities and towns. Architectural schemes also required large quantities of glass for windows, and for the decoration on floors, walls and vaults. Window glass was used in buildings for keeping heat in, letting light into the building and excluding draughts, and in certain situations it may have combined protection from the elements with providing a view for the occupants of buildings (pers. comm. Chris Martins). By contrast, the glass tesserae in wall and vault mosaics were largely decorative though they must also have been valuable for reflecting light within the buildings.

Glazed windows were fitted in high-status private residences in many parts of the Roman world but they occurred principally in public buildings, and especially in bath-houses, from the early first century onwards (Whitehouse 2001). Wall and vault mosaics using glass tesserae also appeared in baths and palatial buildings in the first century AD and their use increased over time (Sear 1976, 234–9; Sear 1977, especially 22–30, 41–3).

The bath-houses at Pompeii and Herculaneum provide much information about first-century glazing patterns. In particular, it is noteworthy that some circular roof windows (*oculi*) were glazed (Allen 2002, 106–8 fig. 8.7) and that some glazed windows had removable frames or were double-glazed (Whitehouse 2001, 35). Less is known in detail about most of the glazing schemes in later civic baths, though they undoubtedly became more complex as larger, more monumental, baths were constructed in the second and later centuries. A papyrus found at Oxyrhynchus indicates that 6000lb of glass were required for the construction of the public baths and gymnasium there in the early fourth AD (Bowman *et al.* 1977, 146 no. 3265) but whether this was to make the windows, or the glass tesserae for wall and vault mosaics, or both, is uncertain.

The numerous imperial bath-houses in Rome and other cities must have consumed very great quantities of glass for their construction and embellishment. A detailed study of the Baths of Caracalla which were built in Rome in the early third century has calculated the quantities of materials, including glass tesserae and window glass, used in this very large imperial project (DeLaine 1997). Glass tesserae[25] decorated more than 16,900 square metres of the interior walls and vaults and parts of the exterior of the central block of the baths; approximately 254 million tesserae were required (at 15,000 to the square metre) (DeLaine 1997, 70, 75, 181, fig. 45),[26] and they weighed approximately 380 tonnes.[27] In addition, it is estimated that glazing the windows would have required at least 3,400 square metres of glass (*ibid*, 318) weighing approximately 50 tonnes.[28]

---

[25] In shades of lilac, blue, turquoise, green, yellow, ochre and red and clear glass with gold or silver leaf backing (DeLaine 1997, 70)

[26] Requiring the services of 220 wall mosaicists plus 70 assistants, and 60 men to cut the glass tesserae (DeLaine 1997, 188)

[27] Taking the average depth of the tesserae as 0.009m (DeLaine 1997, 181) and the weight of glass per m^3 as 2.5 tonnes (*ibid*, 218 fn. 43).

[28] Taking the average thickness of the window glass as 0.006m and the weight of the glass as 2.5 tonnes per m^3 (DeLaine 1997, 218 fn. 43)

Although only a minor part of the range of processes involved in constructing in this complex of buildings, the production, supply, working, shaping and fitting of around 430 tonnes of glass was an immense undertaking, requiring the services of large number of skilled artisans in addition to the 350 individuals estimated to have been working with the glass mosaic tesserae. This striking illustration of the very large quantity of glass needed within a short period for a single imperial public building[29] raises questions about the supply of glass, the organisation of production, the siting of glass workshops and the size of the glass-working community in Rome and elsewhere. It is also a reminder of the yawning gap that exists between the reality of the processes of Roman glass-working and our current knowledge of them from the surviving evidence.

Conclusions

Although comparatively little is known in detail, it is apparent that the working of glass was widespread in the Roman world, and that workshops may have been set up in the vicinity of very many cities and towns. The requirements of the populations of very large cities, such as Rome, must have been served by several glass workshops operating simultaneously. By contrast, the glass produced for smaller towns, such as Mancetter, Leicester or Wroxeter, is more likely to have been made by travelling glassworkers who visited from time to time and worked for a brief period in each place. It is seldom possible to identify the products of an individual workshop, but for everyday vessel glass and large, heavy items such as sheets of glass for windows and mosaics, there would have been distinct advantages in moving the human skills to the intended markets, rather than the finished products. While patterns of glass use varied considerably in different parts of the Roman world, there is little doubt that glass was available to many levels of urban society, and that it was accepted as a relatively useful and inexpensive addition to the amenities and comforts of daily life.

Acknowledgements
In writing this paper I have received assistance from many colleagues and friends, including Heidi Amrein, Don Bailey, Hilary Cool, Barbara Czurda-Ruth, Anna Barbara Follmann-Schulz, Danielle Foy, Yael Gorin-Rosen, Dai Grose, Irena Lazar, Ardle Mac Mahon, Chris Martins, Marie-Dominique Nenna, Marianne Stern and Hugh Willmott, and I would like to thank all of them for information, discussing points with me and answering questions.

I am also very grateful to Yvonne Beadnell and Jeff Veitch in the Department of Archaeology, University of Durham for producing the drawings and photographs.

Bibliography
Abramić, M. 1959. 'Eine römische lampe mit darstellung des glasblasens', *Bonner Jahrbücher* 159: 149–51
Allen, D. 2002 'Roman window glass', in Aldhouse-Green, M. & Webster, P. (eds) *Artefacts and Archaeology*. University of Wales Press, Cardiff; 102–11

---

[29] The quantity, around 430 tonnes, is almost three times the calculated output of the seventeen primary furnaces at Bet Eliezer, near Caesarea in Israel (Gorin-Rosen 1993, 42–3)

Amrein, H. 2001. *L'atelier de verriers d'Avenches. L'artisanat du verre au milieu du Ier siècle apr. J.-C.* Aventicum XI (Cahiers d'archéologie Romande no 87), Lausanne.

Amrein, H. & Hochuli-Gysel, A. 2000. 'Le soufflage du verre: attestations de la technique à Avenches (Suisse) et à Saintes (France) au Ier siècle apr. J.-C', *Annales du 14e Congrès de l'Association Internationale pour l'Histoire du Verre* (Venise-Milan 1998), Lochem: 89–94

Artis, E.T. 1828. *The Durobrivae of Antoninius identified and illustrated in a series of plates, exhibiting the remains of that Roman station, in the vicinity of Castor, Northamptonshire.* Privately printed, London.

Baldoni, D. 1987. 'Una lucerna romana con raffigurazione di officina vetraria: alcune considerazioni sulla lavorazione del vetro soffiato nell'antichità', *JGS* 29: 22–9

Barag, D. 1987. 'Recent important epigraphic discoveries related to the history of glassmaking in the Roman period', *Annales du 10e Congrès de l'Association Internationale pour l'Histoire du Verre* (Madrid-Segovie 1985): 109–16

Barag, D. 1996. 'Phoenica and mould-blowing in the early Roman period', *Annales du 13e Congrès de l'Association Internationale pour l'Histoire du Verre* (Pays Bas – 1995): 77–92

Becker, C. & Monin, M. 2003. 'Fours de verriers antiques des Subsistances, Lyon', in Foy, D. & Nenna, M.-D. (eds) *Échanges et commerce du verre dans le monde antique.* Actes du colloque de l'AFAV, Aix-en-Provence et Marseille 2001. Monographies Instrumentum 24. Montagnac, Monique Mergoil: 297–302

Benet i Arque, C. & Subias i Pascual, E. 1989. 'Rebuigs i restes de fabricació', in TED'A, *Un abocador del segle V D.C. en el Fòrum Provincial de Tàrraco.* Memòries d'Excavació 2. Tarragona, Taller Escuola d'Arquelogia: 343

Bowman, A.K., Haslam, M.W., Stephens, S.A. & West, M.L. 1977. *The Oxyrhynchus Papyri, volume 45.* British Academy, London.

Brown F.E., Richardson, E.H. & Richardson, L. 1993. *Cosa III: The Buildings of the Forum.* Memories of the American Academy in Rome 37, Pennsylvania State University Press, Pennsylvania.

Burnham, B.C. & Wacher, J. 1990. *The 'small towns' of Roman Britain.* Batsford, London

Cabart, H. 2003. 'Productions et importations de verreries romaines dans l'Est de la France', in Foy, D. & Nenna, M.-D. (eds) *Échanges et commerce du verre dans le monde antique.* Actes du colloque de l'AFAV, Aix-en-Provence et Marseille 2001, Monographies Instrumentum 24, Montagnac, Monique Mergoil: 161–76

Calvi, M.C. 1965. 'La coppa vitrea di Aristeas nella collezione Strada', *JGS* 7: 9–16

Chassaing, M. 1961. 'Les barillets frontiniens', *Revue Archéologique du Centre et du Centre-Est* 12: 7–33; 89–104

Cleary, S.E. 1996. 'Roman Britain in 1995: Sites explored', *Britannia* 27: 405–38

Cockle, H. 1981. 'Pottery manufacture in Roman Egypt; a new papyrus', *JRS* 71: 87–97

Coles, R.A., Maehler, H. & Parsons, P.J. 1987. *The Oxyrhynchus Papyri* Vol 54. British Academy, London.

Constable-Maxwell. 1979. *Sale Catalogue of the Constable-Maxwell Collection of Ancient Glass (London, 5th-15th June 1979).* Sotheby Parke Burnett, London.

Cool, H.E.M. 1996. 'The Roman vessel glass', in Cleary, S.E. & Ferris, I.M. (eds) 'Excavations at the New Cemetery, Rocester, Staffordshire, 1985–1987', *SAHST* 35: 106–121

Cool, H.E.M. 1998a. 'Introduction', in Cool, H.E.M. & Philo, C. (eds) *Roman Castleford Volume 1: The Small Finds.* Yorkshire Archaeology 4. West Yorkshire Archaeology Service, Wakefield: 1–10

Cool, H.E.M. 1998b. 'Life in Roman Castleford', in Cool, H.E.M. & Philo, C. (eds) *Roman Castleford Volume 1: The Small Finds.* Yorkshire Archaeology 4. West Yorkshire Archaeology Service, Wakefield: 355–73

Cool, H.E.M., Jackson, C.M. & Monaghan, J. 1999. 'Glass-making and the Sixth Legion at York', *Britannia* 30: 147–61

Cool, H.E.M. & Price, J. 1995. *Roman vessel glass from excavations in Colchester, 1971–85.* Colchester Archaeological Report no 8, Colchester.

Crawford, J.S. 1990. *The Byzantine Shops at Sardis.* Archaeological Exploration of Sardis Monograph no 9, Harvard University Press, Cambridge, MA.

Crowfoot, G.M. 1957. 'The glass', in Crowfoot, J.W., Crowfoot, G.M. & Kenyon, K.M. (eds) *Samaria-Sebaste III: The objects from Samaria.* Palestine Exploration Fund, London: 403–22

Crummy, P. 1997. *City of victory: the story of Colchester – Britain's first Roman town.* Colchester Archaeological Trust, Colchester.

Davidson, G.R. 1952. *Corinth XII: the Minor Objects.* American School of Classical Studies at Athens, Princeton.

de Franciscis, A. 1963. 'Vetri antichi scoperti ad Erculano', *JGS*: 137–9

DeLaine, J. 1997. *The Baths of Caracalla.* JRA supplementary series no 25. Portsmouth, Rhode Island.

Dessau, H. 1892. *Inscriptiones Latinae Selectae*, volume I. Berlin

Dickinson, B. & Hartley, B. 2000. 'The Samian', in Rush, P., Dickinson, B., Hartley, B. & Hartley, K.F. 2000. *Roman Castleford. Volume III; the Pottery.* Yorkshire Archaeology 6, West Yorkshire Archaeology Service, Wakefield: 5–88

Edgar, C.C. 1905. *Catalogue général des Antiquités égyptiennes du musée du Caire. Graeco-Egyptian glass.* Imprimerie de l'Institut Français d'Archéologie Orientale, Cairo.

Feugère, M. 1992. 'Un lot de verres du 1er siècle provenant du Port de Narbonne (Aude) (sondages 1990–1992)', *Revue Archeologique du Narbonnais* 25: 177–206

Feugère, M. & Leyge, F. 1989. 'La cargaison de verrerie augustéenne de l'épave de la Tradelière (Îles de Lérins)', in Feugère, M. (ed.) *Le Verre Préromain en Europe Occidentale.* Montagnac, Monique Mergoil: 169–76

Follmann-Schulz, A.-B. 1991 'Fours de verriers romains dans la province de Germanie inférieure', in Foy, D. and Sennequier, G. (eds.), *Ateliers de verriers de l'Antiquité à la periode pré-industrielle.* Actes de 4èmes Rencontres (Rouen 1989). Association Française pour l'Archéologie du Verre, Rouen.

Foy, D. 2000. 'Technologie, géographie, économie. Les ateliers de verriers primaires et secondaires en Occident esquisse d'une évolution de l'Antiquité au Moyen Âge', in Nenna, M.-D. (ed.) *La Route du Verre. Ateliers primaires et secondaires du second millénaire av.J-C. au Moyen Âge.* Maison de l'Orient Mediterranéen-Jean Pouilloux, Lyon: 147–70

Foy, D. & Nenna, M.-D. 2001. *Tout Feu, Tout Sable. Mille ans de verre antique dans le Midi de la France.* Musées de Marseille. Aix en Provence, Édisud.

Foy, D. & Sennequier, G. 1989. *À travers la verre du Moyen Âge à la Renaissance.* Musées et Monuments départementaux de la Seine-Maritime, Rouen.

Foy, D. & Sennequier, G. 1991 *Ateliers de verriers de l'Antiquité à la periode pré-industrielle.* Actes de 4èmes Rencontres (Rouen 1989). Association Française pour l'Archéologie du Verre, Rouen.

Freestone, I.C., Gorin-Rosen,Y. & Hughes, M.J. 2000. 'Primary glass from Israel and the production of glass in Late Antiquity and the Early Islamic period' in Nenna, M.-D. (ed.) *La Route du Verre. Ateliers primaires et secondaires du second millénaire av.J-C. au Moyen Âge.* Maison de l'Orient Mediterranéen-Jean Pouilloux, Lyon: 65–83

Fremersdorf, F. 1938. 'Römische Gläser mit buntgefleckter Oberfläche', *Festschrift für August Oxé.* Darmstadt: 116–21

Frere, S. 1987. 'Roman Britain in 1986: Sites explored', *Britannia* 18, 302–59

Giacobelli, M. 1997. 'I vetri del rilitto di Grado', *Atti del Convegno Nazionale di Archeologia Subacquea* (Anzio 1996). Bari, Edipuglia: 311–3

Gorin-Rosen, Y. 1993 'Hadera, Bet Eli'ezer', *Excavations and Surveys in Israel* 13, 42–3

Gorin-Rosen, Y. 2000. 'The ancient glass industry in Israel; summary of the finds and new discoveries', in Nenna, M.-D. (ed.) *La Route du Verre. Ateliers primaires et secondaires du second millénaire av.J-C. au Moyen Âge.* Maison de l'Orient Mediterranéen-Jean Pouilloux, Lyon: 49–63

Grose, D.F. 1974. 'Roman glass of the first century AD. A dated deposit of glassware from Cosa, Italy', *Annales du 6e Congrès de l'Association Internationale pour l'Histoire du Verre* (Cologne 1–7 Juillet 1973), Liège: 31–52

Hanel, N. 1995. Vetera I. *Die Funde aus den römischen Lagern auf dem Furstenberg bei Xanten.* Rheinische Ausgrabungen 35, Rheinland-verlag, Bonn.

Harden, D.B. 1935. 'Romano-Syrian glasses with mould-blown inscriptions', *JRS* 25: 163–86

Harden, D.B. 1936. *Roman glass from Karanis found by the University of Michigan Archaeological Expedition in Egypt 1924–29.* University of Michigan Press, Ann Arbor.

Harden, D.B. 1958. 'Glass', in Hull, M.R. (ed.) *Roman Colchester.* Reports of the Research Committee of the Society of Antiquaries of London 20, Oxford: 157–8

Harden, D.B. 1969. 'Ancient Glass, II: Roman' *AJ* 126: 44–77

Hartley, K.F. 2000. 'The "Pottery Shop" Mortaria, in Rush, P., Dickinson, B., Hartley, B. & Hartley, K.F. (eds) *Roman Castleford. Volume III; the Pottery.* Yorkshire Archaeology 6, West Yorkshire Archaeology Service, Wakefield: 183–6

Holwerda, J.H. 1933 Der römische Sarkophag von Simpelveld', *Archäologischer Anzeiger. Beiblatt zum Archäologischer Instituts* 1933 I/II; 56–75

Hull, M.R. 1958. *Roman Colchester.* Reports of the Research Committee of the Society of Antiquaries of London 20, Oxford.

Isings, C. 1957. *Roman Glass from Dated Finds.* Wolters, Groningen.

Isings, C. 1980. 'Glass from the *canabae legionis* at Nijmegen', *Berichten van Rijksdienst voor het Oudheidkundig Bodemonderzoek* 30: 281–346

Jackson, C.M., Cool, H.E.M. & Wager, E.C.W. 1998. 'The manufacture of glass in Roman York', *JGS* 40: 55–61

Jacobson, G.L. 1992. 'Greek names on prismatic jugs', *JGS* 34: 35–43

Jashemski, W.F. 1979. 'The Garden of Hercules at Pompeii (II.viii.6): the discovery of a commercial flower garden', *AJA* 83: 403–11

Kisa, A. 1908. *Das Glas im Altertume.* Hiersmann, Leipzig.

Künzl, E. 1982. 'Medizinische Instrumente aus Sepulkralfunden der römischen Kaiserzeit', *Bonner Jahrbücher* 182: 1–131

Lazar, I. 2004 'Spiegelungen der Vorzeit – Antikes Glas in Slowenien', in Lazar, I. ed., *Die Römer – Glas, Ton, Stein.* Pokrajinski Musej, Celje; 10–81

Lehrer, G. 1979. *Ennion – a First-Century Glassmaker.* Museum Ha Eretz, Ramat Aviv.

Leon, H.J. 1941. 'Sulphur for broken glass', *TPAPA* 72: 233–6

Liversidge, J. 1955. *Furniture in Roman Britain.* Tiranti, London.

Mazor, G. & Bar-Nathan, R. 1998. 'The Bet She'an Excavation Project – 1992–1994. Antiquities Authority Expedition', *Excavations and Surveys in Israel* 17: 7–37

Millett, M. 1987. 'Boudicca, the First Colchester Potters' Shop, and the dating of Neronian Samian', *Britannia* 18: 93–123

Motte, S. & Martin, S. 2003. 'L'atelier de verrier antique de la Montée de la Butte à Lyon et ses productions', in Foy, D. & Nenna, M.-D. (eds) *Échanges et commerce du verre dans le monde antique.* Actes du colloque de l'AFAV, Aix-en-Provence et Marseille 2001, Monographies Instrumentum 24. Montagnac, Monique Mergoil: 303–19

Munier, C. & Brkojewitisch, G. 2003. 'Premiers éléments relatifs à la découverte récente d'un atelier de verrier antique à Besançon', in Foy, D. & Nenna, M.-D. (eds) *Échanges et commerce du verre dans le monde antique.* Actes du colloque de l'AFAV, Aix-en-Provence et Marseille 2001, Monographies Instrumentum 24, Montagnac, Monique Mergoil: 321–37

Naumann-Steckner, F. 1991. 'Depictions of glass in Roman wall paintings', in Newby, M. & Painter, K. (eds) *Roman Glass: Two Centuries of Art and Invention.* Society of Antiquaries of London Occasional Paper no 13, London: 86–98

Naumann-Steckner, F. 1999. 'Glasgefässe in der römischen Wandmalerei', in Klein, M.J. (ed.) *Römische Glaskunst und Wandmalerei.* von Zabern, Mainz: 25–33

Nenna, M.-D. 2000. *La Route du Verre. Ateliers primaires et secondaires du second millénaire av.J-C. au Moyen Âge.* Maison de l'Orient Mediterranéen-Jean Pouilloux, Lyon.

Nenna, M.-D., Picon, M. & Vichy, M. 2000. 'Ateliers Primaires et Secondaires en Égypte a l'époque Gréco-Romaine', in Nenna, M.-D. (ed.) *La Route du Verre. Ateliers primaires et secondaires du second millénaire av.J-C. au Moyen Âge*. Maison de l'Orient Mediterranéen-Jean Pouilloux, Lyon: 97–112

Nordh, A. 1949 *Libellus de regionibus urbis Romae*. Gleerup, Lund

Painter, K.S. 1968. 'Roman glass', in Harden, D.B., Painter, K.S., Pinde-Wilson, R.H. & Tait, H. *Masterpieces of Glass*. British Museum, London 36–90

Parker, A.J. 1992. *Ancient shipwrecks of the Mediterranean and the Roman provinces*. BAR (International Series) 580, Oxford

Peréz-Sala Rodés, M. 2001. 'El estudio del reciclaje del vidrio en el mundo romano: el caso de Guildhall Yard, Londres', in Carreras Rossell, T. (ed.) *I Jornades Hispàniques d'Història del Vidre: Actes* (Sitges 2000). Museu d'Arqueologia de Catalunya, Barcelona 65–72

Price, J. 1974. 'A Roman mould-blown negro-head glass beaker from London', *AntJ* 54: 291–2

Price, J. 1981. *Roman glass in Spain*. Unpublished PhD thesis, University of Wales

Price, J. 1988. 'An Egyptian terracotta group showing Eros beside a glass furnace', *AntJ* 68: 317–9

Price, J. 1991. 'Decorated mould-blown glass tablewares in the first century AD', in Newby, M. & Painter, K. (eds) *Roman Glass: Two Centuries of Art and Invention*. Society of Antiquaries of London Occasional Paper no 13, London: 56–75

Price, J. 1995. 'Glass vessels', in Manning, W.H., Price, J. & Webster, J. (eds) *The Excavations at Usk, 1965–1976. The Roman Small Finds*. Cardiff, University of Wales Press, Cardiff: 139–91

Price, J. 1996. 'A ribbed bowl from a late Iron Age burial at Hertford Heath, Hertfordshire', *Annales du 13e Congrès de l'Association Internationale pour l'Histoire du Verre* (Pays-Bas 1995). Lochem: 47–54

Price, J. 1998. 'The social context of glass production in Roman Britain', in McCray, P. (ed.) *The prehistory and history of glassmaking technology*. Ceramics and Civilisation 8, American Ceramic Society, Westerville, Ohio: 331–48

Price, J. 2002. 'Broken bottles and quartz sand: glass production in Yorkshire and the North in the Roman period', in Wilson, P. & Price, J. (eds) *Aspects of Industry in Roman Yorkshire and the North*. Oxbow, Oxford: 81–94

Price, J. & Cool, H.E.M. 1991. 'The evidence for the production of glass in Roman Britain', in Foy, D. & Sennequier, G. (eds) *Ateliers de verriers de l'Antiquité à la periode pré-industrielle*. Actes de 4èmes Rencontres (Rouen 1989). Rouen, Association Française pour l'Archéologie du Verre, Rouen: 23–30

Price, J. & Cottam, S. 2000. 'Glass tablewares in use at Mytilene in Lesbos in the early-mid 1st century AD', *Annales du 14e Congrès de l'Association Internationale pour l'Histoire du Verre (Venise-Milan 1998)*, Lochem: 58–62

Radić, I. & Jurišic, M. 1993. 'Das antike Schliffswrack von Mljet, Kroatien', *Germania* 71: 113–38

Rush, P. 2000. 'The Coarse Wares', in Rush, P., Dickinson, B., Hartley, B. & Hartley, K.F. (eds). *Roman Castleford. Volume III; the Pottery*. Yorkshire Archaeology 6, West Yorkshire Archaeology Service, Wakefield: 89–166

Rütti, B. 1991. *Die römischen Glaser aus Augst und Kaiseraugst*. Forschungen in Augst 13/1–2. Augst, Römermuseum.

Sagui, L. 1998. *Storie al Caleidoscopio. I vetri della collezione Gorga: un patrimonio ritrovato*. Museo dell'Arte Classica, Rome.

Sagui, L. 2000. 'Produzioni vetrarie a Roma tra V e VII secolo', *Annales du 14e Congrès de l'Association Internationale pour l'Histoire du Verre* (Italia/Venezia-Milano 1998): 203–7

Sagui, L., Bacchelli, B. & Pasqualucci, R. 1996. 'Un patrimoine unique au monde. Les verres de la collection Gorga', *Annales du 13e Congrès de l'Association Internationale pour l'Histoire du Verre* (Pays Bas – 1995): 213–24

Scatozza Horicht, L.A. 1986. *I vetri romani di Erculano*. Ministero per i Beni Culturali ed Ambientali Soprintendenza Archeologica di Pompei, Cataloghi 1, "L'Erma" di Bretschneider, Roma.

Sear, F. 1976. 'Wall and vault mosaics', in Strong, D. & Brown, D. (eds) *Roman Crafts*. Duckworth, London: 231–240

Sear, F. 1977. *Roman wall and vault mosaics*. F.H. Kerle, Heidelberg

Sennequier, G. 1985. *Verrerie d'Époque Romaine. Collections des Musées départementaux de Seine-Maritime*. Rouen

Sennequier, G. 1986. 'Un certain AMARANTUS (ou AMARANTHUS ?), verrier installé en Bourgogne au Ier siècle de notre ère', *JGS* 28: 11–18

Shepherd, J. 1986. 'Glass', in Miller, L., Schofield, J. & Rhodes, M. (eds) *The Roman quay at St Magnus House, London. Excavations at New Fresh Wharf, Lower Thames Street, London 1974–8*. London and Middlesex Archaeological Society Special Paper no 8: 209–10

Shepherd, J. & Heyworth, M. 1991. 'Le travail du verre dans Londres romain (Londinium): un état de la question', in Foy, D. & Sennequier, G. (eds) *Ateliers de verriers de l'Antiquité à la periode pré-industrielle*. Actes de 4èmes Rencontres (Rouen 1989). Rouen, Association Française pour l'Archéologie du Verre, Rouen: 13–22

Steinby, E.M. 1999. *Lexicon Topographicum Urbis Romae, V*. Edizioni Quasar, Rome.

Stern, E.M. 1995. *The Toledo Museum of Art. Roman Mold-Blown glass: the First through Sixth Centuries*. L'Erma di Bretschneider, Rome.

Stern, E.M. 1999. Roman glassblowing in a cultural context. *AJA* 103: 441–84

Sternini, M. 1994. 'Bottiglie in vetro con bolli greci', *Epigrafia della produzione e della distribuzion*. Collection de l'Ecole Française de Rome 193: 567–74

Sternini, M. 1995. *La Fenice di Sabbia: storia e tecnologia del vetro antico*. Edipuglia, Bari.

Stiaffini, D. 2000. 'Vetri', in Bruni, S. (ed.) *Le navi antiche di Pisa*. Edizioni Polistampa, Firenze: 264–89

Swan, V.G. 1984. *The Pottery Kilns of Roman Britain*. Royal Commission on Historical Monuments Supplementary Series 5. Her Majesty's Stationery Office, London.

Taborelli, L. 1996. 'I contenitori per medicamenti nelle prescrizioni di Scribonio Largo e la diffusione del vetro soffiato', *Latomus* 55: 148–56

Tek, A.T. 2003. 'Prismatic glass bottles with Greek inscriptions from Arycanda in Lycia', *Annales du 15e Congrès de l'Association Internationale pour l'Histoire du Verre* (New York-Corning 2001). Nottingham: 82–7

Trowbridge, M.L. 1930. *Philological Studies in Ancient Glass*. University of Illinois Press, Urbana.

von Massow, W. 1932. *Die Grabdenkmäler von Neumagen*. de Gruyter, Berlin.

von Saldern, A. 1980. *Ancient and Byzantine Glass from Sardis*. Archaeological Exploration of Sardis Monograph no 6. Harvard University Press, Cambridge, MA.

Wacher, J. 1978. *Roman Britain*. Dent, London.

Wainwright, G.A. 1924. 'Roman glass from Kom Washim', *Le Musée Égyptien* 3.3: 64–97

Wedepohl, K.H., Gaitzsch, W. & Follmann-Schulz, A.B. 2003. 'Glass-making and Glass-working in six Roman factories in the Hambach Forest, Germany', *Annales du 15e Congrès de l'Association Internationale pour l'Histoire du Verre* (New York-Corning 2001). Nottingham: 56–61

Weinberg, G.D. 1988. *Excavations at Jalame. Site of a glass factory in late Roman Palestine*. University of Missouri Press, Columbia.

Whitehouse, D. 1999. 'Glass in the epigrams of Martial', *JGS* 41: 73–81

Whitehouse, D. 2001. 'Window glass between the first and the eighth centuries', in Dell'Acqua, F. & Silva, R. (eds) *Il Colore nel Medioevo*. Istituto Storico Lucchese, Lucca: 31–43

Whitehouse, D. 2003. 'A mould-blown bottle from the workshop of Titianus Hyacinthus', *JGS* 45: 179–80

Yadin, Y. 1963. *The finds from the Bar Kokhba period in the Cave of Letters*. Israel Exploration Society, Jerusalem.

11

How many lives depended on plants?
Specialisation and agricultural production at Pompeii

Marina Ciaraldi

Urbanisation and archaeobotany at Pompeii

There is little doubt that, at the moment of the eruption of AD 79, Pompeii was a fully developed urban centre, a lively market town with temples, a *Forum*, shops and numerous crafts and industries. So much so, that Jongman claims 'studying Pompeii means studying Roman urbanism under a magnifying glass' (1988, 56). It is, however, less clear when and how Pompeii had become a town and what its role was in the local and regional economy. What we can safely assume is that its economic structure had undergone important changes and that some areas, such as agricultural production, redistribution of food resources and establishment of specialised activities were particularly affected.

Recent archaeological investigations at Pompeii have started addressing questions related to the onset of its urbanism by using the evidence from a number of different disciplines, including topography, sociology and economy (Bon *et al.* 1997, 125–31; Fulford & Wallace-Hadrill 1998, 128–45; 1999, 37–126; Jones & Robinson forthcoming). This paper intends to add to this debate by providing the picture of the plant economy as detected by the study of plant material recovered from new excavations at Pompeii.

Specialisation and the use of plant resources

The emergence of craft specialisations and 'industrial' activities are typically interpreted as evidence of the initial stages of formation of a city (see for instance Childe 1951; Tosi 1984, 22–52; Brumfield & Earle 1987, 125–31; Rosen 1997, 82–91). Most craft categories and industries can be identified in the archaeological context. Historical sources also provide information about technology and the social status of craftspeople. A good example is represented by metal-working. By contrast, the situation of those involved, directly or indirectly, in agricultural-related activities is less clear. Although historical sources have many references to peasants and landlords, they are less informative on the minor or collateral activities associated with agricultural production or the use of wild plants, such as, for instance, the case of the production of perfumes, dyes or medicines. It is in cases such as these that archaeology can help to fill the gap left by the historical record.

Archaeobotany represents a useful tool in the identification of specialised activities on archaeological sites, such as the production of woad (Hall 1995) or of drugs (Ciaraldi 2000). It not only provides evidence of human and animal diet, but often allows the reconstruction of activities which used plants in a variety of ways: as fuel, in the preparation of medicines, perfumes and dyes, as raw material for baskets, mats, roofs, for tanning and many other crafts and industrial processes.

Even when it is possible to detect the presence of specialised activities through the study of the archaeobotanical record, our knowledge of the lives of artisans and craftspeople still remains incomplete. The impact that artisans and craftspeople had on the economy and the social life of urban centres often remains undisclosed. In some cases, however, the picture provided by the archaeological record, though fragmentary, is the only source of evidence available and it often proves to be important, particularly when we attempt to compare

191

willows	*Salix* sp. (bud scale)	river banks
silver fir	*Abies alba* Miller (cone and scales)	mountainous woodland with beech
cypress	*Cupressus sempervirens* L. (seed, scales and leaves)	
walnut	*Juglans regia* L. (shell, buds and bud scales)	
beech	*Fagus sylvatica* L. (bud scales)	nowadays found between 1000–1700m
fig	*Ficus carica* L. (seed)	spontaneous/cultivated
hemp	*Cannabis sativa* L. (seed)	cultivated for its fibres. Adventitious in orchard
stinging nettle	*Urtica dioica* L. (seed)	wastelands; rubbish tips, nithrophile
redshank	*Polygonum persicaria* L. (seed)	weed in irrigated cultures; rarely ruderal
black bindweed	*Bilderdykia convolvulus* (L.) Dumort (seed)	arable; paths
cluster/wood dock	*Rumex conglomeratus/sanguineus* (seed)	
stinking goosefoot	*Chenopodium* cf. *vulvaria* L. (seed)	anthropic, nithrophile
oraches	*Atriplex* sp. (seed)	
common purslane	*Portulaca oleracea* L. (seed)	fields, vegetable gardens, arable
common chickweed	*Stellaria media* (L.) Vill. (seed)	anthropic
hairy buttercup	*Ranunculus sardous* Crantz (seed)	wet environments and fields; acidophile
opium poppy	*Papaver somniferum* L. (seed)	cultivated as medicinal plant and for seeds
greater celandine	*Chelidonium majus* L. (seed)	walls, ruderal
turnip	*Brassica* cf. *rapa* L. (seed)	cultivated, often escaped from cultivation
rose	*Rosa* sp. L. (seed)	
peach	*Prunus persica* (L.) Batsch (stones and stems)	
black medik	*Medicago lupulina* L. (pod)	ruderal; paths; arid arable lands
grape	*Vitis vinifera* L.(seed, berries and tendrils)	
common mallow	*Malva sylvestris* L. (seed)	arable, paths, rubbish tips
bryony	*Bryonia dioica* Jacq. (seed)	hedgerows; wet woodlands; ruderal
myrtle	*Myrtus communis* L. (berries and seeds)	
small bur-parsley	*Caucalis platycarpos* L. (seed)	weed of cereals on limestone
(wild) carrot	*Daucus carota* L. (seed)	arable lands; roadsides
(wild) celery	*Apium graveolens* L. (seed)	arable lands; cultivated
white horehound	*Marrubium vulgare* L. (seed)	ruderal, arable lands, arid pasture
pimpernels	*Anagallis* sp. L. (seed)	
cleavers	*Galium* cf. *aparine* L. (seed)	fields, arable lands, hedgerows
common comfrey	*Symphytum officinale* L. (seed)	wet meadows; woodlands along rivers; banks; hedgerows
vervain	*Verbena officinalis* L. (seed)	roadsides, paths, arable land, sinanthropic
dead-nettles	*Lamium* sp. (seed)	
strawberry tree	*Arbutus* cf. *unedo* (immature fruit)	mediterranean maquis, cultivated
gipsywort	*Lycopus europeus* L.(seed)	wet meadows; banks
black nightshade	*Solanum nigrum* L. (seed)	arable; ruderal
henbane	*Hyoscyamus albus* L. (seed)	ruderal; rubbish tips
alder	*Sambucus nigra* L. (seed)	wet woodlands; hedgerows
nar. leaved cornsalad	*Valerianella dentata* (L) Pollich (seed)	
hemp-agrimony	*Eupatorium cannabinum* L. (seed)	muddy places, wet environments
creeping thistle	*Cirsium arvense* (L.) Scop. (seed)	fields, arable lands, roadsides
prickly sow-thistle	*Sonchus asper* (L.) Hill (seed)	orchards; vineyards
smooth sow-thistle	*Sonchus oleraceus* L. (seed)	manured crops; ruderal; roadsides
sedges	*Carex* sp.	wetland
glaucous sedge	*Carex* cf. *flacca* L. (seed)	meadows, springs, woodland
duckweed	*Lemna* sp. (seed)	water

Table 11.1 List of plants identified from Villa Vesuvio (from Ciaraldi 2000, modified)

different urban situations or to understand the transformation of urban centres.

In this paper the archaeobotanical record will be used to detect industrial activities often unmentioned in traditional sources and to provide information about the existence of various specialists who contributed to the economic and social complexity of ancient towns. Two case

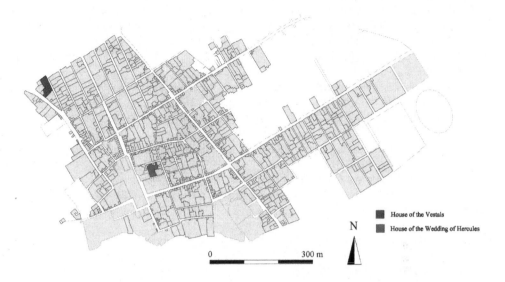

Figure 11.1 *Plan of Pompeii showing the location of the Casa delle Vestali (VI.i.1–6) and the Casa delle Nozze di Ercole (VII.ix.47).*

studies from Pompeii are examined in this paper. The first looks at a well-defined profession, that of the 'pharmacist', which used plants and other natural resources as raw material for the production of medicines. The second considers the more general picture of the production of food and looks at the changes which were brought about by the transformation of the urban economy over time.

Farmer or pharmacist?

In 1996 the Soprintendenza Archeologica of Avellino, Salerno and Benevento undertook a rescue excavation of a *villa rustica* or farmhouse near Pompeii called the Villa Vesuvio. The villa lies in a lowland area, close to what was once the course of the River Sarno, in an area with a concentration of small farmhouses (Soprintendenza Archeologica di Pompei 1992). The *villa*, covered by several metres of lapilli by the AD 79 eruption, had all the architectural elements of a rural house, including a threshing floor and a wine press *(torcularium)* with associated cellar *(cella vinaria)*. The cellar contained seven *dolia,* partly embedded in the ground and a brick fire-place approximately 40cm in height (pers. comm. Marisa Conticello de' Spagnolis).

The contents of one of the *dolia* consisted of a thick organic deposit, which contained numerous waterlogged plant remains (Table 11.1). Fifty-eight per cent of the plants identified were medicinal plants and, of these, seventy-seven per cent were mentioned in ancient sources as being effective against poisons when taken on their own or in combination with other ingredients (Ciaraldi 2000; 2001). Some of the species were medicinal ingredients, known to have been used for millennia (see for instance Pliny *Historia Naturalis* 20–27; Dioscorides *Materia Medica*; Riddle 1985), such as the group of the Solanaceae, comfrey (*Symphytum officinale* L.), hemp (*Cannabis sativa* L.) and opium poppy (*Papaverum somniferum* L.).

It has been suggested that the assemblage could have been related to the preparation of medicines, as is also indicated by the presence of the peculiar fireplace found at the Villa Vesuvio (Ciaraldi 2000; 2001). Similar cooking installations have also been observed by the author in Pompeian workshops associated with medical activities and the production of dyes through associated finds (for VII.iv.37 see Eschenbach 1993; for see VIII.iv.46 see Bliquez 1994; for VII.ii.2 see van der Poel 1977).

A small cooker, similar to the one found at Villa Vesuvio, also appears in a Roman votive stele from Grand in southern France (presently kept at the Museum of Èpinal) (Rostovtzeff 1957, 164). It illustrates a scene in a workshop, and has been interpreted as a pharmacy or a soap factory.

Some of the plants found in the *dolium* at Villa Vesuvio were used both as medicine and in the production of soap and dyes. The overlap of these two extractive activities (soap and dye production) seems to be confirmed by Pliny's use of the word *sapo* (soap), used also for the dyeing of hair (Pliny *Historia Naturalis* 28.191). Interestingly, Rawcliffe (1995, 152) suggests that early drug preparation was closely related to cooking and dyeing, therefore it is possible that drugs and dyes were produced in the same workshop.

In the past, the processing of plants for drug preparation seems to have been different from modern methods. Decoctions (the extraction of the water-soluble substances of a drug or a medicinal plants by boiling), infusions and soaking in wine were common practices. Grinding, powdering and pounding are also mentioned, but perhaps they were not as common as we would expect on the basis of modern references (Ciaraldi 2002).

What could have the drug produced at Villa Vesuvio been? Two compound drugs were recurrently mentioned in the ancient literature: *mithridatium* and *theriac*. The first took its name from Mithridates IV, King of Pontus (120–63 BC). Mithridates, or more probably his personal doctor, the Greek botanist Crataeus, is believed to have prepared an antidote against poisons (Celsus *de Medicina* 5.23.3; Miller 1969, 5). It is said that Mithridates drank a small amount of the drug each day in order to become immune to poisons (Watson 1966, 35).

The written sources mention several different recipes for *mithridatium,* containing between four and fifty ingredients (Watson 1966, 38; Guthrie 1945, 69). *Theriac*, the second compound drug, bears many similarities with *mithridatium*. Its name derives from the Greek *therion*, meaning venomous animal. It was originally used as an antidote to counteract the bites of venomous creatures (Watson 1966, 4) but, in medieval times, it was used as a panacea (Rawcliffe 1995, 152–5). Its ingredients were mixed together with wine and stored for many years (Watson 1966, 12). Galen (*Antidothes* 2.17) and Pliny (*Historia Naturalis* 20.264) say that the Falernian, a renowned Campanian wine, was an important ingredient in the preparation of *theriac*.

We should not be surprised that medicinal production was located in the countryside. Villa Vesuvio is not far away from Pompeii and is favourably located for easy access to the town and its market. Moreover, the location of medicinal activities in the countryside was well known in the Greek world and was exported with success to the Roman world (Nutton 1995, 39–40). The presence of a 'pharmacy' in the Pompeian countryside suggests that specialised activities not directly connected to agricultural production may not have been confined to the city. Practices that involved a deep knowledge of the medicinal properties of the plants might still have been in the hands of those who lived close to the natural environment. Even though specialised activities are often referred to as evidence of urbanisation (as in Rosen 1977) and are often associated with towns, some specialisation might have been stimulated by the close proximity of the town, but have remained located in the countryside. The market must have been the driving force, as its presence would have facilitated the distribution of goods.

In the case of medicinal production, an important element that could have favoured the location of drug production in the countryside was the ease of access to the primary material: plants and animals. Other industries that required easy access to natural resources could have, similarly, been located outside the towns. Factors such as availability of running water, easy access to large open spaces and availability of large storage areas, would all have contributed to render a location in the countryside more attractive for some industries. The feasibility of such choice, however, would have also depended on other factors, such as the distance from the town or from other markets and the efficiency of the transport system.

Changing agriculture, changing society

The production of medicines discussed above is a good example showing how, through the analysis of the archaeobotanical evidence, it is possible to detect the presence of an otherwise undocumented specialised activity. There are other cases in which this is only possible to a limited extent and the information that can be gained from the archaeobotanical evidence is less precise. This is the case, for instance, of the diachronic changes that occur in botanical assemblages, which are very informative about the changes in the economic structure of an urban centre but are less informative about the lives and activities of artisans and craftspeople.

The evidence presented in the following part of this paper is a synthesis discussing examples of this situation. The object of the study is the archaeobotanical material recovered from two Pompeian dwellings, the *Casa delle Vestali* (VI.i.1–6) and the *Casa delle Nozze di Ercole* (VII.ix.47), as well as from older excavations and archival data (Figure 11.1; Ciaraldi 2001). The archaeobotanical evidence will be discussed in three phases, ranging in date from the sixth century BC to the moment of the death of the city, in AD 79.

Phase I (sixth to fifth century BC)

The plant assemblage from this period is very homogeneous and includes staple crops such as emmer, free-threshing wheat, barley, common and Italian millets, fig and grape. The presence of chaff indicates that cereals were probably cleaned daily, just before cooking. The settlement area, though already surrounded by walls, was occupied by scattered houses, interspersed by open land (de Caro 1986, 20; 1992, 72). This, together with the fact that part of the crop processing still occurred in the house, suggests that agricultural activities were very much part of the economy of the town rather than being relegated to the countryside. It is possible that, from an agricultural point of view, each single household represented a self-sufficient unit. What did the inhabitants of Pompeii do during this period? Were they just small farmers who lived in an enclosed settlement for protection? Were they involved in other specialised activities? Were such activities part of an economic system that could already be defined as urban? Although these questions cannot be fully answered, it is at least possible to suggest that, as far as agriculture activities were concerned, there was little specialisation.

Phase II (fourth to first half of second century BC)

The historical events that took place in Campania between the fourth and the second century BC portray a complex political situation, rapidly evolving, which saw the escalation of the contrasting interests between the various ethnic groups that occupied different areas of the region: Greeks, Romans and Samnites. The rising importance of the port of Puteoli, located in the northern part of the Gulf of Naples, not far away from Pompeii, was significant in this period. Puteoli played an essential role in the Mediterranean trade of this period as it was involved in regular contacts with North Africa and Asia. Luxury items, such as perfumes, spices and pearls, as well as religious ideas, arrived in Italy from places as distant as Arabia, India and Sri Lanka (Tram Tan Tinh 1972, xviii; Camodeca 1990, 77–8).

Agriculture, particularly in central and southern Italy, was strongly affected by the continuous request of manpower by the Roman army (Toynbee 1965; Frederiksen 1981, 265). This brought about a substantial depopulation of the countryside. By the end of the Hannibalic war (218–201 BC), the entire *ager Campanus* had became *ager publicus* and land was redistributed amongst the war veterans (Fredericksen 1981, 266–7). The Roman conquests brought great wealth to Italy and slaves started pouring into Italy. The availability of this cheap manpower saw the emergence of profit-oriented agricultural villas. These were specialised in the production of olives and wines and were staffed by slaves. Cereal cultivation and large-scale stock rearing, on the other hand, was relegated to areas with poorer soils. The scarce attention paid to the production of cereals induced a reduction of cereal cultivation and a consequent movement of peasants to Rome and, by the end of the first century AD, growing competition of wine and oil produced in other parts of the empire and the collapse of the supply of slaves, gradually pushed towards a reduction of arboriculture in favour of extensive pastoralism and cereal cultivation in *latifondia* run mainly by tenants (for instance, see Toynbee 1965, 247ff; Rostovtzeff 1957, 77 & 98; Patterson 1987).

The plant assemblage from Pompeii during this period partly resembles that of the previous phase. However, there are also important differences, such as an increase in the types of pulses consumed, some of which were certainly cultivated in the surroundings of Pompeii, whereas others, including lentils and chickpeas, were probably imported from North Africa. The finding of exotic foodstuff, particularly citrus fruit and peppercorn, confirms the existence of trade contacts with distant regions. The existence of a system of long-distance trade (even though it was not necessarily direct) between Pompeii, Africa and the Far East represents a profound change in the role of the ancient town within the trade network of the region, as well as in its social structure. The emergence of this trade must have caused the creation of new specialisations. New types of sellers must have been present in the town market and in the streets of Pompeii. In addition, some people must have acted as intermediaries between the ports and the town, and a new elite who could afford to buy expensive imported foodstuff must have emerged.

The archaeobotanical record shows that the arrival of exotic foodstuff corresponds with a change in the use of local species. Remains of the olive, for instance, occur for the first time in this phase. The small number of pollen records from Southern Italy available for this period show a low frequency of olive pollen (Carter & Costantini 1994). This is partly confirmed by the historical data for the early Classical period, which indicate that olive cultivation was not widespread in Italy. Pliny (*Historia Naturalis* 15.1), quoting Fenestella, writes that during the reign of Tarquinius Priscus (616–579 BC), olive trees were not found in Italy, Spain or Africa. The cultivation of the olive in these regions is generally associated with the presence of Greek colonies (Ampolo 1980, 32–3), the first of which, Cumae in Campania, was founded in the seventh century BC (for instance, see Frederiksen 1984, 54–5). The late date of the evidence for olive cultivation at Pompeii is in apparent contrast with the finding of olive stones from many prehistoric sites in southern Italy (for instance Lacroix-Phippen 1975; Costantini 1981; Castelletti *et al.* 1987; Costantini & Stancanelli 1994). It is therefore conceivable that olive cultivation started much earlier in other areas of the peninsula or that wild olives were extensively exploited well before their cultivation (our present knowledge of the morphology of olive stones does not allow a distinction to be made between wild and cultivated forms). Recent research in the Lepine Hills, in southern Latium, has revealed the existence of platforms built on hill slopes, which were probably related to olive cultivation (Attema *et al.* 1999, 116). They seem to reflect a re-landscaping of the territory, which occurred around the late fourth century BC. This would support the notion that there was an intensification of olive cultivation in this period, in central as in southern Italy. Toynbee (1965, 152) suggests that a system of 'plantation' agriculture, based mainly on the cultivation of grape and olive, was in place in the third century BC. This view, although more recently criticised (for instance, see Jongman 1988; Lomas 1993), seems to find some support in the archaeological evidence.

The historical and archaeological evidence outlined above provides an indication of the rapid transformation of Pompeii. By this period, goods produced in distant countries had become a regular feature of the diet of the city dwellers. The food was probably distributed through a market system, which may also have reached the more internal areas of the region. The arrival of exotic foodstuff is likely to have been accompanied by the arrival of new ideas, people and professions.

Phase III (second half of second century BC to AD 79)
By the middle of the second century BC, the historical situation in Campania had further evolved. Rome gradually consolidated its presence in the region and in 80 BC, Pompeii became a Roman *colonia*. The countryside around Pompeii was, by now, densely populated by productive *villae rusticae* (for instance, see Conticello de' Spagnolis 1994; de Caro 1994) and luxurious residences, with gardens and pools. The redistribution of the land amongst the Roman colonists had accentuated the fragmentation of the land into smaller plots, whose productivity was guaranteed by the fertility of the land (Frederiksen 1981, 270). The existence of wine and oil presses in most of the *villae rusticae* around Pompeii (Day 1932; Casale & Bianco 1979; Oëttel 1996) suggests that these were important products. Some scholars have even suggested that there was a real boom in wine production in the region in the first century AD (Purcell 1985; Tchernia 1986).

Chaff, whose presence in the archaeological deposits of a previous period (Phase I) has been interpreted as evidence of daily activities of crop processing, is not found in the deposits of this late phase. Its absence suggests that crop-processing was now carried out elsewhere, possibly in the countryside. The use of slaves meant that agricultural labour became cheaper and easily available, a factor that probably favoured the shift of most of the agricultural activities from the town to the countryside. The presence of threshing floors in most of the *villae rusticae* around Pompeii is consistent with this hypothesis (for instance Casale & Bianco 1979; Oëttel 1996). The large-scale cereal processing implies, as a consequence, a different strategy for crop storage and distribution.

In phase III, there is a clear increase in the number of plant species represented in the archaeobotanical assemblage, including some of exotic origin, such as cucumber (or melon), peach, sesame, pine, date, walnuts and a species of Cucurbitaceae 0– probably watermelon. Some of these species, for instance the date, were certainly imported, while others, such as peaches, were probably cultivated in the town itself or in its surroundings. The mild climate of Campania and the high productivity of its soils made this region very suitable for the acclimatisation of new species, so much so that Strabo (*Geography* 5.4.8) refers to Campania as the ideal land for fruit growing.

Olive remains become more common in the plant assemblage of this phase (Ciaraldi 2000; 2001). This supports the traditional view of Pompeian agriculture, which portrays the lands around the town as being cultivated mainly with vines and olives (for instance, see Day 1932). Ancient sources seem to agree that there was a growing expansion of olive cultivation in this period. Rees (1987, 187) notes that, while Cato, who was writing in the middle of the second century BC, mentions only seven varieties of olives, Pliny, who was writing in the third quarter of the first century AD, lists fifteen of them. The high frequency of charred olive stones in deposits of this period, however, may be related to a change in the use of olives and their by-products, for instance through the utilisation of lees (the residue of the pressure of the olive) as fuel or fertiliser. If so, this may indicate that such by-products were easily available and cheap. It is worth noticing that, nowadays, olive groves are almost completely absent from the immediate surroundings of Pompeii, as the rich soil is intensively exploited with plantations of more demanding crops.

The presence of a larger variety of plants during phase III must reflect substantial changes in the agricultural practices and in the provisioning of the city. The increase in the number of fruit species, in particular, suggests that these were cultivated as cash crops for the town market. They represented a perfect investment for small owners. The archaeobotanical data from rural sites, though admittedly sparse, confirm that species such as peaches and walnuts were in fact cultivated in the small farms around Pompeii at the time of the eruption (Ciaraldi 2001).

Long-distance trade also becomes more extensive and involved the import of foodstuff, including those of oriental origin such as pistachio and jujube, which featured regularly on the tables of the Pompeian elites.

The changing face of agriculture

The changes in the production and consumption of food observed in the course of the three phases must have been paralleled by a profound transformation of the social organisation of the town, with consequential effects on the production strategies of the countryside.

In the initial stages there must have been little difference between the role of the producers and that of the consumers, a system probably definable as typical of a subsistence agriculture model. As far as the distribution of food was concerned, this was likely to have been organised through a simple network of contacts, probably not of a commercial nature.

The progressive increase of plant species and the arrival of exotic foodstuff imply a transformation and expansion in the trade network, probably as a consequence of the influence of Rome in the region. A new system of access to food must have been put in place, with an increasingly hierarchical relation between producers and consumers. Because of this, new professions and changes in the organisation of the exchange system must have occurred at Pompeii. These include importers and sellers of exotic foodstuff, new types of entrepreneurial land owners who endeavoured to grow the precious new fruits in their plots, a new system of transport and exchange between the town markets and countryside, and an intensification in the use of olives and their by-products. The developments and structures of this multifaceted society are, however, still poorly understood. The evidence for changes in the plant composition, despite their lack of detail, give some indications of how Pompeian society was affected and how it adjusted to those changes. The example of the production processes at Villa Vesuvio, on the other hand, gives us a concrete example of the reality of these changes.

Conclusions

How many lives depended on the production and commerce of these plants? How did this number change during the evolution of Pompeii? How were the lives of those involved affected? Were they located in the city or in the countryside? Where they elites or slaves? Did they have to travel far away for their commerce or just outside the Pompeian gates? Few of these questions can be answered with confidence but the evidence from the plant remains from Pompeii helps us in pinpointing the chronology and nature of these changes.

From the sixth century BC to the volcanic eruption in AD 79 we witness a growing complexity in the structure of the town. New needs and demands were met with the creation of new specialised activities. These affected all sectors of the population, especially those involved in the production of agricultural goods. The city-countryside relationship must have changed dramatically, causing the location or relocation of groups of the population, such as artisans who became based in the town, and a greater compartmentalisation of productive knowledge.

The plant assemblage from Villa Vesuvio has provided an opportunity to look at the issue of specialisation from an alternative point of view. The existence of a farm in which medicines were probably produced suggests that although some specialised activities were better located in the town, others were more appropriately based in the countryside. This slightly alters the perspective that has seen urban centres as 'consumer' or 'service' cities and the countryside as the main food producer and the recipient of the services offered by the city. In fact, some specialised activities had no particular reasons to be located in towns. Some might have required easy access to natural resources such as large quantities of water or herbs, or large open spaces such as threshing floors and storage areas, and consequently were better based in the countryside where these facilities were to hand. The production of medicines, for instance, would have benefited not only from the availability of medicinal plants but also from the country dweller's knowledge of the medicinal properties of certain plants, while the neighbouring town guaranteed access to the market in which the finished products were sold.

Bibliography

Ampolo, C. 1980. 'Le condizioni materiali della produzione. Agricoltura e paesaggio agrario', *Dialoghi di Archeologia* 1: 15–46
Attema, P., Delvigne, J. & Haagsma, B.J. 1999. 'Case studies from the Pontine region in central Italy on settlement and environmental change in the first millennium BC', in Leveau, P., Trement, F., Walsh, K. & Barker, G. (eds) *Environmental Reconstruction in Mediterranean Landscape Archaeology.* Oxbow, Oxford: 105–22
Bliquez, L.J. 1994. *Roman Surgical Instruments and other Minor Objects in the National Archaeological Museum of Naples.* Zeben, Main.
Bon, S., Jones, R., Kurchin, B. & Robinson, D. 1997. *Anglo-American Pompeii Project 1996.* Bradford Archaeological Sciences Research 3, University of Bradford.
Brumfield, E.M. & Earle, T. 1995. 'Specialisation, exchange and complex societies', in Ehrenreich, R.M., Crumley, C.L. & Levy, J.E. (eds) *Heterarchy and the analysis of complex societies.* Arlington, VA, American Anthropological Society 6: 125–31
Camodeca, G. 1990. 'Puteoli, il quadro storico', in Amalfitano, P., Camodeca, G. & Medri, M. (eds) *I Campi Flegrei.* Marsilio Editori, Venezia: 77–83

Marina Ciaraldi

Carter, J.C. & Costantini, L. 1994. 'Settlement density, agriculture and the extent of productive land cleared from forest in Magna Grecia', in Frenzel, B. (ed.) *Evaluation of Land Surfaces Cleared from Forests in the Mediterranean Region during the Time of the Roman Empire.* Fisher Verlag, Stuttgart: 101–18

Casale, A. & Bianco, A. 1979. 'Primo contributo alla topografia del suburbio pompeiano', *Antiqua* 15 suppl. 27: 27–56 + maps

Castelletti, L., Costantini, L. & Tozzi, C. 1987. 'Considerazioni sull'economia e sull'ambiente durante il neolitico', *Atti della XXVI Riunione scientifica dell'Istitituto di Preistoria e Protostoria: il Neolitco in Italia.* Firenze 7 Novembre 1985: 37–55

Childe, V.G. 1951. *Man Makes Himself.* New American Library, New York.

Ciaraldi, M. 2000. 'Drug preparation in evidence? An unusual plant and bone assemblage from the Pompeian countryside', *Vegetation History and Archaeobotany* 9: 91–98

Ciaraldi, M. 2001. *Food and Fodder, Religion and Medicine at Pompeii. The use of plant resources at Pompeii and in the Pompeian area from the sixth century BC to AD 79.* PhD Dissertation, University of Bradford.

Ciaraldi, M. 2002. 'The interpretation of medicinal plants in the archaeological context: some case studies from Pompeii', in Arnott, R. (ed.) *The Archaeology of Medicine.* BAR (International Series) 1046, Oxford: 81–5

Conticello de' Spagnolis, M. 1994. *Il Pons Sarni.* L'Erma di Bretscheneider, Roma.

Costantini, L. 1981. 'Semi e carboni del mesolitico e neolitico della Grotta dell'Uzzo, Trapani', *Quaternaria* 23: 233–47

Costantini, L. & Stancanelli, M. 1994. 'La preistoria agricola dell'Italia centro-meridionale. Il contributo delle indagini paleobotaniche', *Origini* 18: 149–244

Day, J. 1932. 'Agriculture in the life of Pompeii', *Yale Classical Studies* 3: 166–209

de Caro, S. 1986. *Saggi nell'area del Tempio di Apollo a Pompei.* Annali dell' Istituto Universitario Orientale di Napoli, Napoli.

de Caro, S. 1992. 'Lo sviluppo urbanistico di Pompeii', *Atti e Memorie della Società della Magna Grecia* (series 3) 1: 67–90

de Caro, S. 1994. *La Villa Rustica in località Villa Regina a Boscoreale.* L'Erma di Bretschneider, Roma.

Eschenbach, L. 1993. *Gebaundeverzeichnis und Stadtplan der antiken Stadt, Pompeji.* Verlag, Köln.

Fredericksen, M. 1981. 'I cambiamenti delle strutture agrarie nella tarda Repubblica: la Campania', in Giardina, A. & Schiavone, A. (eds) *L'Italia: Insediamenti e Forme Economiche.* Laterza, Napoli: 265–87 + notes

Fredericksen, M. 1984. *Campania.* British School at Rome, Austin & Sons, Hertford.

Fulford, M. & Wallace-Hadrill, A. 1998. 'Unpeeling Pompeii', *Antiquity* 72: 128–45

Fulford, M. & Wallace-Hadrill, A. 1999. 'Towards a history of pre-Roman Pompeii: excavations beneath the House of Amarantus (I.9.11–12), 1995–8', *PBSR* 57: 37–126 + plates

Guthrie, D. 1945. *A History of Medicine.* Nelson & Sons, London.

Hall, A.R. 1995. 'Archaeological evidence for woad (*Isatis tinctoria* L.) from Medieval England and Ireland', in Kröll, U. & Pasternak, R. (eds) *Res Archaeobotanicae.* Proceedings of the 9th Symposium, Kiel 1992, produced by editors, Kiel: 33–8

Jones, R. & Robinson, D. Forthcoming. 'The creation of the Casa delle Vestali (V.i.6–8)', in Dobbins, J. & Foss, P. (eds) *Cities under Vesuvius.* Routledge, London and New York.

Jongman, W. 1988. *The Economy and Society of Pompeii.* Gieben, Amsterdam.

Lacroix-Phippen, W. 1975. 'Vegetal remains', in Holloway, R.R. (ed.) 'Buccino: the Early Bronze Age village of Tufariello', *Journal of Field Archaeology* 2: 79–80

Lomas, K. 1993. *Rome and the Western Greeks.* Routledge, London and New York.

Miller, I.J. 1969. *The Spice Trade of the Roman Empire.* Oxford University Press, Oxford.

Nutton, V. 1995. 'Roman medicine, 250 BC to AD 200', in Lawrence, C.I., Neve, M., Nutton, V., Porter, R. & Wear, A. (eds) *The Western Medical Tradition.* Cambridge University Press, Cambridge: 39–70

Oëttel, A. 1996. *Fundkontexte Römischer Vesuvvillen in Gebiet um Pompeji.* Verlag Phillip von Zabern, Mainz.

Patterson, J.R. 1987. 'Crisis: what crisis? Rural change and urban development in Imperial Appennine Italy', *PBSR* 6: 115–46

Purcell, N. 1985. 'Wine and wealth in ancient Italy', *JRS* 75: 1–19

Rawcliffe, C. 1995. *Medicine and Society in Later Medieval England*. Alan Sutton, Gloucestershire.

Rees, S. 1987. 'L'agricoltura e l'orticultura', in Wacher, J. (ed.) *Il mondo di Roma Imperiale*. Laterza, Napoli: 177–205

Riddle, J. 1985. *Dioscorides on Pharmacy and Medicine*. University of Texas Press, Austin.

Rosen S.A. 1997. 'Craft specialization and the rise of secondary urbanism: a view from the Southern Levant', in Aufrecht, W.E., Mirau, N.A. & Gauley, S.W. (eds) *Urbanism in Antiquity*. Sheffield Academic Press, Sheffield: 82–91

Rostovtzeff, M. 1957. *The Social and Economic History of the Roman Empire*. Clarendon Press, Oxford.

Soprintendenza Archeologica di Pompei. 1992. *Il Territorio Vesuviano nel 79 d.C.*, 4–9 maggio 1992, Pompei.

Tchernia, A. 1986. *Le vin de L'Italie Romaine: essai d'histoire économique d'après les amphores*. L'Ecoles Fançaises de Rome, Rome.

Tosi, M. 1984. 'The notion of craft specialization and its representation in the archaeological record of early states in the Thuranian Basin', in Spriggs, M. (ed.) *Marxist Perspectives in Archaeology*. Cambridge University Press, Cambridge: 22–52

Toynbee, A.J. 1965. *Hannibal's Legacy*, Vols. I and II. Oxford University Press, Oxford.

Tram Tan Tinh, V. 1972. *Le Culte des Divinités Orientales en Campanies*. Brill, Leiden.

van der Poel, H. 1977. *Corpus Topographicum Pompeianorum*. University of Texas Press, Austin.

Watson, G. 1966. *Theriac and Mithridatium*. Clowes & Sons, Austin.

12

The role of doctors in the city

Ralph Jackson

Cities, as places of concentrated population, facilitate the spread of diseases. For a Roman healer they provided a 'market opportunity' rather different from that of the more sparsely populated countryside. While people in rural communities may often have coped with health issues within the (extended) family or by means of peripatetic or 'circuit' doctors, those in urban centres had different health choices. The size of the 'market' might sustain several, or many, healers, and it might also enable some to concentrate on, or restrict themselves to, particular realms of healing, treatments or operations. So, a prospective patient might have access to several healers and to specialists. Such 'specialists' are likely to have been very different from their present-day counterparts, and we need to be vigilant in avoiding superimposing modern medical precepts and validations (or the opposite) on the healers and healing of antiquity. We should be cautious even in applying the term 'doctors' to Greek and Roman medical personnel. To be sure, some of those healers were specified as, or styled themselves, doctor or physician – *medicus* or, if Greek-speaking or of Greek extraction, *iatros* (or *medica/iatrine*, for there were also female healers). However, there were evidently many without such titles, who also practised healing. Scribonius Largus (writing *c.* AD 50) said as much in the introduction to his *Compositiones* where, in examining the role of healers, he contrasted those *medici* who knew only one branch of medicine, or were ineffective or grossly negligent, with '…certain humble, and indeed otherwise unknown, men…greatly skilled in terms of experience, although far removed from the discipline of medicine and not associated with that profession' (*Compositiones* prooemium; Hamilton 1986, 213, 215). Those latter no doubt included part-time healers, *iatraliptae* (medical therapists), masseurs, trainers, ointment sellers (*unguentarii, pharmacopolae, seplasiarii*) and root-cutters, but, above all, those who were acquainted with the numerous time-hallowed folk remedies based on diet, medicinal plants and herbs. In fact, all or any could have called themselves *medicus* for, despite Scribonius Largus' allusion to a medical 'profession' (*professio medici*), there were no courses to be followed, exams to be passed or qualifications to be gained, and no controlling body or general agreement on standards or required skills. 'Medicine was an open market-place, in which there was nothing to stop a cobbler or a barmaid from setting up as a healer, or from reverting at will to their old trade' (Nutton 1993, 56). In what follows, therefore, except in specific instances, the words healer, medical practitioner and medical personnel have generally been used in preference to the baggage-laden 'doctor' or 'physician'.

So who were the healers, what were their roles in the cities of the Roman Empire, and how did health-care strategies work at the level of the general public? Much of our information derives from texts, above all the writings of Galen, but epigraphy and archaeology are important sources, too, and in seeking the urban healers we need to integrate the evidence of all three sources.

The Roman state had involved itself in the provision of urban public health-care at least as early as 219 BC, when the Greek surgeon (*vulnerarius*) Archagathus of Sparta became, briefly, the first state medical employee in Rome (Pliny *Historia Naturalis* 29.12, quoting from the lost writings of Cassius Hemina, *fl. c.* 146 BC.). The third century BC had seen an increasing hellenization of Rome, intensified by the conquest of the Greek lands of southern Italy by 250

BC. In the tradition of the Greek cities, the Roman senate invited Archagathus to come to Rome with the inducement of privileges that included Roman citizenship and the free use of a public surgery (*taberna*) in a prime position (Nutton 1981, 17–18; Jackson 1993, 80–1; Scarborough 1993, 23–4). However, according to Pliny, Archagathus' methods proved not to the liking of the Roman public – he soon gained the nickname *carnifex* ('butcher' or 'executioner') – and he returned to the Peloponnese, leaving behind, if we are to believe the account, a legacy of loathing for doctors and the medical art (Pliny *Historia Naturalis* 29.13).

This brief, celebrated, episode is undoubtedly more complex than Pliny was able to reveal (see especially Nutton 1993; also Marasco 1995). At all events, it appears not to have diminished the flow of Greek physicians to the households of wealthy Roman families. The attraction of the expanding city, a growing taste for Greek culture, and an increasing dependency on healers resulting from rising urbanisation and the consequent loss of contact with rural remedies and medical self-sufficiency, together ensured an expanding market for Greek healers, whether as free agents, prisoners of war or slaves. As Nutton (1992, 38) has observed '...the absence of a theoretical component from Roman domestic medicine was increasingly likely to offend these men of wealth who were experiencing for themselves the delights of Greek culture and philosophy and whose cultural outlook was becoming hellenized. For them Greek physicians were necessary, as much for ostentation as for practical value...'. Unlike the Greek East, however, with its long-established traditions of theory-based healing and civic enterprise, the rising Roman world was relatively unsophisticated. To Greek healers Rome probably compared unfavourably to Athens, Alexandria or even Naples, and those of them who chose to seek their fortune in what has been characterised as a 'frontier town' probably varied widely in competence (Nutton 1993, 59–63). At all events, according to the surviving evidence, some one-and-a-half centuries were to elapse before the Roman state involved itself again in the matter of public health-care.

In *c*. 45 BC Julius Caesar's grant of citizenship to all foreign doctors practising in Rome (Suetonius *Julius* 42.1) was a more general inducement subsequently confirmed by Augustus, who, in gratitude for his cure from a serious disease, was reported to have granted tax-immunity to all doctors everywhere (Cassius Dio 53.30.3; Suetonius *Augustus* 59; Nutton 1993, 59). However, it is doubtful whether it was universally enacted, and its appeal was, in any case, limited. Citizenship, even if it did bring tax concessions, was then, after all, the norm in Rome, and it is unlikely to have proved tempting to the most distinguished healers of the Greek East, where certain concessions and immunities also prevailed. Whatever the precise reason, healers in Rome and the western half of the Empire rarely seem to have ascended to the municipal elite, and a study of inscriptions referring to doctors in the first three centuries AD would appear to demonstrate that their civil status remained generally low, with 80%, 50% and 25% of those recorded on inscriptions lacking full citizen rights in the first, second and third centuries AD respectively (Nutton 1992, 39; 1993, 60; Pleket 1995). In this context it is perhaps instructive to note that while Julius Caesar linked doctors with teachers of the liberal arts Hadrian, who also extended privileges to doctors, accorded the same rights to firemen and transport workers (*Codex Theodosianus* 13.4.1; *Codex Iustinianus* 10.66.1; Fischer 1979, 167).

Acceptance of privileges, whatever their real worth – doctors had to struggle sometimes even to retain their exemptions (Jackson 1988, 57) – required registration, and with it the possibility of official control. This may not have proved a disincentive, for healers in towns, even if their status was hardly elevated, appear to have proliferated. Such is the impression given by the legislation enacted by Antoninus Pius, which restricted the number of 'approved' doctors to maxima of five, seven or ten according to the population of the town (*Digesta* 27.1.6.2–4). It was the *ordo* of towns that had to underwrite the exemptions from taxes and other liturgies, and the statute of Pius was intended to ease an increasing burden. Henceforth, the limited number of legitimised public doctors was a more clearly defined group, though they appear to have had no statutory duties other than that of residency. No medical personnel were involved in their appointment – they simply had to convince a lay magistrate as to their suitability. However, this assessment, by 'future consumer', not 'technical peer', was, in the circumstances, probably the most effective solution (Nutton 1985a, 34; 1992, 53). The civic doctors were appointed and regularly monitored by the councillors of the community in which they practised and news of success, incompetence or failure could be rapidly diffused by word of mouth (see *e.g.* Galen 14.622–4K).

Even in the smaller cities it is likely that the public doctors were part only of a broader-based group of medical personnel that included independent generalists, specialists and pharmacists as well as those we might characterise as 'fringe' healers. At the apex, in terms of fame and fortune, were those healers who attended the emperor, his family and his court. It was one of these, Antonius Musa, whose 'miracle' cure caused Augustus to make his universal grant of tax immunity to *medici*. In 23 BC Augustus was in a desperate condition suffering from 'abscesses of the liver'. Musa, reversing normal practise, cured the emperor through his use of a cold water therapy, a success that brought him immense wealth from a grateful emperor and also resulted in the elevation of hydrotherapy to a fashionable form of treatment. Still more wealthy and influential was Caius Stertinius Xenophon, court physician to Claudius, while Criton, Trajan's physician, was also a historian who wrote an account of the emperor's Dacian Wars. The most celebrated imperial physician was the polymath Galen of Pergamum (AD 129–*c*. 216), who, from AD 169, attended Marcus Aurelius and Lucius Verus and remained in imperial service until his death almost half a century later. The son of a wealthy architect, Galen's long study of medicine – some twelve years – was exceptional. Together with a keen intellect, acute observation and a passionate dedication to both the theory and practise of medicine, it laid the basis for his influential writings on almost every aspect of medicine. A very considerable amount of his prodigious written output has survived. Especially important are his books on pathology, anatomy and physiology, prognosis and diagnosis as well as his interpretation of the works attributed to Hippocrates. Throughout, his work is pervaded by his assertive, often polemical, views, both on medicine and on his medical contemporaries, as well as those of earlier times.

Galen was born in the city of Pergamum, studied in the cities of Pergamum, Smyrna, Corinth and Alexandria, and returned to Pergamum for his first medical appointment as surgeon to a school of gladiators. He subsequently spent most of his life in the city of Rome, first as a high-profile private practitioner renowned for his spectacular cures of 'celebrity' patients and his scintillating and disputatious public dissections and vivisections of animals, and then also as court physician. His very full testimony, albeit as an idiosyncratic member of the urban elite, is thus of fundamental importance to an understanding of at least certain aspects of the role of doctors and healers in Rome and in the cities of the Roman Empire. It is only unfortunate that the sheer volume of his writings is not balanced by that of others: the relatively low survival rate of the works of other medical authors provides no useful corrective.

Although subject to the whim of the emperor and always at his disposal, Galen, as court physician, had the facilities and resources to pursue and record his medical research and to acquire the best *materia medica*. For many other healers, perhaps the majority, such luxuries

Figure 12.1 *This marble tombstone of the early second century AD, probably from Rome, shows the healer Claudius Agathamerus and his wife Myrtale. The Greek epitaph may be translated 'Here lie I, Claudius Agathamerus, a doctor (iatros) who administered fast-working medicines for all kinds of disease. I had this monument erected for me and my wife Myrtale. We are together now with the blessed in Elysium'. (Ashmolean Museum, Oxford.)*

were probably out of the question, although some of the public doctors and some of those healers attached to wealthy patrician families may have had the time and ability to research their field. The latter group, largely freedmen or slaves, were also at the beck and call of their employer and often resided in his household (Celsus *de Medicina* prooemium 23–25, 45–53, 74–5). Most were Greek or from Greek-speaking parts of the world and were often valued both as healers and as learned companions (see *e.g.* Seneca *de Beneficiis* 6.15–16; Pliny *Epistulae* 10.5.1, 10.10.1, 10.11.1). As Nutton (1993, 63) has observed, they tended not to be drawn from the upper social grouping of their home towns and therefore seem not to have been deterred by the relatively low legal and social status that they encountered in Rome. Furthermore, by the first and second centuries AD they will have found in Rome a large and growing Greek-speaking community that is likely to have been congenial. At all events, as the surviving inscriptions reveal, they arrived in numbers from many cities and provinces of the East (Nutton 1986, 37–8; Korpela 1987). A proportion probably established themselves as independent *medici* and *iatroi*. These practitioners, probably the largest single group, were generalists who sought to cure all ills, as, for example, Claudius Agathamerus, '… a doctor who administered fast-working medicines for all kinds of disease…' (Figure 12.1) (*Corpus Inscriptionum Graecarum* 6197).

The few surviving images of such healers, mainly on tombstones, portray prosperous-looking learned men, but there is little evidence for great wealth (Fischer 1979, 168–9; Nutton 1986, 35–6; Hillert 1990). A conspicuous exception is the freedman P. Decimius Eros Merula of Assisi, who amassed a small fortune from his practise as a physician, clinician, surgeon and oculist – *medicus clinicus chirurgus ocularius* (CIL xi.5400). Few will have had the advantage

Figure 12.2 *The centre panel of this fourth century AD marble sarcophagus from Ostia shows a seated healer reading from a scroll, a stock figure-type chosen to align the healer with philosophers and poets. On a cupboard before him an opened box of surgical instruments identifies his healing role, while further scrolls and equipment may be seen on the shelves of the cupboard. (Metropolitan Museum of Art, New York. Neg. no. 145288B)*

of Galen's long years of study and travel. Some, it is said, were trained in six months (Galen 10.4K, 19.804K), but the majority probably learnt by example as assistants or apprentices of an established healer. Although Galen rated book-learning above that of travel and attendance at medical centres (*de Optimo Medico Cognoscendo* 9.3, 9.22; Nutton 1990), the apprenticeship system was always important to those who did not have ready access to libraries or medical texts, and especially to those many healers who, if we are to believe Galen, were illiterate (but note Figure 12.2 for an alternative impression) (Galen 19.9K. On the form and availability of medical books see *e.g.* Kollesch 1973 and Nutton 1990, 247–8). Under these circumstances it is not difficult to understand the conservatism of certain ideas and therapies, notably humoral pathology, cupping, blood-letting and purging. Indeed, the stereotypical healer of Imperial Rome bled his patient, applied a plaster and administered an enema while giving advice on anything and everything (Galen 15.313–315K; Scarborough 1993, 34).

It is hard enough to discern healers archaeologically let alone to differentiate them. However, the discovery of sets of surgical instruments and medical paraphernalia in a number of different contexts has permitted some informed speculation on the form their practise may have taken (Jackson 1995; Künzl 2002). The majority seems to conform to the ancient ideal of a healer who was expected to deal with any medical eventuality. For, most of the largest apparently complete *instrumentaria*, including those from Pompeii, Rimini, Colophon, Nea Paphos, Marcianopolis, Rheims, Paris and Nijmegen, comprise not only essential surgical tools, but also more specialised instruments as well as pharmaceutical implements (Figure 12.3; Jackson 1995, table 1; 2003). We may infer from the sets that the practitioner might have advised on regimen, suggested dietary measures, prescribed and dispensed a drug or carried out surgery, whether in response to wounds, injuries and other emergencies or to resolve specific

Figure 12.3 *This large set of Roman medical instruments from Italy, probably of first century AD date, comprises pharmaceutical implements (medicine tubes, mixing palette, spoon, scoops and spatulae), basic surgical tools (scalpels, forceps, hooks and probes), and a number of specialised instruments (catheters, rectal speculum, cataract needle). (British Museum. Neg. no. GR, PS161840)*

conditions or diseases. Clearly, in the smaller cities and towns where few (if any) other medical personnel were located a general practise of this kind was expedient. It also reflects the unity of medicine advocated by many medical writers, above all by Galen (*e.g. de Optimo Medico Cognoscendo*; Nutton 1990; 1995, 8). However, the composition of some other *instrumentaria* does indicate specialisation, whether broadly in surgery or more specifically in dentistry, bone surgery, eye medicine, lithotomy (Figure 12.4), throat or rectal treatments. Interestingly, the range accords well with with medical specialists attested in literary sources (Jackson 1995, 192, 196–7, table 3), with the addition of ear disorders, hernia, fever, dietetics and hydrotherapy. Even Celsus and Scribonius Largus, who disapproved of the tendency towards specialisation, acknowledged specialists in eye diseases (Celsus *de Medicina* prooemium, 9; 5, prooemium, 2; 7, prooemium, 5; Mudry 1985; Scribonius Largus *Compositiones* prooemium). As Galen observed, however, a wide range of resident specialists could only be supported by cities of the size of Rome and Alexandria (Baader 1967). Elsewhere specialists, if encountered, were likely to have been itinerant healers or circuit doctors.

Clearly, specialisation could benefit patients, either through a healer's long experience and knowledge based on detailed observations of a particular condition or disease and the development of appropriate therapies, as in fevers, or through his manual dexterity, strength, stamina and audacity in performing specific, delicate, hazardous or complex surgical interventions, such as dentistry, cataract surgery, cranial trepanation or lithotomy. Reputation was the sole gauge of a specialist's worth available to a prospective patient, a method as applicable to an itinerant healer following a regular 'circuit' in rural regions as to a resident healer in a town. However, Galen paints a gloomy picture of Rome in his day, where the anonymity of the big city allowed incompetents to prosper and charlatans to avoid exposure

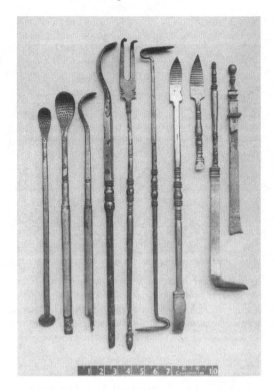

Figure 12.4 The surgical kit of a Roman medical specialist. Believed to have been found in a tomb in the vicinity of Rome the kit comprises roughened scoops, knives, forceps, hooks and levers. These distinctive instruments were designed for use by a lithotomist in the hazardous operation to cut for stone in the urinary bladder. (Museum of Classical Archaeology, Cambridge. Photo: author)

(Galen *de Praecognitione* (CMG 5.8 = 14.621–3K): Nutton 1979, 89–93, 178–180). For the patient who had the wealth and inclination, however, and 'considers his body at least as important as his personal possessions', Galen provided an aid to selecting a competent physician (*de Optimo Medico Cognoscendo* 1.13; Nutton 1990). More positive indicators, too, are the excellence of technique of many of the surgical interventions described in the ancient medical texts and the very high quality of design and manufacture of Roman surgical instruments (Figure 12.5; Jackson 1994; 1997).

Amongst the healers, both as generalists and specialists, were women, though they were always less numerous than men (Jackson 1993, 85–6; Flemming 2000; Künzl 2002, chapter 10). Many were midwives (*obstetrices*) (Figure 12.6), but there was also a long-standing association of women with Roman folk medicine and herbal lore (Pliny *Historia Naturalis* 25.9–10). The social position and status of *medicae* – female physicians – seems to have been as variable as that of the *medici* (King 1986, 55, 59–60; Korpela 1987, 18–20; Jackson 1988, 86–8). Some were specialists in the sense that they confined themselves to or concentrated on women's diseases (Galen 12.250,3K; 13.341,2K; Seneca *Epistulae* 66; Martial *Epigrammaton*11.71.7), but not all were exclusively women's doctors (Baader 1967, 233; Pomeroy 1978; Nickel 1979, 517–8). It is instructive to read the requirement of Soranus of

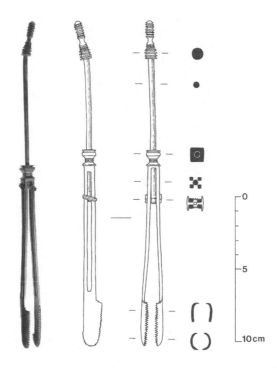

Figure 12.5 *This finely-crafted Roman surgical instrument is a specialised forceps with an ingenious slot-slide plunger mechanism and large, hollow, precisely-interlocking toothed jaws. It was designed for use in the operations for anal fistula, piles and amputation of the uvula, and other roles are likely to have included the removal of growths and tumours as well as deeply-embedded foreign bodies. Length, fully extended, 240mm. (Photo: Ashmolean Museum, Oxford: Drawing: author.)*

Ephesus (*fl.* AD 98–138) that the best midwives should be competent in all three branches of therapy – dietetics, pharmacy and surgery (Soranus *Gynaecia* 1.4), and several recent finds have demonstrated that female healers, like their male counterparts, were sometimes buried with surgical instruments (Künzl 1995; 2002, 93–5).

If the material remains of healers is rare and seldom clear-cut that of their surgeries is even more elusive. It is one thing to know surgeries existed, quite another to recognise and identify unequivocally the architectural settings of medical practise. In antiquity, as today, there was little to differentiate structurally the premises of a healer from those of other individuals. The Hippocratic treatise 'In the Surgery' demanded no requirements of the building other than the provision of sufficient space and of windows to give access to natural light. All else was furnishing, equipment and personnel, most of which is both (re)movable and perishable, whether staff, or chairs, couches and apparatus of wood, leather and textile. Fortunately, medical instruments were made principally of metal and, in a few spectacular instances, where disasters have occurred, suddenly and unexpectedly overwhelming buildings, instruments have survived in a sufficiently recognisable form to disclose the medical context and to permit interpretation of the building as a surgery.

At both Pompeii and Herculaneum 'invisible' surgeries are perhaps represented by the

Figure 12.6 *The epitaph on this simple tombstone to the first century AD midwife Julia Pieris from Trier reads IVLIA PIERIS OBSTETRIX HIC IACET NVLLI GRAVIS – 'Julia Pieris, midwife, rests here. She was in life no burden to anyone'. (Rheinisches Landesmuseum Trier. Photo: author)*

discovery of sets of instruments with individuals – presumably healers – who had been fleeing the eruption. At Pompeii, one of the group of people overcome in the *palaestra* (*Piazza dell'Anfiteatro*) had with him a wooden box containing a set of surgical instruments – scalpels, forceps, hooks, needles and probes – and medicaments in four tubular copper-alloy boxes (Künzl 1983, 12–15; Bliquez 1994, 87–8, 200–1, 207–8). Similarly, at Herculaneum, one of the individuals in the recently-revealed huddled groups trapped in the waterfront vaults (Fornice 12) had selected a box with contents nearly identical to those of the Pompeii set – scalpels, forceps, hooks, needle and probe, stone mixing palette and seven tubular drug boxes (d'Ambrosio *et al.* 2003, 124–7, 135–8, 182–3). These two finds, the equivalent of the doctor's black bag of recent times, may represent the complete medical equipment of the two healers, but it is also possible that they were only the portable component and that large implements and more specialised instruments were left behind in the healer's home/surgery. Certainly, at Pompeii, between ten and twenty houses have yielded sufficient instruments to imply the full- or part-time practise of surgery by their occupants, and it is not impossible that the *palaestra* victim was the healer from one of those houses. The houses vary in size and type, but all are architecturally indistinguishable from other habitations, whether the celebrated House of the Surgeon (*Casa del Chirurgo*: VI.i.9.10, 23), the less well-known but more significant *Casa del Medico nuovo* II (IX.ix.3–5), or the *taberna medica* of Aulus Pumponius Magonianus (VIII.iii.10–12), whose name survives on the lintel above the entrance (Figure 12.7) (Eschebach 1984; Bliquez 1994, 79–89). Pompeii is unique in permitting an estimate of the medical provision for a whole town, and it gives the impression that in AD 79 in this prosperous part of Roman Italy, the inhabitants were rather well-provided with healers. To judge from the surviving instrumentation some were generalists while others appear to have

Figure 12.7 The street frontage of the taberna medica of the Pompeian medicus Aulus Pumponius Magonianus, situated near to the forum on the Via dell'Abbondanza (VIII.iii.10– 12). (Photo: author)

specialised in such aspects as pharmacy or childbirth and women's medicine (Bliquez 1994; 1995; Künzl 1998).

Elsewhere, the surgeries of individual urban practitioners have occasionally been identified, as at Marcianopolis in Bulgaria, where a large and comprehensive set of instruments was discovered in a building destroyed by fire early in the fifth century AD (Minchev 1983; Kirova 2002). The instruments, which include scalpels, uvula forceps, lithotomy scoops, rectal and vaginal dilators, an embryo hook and a trepanning tool, would have enabled a practitioner to perform a wide range of surgery. However, the largest single instrument find is the remarkable assemblage discovered in 1989 in excavations in the Roman town of Ariminium (Rimini) (Figure 12.8). Together with the remains of the house in which he lived and practised, they provide some of the best evidence we have for a Roman healer, his equipment and his surgery (Ortalli 1992; 2000; 2003; Dal Maso 2003, 184–199. Jackson 2002a; 2003). The house, which has become known as the Domus 'del chirurgo', was destroyed in a conflagration in the mid-third century AD, very likely as a casualty of the Alamannic raid of AD 257–8. The ruins were almost immediately sealed by the construction of new town defences, which preserved both standing remains and the destruction debris within. The *domus* was a modest-sized, but richly-furnished, dwelling of half-timbered construction, with a partial upper storey, created in the later second century AD during a radical transformation of a more extensive residence. It

Figure 12.8 One of the fused clusters of surgical instruments from the third century AD assemblage in the Domus 'del chirurgo' at Rimini. Most clearly visible are the sequestrum forceps with decorative handles, a lithotomy scoop, and two folding handles for bow drills (trepans). Two spring forceps, a double-ended hook, a bone lever and a gouge may also be discerned. (Photo: author)

occupied a triangular plot at the end of an *insula* overlooking the Adriatic and comprised six main ground floor rooms (one hypocausted, the others with mosaic floors), with a communicating corridor and a small courtyard garden. The rooms included a *triclinium* and *cubiculum*, but the principal room with Orpheus floor mosaic has been interpreted as a consulting room and surgery. For, within it was found a great profusion of surgical instruments and medical paraphernalia in positions suggestive of their former storage on shelves and in cupboards. The fire had consumed all organic materials and melted the glassware, but over 150 metal instruments were preserved, as well as metal and ceramic medicine pots, stone mortars and pestles and other medical implements. The instruments include numerous scalpels and forceps in a wide variety of forms and sizes; hooks, needles and probes; trepanning tools, chisels, gouges, levers and lenticulars, and many other instruments of bone surgery; dental forceps, uvula forceps and lithotomy scoops (Figure 12.8 & 12.9). Work is still in progress on the final report, but a provisional assessment suggests that the *domus* was, indeed, a healer's residence and surgery, and that the healer was both successful and extremely well-equipped. He appears to have been of Greek extraction or, at least, Greek-speaking, and a fairly prosperous member of the community in which he lived and practised (Jackson 2003).

In the absence of ancient written accounts detailing the day-to-day practise of medicine we may speculate on the forms of medical activity that might have taken place in the Rimini *domus*. Excepting the *valetudinarii* of military units and *latifundia* there were no hospitals in the Roman world. The normal setting for the treatment and care of those who fell ill, therefore – if they received treatment at all – was their home. Healers, from the humblest *medicus* to the great Galen, made house visits to examine, diagnose and treat patients, who were then left in the care of their relatives or friends. The treatment might take the form of instructions for a controlled diet and regimen or, perhaps, the dispensing of a drug, the letting of blood or the administration of an enema or purgative. However, for those who were mobile, especially those

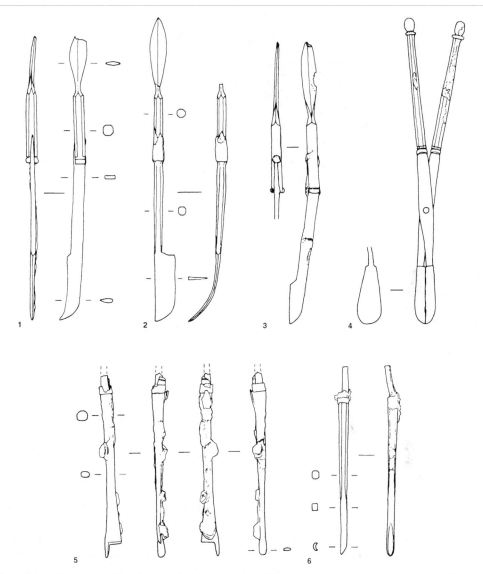

Figure 12.9 *A selection of surgical instruments from the Domus 'del chirurgo' at Rimini. 1–3: copper-alloy scalpel handles with their iron blades intact. 4: copper-alloy staphylocaustes (uvula forceps). 5–6: iron instruments of bone surgery, 5: lenticular (guarded chisel). 6: gouge. Scale 1:2 (author)*

who lived in a very modest dwelling, a visit to a healer's *iatrium* or *taberna medica* may have been more expedient. This would be appropriate to those seeking a draught of medicine or the treatment of a minor ailment. It would also apply especially to those who required surgery involving either bulky equipment or a carefully controlled environment. One thinks, for

Figure 12.10 *Impression of a sard sealstone, of first to second century AD date, showing a healer examining his patient under the watchful eye of the healing god Aesculapius. (British Museum. Neg.no. GR, PS115626)*

example, of the extension and reduction of fractures and dislocations using various mechanical contrivances, including the celebrated Hippocratic Bench (see *e.g.* Majno 1975, figs 4.20 & 10.12; Marganne 1998, 53–6, figs 7–8), or of the operation to couch a cataractous lens (Feugère *et al.* 1985; Jackson 1988, 121–3; 1996). We should imagine all of this medical activity taking place in the Rimini healer's surgery as well as, perhaps, thermal and water therapies in the hypocausted room. It is further possible that he used his *domus* on occasion as a clinic to accommodate those undergoing and recovering from serious surgery when it was critical not to move the patient.

The limited surviving evidence from Rimini and the Vesuvian cities suggests that in general an urban healer based his practise in his home, even if he frequently made house visits to treat patients. In addition to these two settings there is evidence to suggest that medical treatment in towns might also take place at public baths. Seneca's vivid account (*Epistulae Morales* 56.1–2) of the 'assortment of sounds' emanating from the baths above which he had lodgings highlighted the role of several of those employed in the 'service sector' of body care. As centres of cleansing and social intercourse, baths were also an obvious setting for restorative, curative and convalescent treatments. Water therapies, eye treatments and even surgery took place alongside massage, manicure and depilation (Künzl 1986; Jackson 1988, 48–50; 1999; Fagan 1999, 85–103).

What, then, were the day-to-day roles of urban healers in the Roman world? As we have seen, few had any statutory duties other than the residential requirement of the 'approved' public doctors and the twenty-four hour availability of imperial physicians. Medical personnel appear to have had no forensic status in Roman law, the only exceptions being the employment of midwives to certify pregnancy (Amundsen & Ferngren 1979, 46–8) and, in Roman Egypt, the requirement there of public physicians (*demosioi iatroi*) to provide a report in cases of violent or accidental injury or death (Amundsen & Ferngren 1978, 342–53).

A healer's primary role was, of course, to visit and minister to the sick. In examining who were Galen's patients and how he treated them Horstmanshoff (1995) attempted to reconstruct a working day in the life of Galen, which sheds interesting light on Galen and his *modus operandi,* and, to an extent, on the practise of his contemporary healers. Galen was, in

Figure 12.11 *Marble tombstone of the Athenian physician (iatros) Jason, c. AD 100. Even those who could not read the epitaph would be left in no doubt as to the calling of the deceased person: at bottom right an outsize cupping vessel is depicted, the 'badge of office' of Greek and Roman healers; while the main image shows a stereotypical medical scene as Jason attentively examines his patient. (British Museum. Neg. no. GR, C962)*

modern slang, a 'workaholic', and his day, which might include visits to patients, reading, writing, meetings with other physicians, perhaps even a dissection or the preparation of a drug, started before dawn and often stretched well into the night:

> I was enslaved to the obligations of my profession and served my friends, relatives and fellow citizens in many ways. I spent most of each night without sleeping, sometimes because of my sick patients, and sometimes on account of everything that is beneficial to one's study (*de Sanitate Tuenda* 5.1, 6.308–309K; Horstmanshoff 1995, 84–5).

Already by the third hour he visited his first patient, and patients were visited again later in the day. Such visits were at the core of any healer's practise and the form they took was of great importance. Just as a surgery had to be equipped in the correct way so the healer's appearance and bedside manner were critical, and many ancient medical texts included sections on etiquette. The patient might, with reason, be frightened as well as sick and thus in need of reassurance (Figure 12.10). The author of the Hippocratic text 'The Physician' gave a brief, measured account of the appearance, bearing and qualities required of a healer, while Celsus (*de Medicina* 3.6.6) advocated a calm and sympathetic bedside manner. Both the countenance of the healer and his preliminary conversation with the patient should be such as to allay any fears before a formal examination took place. Galen, too, understood and articulated the ways in which a healer should accommodate the wishes of a patient, reassure him, and inspire his confidence, though without ever compromising the most effective treatment, the ultimate benefit to the patient (Hortmanshoff 1995, 94–6).

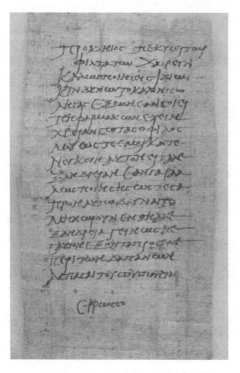

Figure 12.12 *This letter, written on papyrus in the first century AD, highlights both the problem of drug fraud and Alexandria's pre-eminence in medicine. The Greek text may be translated 'Procleius to Persius, his dear friend, greetings. You will please me, if, at your own risk, you can sell a good quality drug from your stock, if you have it, so that my friend Sotas can take it to Alexandria. If you do otherwise, giving him a rotten product, it will not pass muster in Alexandria. You will hear from me about the costs. Greetings to all your family. Farewell' (trans. Lucilla Burn). (Catalogue of Greek papyri CCCLVI. British Library. British Museum Neg. no. GR, PS181598)*

To treat the patient effectively, the healer had to arrive at a diagnosis of the disease and a forecast of its progress and outcome – prognosis. The two were closely connected in classical medicine and they were central to a healer's authority and reputation, but they posed a considerable challenge. An expert and compassionate healer like Galen, who knew and extended Hippocratic methods, would observe all aspects of his patient unhurriedly and intently. For, the evidence of the senses, 'the sensing of the body', was, for Galen, the indisputable starting point, the basic criterion of medical practise (García Ballester 1981, 25). In order to arrive at a considered diagnosis of the disease and its severity, signs were sought in the patient's general appearance and spirits, in his posture, face and breathing, and in the nature of all excreted matter. The character of the pulse and urine were of especial importance, the latter being intimately bound up with Galen's humoral pathology. But all the practitioner's senses were to be employed in determining the appearance, colour, smell, taste, sound, consistency and composition of the various body parts and substances (Figure 12.11). The diagnostic and prognostic value of a sign depended on the sum total of them – 'once there exists between all the symptoms present a harmony like the voices of a choir in tune, one may proceed with confidence' (Galen *ad Glauconem de Medendi Methodo* 1.2: 11.9K). The individual approach was essential, and in addition to the sensory exploration of bodily signs Galen engaged both the patient and his relatives in conversation in order to learn of his habits, activities, character, mental and emotional life, as well as the environment, climate and surroundings in which he lived (García Ballester 1981, 29–31; Horstmanshoff 1995, 94). Finally, and critically, Galen set this sensory knowledge within the framework of a logical system based upon his intimate knowledge of anatomy and physiology, the basic tools of the medical practitioner. 'The starting point was sensory exploration backed up by questioning, but all that was nothing if the doctor did not apply reason to the problem' (García Ballester 1981, 33). Furthermore, 'between what was manifest to the eye and what was obvious to reason, Galen, when it came down to it, chose the latter' (García Ballester 1981, 37).

Observing and listening to the whole diagnostic process was likely to have been at least one apprentice or student, for this was the normal route for those aiming to become practitioners. Galen occasionally refers to students (*e.g.* 8.192–193K; 19.8–12K), they are evidenced in medical papyri (Marganne 1998, 13–34, 85–95, 160–3) and are among the medical butts of the satirist Martial (*Epigrammaton* 5.9).

Having reached a diagnosis and given his prognosis the healer determined a course of treatment. In accordance with the advice of Scribonius Largus he might begin by seeking a cure through diet. Depending on the severity of the illness and the social standing of the practitioner and his patient a joint discussion might ensue in which the two of them debated the relative merits of various exercises and dietetic measures. For, a general understanding of the theories of causation of disease and the principles of medicine was considered desirable as part of a young man's education (Athenaeus in Oribasius *Collectiones Medicae* 54.7; Aulus Gellius *Noctes Atticae* 18.10). Indeed, some patients had, or believed they had, a better knowledge of medicine than their healer (Galen *de Praecognitione* 3 (CMG 5.8, 1, 14.617K): Nutton 1979, 86). If dietetics were inappropriate or to no avail the healer would turn to drugs or, in the last resort, to surgery, unless the condition was one which could only be resolved by an operation, in which case surgery was the sole and immediate option. Depending on the healer's status, he might either prescribe and administer the treatment himself or instruct and supervise an assistant or apprentice or a more junior or practical healer, or perhaps even recommend a specialist. In his long career Galen performed a wide variety of medical roles, from pharmacy through surgery to consultancy, but once established in Rome, for example, he chose to leave 'to those called surgeons' operations like cranial trepanation (*de Methodo Medendi* 6.6, 10.454K).

Pharmacy was integral to the practise of medicine, and there was a huge and lucrative trade in *materia medica* (see *e.g.* Nutton 1985b). The obtaining and compounding of drugs was specialised and time-consuming, and few had Galen's opportunities in this field. Many urban healers, therefore, like their patients, would have been reliant on drug-sellers in the market place. Vigilance was required because adulteration and drug fraud were common, and prices were often regarded as outrageous (Figure 12.12). A healer would need to purchase carefully from trusted sources and perhaps employ simple tests of purity and efficacy. Not surprisingly some patients sought guidance on medication from healers, as, for example, from Galen, whose renown was so great in his own lifetime (Nutton 1984; Hanson 1985) that he received correspondence from patients throughout the empire:

> ...through correspondence I have cured some patients residing in other countries. Some sent me letters from Iberia, from Celtic lands, from Asia, Thracia and other countries, asking me whether I knew and could dispatch a trustworthy medicine against the beginning of suffusion (cataract) (*de Locis Affectis* 4.2: 8.224K; Horstmanshoff 1995, 85–6).

Towards the end of the day and into the night Galen devoted time to study, both reading and composing medical treatises. Like other practitioners he made notes on his patients and recorded clinical observations. While few may have matched his stamina and drive many would have read and possessed medical texts and manuals. It seems very likely, for example, that the missing organic component of the Rimini healer's medical assemblage included medical texts that were consumed by the fire. Such valuable possessions were annotated, amended and supplemented through the practitioner's clinical experience. Passed on from generation to generation, as originals or copies, they would have ensured an essential continuity of medical theory and practise. This commonality of practise appears to have been widespread as well as long-lived, although it was undoubtedly modified by regional traditions in different provinces. Inevitably, too, the level of medical activity and the competence of individual practitioners varied according to circumstance. For example, the discrepancy in size between the likes of Rome, Alexandria, Athens, Antioch, Corinth and Carthage on the one hand and Pompeii, Rimini, Augst, Lyon, Paris and London on the other would certainly have had an effect on the relative scale, availability and quality of medical provision, as Galen's 'healing by correspondence' implies. Nevertheless, the most distinctive surviving physical remains, the medical instruments, vary hardly at all, either in their individual form or in the composition of instrumentaria, from one end of the Empire to the other (Jackson 2002b, 92): the practitioners at Stanway, Rimini and Colophon would have had little difficulty in performing surgery with each other's instruments.

In sum, the principal role of healers was (as it still is) to recognise and describe disease, to explain it to their patients, and to help those patients to get well or to feel better. Irrespective of the various medical theories they may have subscribed to, there appears to have been a strong uniformity and continuity of practise.

Bibliography

d'Ambrosio, A., Guzzo, P.G. & Mastroroberto, M. 2003. *Storia da un'eruzione: Pompeii, Ercolano, Oplontis*. Electa, Milan.

Amundsen, D.W. & Ferngren, G.B. 1978. 'The forensic role of physicians in Ptolemaic and Roman Egypt', *Bulletin of the History of Medicine* 52: 336–53

Amundsen, D.W. & Ferngren, G.B. 1979. 'The forensic role of physicians in Roman law', *Bulletin of the History of Medicine* 53: 39–56

Baader, G. 1967. 'Spezialärzte in der Spätantike', *Medizin-historisches Journal* 2: 231–8

Bliquez, L.J. 1994. *Roman Surgical Instruments and other Minor Objects in the National Archaeological Museum of Naples: with a catalogue of the surgical instruments in the 'Antiquarium' at Pompeii by Ralph Jackson*. Philipp von Zabern, Mainz.

Bliquez, L.J. 1995. 'Gynecology in Pompeii', in van der Eijk, P.J., Horstmanshoff, H.F.J. & Schrijvers, P.H. (eds) *Ancient Medicine in its Socio-Cultural Context*. Clio Medica 27/28, Rodopi, Amsterdam: 209–23

Dal Maso, C. 2003. 'Rimini imperiale (II-III secolo)/Rimini in the Roman Empire (II-III

centuries AD)', in Braccesi, L. (ed) *Rimini imperiale (II-III secolo) / Rimini in the Roman Empire (II-III centuries)*. Musei Comunali Rimini, Le Guide/ I, Rimini: 129–219

Eschebach, H. 1984. 'Die Arzthäuser in Pompeii', *Antike Welt Sondernummer* 15, Raggi-Verlag, Feldmeilen: 2–68

Fagan, G.G. 1999. *Bathing in Public in the Roman World*. University of Michigan Press, Ann Arbor.

Feugère, M., Künzl, E. & Weisser, U. 1985. 'Die Starnadeln von Montbellet (Saône-et Loire). Ein Beitrag zur antiken und islamischen Augenheilkunde', *Jahrbuch des Römisch Germanischen Zentralmuseums* 32: 436–508

Fischer, K-D. 1979. 'Zur Entwicklung des ärztlichen Standes im römischen Kaiserreich', *Medizin-historisches Journal* 14: 165–75

Flemming, R. 2000. *Medicine and the Making of Roman Women: gender, nature, and authority from Celsus to Galen.* Oxford University Press, Oxford.

García Ballester, L. 1981. 'Galen as a medical practitioner: problems in diagnosis', in Nutton, V. (ed) *Galen: problems and prospects.* Wellcome Institute for the History of Medicine, London: 13–46

Hamilton, J.S. 1986. 'Scribonius Largus on the medical profession', *Bulletin of the History of Medicine* 60: 209–16

Hanson, A.E. 1985. 'Papyri of medical content', *Yale Classical Studies* 28: 25–48

Hillert, A. 1990. *Antike Ärztedarstellungen.* Marburger Schriften zur Medizingeschichte 25, Peter Lang, Frankfurt am Main.

Horstmanshoff, H.F.J. 1995. 'Galen and his patients', in van der Eijk, P.J., Horstmanshoff, H.F.J. & Schrijvers, P.H. (eds) *Ancient Medicine in its Socio-Cultural Context.* Clio Medica 27/28, Rodopi, Amsterdam: 83–99

Jackson, R. 1988. *Doctors and Diseases in the Roman Empire.* British Museum Publications, London.

Jackson, R. 1993. 'Roman medicine: the practitioners and their practices', in Haase, W. & Temporini, H. (eds.) *Aufstieg und Niedergang der römischen Welt (ANRW)* II 37.1. Walter de Gruyter, Berlin & New York: 79–101

Jackson, R. 1994. 'The surgical instruments, appliances and equipment in Celsus' *De medicina*', in Sabbah, G. & Mudry, P. (eds) *La médecine de Celse: Aspects historiques, scientifiques et littéraires.* Centre Jean Palerne, Mémoires XIII, St Étienne: 167–209

Jackson, R. 1995. 'The composition of Roman medical *instrumentaria* as an indicator of medical practice: a provisional assessment', in van der Eijk, P.J., Horstmanshoff, H.F.J. & Schrijvers, P.H. (eds) *Ancient Medicine in its Socio-Cultural Context.* Clio Medica 27/28, Rodopi, Amsterdam: 189–207

Jackson, R. 1996. 'Eye medicine in the Roman Empire', in Haase, W. & Temporini, H. (eds) *Aufstieg und Niedergang der römischen Welt (ANRW)* II 37.3. Walter de Gruyter, Berlin & New York: 2228–51

Jackson, R. 1997. 'Medical instruments in the Roman world', *Medicina nei Secoli* 9.2: 223–48

Jackson, R. 1999. 'Spas, waters, and hydrotherapy in the Roman world', in DeLaine, J. & Johnston, D.E. (eds) *Roman Baths and Bathing. Part 1: bathing and society.* JRA, Supplementary Series 37, Portsmouth: 107–16

Jackson, R. 2002a. 'A Roman doctor's house in Rimini', *British Museum Magazine* 44: 20–3

Jackson, R. 2002b. 'Roman surgery: the evidence of the instruments', in Arnott, R. (ed) *The Archaeology of Medicine.* BAR (International Series) 1046: 87–94

Jackson, R. 2003. 'The Domus "del chirurgo" at Rimini: an interim account of the medical assemblage', *JRA* 16: 312–21

King, H. 1986. 'Agnodike and the profession of medicine', *Proceedings of the Cambridge Philological Society* 212: 53–77

Kirova, N. 2002. 'Specialized medical instruments from Bulgaria in the context of finds from other Roman provinces (I-IV c. AD)', *Archaeologia Bulgarica* 6: 73–94

Kollesch, J. 1973. *Untersuchungen zu den Pseudogalenischen Definitiones Medicae.* Schriften zur Geschichte und Kultur der Antike 7, Akademie-Verlag, Berlin.

Korpela, J. 1987. *Das Medizinalpersonal im antiken Rom. Eine sozialgeschichtliche Untersuchung.* Annales Academiae Scientiarum Fennicae Dissertationes Humanarum Litterarum 45, Suomalainen Tiedeakatemia, Helsinki.

Künzl, E. 1983. *Medizinische Instrumente aus Sepulkralfunden der römischen Kaiserzeit.* Unter Mitarbeit von Franz Josef Hassel und Susanna Künzl. Kunst und Altertum am Rhein 115, Köln & Bonn also published in *Bonner Jahrbücher* 182: 1–131

Künzl, E. 1986. 'Operationsräume in römischen Thermen', *Bonner Jahrbücher* 186: 491–509

Künzl, E. 1995. 'Ein archäologisches Problem: Gräber römischer Chirurginnen', in van der Eijk, P.J., Horstmanshoff, H.F.J. & Schrijvers, P.H. (eds) *Ancient Medicine in its Socio-Cultural Context.* Clio Medica 27/28, Rodopi, Amsterdam: 309–19

Künzl, E. 1998. 'Instrumentenfunde und Ärzthäuser in Pompeji: Die medizinische Versorgung einer römischen Stadt des 1. Jahrhunderts n.Chr.', *Sartoniana* 11: 71–152

Künzl, E. 2002. *Medizin in der Antike. Aus einer Welt ohne Narkose und Aspirin.* Theiss, Stuttgart.

Majno, G. 1975. *The Healing Hand: man and wound in the ancient world.* Harvard University Press, Cambridge MA & London.

Marasco, G. 1995. 'L'introduction de la médecine grecque à Rome: Une dissension politique et idéologique', in van der Eijk, P.J., Horstmanshoff, H.F.J. & Schrijvers, P.H. (eds) *Ancient Medicine in its Socio-Cultural Context.* Clio Medica 27/28, Rodopi, Amsterdam: 35–48

Marganne, M-H. 1998. *La chirurgie dans l'Égypte gréco-romaine d'après les papyrus littéraires grecs.* Brill, Leiden.

Minchev, A. 1983. 'Roman medicine in Marcianopolis', in Oliva, P. & Frolíková, A. (eds) *Concilium Eirene XVI. Proceedings of the 16th International Eirene Conference, Prague.* Kabinet pro studia recká, rímská a latinská CSAV, Prague: 143–8

Mudry, P. 1985. 'Médecins et spécialistes. Le problème de l'unité de la médecine à Rome au premier siècle ap. J.-C.', *Gesnerus* 42: 329–36

Nickel, D. 1979. 'Berufsvorstellungen über weibliche Medizinalpersonen in der Antike', *Klio* 61/2: 515–8

Nutton, V. 1979. *Galen: on prognosis.* Corpus Medicorum Graecorum V, 8, 1. Berlin.

Nutton, V. 1981. 'Continuity or rediscovery? The city physician in classical antiquity and medieval Italy', in Russell, A.W. (ed) *The Town and State Physician in Europe from the Middle Ages to the Enlightenment.* Wolfenbütteler Forschungen 17, Herzog August Bibliothek, Wolfenbüttel: 9–46

Nutton, V. 1984. 'Galen in the eyes of his contemporaries', *Bulletin of the History of Medicine* 58: 315–24

Nutton, V. 1985a. 'Murders and miracles: lay attitudes towards medicine in classical antiquity', in Porter, R. (ed) *Patients and Practitioners. Lay perceptions of medicine in pre-industrial society.* Cambridge University Press, Cambridge: 23–53

Nutton, V. 1985b. 'The drug trade in antiquity', *Journal of the Royal Society of Medicine* 78: 138–45

Nutton, V. 1986. 'The perils of patriotism: Pliny and Roman medicine', in French, R. & Greenaway, F. (eds) *Science in the Early Roman Empire: Pliny the Elder, his sources and influences.* Croom Helm, London & Sydney: 30–58

Nutton, V. 1990. 'The patient's choice: a new treatise by Galen', *Classical Quarterly* 40/1: 236–57

Nutton, V. 1992. 'Healers in the medical market place: towards a social history of Graeco-Roman medicine', in Wear, A. (ed) *Medicine in Society: historical essays.* Cambridge University Press, Cambridge: 15–58

Nutton, V. 1993. 'Roman medicine: Tradition, confrontation, assimilation', in Haase, W. & Temporini, H. (eds) *Aufstieg und Niedergang der römischen Welt (ANRW)* II 37.1. Walter de Gruyter, Berlin & New York: 49–78

Nutton, V. 1995. 'The medical meeting place', in van der Eijk, P.J., Horstmanshoff, H.F.J. & Schrijvers, P.H. (eds) *Ancient Medicine in its Socio-Cultural Context.* Clio Medica 27/28, Rodopi, Amsterdam: 3–25

Ortalli, J. 1992. 'Edilizia residenziale e crisi urbana nella tarda antichità: fonti archeologiche per la Cispadana', in *XXXIX Corso di Cultura sull'arte Ravennate e Bizantina: Seminario internazionale di studi su 'Aspetti e problemi di archeologia e storia dell'arte della Lusitania, Galizia, e Asturie tra tardoantico e medioevo', Ravenna, 6–12 aprile 1992.* Edizione del Girasole, Ravenna: 584–90

Ortalli, J. 2000. 'Rimini: la città', in Calvani, M.M. (ed) *Aemilia: la cultura romana in Emilia Romagna dal III secolo a.C. all'età costantiniana.* Marsilio, Venice: 501–6

Ortalli, J. 2003. 'Rimini archeologica: the archaeology of Rimini', in Braccesi, L. (ed) *Rimini imperiale (II-III secolo) / Rimini in the Roman Empire (II-III centuries).* Musei Comunali Rimini, Le Guide/ I, Rimini: 69–116

Pleket, H.W. 1995. 'The social status of physicians in the Graeco-Roman world', in van der Eijk, P.J., Horstmanshoff, H.F.J. & Schrijvers, P.H. (eds) *Ancient Medicine in its Socio-Cultural Context.* Clio Medica 27/28, Rodopi, Amsterdam: 27–34

Pomeroy, S. 1978. 'Plato and the female physician (*Republic* 454 d2)', *AJP* 99: 496–500

Scarborough, J. 1993. 'Roman medicine to Galen', in Haase, W. & Temporini, H. (eds) *Aufstieg und Niedergang der römischen Welt (ANRW)* II 37.1. Walter de Gruyter, Berlin & New York: 3–48

Index

222

Scribonius Largus 180, 202, 207, 217
Second Sophistic 19
Segontium 161
Semita dei Cippi 33–4
Seneca 32, 36, 205, 208, 214
Sens 82
Sentia Secunda 177
Sepphoris 174
Seripola 108
seviri 6
Sheepen 11, 174
shipbuilding 137
shoemaker 63
Sidon 177–8
Silchester 8, 12, 20, 23, 49, 53–4, 58, 63–4, 112
Školarice-Križišče 170–1
Smyrna 204
soap 194
Soranus 208–9
Sousse 182
South Shields 23
Southwark 127, 129–30, 133, 136, 139–42
Sparta 175, 202
St Alban 13–14
St Marcius Stator 109
St Thomas Street 131, 133
Stanway 218
Statius 169
stativae 3
stoa 24
Strabo 30, 169, 177, 198
Suetonius 83, 203
Superaequum 32, 45
supplicationes 5
Swanpool 146
symposium 25

tabernae/tavern 29–30, 32, 34, 36, 38, 40, 42, 45, 48–65, 70–85, 89–99, 180–2, 184, 203, 210–11

tablinum 44, 74, 76, 78
Tacitus 22–3
tanning 63, 135, 191
Tarquinius Priscus 196
Tarragona 10, 174
temple 6–13, 59, 81, 97, 108, 111, 191
Terme dei Sette Sapienti 35
textile 30, 61, 88, 90–8, 98–101, 135
Thamusida 55
theatre 8, 10–12
Theodoros 177
Tiber 33, 36, 38, 106–22, 170
tile-making 138–9
Timgad 76
Tipasa 55
Titianus Hyacinthus 177
Toppings Wharf 127, 129
Towcester 149, 151, 156
Trajan 204
Trier 210
Trimalchio 81, 167
Trinox(tion) Samoni 4
Trophimus Agathobuli 119–20
Tubilustrium 4
Tyre 175

Usk 178

Vaison-la-Romaine 49, 55
Verginius 71
Verulamium 8–9, 12–14, 49–50, 53, 58–9, 62–3, 65, 153, 158
Via degli Aurighi 33, 36
Via dei Balconi 33, 36
Via dei Grandi Horrea 34–5
Via dei Lari 36
Via dei Molini 33–4
Via del Larario 35
Via del Pomerio 33, 38
Via dell'Abbondanza 84, 90, 93
Via della Foce 33–5, 76

Via della Fortuna 34
Via di Annio 34, 42
Via di Diana 35–6, 73
Via Epagathiana 33
Via Est delle Casette Tipo 34
Via Laurentina 38
via Sacra 4
Via Tecta degli Aurighi 33, 35
vicomagistri 36
Viénne 55
vigiles 30, 36
Villa du Bord de Mar 55
Villa Regina 80
Villa Vesuvio 191–4, 199
Villards d'Heria 4
Vindolanda 57
Vitruvius 3
Voghenza 170
Volubilis 20, 55

Walbrook 63, 132, 134–41
Walheim 59
Walton-le-Dale 162
Water Newton 174
Watling Court 49, 127, 138
Watling Street 12, 59–60, 134
Whittington Avenue 138
Wigan 162
Wilderspool 162
Winchester 8
Winchester Palace 138
wine 79–85, 157, 193–4, 196
wood-working 132, 135, 137
Wroxeter 15, 51–2, 58–60, 62–3, 158, 168, 185

York 62, 158–60, 168

Zosimos177